Alberta Culbreath and Vernon Kinney

We are who we are because of who they were

Barbara Kinney Black

ISBN: 978-0615951737

DEDICATION

This book is dedicated to my family: mother, father, brother, niece, nephews, grandparents, aunt, uncle, and all my cousins for inspiring me to dig into our Kinney family history and uncover the hidden gems that make us who we are because of who our ancestors were. May your lives be enriched through the discovery of our ancestors' lives.

Eternally,

Barbara Kinney Black

Barbara Kinney Black

CONTENTS

ACKNOWLEDGEMENTS

A grateful thank you from the bottom of my heart goes to my husband, Bernie Black, for without him none of this would have happened. He rescued the computer when it crashed, drove us to the Midwest for research, tromped through too many graveyards, scanned countless documents in courthouses, and photographed anything and everything that caught my fancy. So, THANK YOU! Also thanks goes to my brother, Roger, for his computer and research advice. Thanks also to our Sunday Bible class at Pines Baptist Church for their prayers through the writing process. Finally, thanks be to my Lord, Jesus Christ, for endowing me with the creative abilities needed to undertake this project.

Preface

by Barbara Kinney Black

"Do you know where you got the skill for your new profession as an auto mechanic?" That was the question I asked my cousin's daughter when I learned she'd just completed a mechanic's course. "No," she replied. "Well, it's from your great, great grandfather," I said. "He was an inventor and a very talented mechanic among many other skills."

Later, as I reflected on my great grandfather, Thomas Sherman Culbreath, I once again wished I'd been just a little older when he died so that I would have had at least a little opportunity to know this fascinating member of my family. The more time that passes, the more my memory of him and my other influential ancestors fades away. And, it's happening far too quickly. Gabriella is just one generation below me, and she didn't even know Thomas' name, let alone the connection between him and her.

This was not right. If Gabriella was missing the riches that come from having knowledge of our ancestors, probably the rest of her generation was as well. We know from DNA today that we are definitely a product of our genes, and that's not just a trite saying anymore. We are who we are because of who they were.

I'd already started a family tree on Ancestry.com when my conversation with Gabriella took place. There had been loads of fascinating discoveries I'd made. But, aside from my husband and brother with whom I'd shared my findings, most of those discoveries were mine alone. They hadn't been shared. It was high time to kick it into high gear. My mission was set: to discover all I could about our ancestry and to pass it along to my family, sort of like the Olympic torch bearer.

My cousin, Sandy Stewart Dolan, says that I'm uncovering the family history. That sounds like an accurate description. So much of our history lies hidden just below the surface just waiting for someone to dig down to discover the precious jewels. Each nugget that's uncovered is like a little treasure chest. And when it's opened, the little jewels shine, revealing their hidden secrets. I wish I could make a necklace of these gems and keep them with me all the time. The truths they reveal have given me an insight into who I am and why. Now I hope to pass those truths along to my family.

Introduction

Organization

When I first started inputting my family history data onto my Ancestry.com tree home page, I was able to view five generations, back to my great, great grandparents, on the home page. This home page became a mental picture of my family. So, it was only natural to organize the chapters around the great, great grandparents and their families. Sub headings within the chapter such as, "The Wife of …", "The Parents of …", and "The Children of …", help the reader to keep track of who is who and how they fit into the family tree. There is also a pedigree family tree chart and individual descendants charts from each great, grandparent on the following pages.

DNA Results

Most every family has its urban legends, myths, and speculations about who they may or may not be related to, and where their ethnicity may have come from. For years I joked that I was a "Heinz 57" variety. Once DNA testing became readily accessible for a reasonable price, I just had to get tested so I could ditch the Heinz 57 label. When the results came back, there were some big surprises and some previous ethnicity beliefs were confirmed. Here are the results.

European – 99% - no surprise there   Pacific Islander, Melanesia – 1% - big surprise!

Here's the breakdown of the 99% European:

Ireland – 51%	Great Britain – 35%	Great Britain Trace Regions – 13%
Italy/Greece – 7%	Western Europe – 2%	Scandinavia – 2%
European Jewish – 2%	Iberian Peninsula – 1%	

Questions

At the beginning of my family history research, I mistakenly thought I'd finish in 2 weeks! It's been 2 years, and I've just scratched the surface. So, here are the results that have been discovered so far. At the end of each person's bio, there is a list of questions which bear further research. I invite readers to participate in this process by helping to answer the questions. Together we can punch through those brick walls.

Contact – Barbara K. Black – bbblack22@bellsouth.net

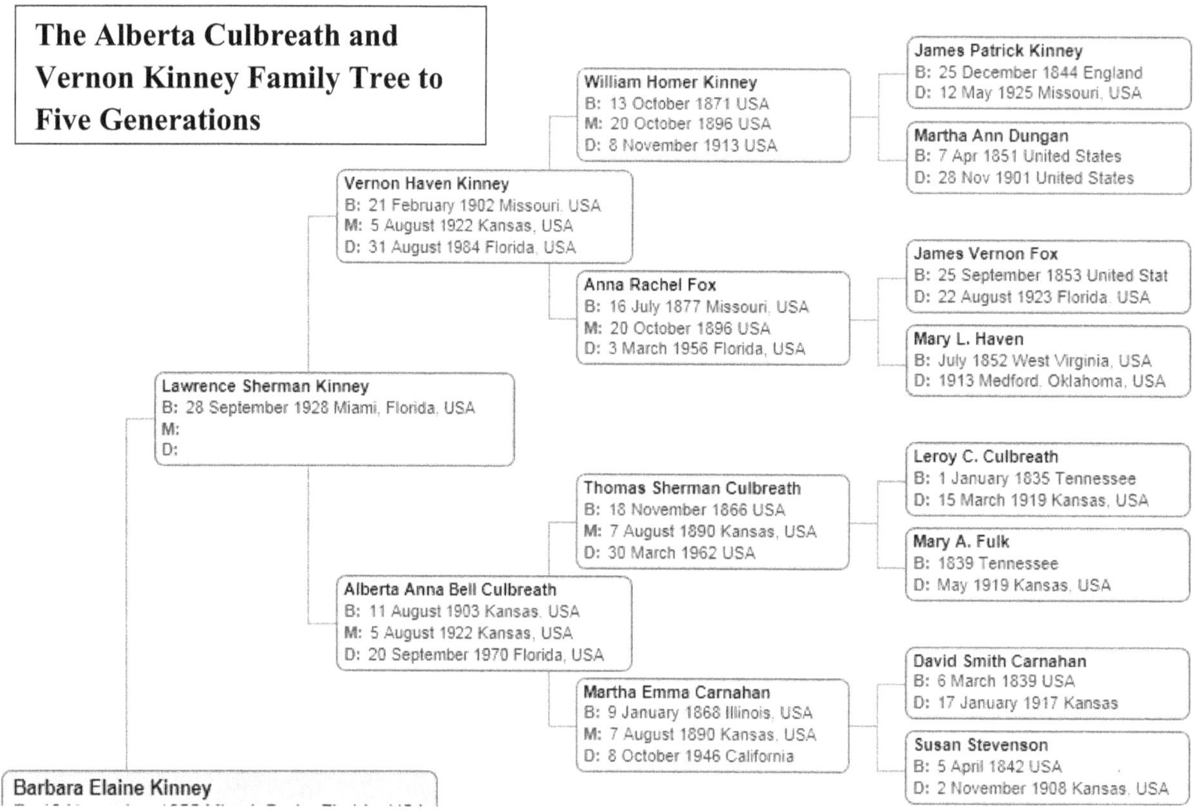

The pedigree chart above gives a bird's eye view of the family tree, while below, the descendants are listed down from each great, great grandparent; Vernon's ancestors are the first four listed, and Alberta's ancestors are the last four listed.

James Patrick Kinney (1844 - 1925)
is your 2nd great grandfather

William Homer Kinney (1871 - 1913)
son of James Patrick Kinney

Vernon Haven Kinney (1902 - 1984)
son of William Homer Kinney

Lawrence Sherman Kinney (1928 -)
son of Vernon Haven Kinney

Barbara Elaine Kinney
daughter of Lawrence Sherman Kinney

Martha Ann Dungan (1851 - 1901)
is your 2nd great grandmother

William Homer Kinney (1871 - 1913)
son of Martha Ann Dungan

Vernon Haven Kinney (1902 - 1984)
son of William Homer Kinney

Lawrence Sherman Kinney (1928 -)
son of Vernon Haven Kinney

Barbara Elaine Kinney
daughter of Lawrence Sherman Kinney

James Vernon Fox (1853 - 1923)
is your 2nd great grandfather

Anna Rachel Fox (1877 - 1956)
daughter of James Vernon Fox

Vernon Haven Kinney (1902 - 1984)
son of Anna Rachel Fox

Lawrence Sherman Kinney (1928 -)
son of Vernon Haven Kinney

Barbara Elaine Kinney
daughter of Lawrence Sherman Kinney

Mary L. Haven (1852 - 1913)
is your 2nd great grandmother

Anna Rachel Fox (1877 - 1956)
daughter of Mary L. Haven

Vernon Haven Kinney (1902 - 1984)
son of Anna Rachel Fox

Lawrence Sherman Kinney (1928 -)
son of Vernon Haven Kinney

Barbara Elaine Kinney
daughter of Lawrence Sherman Kinney

Leroy C. Culbreath (1835 - 1919)
is your 2nd great grandfather

Thomas Sherman Culbreath (1866 - 1962)
son of Leroy C. Culbreath

Alberta Anna Bell Culbreath (1903 - 1970)
daughter of Thomas Sherman Culbreath

Lawrence Sherman Kinney (1928 -)
son of Alberta Anna Bell Culbreath

Barbara Elaine Kinney
daughter of Lawrence Sherman Kinney

Mary A. Fulk (1839 - 1919)
is your 2nd great grandmother

Thomas Sherman Culbreath (1866 - 1962)
son of Mary A. Fulk

Alberta Anna Bell Culbreath (1903 - 1970)
daughter of Thomas Sherman Culbreath

Lawrence Sherman Kinney (1928 -)
son of Alberta Anna Bell Culbreath

Barbara Elaine Kinney
daughter of Lawrence Sherman Kinney

**David Smith Carnahan (1839 - 1917)
is your 2nd great grandfather**

**Martha Emma Carnahan (1868 - 1946)
daughter of David Smith Carnahan**

**Alberta Anna Bell Culbreath (1903 - 1970)
daughter of Martha Emma Carnahan**

**Lawrence Sherman Kinney (1928 -)
son of Alberta Anna Bell Culbreath**

**Barbara Elaine Kinney
daughter of Lawrence Sherman Kinney**

**Susan Stevenson (1842 - 1908)
is your 2nd great grandmother**

**Martha Emma Carnahan (1868 - 1946)
daughter of Susan Stevenson**

**Alberta Anna Bell Culbreath (1903 - 1970)
daughter of Martha Emma Carnahan**

**Lawrence Sherman Kinney (1928 -)
son of Alberta Anna Bell Culbreath**

**Barbara Elaine Kinney
daughter of Lawrence Sherman Kinney**

1

James Patrick Kinney

1844-1925

James Patrick Kinney (1844 - 1925)

is your 2nd great grandfather

William Homer Kinney (1871 - 1913)

son of James Patrick Kinney

Vernon Haven Kinney (1902 - 1984)

son of William Homer Kinney

Lawrence Sherman Kinney (1928 -)

son of Vernon Haven Kinney

Barbara Elaine Kinney

daughter of Lawrence Sherman Kinney

For a long time, the only thing I knew about James Patrick Kinney was his name, his wife's name, and the names of 13 of their 14 children. I knew he was of Irish descent, but for some reason had been born in England. From his obituary, I knew his family had settled in Mt. Pleasant, Iowa, and that James had "returned to near Isadora, Missouri" after the Civil War. There were great gaps in his life story.

Then one day I was browsing my tree connections on Ancestry.com and made a new connection to a descendant of one of James' daughters. This new cousin asked if I had a copy of James' autobiography. Instantly my heart jumped. There was an autobiography? I could hardly believe my ears. I was so excited to learn this information, but would have to wait to get it for several months.

The wait seemed like an eternity, but eventually I met my newly discovered cousin, Jan Bethards, in person and she nonchalantly handed me a transcript of James' autobiography. My husband and I passed a very delightful afternoon getting to know our new cousins. After we parted company, I finally had an opportunity to read the autobiography. What a shock! It read like a Tom Sawyer-type novel. I thought about my new cousin and how she was probably imagining the thrill I was experiencing in discovering my great, great grandfather's story told from his own life experience. I was so grateful to her for sharing this intimate account of James' life with me. So, here it is: the early adventures of James Patrick Kinney as James himself revealed them.

Autobiography of James P. Kinney

"James Patrick Kinney was born Dec. 25, 1844, at Newton, Lancashire, England, the oldest son of Bridget and John Kinney, of the County of Galloway [Galway], Ireland, who came to the United States in 1850, settling for a time in Yates County, New York, near Penn Yan, where my mother died Feb. 3, 1853.

When only four years old my parents came to this country leaving myself and sister two years older in the old country, my sister staying in England with my father's uncle, Peter Lonehat, and I was taken to Ireland by my mother's brother, John Flemming. We remained in the old country till 1852, when my uncle, John and his wife came over with us after the death of my mother. My father married again and moved to Toledo, Ohio, in the fall of 1854. We again moved West in the spring of 1856 and located at Mt. Pleasant, Iowa. When we moved to Iowa my stepmother and my sister didn't get along and sister had to live away from home and couldn't come to see me, so I decided I wouldn't stay and about the last of June, 1856, ran away at the age of eleven years and six months.

I went to Burlington [Iowa] where there were some people that I knew in Ohio by the name of Tally, and while in Burlington I got acquainted with a boy about my age who stole some money from his father and got me a suit of clothes and made me a present of them. When I took the clothes to where I was stopping the boy's mother was there telling about the boy stealing the money and how the father would whip him for it. After she went home Mrs. Tally wanted to know what it was I had in the bundle. I told her it was some clothes I had bought uptown. She then wanted to know where I got the money and I told her the whole story. She was very sorry I had got mixed up in the affair, but told me to keep away from the boy till her husband came home. Well, when he came home we talked the matter over, and he decided to send me on to Chicago clothes and all.

When I got to Chicago I went to the railroad shops and found some friends of my father and told them I wanted to go to Toledo, Ohio. So they made up some money and got me a pass to Toledo. I hadn't been in Toledo but a short time till I heard the man and woman talking about the priest telling at church that a woman and little boy was here enquiring for John Kinney, her husband, so I concluded it was my stepmother, and I would rather die than to fall into her hands, so I ran away and went across the lake to Buffalo, New York.

I was trying to get back to Penn Yan, N.Y., where my mother died. I got on a train one night and went to sleep on the seat of the car. Sometime in the night the conductor waked me and wanted to know where I wanted to go, and when I told him he said I was on the wrong train and was then in Canada. So he put me off at the next station, telling me that another train would be along soon going back to Buffalo and for me to get on it and they would tell me what train to take. Well, I got back to where I started and in the morning I got in with some town boys and bought me a boat. Now at that time there were no bridges across the Buffalo River [probably Niagara River] and sailing vessels and steamers were quite a ways up the river from the lake [probably Lake Erie or maybe Lake Ontario] and all travelers had to be taken across in boats, and in addition to the ferry small boys and men owned skiffs to carry from one to four persons at two cents a trip. Well, I had one of the boats and soon had a pretty good trade. I stayed there till it began to get cold so I went back to Toledo and found that the woman and little boy were still there, so I got in with a bunch of boys that were going to Terre Haute, Indiana, and when we got there some of the boys went on to Milwaukee, Wisconsin, and I went with them.

I went two trips across Lake Michigan before it got too cold to navigate the lake. One trip we were in a storm 3 days and threw the whole cargo of lumber overboard, and when we reached port we heard our ship had gone down with all on board.

At this time, about October 10, 1856, I was taken in at an orphan's home at Milwaukee and stayed one year. One day a man came to the home to get a boy and we were all lined up for him to pick one out. He went the whole length up the line and when he came to me he stopped and asked me how I would like to live on a farm. I told him I didn't know but would be glad to try it. So I went with him to La Crosse, Wis., and stayed with him about a year. But I didn't like him so I left and went to Beaver Dam in Dodge County, Wis., where I lived till the spring of 1859, when I left there and went to La Crosse again and went on a steamboat as waiter to the cook in the pastry department.

We made regular trips from La Crosse to St. Paul, Minn., twice a week till the weather got cold. Then I started to go South with the cook to work on the lower Mississippi river, but when we got to St. Louis there were two families coming up the Missouri river to Kansas City and St. Joe. The one coming to St. Joe was named Thompson and they had two children, a boy and girl about my age. They wanted me to go with them. The man said he would send me to school and do as good part by me as his own son. The other one was a young doctor and his wife. They were going to Kansas and got me to go with them. But when they got to Kansas they went to live with his brother in a one room log cabin and there was several kids so I never went in the house. When the man that hauled us came out of the house he asked me what I was going to do (he knew about my case.) I told him I didn't know but one thing was sure there was no room for me there. He told me to get in the wagon and go home with him so I went and Doctor Chilton does not know to this day what became of the boy he brought out from Kansas City.

My new boss was named Mitchell and he was living with his second wife, a big fine woman. He also had a daughter by his first wife. She was about my age and she did not like her stepmother. We became great friends from the first but his old father was a hard master and I did not stay with him very long.

In the spring of 1860 I went to live with a doctor and merchant at Aubeny, Kansas, 25 miles south of Kansas City. [probably Aubry which is located south of Kansas City] Had a fine place to live. I worked in the store Saturdays and went to school.

During the summer of 1860 I went with a corn sheller, shelling corn and hauling it to Kansas City at 15 cents per bushel, until about the first of July, when the dry winds struck Kansas and dried up the growing crops and the corn we had on hand went to 2 dollars per bushel. About the first of August, Doctor Mann went to Kansas City to buy goods for the store, and when he returned he told his wife that the Republicans had named Abe Lincoln for the office of President and he was going to sell out his business in Kansas at once and go to Illinois and do all he could to elect him president, as he was his friend and neighbor before he came to Kansas. I asked him what he was going to do with me and he said I was going back with him and if Lincoln was elected I would go to school in Washington that winter.

James Patrick Kinney during the Civil War

During the summer a family by the name of Snober came to Auben on their way from Texas to what is now Worth County, and they had a boy about my age that I got chummy with and he told me such wonderful stories about North Missouri that I decided not to go to Illinois or Washington with Doctor Mann but go to North Missouri with the Snober family, and about the first of September, 1860, we drove through with a yoke of oxen from 25 miles south of Kansas City to what is now known as Isadora, but at that time it was a vast wilderness of heavy timber and very few settlers.

An old man named Aaron Hibbs and his two sons, Sam and Jerry, settled on the Grand River bottom north and northwest of what is now Isadora, and he also had five sons-in-law that settled in the same community, named as follows: Thomas Murphin, F. M. West, Alexander Young, Thomas Goodspeed and Joseph Castor. I had not been there but a short time till I got work for some one or another of the Hibbs family.

In the winter of 1860-61 I made my home at F. M. West's and went to school at what was known as the Morgason school house. Aaron Zink was teacher. In the spring of 1861 I went to live with Jerry Hibbs and done his farming as he was afflicted with a bad leg and was not able to do much work. In the fall I went back to Mr. West's and in October, 1861, enlisted in what was known as the Six Months Volunteer Militia and was honorably discharged the 23rd of Feb., 1862 and received 55 dollars for my six months service. I then hired to Jerry Hibbs at 25 dollars per month for the summer, commencing the first of March. I worked till about the 24th of the month and gave up my job at 25 dollars and accepted a three year job at 13 dollars per month with Uncle Sam as he was badly in need of help at that time, as about half of his hired men had gone on a strike and others that stayed on the job were on a standstill what to do and consequently doing nothing.

On October 15, 1861, I enlisted for six months and began to learn something of soldier's hardships. After being discharged in February, 1862, I was hired out to Jerry Hibbs at 25 dollars per month, worked one month and gave him the work for nothing and again enlisted for three years or during the war. I was discharged April 4, 1865.

In July, 1865, I hired to a train of freight wagons and went across the plains to Fort Union, New Mexico and got back to Leavenworth, Kansas, on December 15, and got back to old Isadora December 23rd, just in time to celebrate my 21st birthday. [Probably he took the Santa Fe Trail which left from Kansas City. There were two routes: the main route went through southeastern Colorado while the Cimarron Cut Off went through the Oklahoma Panhandle. They both joined up again at Fort Union.]

Fort Union, New Mexico, probable destination of James Patrick Kinney when he accompanied the freight wagon team to New Mexico, 1865. For more info, visit the website of Fort Union National Monument: http://www.nps.gov/foun/planyourvisit/index.htm

I then made my home with F. M. West and farmed the summer of 1865 and on the thirteenth of January, 1867, was married to Martha A. Dungan, with whom I lived happily until the 28th of November, 1901, when it pleased the Lord to take her from me after having raised thirteen children, seven boys and six girls, to be grown men and women. I am now alone (this 28th day of April, 1921) [probably the date of writing]. Four of the children have gone to join their mother [Ira Edward, William Homer, Effie Jane, and John Hubert]. I only have nine left and they are scattered around in four states and we may never meet, but I hope we may all so live that if we never meet here we may be an unbroken family in that land where death and sorrow are unknown.

And now at the age of 76 I am blessed with 24 grandsons and 16 granddaughters and 12 great grandchildren."

The above was transcribed from an original copy supplied by descendants of James Patrick Kinney's daughter, Cora Clementine Kinney Keyes. Many thanks to my newly discovered cousins, Joyce Stark and Janice Bethards, for this enlightening and exciting autobiography.

~~~~~~

Back in the Day . . . Buffalo, New York, was at the western end of the Erie Canal which made Buffalo a popular place due to the commerce brought in by the Canal. The Niagara River divided Canada and the U.S. Perhaps this was the river on which James operated a skiff transporting passengers back and forth for pay. Buffalo was also an important stop on the Underground Railroad. Escaping African-American slaves crossed the Niagara River to Fort Erie, Ontario, Canada, to freedom. I wonder if our James Patrick Kinney assisted any escaping slaves to their freedom.

James also worked on steamboats on both the Great Lakes and the Mississippi River. For some 1850s era steamboat images, visit the following: http://steamboattimes.com/levee_scenes.html

~~~~~~

The Wife of James Patrick Kinney

Martha Anna Dungan

1851-1901

Martha Ann Dungan (1851 - 1901)

is your 2nd great grandmother

William Homer Kinney (1871 - 1913)

son of Martha Ann Dungan

Vernon Haven Kinney (1902 - 1984)

son of William Homer Kinney

Lawrence Sherman Kinney (1928 -)

son of Vernon Haven Kinney

Barbara Elaine Kinney

daughter of Lawrence Sherman Kinney

Now we will expand upon James' married life. James Patrick Kinney was married to Martha Anna Dungan who was born 7 April 1851 in Missouri. Her stepfather was probably C. H. Banes who signed the marriage certificate giving Martha Anna permission to marry, and his wife, possibly Martha's mother, Jane Banes. At the time of their marriage in Worth County, Missouri, C. H. Banes and Jane Banes were residents of Worth County along with Daley Young who acted as a witness. Other family documents give the name of Martha Anna's step father as Barn.

this is to Certify that the undersigned just of the Peace for union Township in worth County in the state of Missouri did on the 13 day of January 1867 solemise the Marr Contrack betwen Mr James Kiney and Miss Anne Dungan Done by vurtue of a Cirtifacate signed by C.H Banes and Jone Banes and proven to be guenuine by Daley yong all of worth County Mo
Joseph Watson, J.P.

The "Missouri Marriage Records, 1805-2002" Collection, Page 60, lists the following entry for James and Martha's wedding:

"This is to certify that the undersigned Justice of the Peace for Union Township in Worth County in the State of Missouri, did on the 13th day of January 1867 did solemnize the marriage contract Mr. James Kiney [misspelled] and Miss Ann Denigan [misspelled] done by virtue of a certificate signed by C. H. Banes and Jane Banes and proven to be genuine by Dallas Young all of Worth Missouri.

Joseph Watson, J.P. Note: Perhaps the bride's name was Deugan. However, there were Dennigans or Dunnigans in Worth County."

A copy of the original record, in my possession, clearly shows the spelling of "Dungan" for Martha Ann.

This photograph taken during the Civil War era and labeled by family as "Grandfather of Cora Kinney" is thought to possibly be the father or stepfather of Martha Anna Dungan. Note the photo sleeve labeled, "N. E. Daggett, Stockton, Iowa."

C. H. Banes, Probable Stepfather to Martha Anna Dungan Kinney

Another photograph labeled by family as "Martha Dungan Mother of Cora Kinney," appears to be from the same time frame as the previous photo of C. H. Banes. This photo is mounted on a card which reads, "Wray's Studio, Sheridan, MO." Sheridan was a town near Isadora where Martha Anna Dungan supposedly was from.

Other researchers, however, claim her parents were from Howard County, Missouri, which is located southeast from Worth County, halfway across Missouri. A check of a Missouri plat map for Gentry County which is located just west of Daviess County and south of Worth County, reveals there is an area called Howard in the northeast corner of Gentry County. As the marriage took place in Daviess County, perhaps her parents could have been from the next county over in the Howard area of Gentry County, as opposed to Howard County which was located half-way across the State. It bears researching in the future.

Their first child, Ira Edward Kinney, was born near Isadora, Worth County, Missouri, 22 April 1867.

He was followed by Sarah Frances Kinney, born near Smithton, Worth County, Missouri, 21 August 1868.

Next, Cora Clementine Kinney was born near Smithton, 12 January 1870, and was followed by William Homer Kinney, born near Rochester, Andrew County, Missouri, on 13 October 1871.

Jesse Arthur Kinney was born near Isadora, Worth County, Missouri, on 5 February 1875, followed by Effie Jane Kinney, born near Isadora, 19 October 1876.

At the 1880 U.S. Federal Census, son Lindsey Addison Kinney, was listed as 11 months old. He was born in Smithton, Worth County, on 13 July 1879.

Irvin A. Kinney was born next in Grant City, Worth County, on 25 October 1881.

Albert Perlo Kinney was born near Allendale, located just west of Grant City in Worth County, 24 January 1884.

Mary E. Kinney was also born near Allendale, 23 December 1886, as well as John Hubert Kinney, born 10 August 1888.

The last two daughters were born in Harrison County, Missouri, probably on the family farm, which was in the extreme northwest corner of the County. They were Edith Lodema Kinney, 16 June 1890, and finally, Martha Ellen Kinney, 17 May 1893.

Martha Anna Dungan Kinney

Military records, specifically, the Surviving Soldiers 1890 Veterans Schedule, detail James' Civil War service as a private, enlisted 4 April 1862 and discharged 5 April 1865. He was in Company E. 4th Missouri 3. M. Cavalry. His post office was listed as Allendale, Missouri. His disability incurred was "disease of eyes, chronic." There is an unreadable remark on the record. It is confusing, however, because the military service inscribed on his tomb stone is different from this service listed in the 1890 Veterans Schedule. His tomb stone says: "Co. D, 6th MO Mil."

Based on James Patrick's own autobiography describing a wandering lifestyle, it's no wonder I have been unsuccessful to date in locating him in either the 1860 or 1870 U.S. Federal Census records. The first U.S. Federal Census he's located in was for 1880. At that time he was 35 years old and living in Grant City, Worth County, Missouri. Wife, Martha Anna, was 29. The first 7 children were living with them and ranged in age from 11 months to 13 years old. James gave his occupation as a day laborer while Martha Anna as keeping house.

In the 1900 U.S. Federal Census, the family was living in Lincoln Township, Harrison County, Missouri. This was the location of their family farm. The 7 youngest children were living with them, ranging in age from 7 to 22. They had been married 37 years. Martha Anna indicated that 14 children had been born and 13 were currently living. She stated that while she was born in Missouri, her parents were both born in Scotland. James listed his occupation as farmer and he owned his farm with a mortgage.

By the 1910 U.S. Federal Census, Martha Anna was deceased, and James, aged 65, was living in Athens Township, Albany City, Gentry County, Missouri. James was a widower and his 3 youngest daughters were living with him. He did not list an occupation for himself, but 2 of the daughters were working as public school teachers. Only the youngest did not have an occupation listed. Although the script is difficult to read, it appears they were living on Van Buren, and they must have been in the general vicinity of the Gentry County Jail, as the prisoners were enumerated on the same page of the Census record.

The last U.S. Federal Census record for James Kinney was 1920 and he was aged 75, living alone in his own home in Athens Township, Albany City, Gentry County, Missouri. He owned his home free of a mortgage. He indicated he immigrated in 1852 and was naturalized as a citizen in 1854. He stated he was born in England and spoke English as his mother tongue, while both parents were born in Ireland and spoke Irish as their mother tongue in addition to English.

The family farm was purchased in September, 1892, and was described as, "All of the south half of the N.W. Quarter and ten acres off of the north side of the N.W. fourth of the S.W. Quarter. All in Section 6, Township 66, Range 29, and containing 90 acres by government survey." In 2013, this land was located in Harrison County, at the intersection of West Highway HH and West 110 Avenue.

Martha Anna Dungan Kinney died on 28 November 1901, in Athens, Gentry County, Missouri. I have found no death certificate, nor burial location for her. It is my belief that, although there is no grave marker or record, she is buried in the Lott's Grove Cemetery behind the Lott's Grove Church, located between Hatfield, Harrison County and Allendale, Worth County, ½ mile east of the intersection of highways O and HH, on the south side of the highway, and that she lies between husband, James Patrick Kinney, and oldest son, Ira Edward Kinney, Ira's wife Ruby, and their infant daughter. James Patrick's grave is marked with a marble stone inscribed with his name and his military service.

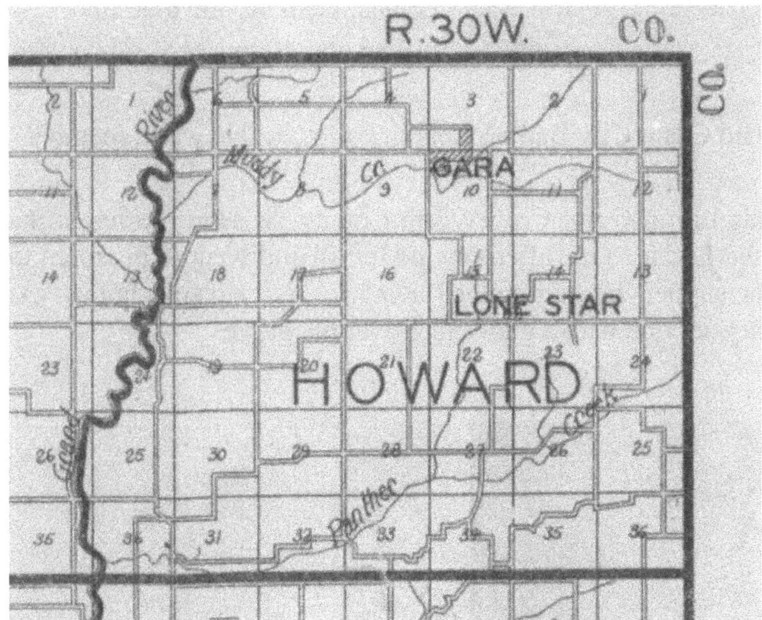

Plat map showing the corner of Grundy County with the area called Howard

After Martha's death, James sold the family farm to son, Albert Perlo, in September 1903, and bought property in Albany, Gentry County, Missouri. At Albany, John Hubert died, however, the 1910 U.S. Federal Census records indicate that at census time, he was living with brother Jesse Kinney in Iowa. Effie met and married her husband, Mr. Scott. Edith, Mary, and Ellen all finished high school, and all 3 taught school until they married according to family tradition.

According to family members, James was also known as a "typical Irishman." For example, one of his descendants recalled an Irish story he had told once: "Two Irishmen came over to this country and were passing a cemetery and Pat noticed a tall stone and written on it, 'Here lies a lawyer and an honest man,' and Pat turned to Mike and said, 'And bejebbers, how can they bury 2 men in 1 grave?'"

In 2013, the location of James Patrick Kinney's farm from 1892-1903

He was remembered as a wonderful, old gentlemen, always cheerful, and a true Christian man who was loved by all very much.

Family recalled he would often say, "Life is sweet and I've been able to do many of the tasks I think the Lord would have me do. And when my time comes, I can lie down on my pillow and go to sleep and be with my Savior."

On 21 October 1923, James joined Grant City Baptist Church by letter. He was a member there until his death in 1925.

James spent the latter part of his life in Grant City, Worth County, Missouri, often at the home of his son, Lindsey, and daughter-in-law, Lizzie. One afternoon he felt ill and went to his room to lie down. When Lizzie went to get him for supper, he had slipped away to his heavenly home. At James' funeral in 1925, he was given a military service with a gun salute over his grave.

2013 location of James Patrick Kinney farm from 1892-1903; note the older barn

James Patrick Kinney grave stone in Lott's Grove Cemetery

Lott's Grove Cemetery beside the Lott's Grove Church, a Baptist church near Allendale, Missouri

Questions:

1. When did James' parents, John Kinney and Bridget Flemming, immigrate to New York?
2. Where is Bridget buried?
3. Who did John Kinney marry after Bridget died?
4. How many children did John have?
5. Where is John Kinney buried?
6. What happened to James' uncle John who brought the family over from Ireland?
7. What was the name of James' sister?
8. Did he ever reunite with his sister?
9. Are there records of the orphan homes in Milwaukee during the 1850s which may include a record of James living there? If so, how to find them?
10. Where did James live in Beaver Dam, Dodge County, Wisconsin in 1859?
11. How did he get a job on a steamboat between La Crosse and St. Paul?
12. Is there a way to identify the Doctor Mann whom James lived with in Kansas City area who returned to Illinois to help Lincoln get elected?
13. Are there Census records for the Hibbs family James met when he first went to northwest Missouri?
14. Was James in the military two different times or three times? Are there military records of his service?
15. Did James take a wagon freight train down the Santa Fe Trail, which was the most widely used in 1865, or, by some chance, did he take a railroad train to New Mexico?

Lott's Grove Church, a Baptist church which, in 2013, was no longer meeting in this building

Last known residence of James Patrick Kinney, 1925, Grant City, Missouri, as seen in 2013

Questions, continued:

16. Is the C. H. Banes on the marriage certificate of James and Martha Anna the stepfather of Martha Anna? If so, what happened to her biological father?
17. Where is Blockton, Iowa, the inscription on the photo of C. H. Banes?
18. Are there records for Wray's Studio, Sheridan, MO, as inscribed on the photo of Martha Anna Dungan?
19. Where was Martha Anna born?
What was her mother's name?
20. How did James Patrick and Martha Anna meet?
21. When did they give birth to the child that didn't live to adulthood?
22. What was the child's sex and where is the child buried?
23. Where is Martha Anna buried?
24. Is there a wedding picture of Martha Anna and James Patrick? If so, where?
25. Where was James Patrick's land in Albany, MO?

The Children of James Patrick and Martha Anna Dungan Kinney

Ira Edward Kinney, Lott's Grove

Ira Edward Kinney
1867-1900

Not much has been learned about the first-born son of James and Martha except that he married Ruby M. and both are buried in the Lott's Grove Cemetery. There is a tower shaped grave stone with this inscription: "Ira E. Kinney died December 31, 1900 aged 33 years 8 months 9 days." On the reverse side of the tower is this inscription: "Ruby M. wife of I. E. Kinney." Next to the tower is a small rectangular stone inscribed: "Infant Son of I. E. and R. M. Kinney, died December 12, 1892, Age 13 days."

Questions:
1. What happened to Ira Edward Kinney? Why did he die so young?
2. Why did the child die?
3. Did he have other children? Family documents indicate he had a daughter.
4. When did wife Ruby die?
5. What was Ruby's maiden name?

Sarah Frances Kinney
1868-1925

Sarah Frances Kinney was born near Smithton, Worth County, Missouri, on 21 August 1868. She was the first daughter. On 27 July 1887 at Grant City, Worth County, Missouri, she married William Riley Ross whose parents were both dead. By the time Sarah was 31 years old, at the 1900 U.S. Federal Census, she had given birth to 6 children with 5 still living. These 5 were: Harry M., Katie, James W., son Leslie H., and daughter Dale. William was a farmer, born in June 1867, and was 32 years old. At the 1910 U.S. Federal Census, 2 more sons had been added to the family: Jessie M. and Clarence L. William was still farming on his own account, even though they had rented the land. The last Census record for Sarah was 1920. The 2 youngest sons were still living with the family, and they were still farming in Smith Township, Worth County, Missouri. Sarah died just 3 months after her father, James, on 20 July 1925. She is buried in Fletchall Cemetery, outside of Grant City, Worth County. Her husband, William Riley Ross, and a number of other Ross family members are buried in Fletchell Cemetery as well.

Sarah Frances Kinney Ross and husband William Riley Ross in Fletchall Cemetery, Missouri

Fletchall Cemetery Grant City, Missouri

Questions:

1. Where was Smithton Township?
2. How did Sarah meet William Riley Ross?
3. Why did she die so young?

Cora Clementine Kinney 1870-1938

Circa 1917 four generations of James Patrick Kinney family, oldest to youngest:

James Patrick Kinney with daughter Cora Clementine Kinney Keyes, granddaughter Sallie Keyes Rinehart, and great grandson Clarence Rinehart Junior.

Granddaughter of James Patrick Kinney, Sallie Keyes Rinehart, as she appeared in the1945 issue of Successful Farming Magazine

The third child of James and Martha Anna was daughter Cora Clementine Kinney, born 12 January 1870, in Smithton Township, Worth County, Missouri. She grew up in Worth County and attended both country schools and Grant City Schools. She married Robert C. Keyes 4 August 1886 in Grant City, Worth County, Missouri.

By the 1900 U.S. Federal Census, Cora and Robert had given birth to 4 children: Sallie Keyes, 1887; Ethel Keyes, 1889; Ralph Keyes, 1890; and Rush Keyes, 1891. The family was living in Bethany, Harrison County, Missouri. Although they were living on a farm, Robert was a traveling salesman. In the 1910 Census, Robert was a farmer and they lived on a rented farm in Glenwood, Mills County, Iowa. Cora had given birth to 6 children with 4 surviving.

By the 1920 Census, many changes had come into the lives of Cora and Robert as they were then living with son, Rush, and his wife, Grace, and their son, Robert R., an infant born in 1920. Rush was farming and they were living in Peterson Township, Clay County, Iowa. Robert was also farming, presumably with son Rush.

The 1930 Census revealed big changes again for Cora and Robert as they were then living in Silver Creek, Dixon County, Nebraska. Robert was still farming at age 66.

At Cora's death, 22 July 1938, they were residing in New Castle, Nebraska. Cora was returned to her daughter's home in Ridgeway, Missouri, for burial in the Rose Hill Cemetery. Cora's obituary dated 12 October 1938 (unknown source) states that she "was converted in early girlhood and lived the life that symbolized her true faith, so that her children, grandchildren, other relatives and friends 'may rise to call her blessed.'" The funeral service was held at the Ridgeway Christian Church and officiated by Rev. W. A. Tandy of Hamburg, Iowa, a nephew of Cora's.

Cora Clementine Kinney Keyes' legacy lives on through her children, particularly daughter, Sallie Keyes, and husband, Elmer Clarence Rinehart, grandchild, Clarence Rinehart Junior, great granddaughters, Joyce Ann, and Janice Sue Rinehart, and great, great grandchildren, Janice's children: Julie Ann Rhea, John William Rhea, and Justin Craig Rhea.

2013 two times great granddaughter of James Patrick Kinney, Janice Rinehart Bethards, center, surrounded by her family

Circa 1915, James Patrick Kinney and great grandson Clarence Rinehart, Junior

William Homer Kinney

1871-1913

The fourth child of James Patrick and Martha Anna Kinney, William Homer Kinney, was born in Rochester, Andrew County, Missouri in 1871. He joined 1 older brother and 2 older sisters. William Homer Kinney is my great grandfather. See page 29 for his life story and his descendants.

Jesse Arthur Kinney

1875-1959

Just before writing, I had absolutely no information on Jesse other than an approximate birth date. My newly-met cousin, Janice, shared his obituary and life story as told by his wife, Nora. It was as if I'd struck genealogical gold! Here is the account now.

The fifth of February 1875, Grant City, Worth County, Missouri was the birth date and location for Jesse Arthur Kinney, the fifth child born to James Patrick and Martha Anna Dungan Kinney.

In 1880, Jesse lived with the family in Grant City, Worth County, Missouri. He was 5 years old. His obituary states that his education came mostly from his father, James, who had traveled extensively and read much history.

Around 1896, Jesse began working as an Assistant Manager for one of David Rankin's 3,200 acre ranches. Rankin operated several ranches in the Tarkio, Atchison County, Missouri area. Supposedly, he was the largest cattle feeder in the U.S. and one of the first to use "riding cultivators." Cattle on just one of his ranches ate 900 bushels of corn daily to fatten them up for market.

Mt. Rushmore, near where Jesse lived in South Dakota

Around 1898, Jesse attended a "Singing School," along with Nora M. Deel, who would become his wife on 16 September 1900, in Westboro, Atchison County, Missouri. Following their wedding, the couple lived on one of David Rankin's ranches and farmed there for 2 years.

Nora Deel Kinney wrote an account of her life history entitled Memories of the Past, in which she detailed her childhood experiences growing up along the Tarkio River in Northwest Missouri. In this document, she states she and Jesse moved on from Missouri about 1903 to Silver City, Mills County, Iowa where they farmed for 7 years.

The 1910 U.S. Federal Census located the family farming in Keg Creek, Pottawattamie County, Iowa. The oldest daughter, Thelma E., 7, had been born in Missouri in 1903. Zelda M., 6, was born in 1904 in Iowa. Son, Frank E., 4, was born 1906 in Iowa. Also living with Jesse and Nora was Jesse's brother, Hubert John Kinney. He was 22 years old. A sad fact is revealed by this Census: Nora listed herself as mother of 5 children with 3 living. So, in just 10 short years of marriage, they had grieved the loss of 2 of their children.

Sometime after 1910, they bought a farm near Carns, Rock County, Nebraska, on the Niobrara River. Carns is no longer in existence in 2013, but it probably was located in today's Keyapaha County on the north side of the river, probably northeast of present day Bassett. There is a ghost town called Meadville marked on the 2013 Nebraska highway map along the river nearby.

Daughter, Lucille, was born here in 1915. In Carns, Nora says in Memories of the Past, "When drought and hail destroyed our crops we traded for some timber land, a farm, and property near Whitewood, South Dakota." Apparently, there were good schools in South Dakota, so they bought a farm in Spearfish Valley near Spearfish, South Dakota, and spent the next 17 years there. All 4 of the children completed high school and some attended college at the Spearfish Training School and Normal School. The family also attended the Congregational Church during this time.

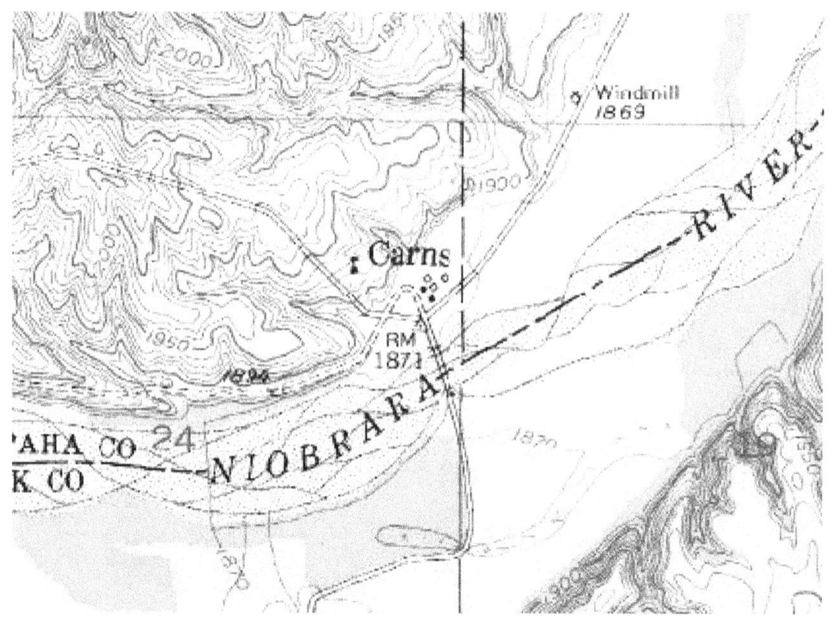

The 1920 U.S. Federal Census for Wells, Lawrence County, South Dakota, listed Jesse and Nora with 4 children. Jesse gave his occupation as truck farmer. This area was located in 2013's Black Forest near Mt. Rushmore, Jewel Cave, and Wind Cave. They were still living here, according to father James' 1925 obituary, which listed Jesse of Spearfish, South Dakota.

For the 1930 U.S. Federal Census, Jesse and Nora, both 55 years old, were living in Township 6, Lawrence County, South Dakota, with their 2 youngest children, Franklin and Lucille. Jesse was still farming. For some reason, Jesse stated his mother, Martha Anna Dungan Kinney, had been born in Scotland. On one Census record, Martha Anna stated her parents were born in Scotland, but some researchers claim they were from Howard County, Missouri. It is still unclear to me where the parents of Martha Anna Dungan were from.

Back in the Day . . . Although Carns is no longer in existence, the historic Carns Bridge over the Niobrara River, completed in 1913, is the oldest remaining bridge structure that was built under Nebraska's state aid bridge program. It replaced the timber bridge over the Niobrara River that was destroyed by ice during the winter of 1910. The bridge is located 10.8 miles northeast of Bassett, Nebraska, in a rural setting. To view a picture of the Carns State Aid Bridge, visit http://bridgehunter.com/ne/rock/c007522105/.

At the 1940 U.S. Federal Census, Jesse and Nora were living in Garfield Township, Jackson County, Kansas. They lived in this same place in 1935. Jesse again, was farming.

Nora's account of their lives, Memories of the Past, did not mention living in Garfield. She does state they lived for one year in Cawker City, Osborne County, Kansas, while caring for her aged parents, after which they lived the next 11 years farming in Holton, Jackson County, Kansas. Perhaps Garfield is near Holton.

Brother, Irvin A. Kinney's obituary in the 12 September 1945 issue of the Lincoln Nebraska State Journal, names Jesse as being from Holton, Kansas.

Probably sometime around 1946, Nora reports that regrettably, they had to sell their last farm in Kansas because of her inability to do her part of the work. They then moved to Tripp, South Dakota, to farm near daughter, Thelma, and her husband, Edwin. It was in Tripp they celebrated their golden wedding anniversary in 1950.

Nora attended the Methodist church while in Tripp. She described the town as, "progressive…but spiritual progress is a slow process in any town or community. There is always a contest between constructive and destructive forces and because of our indifference, good works are delayed. Our country has been involved in three wars in the last forty years and many homes have been saddened by the loss of their sons and brothers. Now in August 1954, it seems the whole world is at war. But we have the promise that eventually the right forces will overcome the wrong." She closes her family history account by quoting Psalm 23, "My cup runneth over."

~~~~~~

Psalm 23 – 1. The Lord is my shepherd, I lack nothing. 2. He makes me lie down in green pastures, he leads me beside quiet waters, 3. He refreshes my soul. He guides me along the right paths for his name's sake. 4. Even though I walk through the darkest valley, I will fear no evil, for you are with me; your rod and your staff, they comfort me. 5. You prepare a table before me in the presence of my enemies. You anoint my head with oil; my cup overflows. 6. Surely your goodness and love will follow me all the days of my life, and I will dwell in the house of the Lord forever." New International Version of the Holy Bible

~~~~~~

Around 1953, Jesse and Nora recorded records of the songs they had sung together 55 years earlier.

Jesse died 10 November 1959, in Tripp, Hutchinson County, South Dakota. He had been ill for 9 months. He was survived by wife, Nora Kinney, and his 4 children, Thelma, who married Edwin Mayer of Tripp, South Dakota; Zelda, of Bakersfield, California; Franklin, who married Edythe Clausen and lived in Rapid City, South Dakota; and Lucille, who married George Wendt, and lived in Wisconsin Rapids, Wisconsin.

Questions:

1. What happened to the 2 children they gave birth to according to the 1910 U.S. Federal Census that did not survive? What was the sex of the children? Where are they buried?
2. What was the name of the record they recorded around 1953-1955 of the songs they had sung before they were married?
3. Where was the Singing School located?
4. What parts did each sing: soprano, alto, tenor, or bass?

Effie Jane Kinney

1876-1919

Born 19 October 1876, near Isadora, Worth County, Missouri, Effie Jane was the sixth child of James and Martha. In the 1900 U.S. Federal Census for her family, she was living in Lincoln Township, Harrison County, Missouri. Following the death of her mother, Martha Anna Dungan Kinney, Effie moved from the farm with her father and younger sisters to Athens Township, Albany City, Gentry County.

On 27 July 1906, she married Stephen Alfred Scott who was born in 1860. Effie would have been 30 years old and Stephen 46 when they married. This was the second marriage for Stephen.

He had a son named Byron Scott, 14, who was living with the family. Effie and Stephen had 2 sons and 1 daughter: Noel Gard Scott, born 18 August 1907; Vida Marie Scott, 1911-1912; and James E. Scott, born 1918.

In the 1910 U.S. Federal Census, the family was living in Cooper Township, Gentry County, Missouri, and Stephen's widowed sister, Lib Scott, was living with them, as well as Stephen's son from his first marriage, John Byron Scott, who was 15 years old. Stephen was a farmer working on his own account on a rented farm.

Just 9 months after giving birth to son, James, Effie succumbed to pneumonia with influenza and died 22 March 1919. She is buried either in Grandview Cemetery, Albany, Gentry County, Missouri, or in Gribble Cemetery, Darlington, where Stephen and daughter, Vida Marie, lie side by side.

Questions:

1. Where exactly is Effie Jane buried?
2. Why did daughter Vida Marie die?

Lindsy A. Kinney

1879-??

Lindsy A. Kinney was born 13 July 1879, near Smithton Township, Worth County, Missouri. His middle name was either Addington, as he listed on his World War I Draft Registration Card, or Addison, as he signed in his own hand on his WWI Draft Card. The author has seen both names referenced in various sources. When he served as administrator of his father James' estate in 1925, he was going by L. A. Kinney. His WWI Draft Card described him as medium height and build, with blue eyes and gray hair.

Lindsy first appeared in the 1880 U.S. Federal Census at age 11 months, the seventh child of James and Martha Anna. The family was living in Grant City, Worth County, Missouri.

He was not listed in the 1900 U.S. Census with his family, nor have I located a separate Census entry for Lindsy.

On 24 February 1904, Lindsy Kinney married Elizabeth Noe in Burlington Junction, Nodaway County, Missouri.

The 1910 U.S. Federal Census showed Lindsy and Elizabeth living in Oak Township, Mills County, Iowa. They had 2 sons: James H., 4; and Ralph H., 7 months. Lindsy was farming and had a 17 year old hired man by the name of Hans Ernest living with him.

At the 1920 U.S. Federal Census, added to the family were a daughter, Faye, 7; and two more sons, Clarence, 2; and Kenneth, who was either 11 months old, or 2 years and 11 months. The record is unclear. They had relocated back to Worth County, Missouri, in Fletchall Township. We do know that at the end of his father, James Patrick's, life in 1925, Lindsey and wife, Lizzie, were providing care for James. Family tradition states that James died in Lindsy's home. Lindsy also administered James' estate, according to records accessed at the Worth County Courthouse in 2013

They continued farming in the 1930 U.S. Census and were living in Fletchall Township, Worth County, Missouri. Daughter Faye, 17, was the last child in the home.

During the 1930s, the Great Depression combined with the Dust Bowl which affected the Midwest farming community, forced many farming families to seek other occupations. These circumstances may have influenced Lindsy and Elizabeth, as in the 1940 U.S. Federal Census, we see they had returned to Iowa, in Buena Vista Township, Marathon County. They were living in a rented home with at least 2 sons, Ralph and Kenneth. They also lived there in 1935. Lindsy was working as a caretaker for a cemetery. He only worked 26 weeks during 1939 with an income of just $270. He indicated he had income from other sources. Sons, Ralph and Kenneth, were listed as proprietors and attendants of a gas station, working on their own account. Perhaps they had purchased a gas station. This was apparently hard work as each indicated they had worked 84 hours the week prior to the Census taking. On the Census record, son, Clarence, had been listed, but crossed off and replaced by the wording "extra line". It's unclear what this may mean.

As of 2013, I have not yet located a death certificate for Lindsy, nor wife, Elizabeth.

Questions:

1. Where is Lindsy in the 1900 U.S. Federal Census?
2. Is his middle name Addington or Addison?
3. Where did he meet his wife Elizabeth Noe?
4. Where and when did Lindsy and Elizabeth die?
5. Where are they buried?

Irvin A. Kinney

1882-1945

On 25 October 1882, Irvin A. Kinney was born in Grant City, Worth County, Missouri. He joined 7 older siblings in the James Patrick and Martha Anna Dungan Kinney household. He was listed as "at school" in the family's 1900 U.S. Federal Census, although he was 19 years old at the time.

On 1 October 1903, Irvin married Addie Bell Humphrey of Allendale, Worth County.

In 1910, Irvin and Adalaide had relocated to Edna Township, Barnes County, North Dakota, where Irvin was farming on rented land. Three children had been added to the family in the 6 years since they had married: son, Wayne J., 6; daughter, Mable L., 4; and son, Weldon B., 6 months old.

We find them next in Cass, Nebraska as recorded on Irvin's World War I Draft Registration Card of 1918. Their address was R.F.D. 2 Weeping Water, Cass, Nebraska. Irvin was a self-employed farmer. His description was medium height and build, with blue eyes and brown hair.

In 1920, they were still in Cass, Nebraska, farming on rented land. Interestingly, the family next door was named Fleming, the maiden name of Irvin's grandmother. There's no indication, however, these 2 families were related to each other that I have been able to uncover, but it does bear investigating at a later date. Two more children had joined the family: a daughter, Doris, born in 1915, and a son, Merle, who was about 5 months old.

In father James' 1925 obituary, Irvin was listed as living in Alvo, Nebraska, at that time.

At the 1930 U.S. Federal Census, Irvin and Addie had been married 21 years, and they no longer lived on a farm, yet Irvin's occupation was general farm laborer. They were living in the

MARRIAGE LICENSE.

STATE OF MISSOURI

COUNTY OF Worth

This License authorizes any Judge of a Court of Record, or Justice of the Peace, or any licensed or ordained Preacher of the Gospel, who is a Citizen of the United States, to solemnize Marriage between Irvin A. Kinney of Allendale, in the County of Worth and State of Mo., who is over the age of twenty-one years, and Addie Bell Humphrey of Allendale, in the County of Worth and State of Mo, who is over the age of eighteen years.

*

Witness my hand as Circuit Clerk and Ex-Officio Recorder of Deeds, with the Seal of Office hereto affixed, at my Office in Grant City Mo. this 1st day of October 1903

By [illegible] DEPUTY. [illegible] CIRCUIT CLERK AND EX-OFFICIO RECORDER OF DEEDS.

*NOTE - If the man is under twenty-one, or the woman under eighteen, add the following: The Father (giving his name, or Mother or Guardian, as the case may be) of the said A.B. (or C.D. as the case may require) has given his (or her) assent to the said Marriage.

State of Missouri, COUNTY OF Worth } SS. This is to Certify, that the undersigned M. P. Glenn did, at Grant City, in said County, on the 1st day of October, A.D. 1903, unite in Marriage the above named persons, and I further Certify, that I am a Citizen of the United States and legally qualified under the Laws of the State of Missouri to solemnize Marriages.

M. P. Glenn

NO. 1.

Marriage License for Irvin and Addie Bell Kinney

Greenwood Precinct of Cass County, Nebraska. The 2 youngest children were still living with the family.

I have not yet located Irvin and Addie in the 1940 U.S. Federal Census, but an obituary for Irvin appeared in the Lincoln Nebraska State Journal 12 September 1945 ,which stated that Irvin, 63, of Alvo, died in Elmwood. He was survived by wife Adalade Bell, sons Wayne of Elmwood; Weldon of Portland; Merle of Seattle; and 2 daughters listed by their married names: Mrs. Carrol Foreman of Cheyenne and Mrs. Jack Herganrader of Lincoln.

Questions:

1. Where were Irvin and Addie in the 1940 U.S. Federal Census?
2. Which daughter, Doris or Mabel, married which man as listed in Irvin's obituary: Mrs. Carrol Foreman of Cheyenne and Mrs. Jack Herganrader of Lincoln

Albert Perlo Kinney

1884-??

Albert Perlo Kinney was born near Allendale, located just west of Grant City in Worth County, 24 January 1884. He was the next to the last son. Perlo grew up on the family farm, so it is not surprising that when James decided to sell in 1903, Perlo agreed to purchase on 12 September 1903. Interestingly enough, we find that Perlo sold the farm less than 2 years after buying it on 31 December 1904.

Also in 1903, on 11 August, Perlo married Manerva M. Pinkerton in Worth County. Since Perlo was not yet 21 years old, he had to have permission from his father, James, to marry.

In his father, James Patrick Kinney's, obituary of 1925, Perlo's residence was Aurelia, Iowa. In his brother, Irvin A. Kinney's obituary of 1945, Perlo wasn't mentioned.

One family document indicated Perlo had 3 children. There was a 1920 U.S. Federal Census for Albert P. Kinney with a wife named Bessie Kinney. They were living in Logan, Clay County, Iowa, and had 3 children: Lucile R., 9; Harold, 6; and Clark, 1½ years old. There was also a 1910 U.S. Federal Census for A. P. Kinney with wife Bessie, living in Nebraska.

If this is our Perlo in the 1910 and 1920 Census records referenced above, then what happened to wife Manerva Pinkerton?

As of 2013, I have found no death certificate for Perlo, nor any death certificate for Manerva Pinkerton Kinney.

Consent for Marriage from James Kinney for his Son Albert Perlo Kinney

To all who shall see these presents.
Know ye that I James Kinney father of Albert P. Kinney a minor under the age of 21 years do hereby consent that he may marry Minerva M. Pinkerton and that a license issue therefor.

James Kinney

Subscribed and sworn to before me this 11 day of Aug. [illegible]
G. K. Conklin, J.P.

Albert Perlo Kinney with his cousin Ethel Keyes Tye

Questions:

1. When did Perlo die and where?
2. Did his first wife Manerva Pinkerton Kinney die young?
3. Did Perlo marry a second time to a Bessie Kinney?
4. Could Manerva be going by the name of Bessie?
5. Where is Perlo in the 1930 and 1940 U.S. Federal Censuses?

Mary E. Kinney

1886-??

Mary E. Kinney was born 23 December 1886, near Allendale, Missouri. She lived at the family farm in Harrison County at the 1900 U.S. Federal Census. The Ledger newspaper, Gentry County, issue 25 December 1912, listed a marriage license issued for R. R. Rouse of Darlington, Gentry County, and Mary E. Kinney, from Albany, Gentry County. Family tradition states that R. R. Rouse died just 4 months after marriage, and Mary Rouse gave birth to a son later.

In the 1920 U.S. Federal Census, Mary was living with her mother-in-law, Catherine Rouse, in Cooper Township, Gentry County, Missouri, on Seventh Street. A son, Donald E. Rouse, was living with the family. Mary was working as a clerk in a bank.

In the 1925 obituary of her father, James Patrick Kinney, Mrs. Mary Rouse of Darlington, Missouri, was listed among the surviving children. Again, in the 1945 death obituary for her brother, Irvin A. Kinney, among the surviving siblings was Mrs. Mary Rouse, Darlington, Missouri.

A check of the 1930 U.S. Federal Census listed Mary E. Rouse, widowed head of house, with her 16 year old son, Donald E. Rouse. She was living in her own home and valued it at $700. She listed her occupation as bookkeeper at a bank, although she was actually unemployed at the Census time.

In the 1940 U.S. Federal Census, we find Donald had married Lavonne, and they were living in Cooper Township, Darlington, Gentry County, Missouri. Donald was doing road construction for the government. There was no mention of his mother, Mary Rouse.

In 2013, while driving through Darlington, Missouri, I located a cemetery named "Darlington Rouse." It was located outside of the town surrounded by corn fields. As it was almost sunset, we took a quick drive through on the lane reading grave stones as we passed , but did not see any Rouse grave stones.

Questions:

1. What was the full name of Mary's husband, R. R. Rouse?
2. When did he die and what was the cause of his early demise?
3. Where is he buried?
4. When did Mary die and where is she buried?
5. What became of her son, Donald?

Hubert John Kinney

1888-1913

Child No. 11 was born 31 August 1888. At the 1900 U.S. Federal Census, he was living with the family on their farm in Lincoln Township, Harrison County, Missouri. By the 1910 Census, he was living with his brother, Jesse, and family in Keg Creek, Pottawattamie County, Iowa. He probably returned to his father's place in Albany, Gentry County, Missouri, sometime after the Census, as he died there 19 January 1913, at the young age of 24. He was buried in the Grandview Cemetery, Albany, Gentry County, Missouri. His Find A Grave Memorial No. is 32327201.

Entrance to Grandview Cemetery, where Hubert John Kinney is buried.

Questions:

1. Is Hubert John or John Hubert the correct name order?
2. How did he die so young?
3. Did he ever marry?

Edith Lodema Kinney

1890-1964

Edith Lodema Kinney Mayberry's grave stone

Edith Lodema Kinney was born 16 June 1890, Worth County, Missouri, to James Patrick and Martha Anna Dungan Kinney. At the 1900 U.S. Federal Census, Edith was 9 years old and living with the family on their farm in Lincoln Township, Harrison County. In the 1910 Census, we find she was living with her father and 2 younger sisters in Athens Township, Gentry County, Missouri. Her mother had passed away when she was just 10 years old.

According to her obituary in the Opinion/Tribune, Glenwood, Iowa, 16 July 1964, Edith graduated from a Missouri college and taught at Glenwood State School, Glenwood, Iowa for many years. The 1920 Census located her living in Oakwood, Mills County, Iowa, with her husband and first child, Mary, who was 11 months at Census time.

The 1925 Iowa State Census listed the oldest daughter as Mary C., 5; along with Virginia, who was 3.

At the 1930 Census, there were 5 children living in the home: Catherine, 10; Virginia, 7; Anna, 5; James, 3; and Forest, 1½. Husband, Ralph, seems to have had a title of Rev. although his occupation was listed as farmer, and the family was residing on a farm. There was no mention of their first daughter, Mary, who would be about 11 years old at this time.

In the 1940 Census, Ralph and Edith were in their late 40s, and daughter, Mary, reappeared on the Census, along with Virginia, 17; Emma, 14; James, 13; Forrest, 11; and Beth Ellen, 9. Probably, "Anna" in the 1930 Census was a misspelling of "Emma". Daughter, Catherine, does not appear. Perhaps Catherine was "Mary Catherine."

Edith died 13 July 1964 in Council Bluffs, Iowa. Her Find-A-Grave Memorial No. is 73283593. She is buried in Glenwood Cemetery, Glenwood, Mills County, Iowa.

There are Find-A-Grave memorials for husband, Ralph H. Mayberry, and 4 children: Emma E. Mayberry Gilson; Virginia Rose Mayberry Scott; Mary Catherine Mayberry Jackson; and James Harvey Mayberry.

Ralph Mayberry's obituary in the Opinion/Tribune, Glenwood, Iowa, 3 March 1971, p. 12, states that he died 26 February 1971, in Glenwood, Iowa. He was a farmer most of his life and an Assessor for the Township of Glenwood. In addition, he worked at the Glenwood State Hospital School. He had been a member of the First Christian Church in Glenwood for more than 50 years. We also learn of a daughter, Margaret Emily, who died in infancy.

Questions:

1. Which "Missouri college" did Edith graduate from and what year?
2. Was husband, Ralph Mayberry, a minister or some type of lay pastor?
3. What happened to infant daughter, Margaret Emily? Why did she die, and where is she buried?

Martha Ellen Kinney

1893-1957

The last child who survived past the 1900 U.S. Federal Census, of James Patrick and Martha Anna Dungan Kinney, was born 17 May 1893, Martha Ellen Kinney, in Harrison County, Missouri, presumably at the family farm. According to the 1910 U.S. Federal Census, she moved with her father and sisters who remained in the home, to Athens Township, Albany City, Gentry County, Missouri.

The 11 July 1912 issue of The Ledger newspaper from Gentry County, announced her marriage on 9 July 1912, to Gail DeWitt Dalton of Glenwood, Iowa. The marriage was performed by Rev. F. C. Fay. Her father was titled "Squire" James Kinney! I suppose by the time his 13th child married, he was entitled to be called Squire.

On Gail's World War I Draft Registration Card, we find that he had served 3 years as a noncommissioned infantry officer in the Iowa National Guard. He was described as medium height and build, with dark brown eyes and hair.

At the time of the 1920 U.S. Federal Census, Martha Ellen, and husband, Gail, were living in the Glenwood Township, Mills County, Iowa. They had 2 children: son, Gail D. Junior; and daughter, Meredith K. Gail was a mechanic at a garage.

In 1930, they were still living in Glenwood. The U.S. Federal Census listed their address as 8 North Hazel Street. Gail D. Dalton was born in Iowa, his father born in Illinois, and his mother also born in Iowa. A third child, daughter, Patricia K., had joined the family. She was 10 years old. The family was renting their house for $25 per month, and Gail continued as a mechanic in a garage. An interesting point is that Martha Ellen listed her father, James Patrick Kinney's birthplace, as "Ireland Free State". This comment perhaps gives some insight into the views of James regarding early 1900s political upheaval in Ireland.

By 1940, we find a change as the family had moved to Eugene, Oregon, as per the Eugene City Directory: Gail D. Dalton and wife Martha Ellen, mechanic for Motor Sales and Service Company. They lived at 1772 Lawrence Street. Also, we find a listing for Gail D. Dalton, Jr., and his wife, Genevieve A. They lived at the same 1772 Lawrence address, and he has apparently followed in his father's footsteps, as his job was "body man" for Frink's Auto Refinishing Shop.

Although the City Directory listed one employment for Gail, in the 1940 U.S. Federal Census, Gail Senior, listed a different employment as a mechanic at a Packard Garage, and he made $1,200 for the year. His son, Gail D. Dalton, Jr., made $912 for the year. Geneivieve, was a waitress at Dean's Place and made $120. She worked just 12 weeks, while her father-in-law and husband worked 52 weeks each. A grandson, Frederick, the son of Gail Junior and Geneivieve, was living with the family. He was born in 1937. The Census also revealed that in 1935, Gail and Martha Ellen still lived in Glenwood, as well as son Gail, Junior, but Geneivieve and son, Frederick, lived in Silver City, Mills, Iowa. Who knows what this may mean.

At age 47, we see that Gail Dalton had to register for the World War II Draft. At that time he listed his employer as Motor Sales and Service, 805 Pearl Street, Eugene, Oregon. I wonder if this record was, in fact, for his son, Gail, Jr.

Martha Ellen Kinney Dalton passed away 10 January 1957, in Eugene, Lane County, Oregon. Husband, Gail DeWitt Dalton, followed her 19 July 1958, also in Lane County, Oregon.

The Parents of James Patrick Kinney
John Kinney and Bridget Flemming
of County Galway, Ireland

I know very little of James' father, John Kinney, except what has been gleaned from James' autobiography. John Kinney was born in County Galway, Ireland, around 1811. He married Bridget Flemming. At some point, they migrated to England, as James Patrick was born in Newton, Lancashire, England, as their oldest son. James stated his sister lived with John Kinney's uncle, Peter Lonehat, in England, while James went to Ireland with his mother's brother, James' uncle, John Flemming. James writes that John and Bridget went to the U.S. in 1850 and settled in Yates County [New York]. While there, Bridget died, 3 February 1853. James says his Uncle John brought him and his sister to the U.S. in 1852. He also says that he came after the death of his mother. So, perhaps James left Ireland in late 1852 for the journey by a sailing vessel across the Atlantic, and he did not arrive before his mother's death in February 1853.

James also stated his father, John Kinney, remarried and moved to Ohio in 1854, and then on to Iowa in 1856. Presumably, James moved with the family, at least to Iowa, as his account of running away from home began in Iowa. We also know that John Kinney had children by his second wife. At the time of this writing in 2013, I have not been successful in discovering anything further on John Kinney or Bridget Flemming.

Questions

1. What happened to John Kinney after he immigrated to the U.S.?
2. Who was his second wife?
3. Where did he live?
4. Did he ever see his son, James Patrick Kinney, again in this life?
5. What was James' older sister's name? What became of her?
6. Where is Bridget Flemming buried?
7. Is there a death record for Bridget?
8. What ship did James' uncle sail on when he brought James and his sister to the U.S.?

2

William Homer Kinney

1871-1913

William Homer Kinney (1871 - 1913)

is your great grandfather

Vernon Haven Kinney (1902 - 1984)

son of William Homer Kinney

Lawrence Sherman Kinney (1928 -)

son of Vernon Haven Kinney

Barbara Elaine Kinney

daughter of Lawrence Sherman Kinney

William Homer Kinney sometime before 1913

When William Homer Kinney was born on 13 October 1871, in Independence, Missouri, his father, James Patrick Kinney, was 26 years old and his mother, Martha Ann Dungan Kinney, was 20. This birth place was recorded in the Bible of his daughter-in-law, Alberta Anna Bell Culbreath Kinney. Another researcher states he was born near Rochester, Andrew County, Missouri, which in 2013 was located northeast of St. Joseph, Missouri, at the intersection of U.S. highway 169 and State highway V.

By the 1880 U.S. Federal Census, William Homer's family was living in Grant City, Worth County, Missouri. William Homer was the fourth child born of seven living at the time of the Census.

On 20 October 1896, William Homer married Anna Rachel Fox in Daviess County, Missouri, at her father's home. Their marriage license states that William Homer was from Grundy County, while Anna Rachel was from Grand River Township, Daviess County. Perhaps William Homer was living and working in Grundy County. They were married by Elder Thompson Penn of the Methodist church.

By the 1900 U.S. Federal Census, they were living in Tarkio City, Atchison County, Missouri, and had already given birth to son, Homer Veigh, born in Gallatin, Daviess County on 28 August 1897, and daughter, Valeria, born in January 1900, presumably in Tarkio City, which in 2013, was located just east of the intersection of U.S. highways 136 and 59. William Homer listed his occupation as farmhand. He rented his home and it was classified as a house.

In 1902, we find the family was living in Coffeysberg, Daviess County, where son, Vernon Haven, was born on 21 February 1902. In 2013, Coffeysberg was known as Coffey, and was located in Daviess County at the intersection of State highways H and B.

Sometime before 1904, the family moved to Grant County, Oklahoma Territory.

On son, James August's, certificate of birth, under the question of father's occupation, the response was that William Homer was a landowner. In addition to farming, based on various newspaper articles from 1904-1913 in The Medford Star and The Medford Patriot, we find evidence that William Homer also sold hail insurance and farm land.

For example, in The Medford Star (Medford, Oklahoma), Vol. 11, No. 24, Ed. 1 Thursday, November 24, 1904, we see the following advertisement: "Farm Loans. We solicit your business. We have as cheap rates and as quick money as any in the county. We also want 10 well improved farms to sell to eastern buyers. – W. H. Kinney, Medford." This same ad appeared at least 25 more times during 1904 and 1905.

The Medford Star (Medford, Oklahoma), Vol. 14, No. 15, Ed. 1 Thursday, September 12, 1907, reported: "For Sale. A span of sucking mule colts, call at my farm 3 miles north of Medford or drop me a line and will have them in Medford any Saturday. W. H. Kinney."

William Homer solicited business with this ad in The Medford Patriot (Medford, Oklahoma Territory), Vol. 6, No. 33, Ed. 1 Thursday, May 26, 1904, "Hail Insurance. Protect your growing crops from hail in the El Reno Insurance Co. Call on us at F. S. Fisher's office or drop us a card and we will call on you. W. H. Kinney, Medford, Oklahoma."

This announcement appeared in The Medford Patriot (Medford, Oklahoma), Vol. 18, No. 39, Ed. 1 Thursday, July 6, 1911, "W. H. Kinney living north of town reports threshing going on in his vicinity and yield below normal. Says that his father-in-law Mr. J. V. Fox, has 25 acres of fine oats, that will yield over forty bushels per acre. Mr. Kinney also does a little real estate business on the side, and reports the sale of the Mrs. Bena Somers farm, 8 miles N.E. of Medford to Geo. Bennett for $7,000."

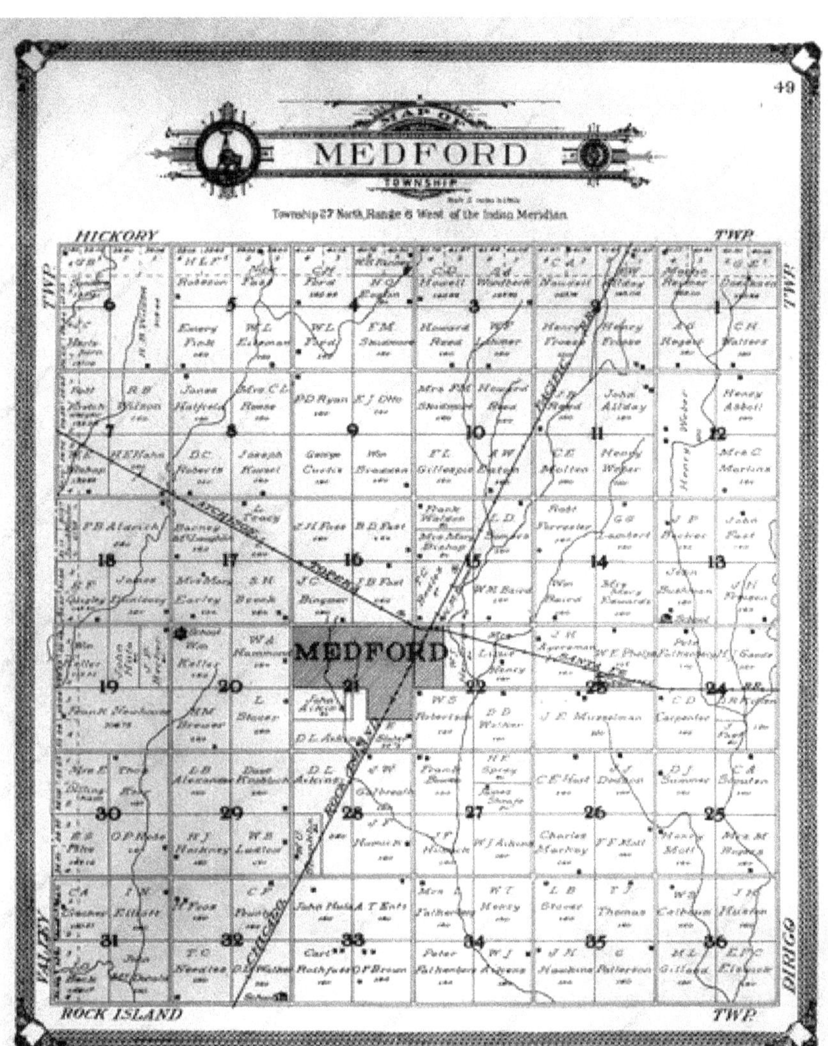

Plat Map of Grant County, showing W. H. Kinney on Lots 1 & 2, in the north half of the N.E. Quarter of Section 4, map accessed at HistoricMapWorks.com in 2013 2013 land formerly belonging to W. H. Kinney or his wife, Anna Rachel Fox Kinney, during the 1900s and 1910s.

In the 1910 U.S. Federal Census, William Homer listed his occupation as "farmer, home farm, working on his own account." He owned the farm with a mortgage. Anna's response to the census question, "Mother of how many children: number born" is "five." Her answer to the next question, "Mother of how many children: number living" is "four," which reveals a sad fact about the family's experience. Although no birth certificate has been located as of 2013, it is calculated that a child could have been born sometime between 1903 and 1908. In an application for life insurance dated 1918, Vernon Haven lists an "infant brother". As no name is given, perhaps the child died shortly after birth.

At age 42, William Homer Kinney died of a gunshot wound to the stomach. He had been suffering with cancer of the stomach according to family tradition. Also on Vernon Haven's life insurance application, the answer to a question about father's death was, "father, 42, dead, stomach cancer, sick 2 years." William Homer left behind his wife, Anna, and 4 children ranging in age from 5 to 15.

Two different inquiries in 2013 to Vital Records in Oklahoma City failed to produce a death certificate. It has been suggested a check for records at the Grant County Coroner's Office might prove useful as suspicious death, such as a gunshot, were often investigated with an autopsy.

William Homer is reportedly buried in Rosemound Cemetery, Medford, Grant County, Oklahoma according to the book, Silent Cities of Grant County, Oklahoma, by Pearcy and Talkington, 1993. The book states the incorrect spelling of "W. H. Kiney" buried in Rosemound Cemetery. Records located at the entrance to the cemetery list "Witt Kiney" which easily could be a misprint of W. H. Kinney. During a search of the Rosemound Cemetery in October, 2013, I could find no tombstone, although cemetery records indicate he is buried directly behind his in-laws, James Vernon and Mary Haven Fox. Both the James Vernon Fox 4-grave plot and the 4-grave plot where W. H. Kinney is buried are outlined with concrete borders. According to the cemetery director, Mr. Cink, such concrete borders are currently against regulations as they interfere with the large commercial grass mowers used to maintain the cemetery grounds. The fact that no other concrete borders appear anywhere in the cemetery leads me to believe the two 4-grave plots are related to each other and were bordered with concrete probably when they were initially purchased.

Questions:

1. How did William Homer Kinney meet Anna Rachel Fox, his wife?
2. When did they move to Oklahoma?
3. Did they own land in any place in Missouri?
4. When was the child born that was listed as dead by the 1910 U.S. Federal Census?
5. What was the sex of this child and where is the child buried?

6. Why was there no death certificate found in the State of Oklahoma records for William Homer when searched in July, 2013?
7. Why was there no warranty deed found for the land in Medford township, Grant County, Oklahoma, that William Homer supposedly owned when searched in October, 2013, even though his name appeared on a 1907 Grant County plat map? In addition, his widow, Anna Rachel Fox Kinney, appears to sell the same land on which his name appeared in the plat map, after his death.
8. Was there a coroner's report on a possible autopsy filed in the county medical examiner's office? If so, this could possibly explain why 2 different requests for a death certificate from Vital Statistics failed to turn up any record.

2013, Rosemound Cemetery, Grant County, Oklahoma. W. H. Kinney's plot is reportedly in the 4-plot grave outlined by the concrete border at the upper left corner of the picture. See where the ground has been dug up inside the lower left corner of the upper left 4-plot grave's concrete border.

The Children of Anna Rachel Fox and William Homer Kinney

Homer Veigh Kinney

1897-1992

The first child born to Anna Rachel Fox and William Homer Kinney was Homer Veigh Kinney on 28 August 1897 in Gallatin, Daviess County, Missouri.

In the 1900 U.S. Federal Census, Homer was 2 years old and living with his family in Tarkio City, Atchison County, Missouri. His father, William Homer, was a farmhand and living on rented land. Perhaps he may have been working at the same location as his brother, Jesse A. Kinney, who was an Assistant Manager for a 3,200 acre ranch in the Tarkio area.

Sometime around 1904, his family moved to Grant County, Oklahoma, where his father, William Homer, pursued real estate, insurance sales, and farming. Veigh attended school, probably in Medford.

209 Mathewson Avenue, Wichita, Kansas as seen in 2013, the former home of William Allen Anderson, where Veigh, Vernon, and James lived with their mother, Anna Rachel Fox between 1918 and 1920

205 Mathewson Avenue, Wichita, former home of Mamie Alice Drum who married Veigh Kinney

For example, in The Medford Patriot, (Medford, Oklahoma, Vol. 20, No. 33, Ed. 1 Thursday 22 May, 1913 it was reported that Veigh graduated from the eighth grade and his class was among the largest ever graduated in Medford.

In the 1910 U.S. Federal Census, Veigh, 11, was listed with his family in Medford Township, Grant County, Oklahoma. Father, William Homer, was farming at this time.

In 1913, Veigh, at 14 years old, experienced the loss of his father, William Homer. I wonder if Veigh felt the weight of providing for his mother and younger siblings.

Sometime around 1915 or 1916, the family made a move to Wichita, Sedgwick County, Kansas

In 1918, Veigh, then 21 years old, completed his World War I Draft Registration Card and listed his residence as 209 Mathewson Avenue, Wichita, Kansas. He stated his employment was as a truck driver for the Carter Oil Company "on the Porter Lease" in Butler County, Kansas. He also described himself as tall, medium build, with blue eyes and brown hair. He must have been a handsome man, because he soon attracted the attention of Mamie Alice Drum.

She lived next door at 205 Mathewson Avenue with her mother, Lillie E. Drum. Both mother and daughter had to work as Lillie was a widow. Lillie was working at Domestic Laundry Company, while Mamie Alice was an operator. Mamie Alice Drum and Homer Veigh Kinney were married 4 December 1919 in Wichita, Sedgwick, Kansas. Veigh's occupation was a mechanic for Western Motor Car Company, according to the 1919 Wichita City Directory.

Shortly after their marriage, the couple relocated to El Dorado, Butler County, according to the 1920 U.S. Federal Census. They were renting a home while Veigh worked as an automobile machinist. I wonder if he was still working in the oil industry.

On 10 January 1922, their first son was born, Veigh Alva Kinney, in Pawhuska, Oklahoma. Today, Pawhuska is the county seat for Osage County, and the entire area is the Osage Indian Reservation. They welcomed their first daughter, Betty Nell Kinney, on 16 August 1924, while living in Pawhuska.

By January of 1927, Veigh and family had relocated to the Texas Panhandle where daughter, Juanita Naoma, was born on the second of January.

Above: Barbara looking at a gigantic belt drive used in oil drilling, circa 1920s

Part of an oil drilling rig circa 1920s

Part of a 1920s oil drill, the "bull wheel" controlled the cables to raise and lower the bit out of the hole. The drilling crew could gauge the progress by watching the cable.

~~~~~~

Back in the Day . . . El Dorado, Butler County, Kansas, was a booming oil production center during the 1860s and into the 1930s. The Kansas Oil Museum preserves the history with exhibits including a 100-foot steel derrick and cable-tool drilling rig among other full-sized pieces of oil drilling equipment. For more information, contact Butler County History Center, El Dorado, Kansas.

~~~~~~

Their fourth child, Victor Homer, was born 17 February 1930 in Odessa, Ector County, Texas. The 1930 U.S. Federal Census recorded their address as 188 South Avenue, Odessa, Ector County, Texas. Although they were living on a farm, Veigh was working as a trucker in the oil fields.

Sometime later, Veigh would take up farming near Seagraves, Texas. His nephew, Lawrence Sherman Kinney, was stationed in nearby Lubbock, Texas, during the Korean War from 1951-55. Lawrence and wife, Betty Mae, often spent holidays with Veigh and Alice on their farm. My family would later visit Veigh and Alice in the summer of 1969, and again in May of 1982.

Ava Joyce with mother Betty Kinney Hudson and grandfather Veigh Kinney

Alice and Veigh admire baby chicks

Christmas Day 1952

Christmas Day 1952

Veigh and Alice Kinney with Betty Mae and Lawrence Kinney on Christmas Day, 1952

Betty Kinney Hudson and her parents Veigh and Alice Kinney on Christmas Day, 1952, near Lubbock, Texas

Veigh and Alice's daughter, Betty Kinney, married Ben Hudson. They had 3 daughters. Their oldest was Ava Joyce Hudson, pictured above left with her mother and grandfather, Veigh. The other 2 daughters were Carolyn and Darlene.

At the age of 95, on 11 November 1992, Homer Veigh passed away in Lubbock, Lubbock County, Texas. His Find A Grave Memorial No. 20457110, shows he is interred in the mausoleum at Resthaven Memorial Park in Lubbock, Lubbock County, Texas.

His wife, Mamie Alice Drum Kinney, preceded him in death on 21 September 1984, as well as his oldest son, Veigh Alva Kinney, on 16 February 1958, youngest daughter, Juanita Naoma, on 10 October 1974, youngest son, Homer Victor, on 11 August 1988, and finally, his oldest daughter, Betty Nell Kinney Hudson, on 22 January 1992. I cannot fathom what sorrow he must have endured to have lost his entire family to early death. It is in times like these that one's faith in God gives the strength to go on living.

~~~~~~

In the Present . . . The Nature Conservancy's Tall Grass Prairie Preserve is located north of Pawhuska, Oklahoma on the Osage Indian Reservation. It preserves 37,500 acres of the original unplowed tall grass prairie that once covered more than 142 million acres in 14 states. The Preserve features native big bluestem grass, Indian grass, switch grass, and little bluestem grass in addition to a variety of prairie wildflowers, songbirds, venomous snakes, the endangered prairie-chicken, raptors, and, most impressively, a huge herd of American bison.

~~~~~~

Tall Grass Prairie wildflower

American bison roam the prairie grass preserve

Prairie grass includes little blue stem and wire grass

Near Pawhuska, Oklahoma, 2013

Oil truck
Sunset while driving near Pawhuska
Veigh and Alice with grandchildren
Veigh in Miami 1955

Valeria Kinney

1900-1918

William Homer and Anna Rachel welcomed a beautiful baby girl, Valeria Kinney, in January of 1900. She joined older brother, Veigh, to complete the young family.

At the 1900 U.S. Federal Census, her family was living in Tarkio City, Atchison County, Missouri, and she was just 5 months old.

By the 1910 U.S. Federal Census, Valeria was living with her family who were farming in Medford Township, Grant County, Oklahoma.

Valeria attended school in Medford as evidenced by her eighth grade graduation announcement in The Medford Patriot, (Medford, Oklahoma), Vol. 20, No. 33, Ed. 1 Thursday 22 May, 1913. Her father, W. H. Kinney, must have been very proud of her accomplishment.

She was also listed among graduates of School No. 54, with her teacher's name, L. Dervage, in The Medford Patriot, (Medford, Oklahoma), Vol. 20, No. 38, Ed. 1 Thursday 26 June 1913.

In the fall of 1913, Valeria, aged 13, experienced a great loss when her father, William Homer, succumbed to cancer.

She continued high school in Medford and shortly thereafter, we read of her wedding in a May issue of The Medford Patriot Star:

"Miss Valeria Kinney of Medford and Mr. Richard W. Winfield of Renfrow were united in marriage at Wichita, Kansas, May 16th at 3 p.m. Miss Valeria is the only daughter of Mrs. W. H. Kinney and has a host of friends, having attended the Medford High School for several years.

Mr. Winfield is a young man of sterling qualities and is connected with the Winfield Hardware store of Renfrow. He is to be congratulated in getting a helpmate of such a noble character as Miss Valeria.

Mr. and Mrs. Winfield will be at home at Renfrow after June 1st. May their life be happy and prosperous is the wish of their many friends."

We find Valeria and Richard's Marriage License from Sedgwick County, Kansas, dated 16 May 1916. Richard Winfield's parents had to give consent as he was only 20 years of age, and Valeria's mother also had to give consent as she was only 17 years old.

~~~~~~

The line from the newspaper article, "a wife of noble character," is a quote from Scripture found in Proverbs 31, verses 10-31, and is often used to describe hard-working, virtuous wives; a model for married women: "The Wife of Noble Character – 10. A wife of noble character who can find? She is worth far more than rubies. 11. Her husband has full confidence in her and lacks nothing of value. 12. She brings him good; not harm, all the days of her life. 13. She selects wool and flax and works with eager hands. 14. She is like the merchant ships, bringing her food from afar. 15. She gets up while it is still night; she provides food for her family and portions for her female servants. 16. She considers a field and buys it; out of her earnings she plants a vineyard. 17. She sets about her work vigorously; her arms are strong for her tasks. 18. She sees that her trading is profitable, and her lamp does not go out at night. 19. In her hand she holds the distaff and grasps the spindle with her fingers. 20. She opens her arms to the poor and extends her hands to the needy. 21. When it snows, she has no fear for her household; for all of them are clothed in scarlet. 22. She makes
~~~~~~

coverings for her bed; and she is clothed in fine linen and purple. 23. Her husband is respected at the city gate, where he takes his seat among the elders of the land. 24. She makes linen garments and sells them, and supplies the merchants with sashes. 25. She is clothed with strength and dignity; she can laugh at the days to come. 26. She speaks with wisdom, and faithful instruction is on her tongue. She watches over the affairs of her household and does not eat the bread of idleness. 28. Her children arise and call her blessed; her husband also, and he praises her: 29. "Many women do noble things, but you surpass them all." 30. Charm is deceptive, and beauty is fleeting; but a woman who fears the Lord is to be praised. 31. Honor her for all that her hands have done, and let her works bring her praise at the city gate."

~~~~~~

STATE OF KANSAS, COUNTY OF SEDGWICK 64763.

Office of the Probate Judge of Said County

BE IT REMEMBERED, That on the 16 day of May A. D., 1916, there was issued from the office of said Probate Judge a Marriage License, of which the following is a true copy;

(Seal)

Marriage License

State of Kansas, County of Sedgwick

Wichita, Kansas, May 16 1916

To any person authorized by law to perform the Marriage Ceremony, Greeting:

YOU ARE HEREBY AUTHORIZED TO JOIN IN MARRIAGE

R. W. Winfield (Groom) of Renfrow, Okla, aged 20

Valeria Kinney (Bride) of Medford, Okla, aged 17

with the consent of R. Q. Winfield + Mrs. R. Q. Winfield parents of R. W. Winfield + Mrs. Kinney mother of Valeria (Name of parent or guardian consenting) and of this license, duly endorsed, you will make due return

(Name of parent or guardian consenting)

to the office of the State Registrar of Vital Statistics, at Topeka, immediately after performing the ceremony.

(Seal) K. W. C. Jones Probate Judge

ENDORSEMENT

TO THE STATE REGISTRAR OF VITAL STATISTICS, Topeka, Kansas

I hereby certify that I performed the ceremony joining in marriage the above-named couple on the .... day of .... 191 ..., at ....

Signed........

Title........

Address........

Richard Webster Winfield was born 12 October 1896, in Latham, Kansas. In the 1900 U.S. Federal Census, his family was living in Union, Butler County, Kansas. By the 1910 Census, they were in Renfrow, Grant County, Oklahoma, where his father was a merchant with a hardware store.

In 1917, the couple was living at 715 North Main, in Wichita, Sedgwick County, Kansas, as recorded in the Wichita City Directory. In 2013, this location was the offices of the American Red Cross. Richard's World War I Draft Registration Card indicated his occupation was driving a car for Orrie Wagner. He describes himself as medium height, slender build, with black hair. There is no date on this card, but the registrations were completed in 1917-1918.
~~~~~~

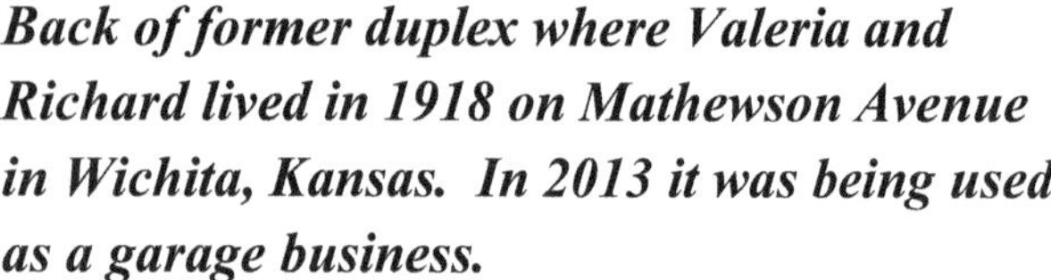

Back of former duplex where Valeria and Richard lived in 1918 on Mathewson Avenue in Wichita, Kansas. In 2013 it was being used as a garage business.

Valeria Kinney Winfield maybe on her wedding day circa 1916

Whether the couple lived in Oklahoma or Wichita is unclear. Richard and Valeria appear in the 1918 Wichita City Directory living at 233 North Mathewson Avenue. According to the librarian at the Wichita Public Library, index cards would have been distributed between September and November of the previous year for residents to complete their personal data for inclusion in the 1918 edition of the directory. So, I assume the couple was living at the Mathewson Avenue address during late 1917. This address is just down the street from the 209 Mathewson address of William Allen Anderson who, in 1920, would marry Valeria's mother, Anna Rachel Fox Kinney. Additionally, two of her brothers were already living at the William Allen home in 1918.

Family tradition states that Valeria tragically died in child birth after being sick for a week with peritonitis, sometime before December of 1918. The author has not been able to discover where she died, or what became of the child. A check of vital records in Topeka, Kansas, did not reveal any death certificate for Valeria. A check of funeral records in Medford, Grant County, Oklahoma, didn't turn up any information. Calls to the cemeteries of Wichita that were in existence in 1918 did not show any interments for Valeria Kinney Winfield. So, it is a great mystery what became of her.

Richard did not appear in the 1919 Wichita City Directory. He turned up again in the 1920 U.S. Federal Census as a widower back with his family in Grant County, Oklahoma. There was no mention of a child. We do know that he went on to marry again and had 3 children. Richard died in 1973 in Los Angeles, California. In 2013, I had the privilege of meeting Richard's son, Richard Junior, in Los Angeles.

Questions:

1. When did Valeria die?
2. What became of her child?
3. Where is Valeria buried?
4. Why did she die?
5. Where was the photo of Valeria, above, taken and was it taken on her wedding day?

Richard Winfield, 2013, the son of Richard Winfield who was married to Valeria Kinney Winfield in 1918

A house on McKinley, the street Richard lived on in 1910, Renfrow, as seen in 2013

Grain elevators dot the Midwest as this one in Renfrow, Grant County, Oklahoma. Sometimes they are in use in 2013, but more often they sit empty, a silent testament to a bygone age when the Midwest was the bread basket for the world. In 2013, we grow just as much corn to be turned into fuel for our cars and trucks as we grew to feed the nation a century ago. And while fuel costs for our vehicles is kept relatively affordable, the real pinch is felt when we go to the supermarket where we find increased prices for almost everything we eat. The rest of the world that used to depend on the U.S. for food, now pays prices unheard of a century ago.

Vernon Haven Kinney
1902-1984

The third child of William Homer and Anna Rachel Fox Kinney was Vernon Haven Kinney, born in Coffeysberg, Daviess County, Missouri, on 21 February 1902. He probably only lived a short time here, because the family relocated to Grant County, Oklahoma, by 1903.

At the 1910 U.S. Federal Census, Vernon was 6 years old and was living with 2 brothers and 1 sister plus his parents in Medford Township, Grant County, Oklahoma. He had experienced sadness already with the tragic death of an infant sibling, perhaps a boy, as he later mentioned in his application for life insurance, dated 1918.

Sadness struck again in 1913 when Vernon was just 11 years old. His father, William Homer, died of cancer.

Vernon Haven Kinney about 18

Once while I was traveling, I met a girl with the last name of Kinney. We started trading stories about the family. Soon, I called Vernon, my grandfather, to try and get some information that may connect me with this girl. This inquiry prompted Vernon to tell me a story. When he was a young boy, he went with his grandfather, James Vernon Fox, to Claremore, Oklahoma, and while in Claremore, their wagon got stuck in the mud. James Vernon stated vehemently that he would never buy land in that place. This story stuck in my head, and when I was researching Oklahoma newspapers for articles about the family, I came across a piece in The Medford Patriot, Medford, Oklahoma, Vol. 20, No. 26, Ed. 1 Thursday 21 August 1913, which read: "J. V. Fox left Tuesday for Claremore, Oklahoma, to get a team he left there some time ago." This, I believe, validated the story Vernon had told me some 30 years ago.

In the 1918 Wichita City Directory, Vernon was living with his mother who had remarried in 1916, at 320 North Seneca Avenue. Vernon completed an application for a life insurance policy in 1918 which gave crucial information about his family. For example, I first noticed his beneficiary was listed as his mother, Anna Gregory. This Gregory name was new to me and began my search to find the story behind it. I discovered she had been married after the death of Vernon's father in 1913, and before she married William Allen Anderson in 1920. This information caused me to search for her second husband's identity. Also, an infant brother was mentioned on the application which none of the family knew existed. A check of the U.S. Federal Census for 1910, confirmed that Anna Rachel did indicate she had given birth to 5 children, yet only 4 were surviving in 1910. Vernon also revealed his sister had died as a result of childbirth in 1918. Also, it was confirmed that Vernon's father, William Homer, had stomach cancer at the time of his death. Vernon, himself, had suffered for two weeks with influenza. This was during the time of the world wide influenza pandemic.

~~~~~~~~~~~~~~~~~~~~~~~~~~~

Back in the Day . . . The worldwide Spanish Flu pandemic broke out at the close of World War I in 1918. It attacked anyone and everyone, but especially young adults. An estimated 675,000 Americans died of the Spanish Flu which was 10 times more than the number who had died in World War I.

~~~~~~~~~~~~~~~~~~~~~~~~~~~

The house in Wichita at 320 North Seneca Avenue where Anna Rachel lived with her second husband, Orley Gregory. During 1917, her father, James Vernon Fox, and some of her sons also lived here.

In the 1919 Wichita City Directory, Vernon was living at 209 Mathewson Avenue and was a press feeder for the Western Newspaper Union, owners of the Wichita Daily Eagle.

In the 1920 Wichita City Directory, we find Vernon H. Kinney was a student at Dague Business College, as well as his step-brother, William Dimple Anderson. His mother, Anna Rachel Fox Kinney Gregory, had married William Allen "Billy" Anderson shortly after the 1920 U.S. Federal Census was taken.

Not long after Vernon and Alberta's arrival in Miami, Vernon was baptized on profession of faith into the fellowship of the First Baptist Church of Miami, 10 June 1923. The pastor was J. L. White. Sometime later about 1942, they moved their membership to the Stanton Memorial Baptist Church.

Vernon and Alberta purchased a home described as: "South 43 ½ feet of Lots 11 and 12 of Block 9 Northern Boulevard Tract, an addition to the City of Miami, Florida, as per plat book 2, page 29 of the Public Records of Dade County, Florida." The address was 3051 N.W. Sixth Avenue, Miami, Florida.

As one can see from the photograph, pg. 44, the house was virtually on the edge of the City of Miami, with much undeveloped land nearby. Vernon made the down payment on this house with the savings he had carefully accumulated ever since he had begun working. The original house consisted of a living room, kitchen, bedroom, and bathroom.

Now that they had a nice house it was time to fill it up with children. Vernon and Alberta welcomed their first child, Lawrence Sherman, 28 September 1928. Daughter Valeria La Verne Kinney, completed the family on 21 September 1930.

Before World War II, there was no hot water plumbing in the house, so whenever a bath was required, they would heat two tea kettles full of water, carry them around to the bathroom, and fill up the tub with the boiling water mixed with cold.

During the mid-1930s, Vernon's father-in-law, Thomas Sherman Culbreath, added a dining room and another bedroom onto the back of the house, almost doubling it in size. Over the years they lovingly increased the size to accommodate the needs of their growing family. In the mid-1920s, when Thomas Sherman was in his 80s, he added a third bedroom and shower room on the back of the house.

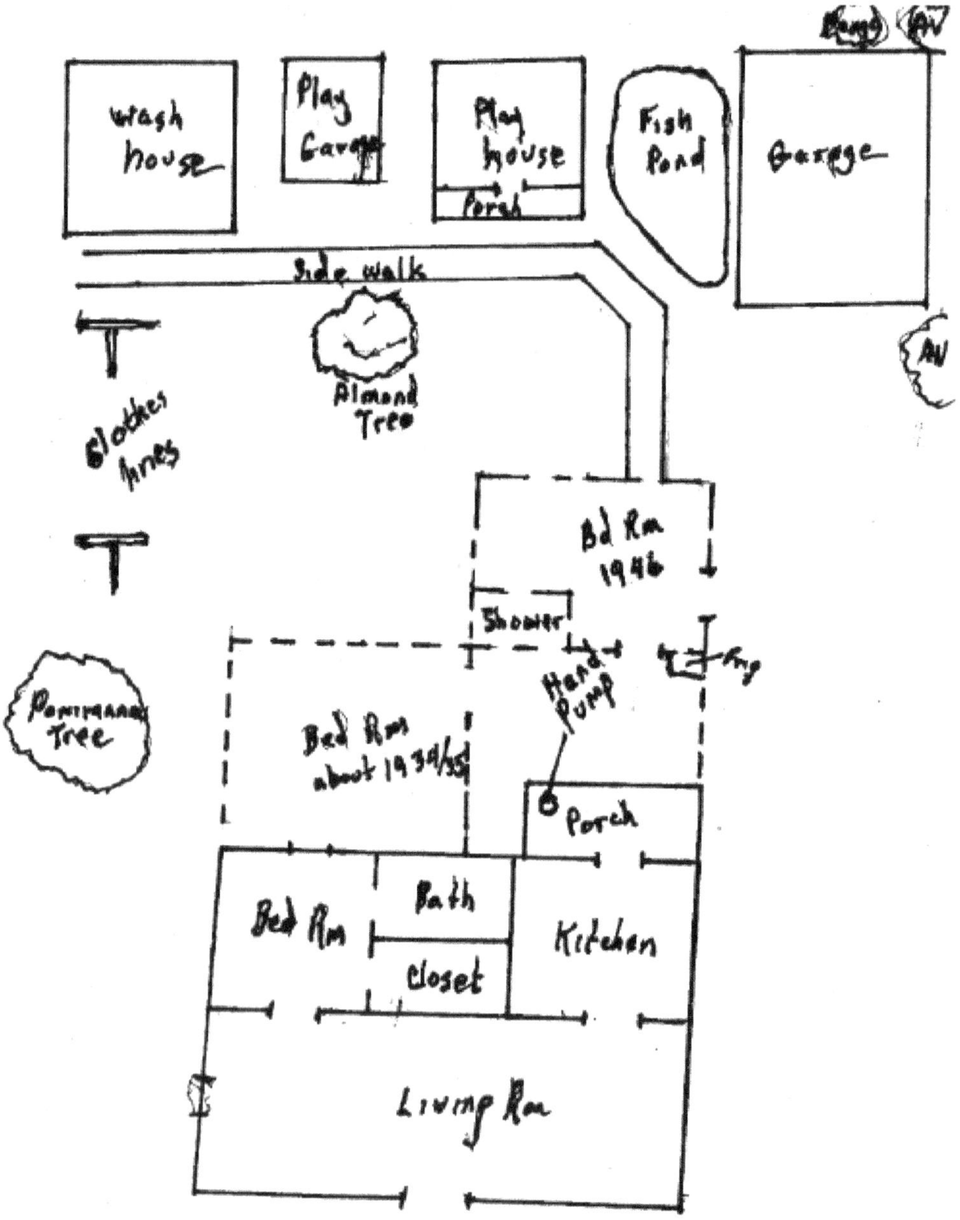

Mango AV
wash house
Play Garage
Play house
Porch
Fish Pond
Garage
Side walk
Almond Tree
Clothes lines
AV
Bd Rm 1946
Shower
Hand Pump
Frig
Poinciana Tree
Bed Rm about 1934/35
Porch
Bed Rm
Bath
Closet
Kitchen
Living Rm

The house doubled in size over the years from the original one pictured below. Mature trees included a Royal Poinciana with flame orange blossoms, an almond tree, Hayden mango, and two avocado trees with dark purple skin. Eventually, the hand pump was replaced by indoor plumbing and a refrigerator moved into the dining room which replaced the original back porch. Notice that no electrical lines run to the original house below.

Vernon and Alberta's first house in 1923, Miami, Dade County, Florida. Over the years they added on to it as their needs required. The additions were always done by Alberta's father, Thomas Sherman Culbreath. The house is built from coral rock. Later it was plastered over.

Lawrence Sherman Kinney and sister, Valeria La Verne "Dee Dee" Kinney, circa 1938

As we see from the drawing, pg. 44, off of the living room were 2 doorways. The doorway to the south entered into a narrow pass through kitchen. The kitchen had a window above the sink which looked out onto the apartment tenement building on the south side. The other doorway off the living room on the north side entered into a pass through bedroom with an interior bathroom and closet. The windows on the north side of the room were looking out to the side yard and neighbor, Mrs. Geroni's house. From this bedroom, a doorway led into the second bedroom at the back of the house with windows on the north and east sides. This bedroom contained the house's only air conditioner during the 1960s. In this bedroom, the single-hung windows were propped open with sticks. We grandchildren always liked to use the sticks to play "horsie". Once when I pulled out "my stick horse", the window came crashing down on my little 3-year old hand, crushing and breaking my ring finger. My Aunt Dee Dee (Valeria) came to my rescue.

The neighbor, Mrs. Geroni, was of Italian descent. She had moved to Florida from New Jersey. She and Alberta were great friends. I recall visiting her inside the tiny kitchen and enjoying the sweet Italian treat, pizzelles, which she made in a special press called an iron. The iron impressed a 6-petal flower design onto each flat wafer. They tasted of anise and vanilla. These cookies were so different from Alberta's, but I loved them all the same. Now that I know we have some Italian DNA in our Kinney genes, I can see why I embraced the pizzelles so heartily.

Alberta's "company dishes"

Back in the pass through kitchen, through the east door, one would enter the dining room containing a large wooden dining table, a china cabinet, a serving buffet, and a bank of windows on the south side looking out onto the driveway to the garage. Many family gatherings were enjoyed in this dining room. It was also the room where we cousins would periodically receive our "punishment" in the form of a spatula, or "pancake turner," to the back side whenever we were disobedient. How could one room be used to experience both pleasure and pain?

Once, James August and brother, Vernon Haven, went fishing and caught a rather large lobster. When they returned home after midnight, they put the lobster on the kitchen floor with an overturned dish pan on top. When their mother, Anna Rachel, got up in the morning to cook breakfast, she was upset to find her dish pan on the middle of the floor. She picked up the dish pan, and lo and behold, the entire household woke up startled by her screams. The lobster was probably dispatched for breakfast after the initial shock of its presence wore off.

Leading off the back of the dining room and down two cement steps we would go into the third bedroom and shower room. This was where Alberta kept her canaries in a large wire cage. I always enjoyed watching the birds. Alberta often sent me in search of "pepper grass," a weed which grew prolifically in the neighbor's yard around the corner. The canaries loved this grass attacking it with enthusiasm, both eating it and rubbing it all over their bodies as if it were some sort of deodorant. None of us cousins ever liked to sleep in this back room. We preferred to sleep in the living room near to Grandma.

During the mid-1940s, Lawrence was assigned this back room as his bedroom. There was a door to the back yard, and then a door for the cat to enter. This door was directly under Lawrence's bed. One night, the cat was involved in a fight with another cat and he made his escape into the house through the cat door. Unfortunately, the opponent cat followed right on in and continued the fight in the bedroom under Lawrence's bed. What a ruckus that caused!

In 2013, the sight of Alberta and Vernon's house in photographs always takes me right back to the 1950s and 1960s when we cousins passed carefree and happy days in our grandparents' home. In addition to the sight of the house in photos, certain sounds and smells take me instantly back to that house. The banging of a screen door takes me back 50 years in an instant. Likewise, the smell of baking bread will put me in Alberta's house immediately. The Holsum or Merita Bread Bakery was located just a block away. The constant smell of baking bread permeated our grandparents' home.

The back yard was a magical place containing a garage complete with the musty smell of an old garage and workshop, a garden shed with an even mustier smell, a patio table with benches so popular in the 1950s made of bits of broken tile set in cement, a swing glider, a bird bath which Alberta crafted herself using a metal garbage can lid for the concrete mold and broken tiles to make it match with the patio table, and, of course, the most huge avocado tree ever. The tree produced large, pear shaped, purplish wrinkled skinned avocadoes which Alberta called alligator pears. As a child, the name, "alligator pear," frightened me off from trying the delicious fruit. As an adult, I often wish that I'd conquered my fear and sampled her tree fruit, as I dearly love avocadoes today.

The birdbath was beckoning. Success! What a way to cool off on a summer's day, 1957, Barbara Kinney in Alberta's birdbath.

A neighbor boy named David Carnafix and Lawrence, went up the avocado tree with the horn shaped speaker from a Victrola. They proceeded to "broadcast" every song they knew how to sing to the neighborhood from that speaker.

There was also a huge almond tree in the yard from which Lawrence decided to swing from branch to branch. Alberta said he was playing Tarzan. Once he put his shoulder out of joint. The tree was popular with the neighborhood boys as they could hang upside down from it.

A mango tree also grew behind the garage. Now that's one fruit which I never developed any sort of taste for, but the rest of the family salivated at the mention of the word, mango.

Lawrence in his pedal car, 1930, age 2

Vernon's Ford in the pine woods, circa 1923

There was a fish pond which T. S. built located between the play house and the garage. Inside the fish pond were 3 pots with water hyacinths in 3 different colors. The pond was stocked with gold fish. Once T. S. decided to raise frogs, so he brought a bull frog and some other frogs and installed them in the pond. Everything went along well until Alberta grew tired of the incessant croaking.

The wash house contained a washing machine and 3 tubs sitting on a bench. One tub held hot water. A fire had to be built in the fire pit and a pan put on top to heat water. Then water was transferred to the washing machine and soap flakes were added. Then the washer was run. Clothes were then taken out with a large stick and put into the hot rinse soaking tub and agitated by hand. Then they would be run through the ringer taking care to keep fingers out of the way. Then the clothes went into the cold water tub followed by the ringer again. The clothes were put into a wicker basket and taken to the clothes line where they were hung from wooden pegs. A long support pole would be used to lift up the line so the sheets wouldn't touch the ground.

Vernon would tinker in the garage. He at one time experimented with hydroponic gardening. Among his papers I found notes he had taken from a book called Complete Guide to Soilless Gardening by William F. Gericke. He listed formulas for hydroponic gardening. I don't recall ever eating anything grown in this manner, however. As there were quite extensive instructions for how to mix the growing formula, build wooden gardening boxes, and for testing the soil for the correct Ph level, I wonder if he actually got around to the gardening at all. He was a farmer as a child, so he was familiar with working the soil and producing something from it.

Vernon had a nice Ford car in the 1920s. He'd take it out to the pine woods. This car was upmarket because it had glass all around rather than just a windshield and canvas sides. Next, he owned a Willis Overland Redbird touring car with canvas top and sides and a glass back window. Lawrence still has the frame of the back window from this car.

After that, he owned a Whippet, around 1927. Vernon had a Hupmobile car and during World War II, he put it in the garage on blocks because tires were not available to the public. The car stayed here for the duration of the war.

Vernon also had a shop in the garage with a lathe. One day as Lawrence was experimenting with how to use the lathe, he got his hair caught in it and lost a whole bunch. That was when his hair started to fall out! By the time I was born, there was very little left.

Poinciana tree blossoms and seed pods

Alberta made this rose ribbon corsage for Barbara Kinney's wedding because she knew she'd not live to see the day.

The house was surrounded by bushes including a delicate fern Alberta called asparagus fern. She always used this to provide a backdrop for her beautiful rose corsages. When she didn't have live roses for flower arranging and corsage making, Alberta created ribbon roses. She created several for me. On my wedding day in 1988, I honored my grandmother by placing one of her ribbon rose corsages on the table with my unity candle.

A beautiful Poinciana tree was on the north side of the house. It produced long seed pods which withered up and dropped on the ground. I imagine Alberta probably thought of some craft to make from the seeds, though I don't recall anything.

Once T.S. had moved to California, he left a car sitting under the Poinciana tree. It stayed there for several years. After a while, Lawrence decided to fill the gas tank as they did at the filling station. The trouble was that he only had a water hose. Lawrence thought he was doing a good thing until Vernon got home and discovered what he'd done.

Lawrence evidently understood the importance of water for his survival as evidenced by his reaction to the following event. One day the fire department was flooding the street with water from a hydrant. Lawrence thought there wasn't going to be any more water, so he rushed home and told Alberta to get out all the jars and bowls to fill up with water before it was all gone.

Their front yard grew coconut palms, ferns, and Alberta's famous rose bushes. The coconuts were harvested to make coconut candy and coconut head piggy banks for the grandchildren.

Both Vernon and Alberta created various handicrafts to sell which would provide additional income during the lean times and the Great Depression. Many industrious families engaged in various cottage industries to help make ends met during those financially difficult times. Vernon, for example, had a mold which accepted molten lead. He would melt the raw material in a smelter, then

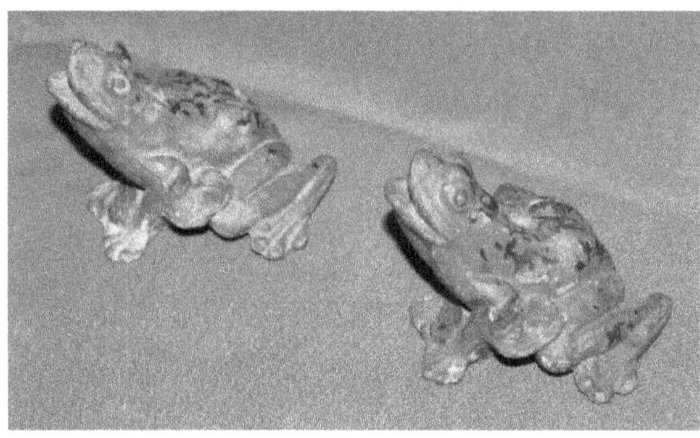

Lead frog paperweight pen holders. Vernon made these during the Depression to supplement the family income. A pen was inserted into the frog's mouth. Vernon helped me make these frogs about 1973.

pour it into the mold. When the mold cooled, out came a lead frog pencil holder/paper weight. He'd paint them green with black dots on their backs, red lips, and a red lily pad. These were peddled to businessmen and anyone who would buy them. During the 1970s, I got Vernon's help in producing these frogs once more. I then mounted each one on a wooden disk, painted the frogs, and gave them to all the men with whom I worked in an office for Christmas. I don't know if they really appreciated the uniqueness of that gift.

They finished paying for their house in April 1941, just in time for World War II. Vernon continued working in the printing industry. Throughout his career, he was employed at Real Estate Journal Publishing Company, Strange Printing Company, McMurray Printing Company, and Franklin Press. In 1936, Vernon applied for a Social Security card and listed his employer as McMurray Printing Company of 2136 N.W. Miami Court, Miami, Florida.

An application for delayed certificate of birth filed in June 1942, listed Vernon's address as "temporary" Apt. No. 15 Elizabeth Apartments, Chattanooga, Tennessee.

During World War II, Vernon's job in Miami closed. He was mainly printing the racing forms. During the war, with more pressing issues at hand, entertainment such as racing was put on hold. So, Vernon's union found him a position in Chattanooga, Tennessee. So, Vernon went there alone to work. He took an apartment, likely the Elizabeth Apartments detailed above, and worked on McCollie Avenue, just a few blocks away from his employment at the Target Printing Company.

In 2013, I visited McCollie Avenue in the block where Vernon's employment would have been located. This building, above left, appeared to be old enough to have been there in the 1940s. Whether or not it is the Target Printing Company former building, I do not know.

Above right, a beautiful lake in the East Lake suburb of Chattanooga where the family lived in 1943.

It was more than a year before Alberta could save enough money to take the kids and go visit Vernon in Chattanooga. In addition, Lawrence and Dee Dee were attending school in Miami. Finally, the day of departure for Chattanooga arrived and the family of 3 boarded a Greyhound bus bound for Tennessee. Once she got there, Alberta decided they would all stay in Chattanooga. Lawrence shipped his bicycle so he would have transportation while living in Chattanooga. The family moved into an apartment at 1405 Bailey Avenue. This was a residence that had been converted to 3 or 4 apartments. They moved into a downstairs apartment off the side of the building. In 2013, that address was just an empty lot, but there were some stone steps leading up from the sidewalk delineating where the apartment house once stood.

Soon the family moved out to the suburbs to East Lake and took a house at 3104 East 36 Street. This was across from a nice large city park with a fountain in the lake and ducks paddling about. Vernon's daughter, Valeria, recalls the tennis courts being right in front of their house.

The family returned to Miami some time before the 1945 Florida State Census. The war was over and life continued.

Vernon, Valeria, Alberta, and Lawrence in Chattanooga, 1943

Both Vernon and Alberta were active in their church, Stanton Memorial Baptist, located at 2948 N.W. Second Avenue, Miami. One of Vernon's jobs was as usher. He greeted people at the door and handed out bulletins with the morning worship program. He attended a men's Sunday School class.

They liked to entertain friends in their home with card parties. Sometimes guests would come dressed in costumes. Vernon would play practical jokes sometimes. The goings on in these parties did not go unnoticed by their children. For example, one day while Alberta was working in the kitchen, she heard loud screaming from the living room where a house full of kids had gathered for the joint birthday party of Lawrence and Dee Dee. When Alberta reached the living room, she saw all the children holding hands in a circle and screaming. Lawrence had instructed everyone to hold hands and then he gave one boy one end of a wire from the extension cord. Then he split the cord and gave the other end to another boy. Then Lawrence had plugged in the cord to the outlet. Everyone was shocked! This was a practical joke he'd observed either Vernon or his friend demonstrating at one of their parties.

REDDY KILOWATT

Reddy Kilowatt gave us a shocking time at Lawrence's birthday party!

Vernon Kinney, back row, second from left, in Sunday School at Stanton Memorial Baptist Church, circa 1950s

Daughter, Valeria, married in 1950 and son, Lawrence, in 1951. Grandchildren came regularly from 1952-1969.

Vernon's mother, Anna Rachel Fox Kinney Gregory Anderson, a widow since 1928, had alternated between living with Vernon, and his brother, James August, on and off until her death in 1956.

September 1950 wedding reception for Valeria La Verne Kinney and James H. Stewart, left to right: Julia Kint Rice, her daughter Julia Karen Rice, Alberta Anna Bell Culbreath Kinney, Mr. and Mrs. Stewart, Valeria, James, Vernon Haven Kinney, Anna Rachel Fox Kinney Anderson, and Lawrence Sherman Kinney

Lawrence Sherman Kinney and Betty Mae Williams' wedding 18 May 1951, left to right: Roger E. Williams, Sr., Mary Belle Culp Williams, Betty Mae Williams Kinney, Lawrence Sherman Kinney, Alberta Anna Belle Culbreath Kinney, and Vernon Haven Kinney. The wedding took place in the yard of the bride's family. Roger Williams was a gardener, so the outdoor wedding had a beautiful setting.
Lawrence made the lattice structure and trimmed it with Alberta's red roses and asparagus fern.

Four generations: left to right: Vernon Haven Kinney with grandson Jimmie Stewart, Anna Rachel Fox Kinney Anderson, mother of Vernon; Lawrence Sherman Kinney, son of Vernon; Betty Mae Williams Kinney, wife of Lawrence, 1953

The first grandchildren of Alberta and Vernon, circa 1960: left to right: Jimmy Stewart, Sandra Stewart, Roger Kinney, Barbara Kinney, Johnny Stewart

The family always enjoyed so much gathering at Alberta and Vernon's house. It seemed every Christmas, every Easter, every Mother's Day and Father's Day, ordinary weekends in the summer, sleep overs for the grandchildren, babysitting, etc. For all of us grandchildren cousins, no matter what else was happening in our lives, we knew we would have a good time and feel warm and loved in Grandma's house.

After having lived in their home for 46 years, making many improvements and enjoying many memories as well, imagine Alberta and Vernon's horror upon receiving the following letter:

"Dade County Public Schools
Administration Offices
Lindsey Hopkins Building
1410 N.E. Second Avenue
Miami, Florida 33132

December 9, 1968

Mr. and Mrs. Vernon Kinney
3051 N.W. 6 Avenue
Miami, Florida
Dear Mr. and Mrs. Kinney:

RE: Site A1039, Add Land Robert E. Lee Junior High School

According to the tax records you own the following legally described property:
South 43.8 feet of Lots 11 and 12, Block 9, Northern Boulevard Tract, PB 2, P. 29, of the Public Records of Dade County, Florida.
The Board of Public Instruction is interested in making a survey to determine the approximate cost of the entire block south of Robert E. Lee Junior High School.
Your help with this plan will be greatly appreciated. Please advise the lowest cash price which you will be willing to accept for your property.
Should you desire more information, or desire to contact the writer, you may do so by telephoning 350.3571 or 350.3572.
A self-addressed envelope is enclosed for your prompt reply.

Yours most sincerely,
Assistant Director
Site Planning"

3051 N.W. Sixth Avenue, Miami, Florida, 1969

Here is their response to the above letter:

"J. H. Matteson:

In regards to the letter of December 9, concerning the property which we own and are making our home as we understand the School Board would like to get us to tell them what we would like to sell our property for.

First of all we do not want to sell and have to move for several reasons. First, because this property is something more to us than just a home. We came into this property October 3, 1922, just as a Bride and Groom, and have endured hardships about as bad as any pioneer. We had no city lights, water, sidewalks, and we waited until 1928 for a sewer. In the meantime, we had an outside toilet with a city pick up at midnight.

We have worked awful hard to keep this place livable and now that we are both not well and have the place where we might enjoy the last few years we have, it looks like we may have to move.

Mr. Kinney has retired this last year and we are living on Social Security, and it is impossible for us to make payments on another home. He was looking forward to enjoying working in his workshop which he has in our garage. I know this lot isn't very large, but we have a home plenty large: three bedrooms, dining room, large living room, full bath and extra shower room, and kitchen, and a garage and work shop. For these reasons we will have to get enough for this home to buy another and we think it only fair to ask enough to do so.

The trees on this place cannot be replaced. Two of the finest avocados that grow; a fine Haden mango; the avocadoes were planted in about 1924, and are too large to move. We also have thirteen small palm trees which we would like to move, along with small shrubbery.

We want to cooperate with the school board, but at the same time, we want a home as good and as large as we have, and in a location that is as convenient as this one is."

Well, the School Board did not honor their request to stay in their home. So, they had to move to Miami Springs.

372 La Villa Drive, Miami Springs, Florida, 1972

Even though the house in Miami Springs had a beautiful yard for gardening, and a large kitchen for Alberta to cook in, she would never have opportunity to enjoy it fully. By the time they moved in,

Alberta had already been suffering lung cancer for a year, and it was getting the best of her. She died in 1970, and Vernon continued alone in that house for 14 more years until 1984.

Left: Vernon at Alberta's grave site in Woodlawn Park, Miami, Dade County, Florida
Right: Three generations: Roger Vernon Kinney, Vernon Haven Kinney, Lawrence Sherman Kinney, circa 1971

Sometimes I believe the Lord lets a person know when he's about to die. I think this may have been the case with Vernon. One day I went to pick him up after being discharged from the hospital. He sat down on the bed and began telling me stories from his past that I had never known before. Dee Dee had a similar experience when she went to his house to take him out to lunch, instead, he began talking about his life and she spent 6 hours listening. She never got lunch. As I'm writing these memories now, I often long to have those days back and to have realized the significance and urgency of what was being communicated to me. Oh, to be able to have that discernment. Instead, we lead such busy lives that we often miss those gems.

Vernon's obituary appeared in the 3 September 1984 edition of The Miami Herald on page 3B: "**KINNEY VERNON H**., 82, of Miami Springs passed away 31 August 1984. He came here in 1922 from Kansas and was a pressman with Franklin Press, having retired in 1972 after 28 years of service and was a member of Stanton Memorial North Shore Baptist Church since 1942. Survived by son, Lawrence S., of North Miami, daughter, Mrs. Valeria Stewart, of Hollywood, Florida, 7 grandchildren, 2 great grandchildren, and brother, Veigh of Seagraves, Texas. Funeral service Wednesday, 10:00 a.m. at Stanton Memorial North Shore Baptist Church under direction of Joseph B. Coffer Funeral Home, 10931 N.E. Sixth Avenue, where friends may call Tuesday 7-9 p.m. Interment at Woodlawn Park."

Although Vernon suffered from colon cancer, he actually died of cardiac arrest.

After Vernon's death, our family went to clean out his house. I was given the task of processing the mail which had been stacked on the dining table. As I worked my way down through 14 years of mail, I finally came to the table cloth. This last layer contained Alberta's hand written list of ingredients for peach ice cream which she had made for all her family on her last Mother's Day of 1970. That was the last time she cooked for her family, and the last time Vernon enjoyed all the family gathering in his home. He lived the rest of his life involving himself with various senior's clubs where he seemed to attract one or two admiring ladies. Every Sunday he would come to church, then drive up to our house in North Miami for lunch, after which he'd drive home to Miami Springs.

When he died, he was cutting the grass. The mailman found him the next morning sitting on the front porch and the lawnmower nearby parked at the end of a swath of cut grass. Apparently, he'd suffered a heart attack, sat down on the porch, and went home to be with his Lord.

Vernon Haven Kinney, circa 1980

Vernon Haven Kinney grave marker in Woodlawn Park, Miami, Dade County, Florida

The Children of Vernon Haven and Alberta Anna Bell Culbreath Kinney

Lawrence Sherman Kinney
1928 –

Lawrence Sherman Kinney was the first child born to Vernon Haven and Alberta Anna Bell Culbreath Kinney, 28 September 1928, Miami, Dade County, Florida. By the 1930 U.S. Federal Census, he was joined by his sister, Valeria La Verne Kinney. Lawrence had difficulty saying Valeria's name, so he simply called her "Dee Dee," and the nickname has stuck for her entire life.

Lawrence Kinney, age 2, in the suit Alberta made

Lawrence and his sister, Dee Dee, circa 1931

Lawrence enjoyed a childhood filled with many friends and visits from family. He grew up with an open invitation to explore his Dad, Vernon's, workshop in the garage and mess about with the tools. So, he did, and as a result, he developed into one of the most creative inventive individuals I've ever met anywhere.

For high school, he chose to attend Technical High, and study aviation. As a child, he'd watched the development of the aviation industry first hand. Seaplanes regularly landed in the waters of Biscayne Bay, just a mile or so from his house.

Seaplane on the beach, 1912, from Historic Photos of Greater Miami, by Bramson, p. 60

~~~~~~

Back in the Day . . . Glenn Hammond Curtiss (May 21, 1878 – July 23, 1930) was an American aviation pioneer and a founder of the U.S. aircraft industry. Curtiss made the first long-distance flight in the United States. His company built aircraft for the U.S. Army and Navy, and, during the years leading up to World War I, his experiments with seaplanes led to advances in naval aviation. In this photo he's landed on the beach in Miami. For more info, see http://en.wikipedia.org/wiki/Glenn_Curtiss

~~~~~~

As a teenager, he built an airplane with a couple of friends and enjoyed flying it above Miami. He tells a story of a time when his friends had taken the plane up for one last flight of the day and were gone for a long time. Before they returned, the father of one of the boys showed up at the air field asking Lawrence where his son was. When the father learned his son hadn't returned yet from a flight, he became very agitated. Apparently, there had been a plane crash near his house and the 2 occupants were so badly burned they were not recognizable. They had been taken to the hospital. I can't imagine the shock that father received when it dawned on him that one of the burned boys was his own son. This experience helped to turn Lawrence away from being a pilot and steered him more towards being an airplane mechanic.

Lawrence began his work career in the airline industry at Eastern Airlines in Miami. He worked most of his career in the landing gear division.

One of his work colleagues, Roy Rudolph, who had gone through the apprenticeship program for Eastern Airlines with Lawrence, bought an old taxi cab with a hole in the roof where the sign had been. He and Lawrence decided to repair it. So they took the taxi to Davie. Another colleague, Earl Dodge, had built a hangar at an auxiliary field the Navy used for emergency landings. Earl had worked for Pan American and Eastern Airlines, and built the hangar at this field. The hangar was open on the front side, facing west, and was built from galvanized tin.

So, Roy and Lawrence proceeded to plug the hole in the roof of the taxi and then paint the taxi. Suddenly, a big rainstorm came up. They went into the hangar to stay dry. There was a twin engine Cessna inside the hangar waiting for the fabric wings to be recovered. The rain turned to hail and it was deafening on the tin roof. Lawrence was standing at the back door of the hangar leaning against the door jamb when it started moving and leaning over. Earl shouted, "There goes the hangar!" Lawrence looked up to see the hangar right above them and breaking apart into a million pieces. Lawrence ran over to a Piper Cub that was sitting outside and got under the wing. He was only there a few seconds when it occurred to him that may not be the safest place to be. As he ran away, he looked back to see if the Piper Cub was tied down and was startled to see that it was gone. It was over his head with a 5 gallon can of concrete tied to the tail swinging around like a pendulum. The airplane kept swirling higher and higher and then disappeared. Then Lawrence crouched down behind a large crate that an engine had been shipped in and was being used to house an air compressor and paint supplies. A minute later, Roy and Earl hunkered down with Lawrence behind the crate. When the storm was over, the Piper Cub had been tossed out in the field, crumpled like a discarded tin can. The Cessna was still standing completely untouched where it had been inside the hangar. A bomber which had been parked across the street was turned completely around and was heading into the wind. All traces of the hangar building were gone. The airport management lost 14 airplanes in the storm, but it was all over in just one minute. Sounds like a tornado danced around there. I can't vouch for Lawrence's companions, but Lawrence sure thought a lot about how precious life was and was very grateful to God that his life had been spared through that storm.

Lawrence's job at Eastern Airlines brought him into contact with some of the pioneers of aviation. Once, at a picnic, he met Eddie Rickenbacker, Al Williams who was the President of Gulf Oil, and Arthur Godfrey who flew a Bonanza airplane. Arthur Godfrey bought a DC3 from Eddie Rickenbacker for $1 and Lawrence's shop did the maintenance on it.

On New Year's Eve 1949, Lawrence attended a party for the young adults at his church, Stanton Memorial Baptist. As he was standing at the top of the stairs looking down, coming up the stairs he saw Betty Mae Williams for the first time. Little did he know the direction his life was going to take by that simple walk up a staircase! The pastor of the church asked Lawrence to give Betty Mae a ride to the New Year's Eve party. He agreed.

2012 Barbara on the staircase where her parents Lawrence Kinney and Betty Mae Williams met in 1949

Before Lawrence took Betty home, however, they stopped at Howard Johnson's for something to eat. I'm sure this event was what started our family tradition of going to Howard Johnson's for ice cream after Sunday night church services when I was a child. My favorite was Swiss Chocolate Almond, while my brother, Roger's, was Pistachio.

Betty and Lawrence were married 18 May 1951, and just 4 short months later, Lawrence was off to Texas for Air Force basic training.

He missed the draft for the Korean War, primarily because of good timing. He had recently had his teeth removed in preparation for a set of dentures. The examiner said he would be "unable to masticate rations" so they gave him a rating of 4F. Lawrence then decided to get married, but the draft came back recruiting a second time. His boss at Eastern Air Lines suggested he enlist and the airlines would keep his job open for his return after military service.

Left, airplanes Lawrence maintained in the Air Force, 1953

Right, airplane Lawrence maintained at Eastern, 1950s

Since he already had considerable experience as an airplane mechanic already under his belt, the Air Force assigned him to airplane maintenance stateside. He was stationed at Reece Air Force Base in Lubbock, Texas. Betty Mae joined him there. They lived in 3 different apartments, each of which left out many of the comforts of home that they were used to having, such as easily accessible hot water, and a heater to take the chill out of those West Texas winters.

While in Lubbock, Lawrence got reacquainted with his Uncle Veigh, Aunt Alice, and his cousin, Betty Kinney. Yes, there were now 2 Betty Kinneys in his life. Veigh and Alice lived in Welman, about 60 miles south of Lubbock. Veigh and Alice by this time were growing watermelons and raising chickens on their farm. After 3 years of trying to grow cotton on "dry land" without irrigation, and having it burn up from the heat, they made the switch to the chickens and watermelons. Once their kids found a human skull on the farm.

As always, they found a great church to attend while in Lubbock: Central Baptist. They involved themselves with the young adult class. For Christmas one year, they built a float for a nativity parade utilizing the carpentry skills Lawrence had inherited from his grandfather, Thomas Sherman Culbreath.

They lived frugally and saved money so they could travel the western states while on leave. They visited New Mexico, Colorado, Wyoming, and Montana. Lawrence sewed a tent using the skill he'd inherited from his mother, Alberta. The tent attached to the side of the car. This allowed access into the car easily avoiding inclement weather. They borrowed cots and sleeping bags from the Air Force.

Their travels were wonderfully detailed in a journal kept by Betty Mae. It's nostalgic to look back through that journal now and read such lines as, "Today we took one colored picture.....In Yellowstone, the bear put his paws up on the open car window.....We went on the roller coaster in Lakeside Park in Denver and I will never go on another one as long as I live.....We saw snow for the first time today.....We ate fried chicken, coleslaw, and a blueberry muffin with apple pie and ice cream for dessert.....Our motel was $3 last night." This is when our family's love for the mountains, travel, and camping was born.

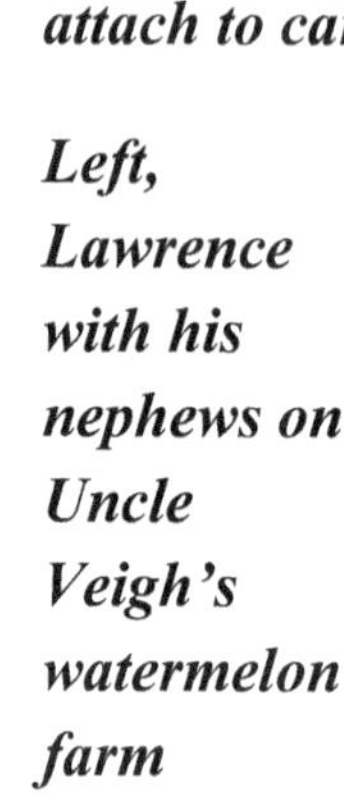

Left, Lawrence cooks in a 5 gallon can grill he made

Tent Lawrence sewed to attach to car

Left, Lawrence with his nephews on Uncle Veigh's watermelon farm

Lawrence and Betty's second anniversary

When Lawrence was discharged from the Air Force in 1955, they returned to Miami, and just 6 weeks later, their daughter, Barbara Elaine Kinney, was born.

Lawrence designed their house and had it built. We moved in when I was 3 months old. Just 2 short years later, suddenly, the little pink house, with only 2 bedrooms, became too small when Roger Vernon Kinney was born. So, the hunt for a larger piece of property began. We moved to a rental house and Lawrence set out to fulfill one of his lifelong goals—to build his own house, following in the footsteps of his grandfather, Thomas Sherman Culbreath.

The new house was located further north in the community of Biscayne Gardens. It was built on almost an acre lot filled with palmetto bushes, Dade County pine trees, saw grass growing wild, and a grove of 40 or so little live oak trees. Lawrence cleared the land to make way for a 3 bedroom 2 bathroom ranch style house. He built a fishpond landscaped with coral rock which doubled as a waterfall emptying into the pond. Goldfish swam in the pond alongside the ugly bullfrogs which my mother, Betty Mae, hated so much. We had a beautiful living room and dining room with a stone dividing wall Lawrence constructed between the living room and the den. There were 3 bedrooms down the south side of the house. Across the back of the house there was a huge covered porch looking out onto the back yard. We had a picnic table set up there and enjoyed family meals in the summer. The back yard had a huge swing in the pine tree and a see-saw for us to play on. But, with all the trees and bushes, we usually played hide and seek. Roger's birthday parties always featured an Easter egg hunt.

The 4 of us moved into the new house at 14551 N.W. 13 Court, Miami, during the summer of 1961.

Above, first house. Below left, Barbara Elaine Kinney with Betty Mae Kinney on wrought iron couch Lawrence made. Above right, the house Lawrence built

Even though Lawrence was busy with his shift work at Eastern Airlines and his volunteer work at North Shore Baptist Church, the spirit of invention had bitten him spurred on by the wanderlust of travel. The idea to build a camper was born. Every Saturday as a family we had an exciting excursion to the city dump, which was located in northwest Dade County. In 2013 the Amelia Earhart Park was located in place of this former dump. As we drove the green Studebaker along the winding trails of the dump, we were hunting discarded washing machines. Once Lawrence got these home, he'd cut up one corner and spread open 8' of sheet metal on the floor of the carport. This was fashioned into supports shaped like covered wagon hoops. The camper was taking shape.

After much exterior construction, Lawrence was offered a different engine by his sister, Valeria La Verne Kinney Stewart. In order to install it, his nephew, Jimmy Stewart, came to assist. They constructed a tower with a steel beam balanced across the top. On the ends of the steel beam were fastened two heavy chains. One chain went around the engine, while the other chain had two 55 gallon drums attached. The drums were filled with water and the engine slowly rose up through the skylight of the camper, as the heavy drums lowered to the ground. In the process, the entire rig buckled. Fortunately, Lawrence and Jimmy were watching from the shade of a tree, and not in harm's way.

Through much experimentation, the camper was finally finished, and the family set out for Texas and New Mexico with only 20 miles of test driving on the camper. Lawrence had a lot of confidence in his invention. That inspired confidence in all of us. We had a fantastic summer. Lawrence's wife, Betty Mae, continued recording her detailed journals of our journeys in Lawrence's "Summer House." Whenever Roger and I have a dispute over our memories of some detail of a summer vacation, all we need do is consult those journals for the definitive answer!

T. S. Culbreath's road grader, 1920

Lawrence Kinney's camper, 1975

Lawrence inherited a wealth of creative and inventive genes from his mother and grandfather, Thomas Sherman Culbreath. Both in their day designed and built ingenious vehicles which were ahead of their respective times. The camper had dual controls so it could be driven from either side. My brother and I learned to drive from the right hand side at age 12.

The camper was made from washing machines, bicycle parts and chains, old airplane windows, chicken wire, plywood, and fiberglass. Inside, it featured a long couch which would seat all 4 of us. At night, the back of the couch was suspended from the ceiling by strong cables and it made a bunk bed for Roger and I. Betty and Lawrence enjoyed a large double bed in the rear which was made up each night from the dining table and bench seats. There was a kitchen counter, but all cooking was done outside on a portable cook stove. There was an ice box which drained the melt water down through a tube to the ground below. There was 1 small clothes closet and 1 bathroom added as an after-thought. The first year we went with a "toilet" fashioned out of a plastic jug which formerly held antifreeze. It was turned upside down, the bottom cut out, and the neck of the bottle screwed into a length of black plastic pipe. The pipe went down to the street below. Of course it was only used for one purpose, and had to be rinsed out with strong toilet cleaner after every use. It was convenient when there was an emergency, but required special aim when used while driving down the highway. We bid a fond farewell to it the second year as it was replaced with a modern marine toilet. Our family had very special times in the camper. We visited all 48 states and most of the Canadian provinces. We dipped into Mexico, as well.

This article written by Lawrence's wife, Betty Mae Williams Kinney, appeared in the Sunday, 7 November 1976 edition of The Miami Herald, page 11-J.

Handmade Motor Home Took Them 51,114 Miles

This story is more about a vehicle than it is about a trip, but since it was the means by which we toured 48 of our United States, it is worthy of recognition. (Alaska and Hawaii were visited by air this Bicentennial year, completing our tour of the United States.)

A strong desire to travel, coupled with a creative personality, enabled my husband to build a motor home named "Summer House." It began in 1966 with a 1957 Ford Fairlane. The chassis was lengthened four feet and all but the front end discarded. The metal from 40 washing machines and lots of welding became the frame. To this was added 10 sheets of plywood, 15 pounds of glue and gallons of sticky resin, resulting in a fiberglass over plywood body. A unique feature is the dual controls.

We ventured forth in the summer of 1969, my husband Lawrence, myself, daughter Barbara and son Roger. "Summer House" has since taken us 51,114 miles, from the Atlantic to the Pacific, into Canada and Mexico; she climbed to the top of Mt. Evans in Colorado, (14,264 feet), doing a little complaining but finally reaching the summit; she rode a ferry to Prince Edward and Vancouver Islands, Canada; she has been photographed between two large snow banks as well as the desert.

She has not been without breakdowns, but never once have we needed a tow truck. Our most "memorable" breakdown occurred in 1970 when we spent six days trying to get out of Florida. Faced with three flat tires at once, you can't go very far unless you are towing a load of tires behind you. Our home-built wheels were cracking at the welds and the tires would not hold air. After much doctoring, my husband reluctantly discarded his wheels and purchased others.

During that same trip, "Summer House" did embarrass us at one point. We were stalled at an intersection in Estes Park, Colorado. A soft-spoken policeman drove up and said, "I'm going to have to ask you to move, you are blocking our busiest intersection. Is this thing pushable?" We managed to get out of the intersection with all haste.

Our 20-foot "Summer Home" brings out smiles in people and has been photographed from passing cars. We think of "Summer House" as our goodwill ambassador and an example of American ingenuity. Not only has God given us a beautiful country in these United States, but our government guarantees freedom of movement to enjoy this beauty. God bless America! BETTY KINNEY

The camper was even on television once. Roger had taken it to the gas station for a fill up when a television news crew from the local ABC station spotted the camper. As it was Halloween, they were looking for appropriate stories. The news reporter got into the camper and filmed it driving down the street with nobody in the driver's seat. You could clearly see the passing cars and scenery and the steering wheel turning as the vehicle turned. The reporter was intimating that a ghost was driving when in actuality, Roger was driving off camera from the right hand driver's side! Lawrence was thrilled to see his invention featured on television.

During the 1970's Lawrence and Betty returned to night school. They took up painting classes. Lawrence specialized in watercolors and acrylics, while Betty stuck with acrylics.

Paintings by Lawrence
Watercolor study of daisies
Hiking in the autumn woods

Lawrence retired in 1986 from Eastern Airlines. He continued with painting and took up photography. He and Betty continued traveling in the Summer House until about 1993 when they moved to Sebring, Highlands County, Florida.

Meanwhile, in 1986, son Roger Vernon, married Mary Ann Hallberg. They had 3 children: Brian, Jonny, and Rebecca.

Roger Kinney and family, left to right, Jonny, Brian, Mary Ann holding Rebecca circa 2004

MaryAnn Hallberg was the youngest of 3 brothers and 3 sisters. In fact, she was a twin and came as a surprise to her mother! She attended Norland High School and the Florida Bible College before transferring to Miami Christian College where she met Roger. They participated in a mission trip where they did vacation Bible schools for Indian children across the Eastern U.S. They were married on 12 July 1986. God has blessed them with three talented and sweet children.

In 1988, daughter, Barbara Elaine, married Bernie Black. We did not have children, but I have more ESL students than one can count and plenty of nieces and nephews.

Bernie and Barbara Black

Our wedding was very unique and fun. We approached it like a combination theater production and surprise party, all along celebrating the lives God had given each of us individually and now together. We had both been Christians for 11 years and we had known each for 11 years, as well. So, we had 11 bridesmaids, and 11 groomsmen in the ceremony.

During the beginning of the ceremony, we shared a slide show featuring pictures of each of us as we were growing up and of our lives together. This gave us opportunity to feel like our special persons who had passed away could be present with us: my grandmother, Alberta Culbreath Kinney, and Bernie's father, Francis Bernard Black.

After the ceremony, we walked out as the organ played the Hallelujah Chorus. We left the church in a canoe carried by our groomsmen.

Sadly, in January of 2008, just after her 80th birthday, Betty Mae Williams Kinney went home to be with the Lord. But Lawrence was not alone in his sorrow, as a lifelong family friend, Joyce Brown Rosier Lasseter was there for him. They spent a lot of time together and in 2010, they married.

Joyce and Lawrence Kinney, 2010

Joyce Brown's mother, Mildred Brown, and my grandmother, Alberta Kinney, were good friends. Joyce grew up in Miami and married Walter Rosier, who became a pastor. They had 2 children: Sharon and David. Walter was killed in an auto accident. Joyce survived. She worked from her home as a ceramics instructor, and I was one of her students.. She then had a full career with the Coast Guard.

I have been blessed to have been born into the family I was, and I am grateful to the Lord for choosing Lawrence and Betty Mae for my parents.

Valeria La Verne "Dee Dee" Kinney

1930 –

Valeria La Verne Kinney was born 23 September 1930, the second and last child of Vernon Haven and Alberta Anna Bell Culbreath Kinney, in Miami, Dade County, Florida.

Since Alberta had named Lawrence, it was Vernon's turn to name Valeria. She was named for his sister who died in childbirth. Unfortunately, Lawrence couldn't pronounce Valeria, so he called her Dee Dee. Everyone called her that thereafter.

Her childhood is intimately detailed in a book called, My Life, A Memoir of 80 Years which was so lovingly published by my cousin, Sandy Stewart Dolan, Valeria's daughter. She describes her Grandmother Anderson, Grandfather Culbreath building her a playhouse, hurricanes, school plays, their first electric refrigerator, surviving diphtheria, living with no air conditioning, going to Sunday School, supper at Woolworth's 5 & 10 cent store, Alberta's special Christmas celebrations, fishing with Alberta, living in Chattanooga during World War II, and many other wonderful times.

Dee Dee attended Tech High where she studied photography and apparel manufacturing and design.

After high school, she married Jimmy Stewart 15 September 1950. They had a one night honeymoon and then bought a house by the end of the week. They moved in and lived at 265 N.W. 133 Street, Miami for 8 years. Then the children started coming: James Herbert Stewart Junior, John Kinney, Sandra Leigh, David Mark, and finally Thomas Jay Stewart. They moved to North Dade and then Hollywood.

Jimmy was the first to marry, and had 1 girl. Next, John and Rose, had a boy and a girl. Jimmy found himself single again, but not for long, as God brought him another helpmeet, Paula. They had 2 girls and 1 boy. Next, Sandy married George Dolan. Sandy became instant mother to George's boy. David married next and had a boy and a girl. Finally Tom married and had a girl and a boy.

Jim with a fish

Dee Dee with Jimmie and Johnny Stewart

Dee Dee's lifelong love, Jim, went home to be with the Lord in 2003. Dee Dee filled her days by caring for her youngest grandchild, born just 7 weeks after Jim's departure.

Dee Dee still lives in Broward County, and all her children live close by except for John. I feel blessed to have such a loving and fun Aunt. She has been an inspiration to all her family and to me, her niece, as well.

James August Kinney

1908-1965

The last child born to William Homer and Anna Rachel was James August Kinney, born in Medford, Grant County, Oklahoma, on the fourth of August 1908.

James August first showed up in the 1900 U.S. Federal Census, living with 2 older brothers and 1 sister in Medford Township, Grant County, Oklahoma. James was the only child to be born in Oklahoma.

As a young boy of 5, James August suffered the loss of his father to cancer. I wonder what impact this event may have had on his future life.

James enjoyed good health as a young boy according to a notation on brother, Vernon's, application for life insurance completed in 1918.

In the 1920 U.S. Federal Census, James was living with his mother, Anna, and brother, Vernon, in a home at 209 North Mathewson Avenue, Wichita. Anna was employed as a housekeeper in this residence, while Vernon and James were listed as lodgers.

Sometime around 1921, James moved with his mother and her new husband, William Allen Anderson, to Dade County, Florida. Anna's father, James Vernon Fox, also moved to Florida. In James Vernon Fox's obituary of 1923, he had been living in Goulds, Dade County, Florida since 1921. Daughter, Anna Anderson, and grandson, James, also lived in Goulds.

The 1927 Miami City Directory listed James living at 62 N.W. 62 Street, Miami in the residence of W. A. Anderson. His occupation was "driver for Burdines." At 18 years old, one would think that he was driving a car, but as we see later, he was a pile driver in the booming construction industry of South Florida. Perhaps he learned his skill early on. Burdines was a large department store with a long history in Miami. The Burdines were one of the early pioneer families. It's possible he was part of the construction of a Burdines store.

At the 1935 Florida State Census, James was living with mother, Anna Anderson, at 260 N.W. Fourth Street, Miami, Dade County, Florida.

James married Erma L. Hillard who was born about 1910. Erma moved to Miami around 1922 from Stanford, Florida. Her first husband was a Mr. Hillard. Erma had 3 children by her first husband: Edris, Zada, and Jack. These children became the step children of James August Kinney. Erma and

James gave birth to Ann Laura Kinney, 27 December 1937, in Miami, Dade County, Florida. A brother, James Norman Kinney, known as "Tuffy," was born 16 November 1941.

Anna Rachel Fox Kinney Anderson, James Kinney, and daughter Anne at her high school graduation.

James Norman Kinney was known as "Tuffy". He was born 16 November 1941 in Miami, Dade County, Florida. He died 15 January 2008, in Maine. His sister, Anne, received two phone calls with sad news of loved ones passing on the same day: for Tuffy and Betty Mae Kinney.

Tragedy struck on 9 July 1946, when Erma passed away from complications during child birth when she was just 36 years old. The child did not survive. James August was now a single father.

He was not alone, as his mother, Anna Rachel Fox Kinney Anderson, and his sister-in-law, Alberta Anna Bell Culbreath Kinney stepped in to lend a helping hand and to offer guidance to the children.

And, it paid off. Anne graduated high school, then married Joseph Myles. They had 4 children: Helen Myles, who married Gene Henning; Joey Myles, Bobbie Myles, and Joann Myles Hawthorne. Helen and Gene had 2 children: Monica and Brandon. Joann also had 2 children: David and Vicki. Sadly, Anne lost both her sons at early ages.

Eventually, James, remarried, but I do not know anything of this relationship.

James passed away on 24 June 1965, following a hospital stay. His cause of death was actually a slip and fall while he was using crutches on a Miami street. At the time of death, he suffered from peripheral vascular collapse, squamous cell carcinoma of the lung, and a "fracture of the left femoral neck." He was interred in Woodlawn Park Cemetery, Miami, Dade County, Florida.

James August Kinney, 1955

James August Kinney grave marker in Woodlawn Park Cemetery, Miami, Dade County, Florida

Anne Kinney and Joe Myles, 1955

1965: Helen Myles, 8 *Joey Myles, 6*

Joe and Anne raised their children in Hialeah, Dade County, Florida, where Joe was a police officer for the City of Hialeah. Anne became a nurse and worked for many years in that capacity. After retirement, Joe and Anne moved to Okeechobee, Florida, where they enjoyed life near Lake Okeechobee. Anne continued her nursing career in Okeechobee by working in hospice care. All her patients loved her dearly. But, sadly, Anne developed cancer herself. In her last days she was lovingly cared for at home by her 2 daughters, Helen and Joann, and her granddaughter, Vicki.

In 2011, the Kinneys, Stewarts, and Myles families had a get together in Okeechobee, Florida. We talked about memories of the good 'ole days and loved ones we missed, and in the process made some new memories.

Anne passed away 24 February 2012, in Okeechobee, Florida. At her funeral service, this poem was shared: "I'm Free. Don't grieve for me, for now I'm free; I'm following the path God laid for me. I took His hand when I heard Him call; I turned my back and left it all. I could not stay another day, To laugh, to love, to work or play. Tasks left undone must stay that way; I found peace at the close of day. If my parting has left a void, Then fill it with remembered joy. A friendship shared, a laugh, a kiss; Ah yes, these things, I too, will miss. Be not burdened with times of sorrow; I wish you the sunshine of tomorrow. My life's been full, I savored much; Good friends, good times, a loved one's touch. Perhaps my time seemed all too brief; Don't lengthen it now with undue grief. Lift up your heart and peace to thee; God wanted me now, He set me free."

Left to right, back:* *Barbara Kinney Black, Roger Vernon Kinney, Vicki Hawthorne, Lawrence Sherman Kinney, Sandy Stewart Dolan, George Dolan
Left to right, front:* *Anne Kinney Myles, Joann Myles Hawthorne, Valeria La Verne "Dee Dee" Kinney Stewart, Joyce Brown Rosier Lasseter Kinney, Gene Henning, and Helen Myles Henning

Cousins: Barbara Kinney Black, Sandy Stewart Dolan, Helen Myles Henning, 2011

Cousins: Lawrence Sherman Kinney, Anne Kinney Myles, and Valeria Kinney Stewart

3

James Vernon Fox

1853-1923

Born 25 September 1853, in Platte City, Platte County, Missouri, James Vernon Fox was the next to the last child born to William Abner Fox and Sarah Jane Cravens Fox. Sarah's grave marker in the Fox Family Cemetery in Platte County lists 6 children who all died before adulthood. Four children survived to adulthood including James Vernon Fox.

James was most likely named after his grandfather, James Fox.

At the 1860 U.S. Federal Census for his family, James Vernon was listed as 7 years old, and his younger brother, George Dorriss Fox, was 5.

In the 1870 U.S. Federal Census, he was 17, and working as a farm hand on his father's farm. The Census, however, was now for Pettis Township, rather than Carroll, so I wonder if the family had moved to another of their holdings.

On 19 September 1876, James Vernon Fox married Mary L. Haven, daughter of John D. and Margaret Ann Harmon Haven of Grand River Township, Daviess County, Missouri.

CERTIFICATE OF MARRIAGE.

U. S. Revenue Stamp
5 Cents.

STATE OF MISSOURI,
County of Daviess.

This certifies, that on the 19th day of September A. D. 1876, at ______ in said County, according to law, and by authority, I duly Joined in Marriage Mr James Fox of Platte Co. and Miss Mary Havens

Given under my hand the 16th day of October A. D. 1876

Filed for Record this ... day Octr 1876
Wm S. Abell
Recorder

J. H. Thompson (seal)

Marriage Certificate for Mary L. Haven and James Vernon Fox

Their first child, Anna Rachel Fox, was born in Platte City, Missouri, 16 July 1877. After her birth, in the 1880 U.S. Federal Census, the family was counted back in Daviess County living with Mary's father, John D. Haven. It appears they were farming together.

At the death of Mary's father, John D. Haven, in 1891, Mary inherited land which the family probably farmed.

Then on 20 October 1896, Anna Rachel married William Homer Kinney of Grundy County, Missouri. Grundy County perhaps was where William Homer was working at the time of his application for a marriage license, because family tradition states he was born in Rochester, Andrew County, Missouri. The wedding ceremony took place in Anna Rachel's father, James Vernon Fox's, home in Daviess County. The Elder, Thompson Penn, of the Methodist church presided. Marriage records indicate that the John D. Haven family were members of the Gallatin Methodist Church, as Mary's oldest sister, Martha Jane Haven, was married in that church in 1861. Perhaps this is the same church the elder was associated with.

We see from the Daviess County court records viewed at the Gallatin Courthouse in 2013, after James Vernon's father-in-law, John D. Haven, died in 1891, that in May 1892, Margaret petitioned the court to be able to sell part of her late husband's land to satisfy his debts. James Vernon Fox bought the land for $200. We also see a series of real estate transactions where James Vernon was apparently selling this land as individual house lots, as the land had become part of the City of Gallatin sometime after John D. Haven's death. We can see what land remained with Margaret Haven by the plat map.

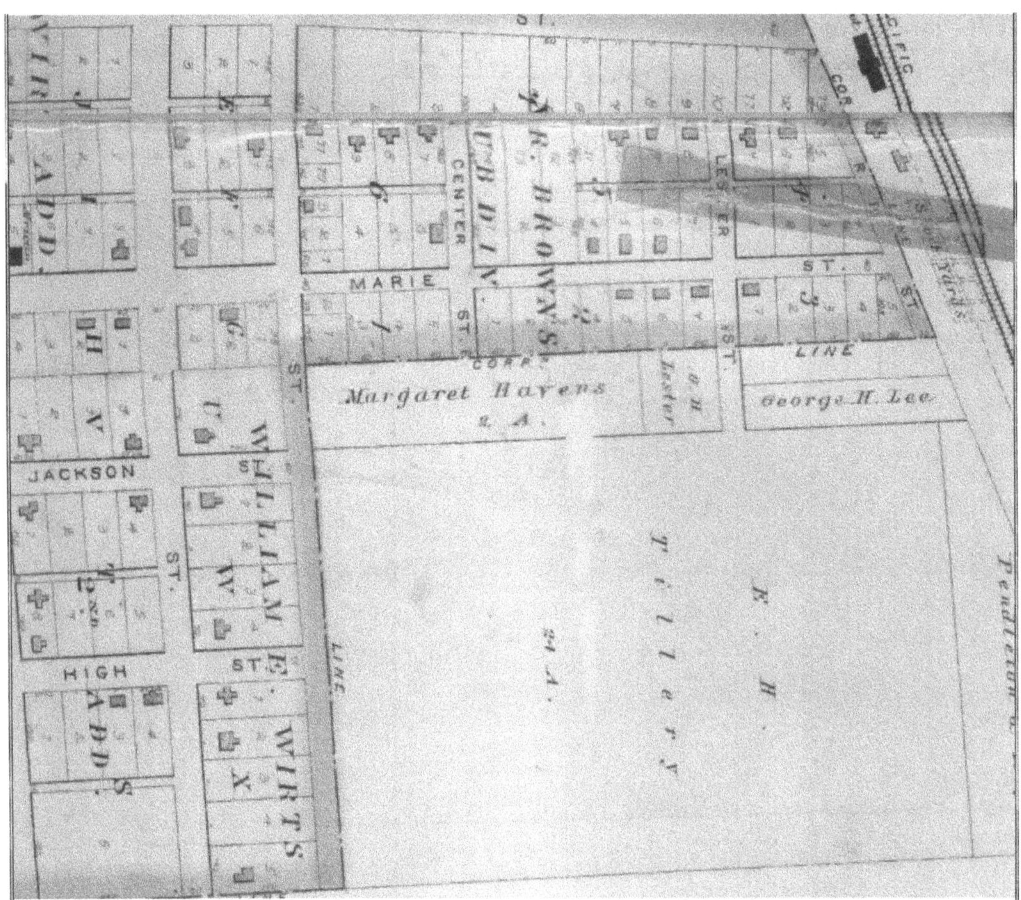

Plat map viewed at the Daviess County Courthouse, Gallatin, Missouri, September 2013

The following names were associated with real estate transactions of James Vernon and/or Mary L. Haven Fox between the dates of 1892 and 1903:
Ames Musselman, Overton Ridings, Wood Hamilton, Cora Dinsmore, Charles G. Yates, John Erwin, Madison Stewart, Brown Cemetery, J. Musselman, M. A. Haven, Anna McNeill, Ed Brown, N. Baker, F. M. Gown, G. W. Fredricks, and R. H. Alderson.

At the 1900 U.S. Federal Census, we find James Vernon and Mary L. living in Washington Township, Daviess County, Missouri. A Charles Bonham, listed as a boarder, 25 years old and single, was living with them. James Vernon owned his farm with a mortgage. This area was located almost directly north of Gallatin, and above Grand River Township where Mary L. Haven Fox was born and raised.

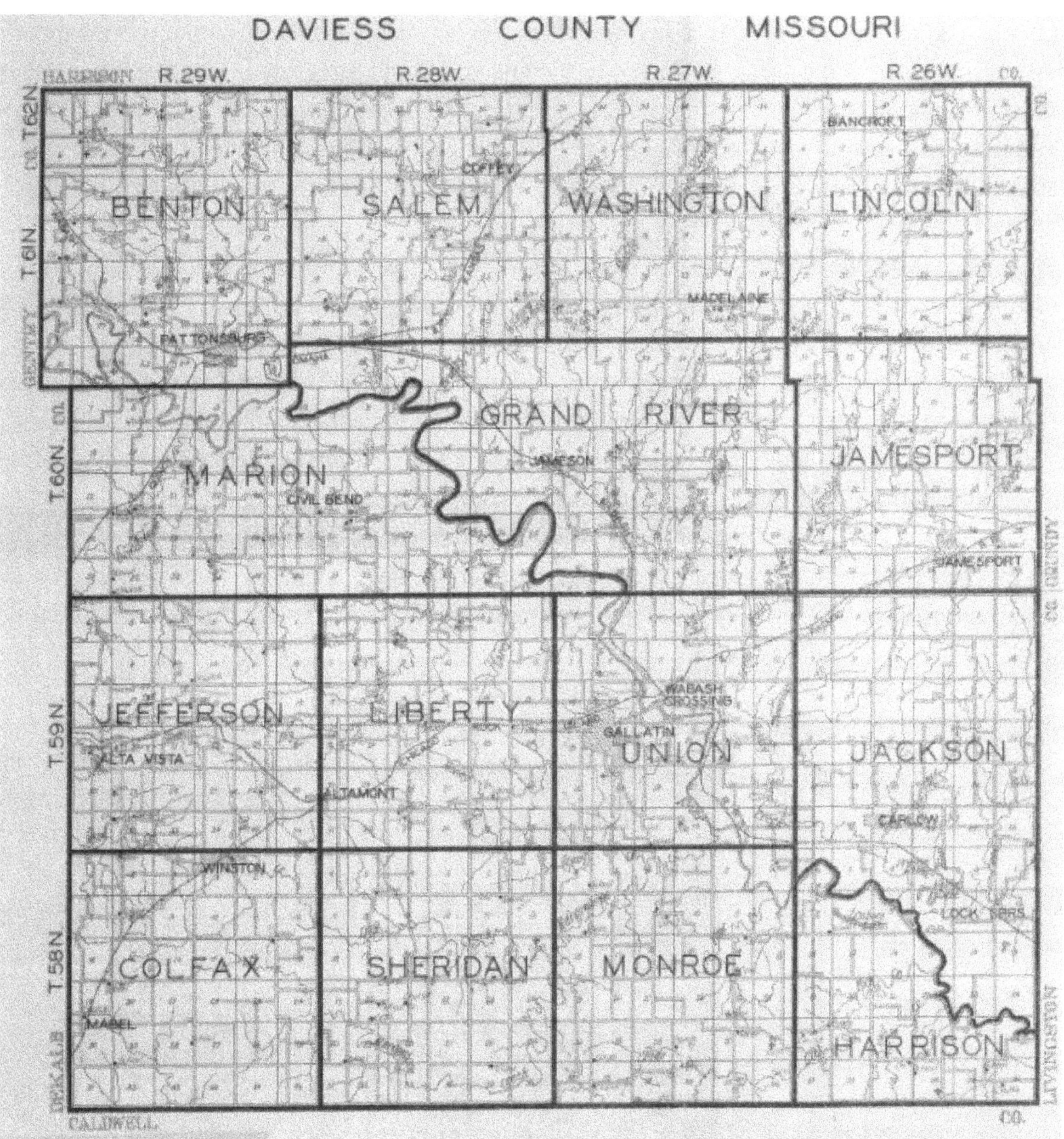

From the Plat Books of Missouri, accessed 2013 from the University of Missouri Library Systems Digital Library at: http://digital.library.umsystem.edu/cgi/i/image/image-idx?type=boolean;view=thumbnail;c=platic;rgn1=platic_ti;corig=platic;start=1;size=20;sort=platic_ti ;q1=daviess

Additionally, on the 1900 Census Mary L. Haven Fox stated she had given birth to 2 children, but only 1 child survived at the Census time. We know the surviving child to be Anna Rachel Fox.

In 1901, Mary's mother, Margaret Ann Harmon Haven, died. Court records indicate her land which remained at her death was ordered sold to cover her debts. James Vernon Fox was the highest bidder purchasing the land for just $35.

The last real estate transaction for James Vernon Fox and Mary L. Fox recorded in Gallatin, Daviess County, was for the sale of "Lot number Six (6) in block number Two (2) of Julia A. Richardson's subdivision of Out Lot number Eleven (11) in the City of Gallatin, as shown by the plat of said subdivision and Out Lot, now of record and on file in said Daviess County." It was sold to Richard H. Alderson, for $80, 14 December 1903. James and Mary were already residents of Grant County, the Territory of Oklahoma, at this time as per the notary public's entry on the document. This piece of property was located at the corner of Prospect Avenue and South Street in 2013. The court document was filed in Book 89, p. 362. This transaction of selling the Gallatin property, coupled with the 9 May 1903 transaction that follows of purchasing the farm in Grant County, Oklahoma, I believe give evidence that James Vernon and Mary Haven Fox moved from Missouri to Oklahoma between 1901 and 1903.

On 9 May 1903, we find a Deed was issued to Mary L. Fox for 160 acres of land in Grant County, Oklahoma. She paid $5,300 for the property. Presumably, there were growing crops, and a vegetable garden, plus fruit trees as described in the Deed transcribed below.

"All of the N.W. Quarter (NW ¼) of Section number twenty-one (21), Township number twenty-eight (28), north of Range number five (5) west of the Indian Meridian containing 160 acres more or less according to the United States Government Survey. All crops, garden and fruit pass with the title to the farm. Grantee assumes and agrees to pay the taxes on said land for the year 1903."

The Articles of Agreement for the Warranty Deed dated 9 May 1903, further outlines property to pass to Mary L. Haven: "...loose and attached lumber, troughs, barrels, wood and broken lumber, tanks, and all other goods, chattels, and lumber, bought and used on the realty, not to include any livestock."

On 9 February 1909, Mary Haven Fox sold the above land.

In 2003, the land appeared to have just been prepared for planting. One of the crops James Vernon Fox grew was oats.

Land purchased by Mary L. Haven Fox in 1903, Hickory Township, Grant County, Oklahoma, as it appeared in 2013

Look closely to see the stone foundations of the former school house. I wonder if W. H. Kinney's kids went here.

Across the road from Mary L. Haven Fox's farmland was a school located near the line of trees, Hickory Township, Grant County, Oklahoma, as it appeared in 2013

While living in Grant County, various newspaper articles appeared about James Vernon Fox in the Medford, Oklahoma papers. For example, in the edition of The Medford Star, Medford, Oklahoma, Vol. 11, No. 33, Ed 1 Thursday 19, January 1905, we read, "J. V. Fox, a prosperous farmer living north of town, bought a fine 80 acre farm for $2,500 Monday. Mr. Fox has sold some of his Missouri property and is investing in Oklahoma property."

A piece of Oklahoma property was purchased by James Vernon Fox using the proceeds from the sale of a piece of property in Platte County, Missouri. This was the 80-acre farm referenced in the above newspaper article. In the will of James Vernon's grandfather, James Fox, land was to be purchased for investment in Platte County, Missouri, on behalf of James Vernon Fox. So, the property in question in Platte County was sold and the money used to purchase these 2 adjacent tracts of land totaling 80 acres in Grant County, Oklahoma. This transaction took place 1 May 1905, for land described as:

"North ½ of the N.E. Quarter, Lots 1 & 2, Section 4, Township 27 North, Range 6 West of the Indian Meridian." Lot 1 consisted of 40.30 acres and Lot 2 of 40.72 acres, so a total of just over 80 acres. A visit to this property in 2013 revealed a little pond, a creek, and an old railroad apparently ran through the northeast corner of Lot 1.

The plat map published around 1907 shows the name of W. H. Kinney on this tract, but a check of records in the Grant County Courthouse in Medford, Oklahoma, 2013, did not show any real estate holdings in the name of W. H. Kinney. This was a mystery to me until I found the Deed describing the purchase as having been made by James Vernon Fox. On 3 January 1916, Anna Rachel Fox Kinney, the widow of W. H. Kinney since 1913, bought this land from her father, James Vernon Fox, for $1. She also took on a mortgage of $1,500.

It appears a transaction may be missing from my records, because the next time we see this land referenced, James Vernon Fox is selling it on 11 June 1918, apparently for a $2,000 life insurance policy with the National Life Insurance Company.

Imagine having your name in the paper just because you use a brand of binding twine. That's what we read in The Medford Star, Medford, Oklahoma, Vol. 11, No. 49, Ed. 1 Thursday 11 May 1905. James Vernon Fox uses the brand Plymouth Twine and it's sold at Fisk & Tharp.

Another interesting article appeared in The Medford Star, Medford, Oklahoma, Vol. 12, No. 15, Ed. 1 Thursday, 14 September 1905: "J. V. Fox, who lives 5¼ miles northwest of town, was in Saturday and made this office a pleasant call. He brought with him a head of cabbage and some fine sweet potatoes which he left at this office. We took them home where they were properly cooked and during the time of eating our thoughts turned very kindly to Mr. Fox. They were fine and we heartily appreciated them, not alone for their intrinsic value and excellence alone, but for the fact that there are at least a few people who appreciate the efforts of the printer, Mr. Fox among that number. Many thanks."

James Vernon received 2 more mentions in the paper during 1907, when The Medford Star included him in their "Roll of Honor" as a reader of their paper. This piece appeared in the 17 January 1907 issue, Vol. 13, No. 33. Again in the 19 September 1907 issue, The Medford Star announced his prizes awarded at the Medford Carnival and Fair held September 5-7. J. V. Fox had the largest ham of meat and received first prize for his black oats.

This following article mentions both W. H. Kinney and J. V. Fox: "W. H. Kinney living north of town reports threshing going on in his vicinity and yield below normal. Says that his father-in-law Mr. J. V. Fox, has 25 acres of fine oats that will yield over forty bushel per acre. Mr. Kinney also does a little real estate business on the side, and reports the sale of the Mrs. Bena Somers farm, 8 miles N.E. of Medford to George Bennett for $7,000," The Medford Patriot, Medford, Oklahoma, Vol. 18, No. 39, Ed. 1 Thursday 6 July 1911.

While the newspapers printed little pieces about the ordinary daily lives of their citizens, they also included sad information as the following article conveys: "Mr. J. V. Fox Has a Brother Die. A telegram received Friday evening from Platte City, Missouri, conveyed the sad intelligence to J. V. Fox that his brother, George D. Fox, died suddenly after a protracted illness, covering several months, in which the deceased was able to be up and about. The evening train having gone when the message arrived, Mr. Fox did not attend the funeral, which was held Saturday at the Missouri home. Mr. and Mrs. Fox have the sympathy and condolence of their Grant County friends in their sad thoughts and tribulations," The Medford Patriot, Medford, Oklahoma, Vol. 18, No. 46, Ed. 1 Thursday, 24 August 1911."

The 12 January 1912 edition of The Medford Patriot, Vol. 19, No. 15, reported that "J. V. Fox living north-west of town has bought of Stewart Brothers a tubular cream separator, having become convinced that his was one of the greatest money savers on a farm."

Do you know what your ancestors did on the 18 of May 1912? I do, because The Medford Patriot, Vol. 19, No. 33, Ed. 1 Thursday 23 May 1912 recorded, "J. V. Fox and wife were in from the farm, Saturday."

Perhaps one of the saddest articles published about James Vernon Fox, appeared in The Medford Patriot, Vol. 20, No. 5, Ed. 1 Thursday 7 November 1912:

PUBLIC SALE!

Being compelled to change climate on account of health, I have decided to quit farming, and will sell at public auction, at my farm three miles north and one and a half miles east of Medford, Oklahoma, commencing at 10 o'clock a. m., with Free Lunch at noon, on

Tuesday, November 12, 1912

the following described property, to-wit:

7 HORSES

One bay mare, 10 years old, weight 1300, with foal by jack
One bay mare, 5 yrs. old, wt. 1200, with foal by jack
One sorrel horse, 10 years old, weight 1300 pounds
One bay mare, 8 years old, weight 1100, with foal
One bay mare, 10 yrs. old, wt. 1100, with foal by jack
One yearling mare mule
One last spring colt

10 CATTLE

1 cow four years old, will be fresh in three weeks
1 cow four years old, will be fresh in four weeks
1 cow six years old, will be fresh in February
1 cow three years old, will be fresh in January
1 cow four years old, will be fresh in February
1 cow four years old, will be fresh in March
1 Shorthorn bull, two years old and 3 calves

3 Hogs Weight about 200 pounds, one a high grade boar

FARMING IMPLEMENTS

CONSISTING OF

McCormick Binder, 6 ft., used 3 years
Rock Island lister
1 walking cultivator
1 five tooth cultivator
1 harrow and 1 disc harrow
1 buggy
1 big iron kettle
One hole Racine corn sheller
Hodges Mower, used 4 years
One 14 inch gang plow
1 John Deere lister
1 double and 1 single shovel
1 good 3 inch Birdsell wagon
Set of single harness
1 set of lister trucks
100 bu. oats and some corn fodder
Cassady 16 inch plow
1 hay rake
1 Riding Cultivator, 6 shovels
1 go-devil and 1 fodder sled
1 feed wagon and rack
Set of double work harness
1 good scraper
Kaffir corn fodder and alfalfa

HOUSEHOLD GOODS, ETC.

Including Upright Folding Bed, Double Couch, Incubator, Marble Top Stand Table, 2 Good Rockers, 6 Dining Room Chairs, 2 Bedsteads, 2 Carpets, Heating Stove, Gasoline Stove (2 burners), Set of Springs, Cupboard, Kitchen Cabinet, and Other Articles too numerous to mention.

TERMS OF SALE

Sums under $10, cash in hand. $10 and over a credit of 8 months, purchaser giving bankable note drawing 10 per cent interest from date. 5 per cent discount for cash on sums over $10. Settlement before removal.

WILLIAMS BROTHERS
AUCTIONEERS
I. R. HEASTY, Clerk

J. V. FOX

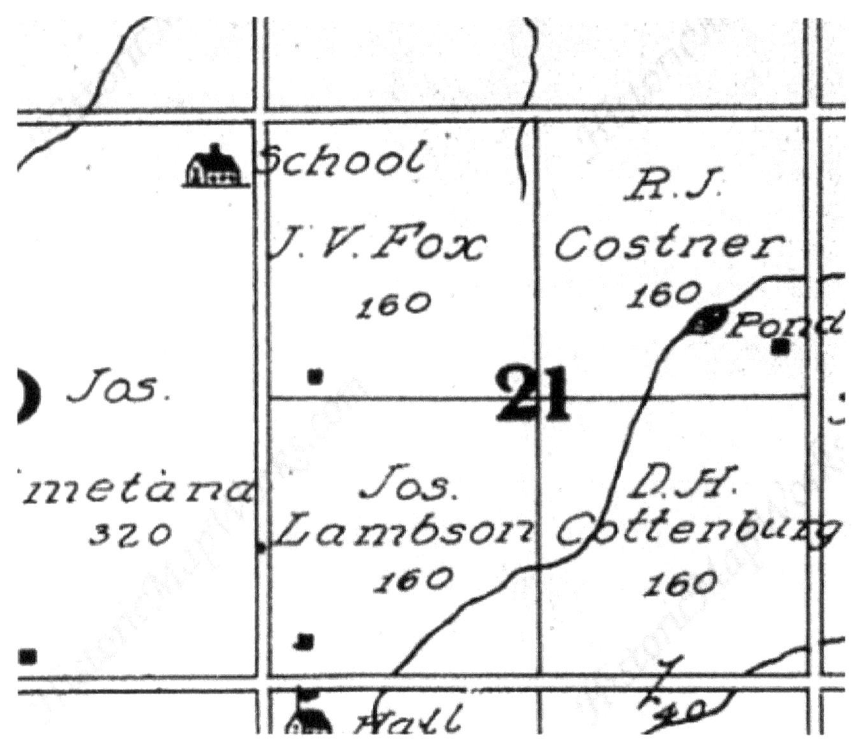

Plat map showing location of school and of J. V. Fox's house in Hickory Township, Grant County, Oklahoma between 1903 and 1913

~~~~~~~~~~~~~~~~~~~~~

A plat is a map, drawn to scale, showing the divisions of a piece of land. U.S. General Land Office surveyors drafted township plats of Public Lands Surveys to show the distance and bearing between section corners, sometimes including topographic or vegetation information. Further refinement often splits blocks into individual lots, usually for the purpose of selling the described lots.

~~~~~~~~~~~~~~~~~~~~~~~

Although it was sad that he had to sell out his farming implements and, in essence, retire, the notice does give us a snapshot of his farming life. For example, he had horses, cattle, and hogs, and he grew corn, alfalfa, hay, and oats, and he had a marble top stand table.

The next article gives us further insight into a possible reason for the sale of his farming goods: "Mrs. Fox Dead – Passed Away at Arkansas City Tuesday. Walter Waldie, secretary of the Odd Fellows lodge, received a telegram Wednesday from J. V. Fox, announcing the sudden death of Mrs. J. V. Fox, his wife, at Arkansas City Tuesday. The remains will be brought here today and the funeral services will be held Friday afternoon at 2 o'clock at the M. E. Church of which Mrs. Fox was a member. Mrs. Fox had been in ill health for some time. Mr. and Mrs. Fox went to Arkansas City recently for Mrs. Fox's health. She is the mother of Mrs. W. H. Kinney on Route One." This appeared in The Medford Patriot, Medford Oklahoma, Vol. 20, No. 43, Ed. 1 Thursday 31 July 1913. Probably Mary L. Haven Fox died on 29 July 1913.

A few weeks later, a Card of Thanks appeared in The Medford Patriot, Medford, Oklahoma, Vol. 20, No. 45, Ed. 1 Thursday 14 August 1913: "We desire to express our deep appreciation and thanks to the Odd Fellow lodge and to our friends for the flowers, the services, and their kindly ministrations during the death and burial of our beloved wife and mother. J. V. Fox and Mrs. W. H. Kinney."

One month after the death of his wife, we find the final article on James Vernon Fox published in the Oklahoma papers: The Medford Patriot, Medford, Oklahoma, Vol. 20, No. 46, Ed. 1 Thursday 21 August 1913 "J. V. Fox left Tuesday for Claremore, Oklahoma, to get a team he left there some time ago." As a young person, I recalled a story that my grandfather, Vernon Haven Kinney, grandson of James Vernon Fox, told me. He said that as a young boy, he once went with his grandfather to somewhere in Oklahoma, he thought Claremore, and the wagon with the horses got stuck in the mud.

James Vernon remarked that he would never buy land in that place because the soil was bad. Once I read this article in the paper, it all made sense. My grandfather, Vernon Haven Kinney (named after his two grandfathers), probably went with James Vernon Fox to pick up the team referenced in this article. Having Vernon Haven's personal reflection on this news item made it all seem more real to me.

Sometime after 1913, probably 1916-1918, James Vernon Fox relocated to Wichita, Sedgwick, Kansas, as he appeared in the City Directory there in 1918, 1919, and 1920.

Also, we know that he moved to Goulds, Dade County, Florida probably during 1921, because his obituary states that he died there in 1923 and had been a resident of Dade County for the past 2 years.

His obituary, published in The Miami Herald 23 August 1923, reads: "James Vernon Fox. The body of James Vernon Fox, 70, who died in his home at Goulds Tuesday, was shipped last night to Medford, Oklahoma, accompanied by his daughter, Mrs. Anna R. Anderson, also of Goulds. The W. H. Combs Company was in charge. Mr. Fox, a retired farmer, had been in Goulds for about two years, coming from Medford, Oklahoma. He was born 25 September 1853, in Platte County, Missouri. He leaves his daughter, Mrs. Anderson, and three grandsons, Vernon H. Kinney of Miami; James Kinney of Goulds; and Veigh Kinney of Pawhuska, Oklahoma."

James Vernon Fox was buried in Rosemound Cemetery outside of Medford, Grant County, Oklahoma, alongside Mary L. Haven Fox, his beloved wife. The cemetery contains two four-grave site plots next to each other, each ringed with about 6" wide concrete borders.

James Vernon Fox a and Mary L. Haven Fox grave stone in Rosemound Cemetery, Medford, Grant County, Oklahoma

Questions

1. How did James Vernon Fox meet Mary L. Haven since he was living in Platte County, and she in Daviess County?
2. What was the birthdate, name, and sex of their child that was listed as dead by the 1900 U.S. Federal Census?
3. How many pieces of land did James Vernon and Mary L. Haven Fox own in Oklahoma?
4. Since in 1909 Mary Haven Fox sold the 160 acres she had purchased in 1903 Grant County, Oklahoma, and James Vernon Fox referenced selling his farm equipment in a 1912 newspaper article, is it possible they owned 2 different farms? If not, where did they live after selling the farm which was in the name of Mary Haven Fox?

Questions, continued:

5. It would appear from the court documents and newspaper articles that James Vernon Fox purchased the 80 acre property upon which William Homer Kinney and family lived in 1905. It also appears that he sold this property to his daughter, Anna Rachel Fox Kinney, in 1916. Later, he sold the same property in 1918. So, did he buy back the property from Anna Rachel between 1916 and 1918?
6. Did he own property in Goulds, Florida, as suggested?
7. Did he leave a will in Florida, Oklahoma, or Missouri?
8. Where was Arkansas City which is listed as the place of residence when Mary L. Haven Fox died? On the 2013 Arkansas highway map, there is a small town called Arkansas City located in southern Arkansas along the Mississippi River. Conversely, there is an Arkansas City, Kansas, just north of Grant County, Oklahoma. Perhaps the Kansas location is more likely.
9. What was the cause of death for Mary L. Haven Fox?
10. Is the Methodist Episcopal Church which Mary L. Haven Fox was a member of upon her death still in existence in 2013?

The Wife of James Vernon Fox
Mary L. Haven
1852-1913

Mary L. Haven was probably the youngest child of John D. and Margaret A. Harmon Haven of Virginia. Mary was born in July 1852 in Tazewell County, Virginia. In later Census records, she stated she was born in West Virginia. Without a birth record, it is difficult to know for sure because the area where her family lived was right on the state line when West Virginia was created out of Virginia. What we do know is that her family migrated to Missouri and was present there for the 1860 U.S. Federal Census in Grand River Township, Daviess County.

She married 16 October 1876, James Vernon Fox of Platte County.

In the 1880 U.S. Federal Census, she and James Vernon were living in the household of her father, John D. Haven, and they had a daughter, Anna Rachel Fox, who had been born 16 July 1877, in Platte County, Missouri.

When Mary's father died in 1891, she inherited a piece of land as described:
"All of the west half of the N.W. Quarter of Section thirty-four (34), in Township sixty (60), of Range twenty-seven (27), except one and one half acres on the south end and three and one half acres on the east side. Also seventeen and a half acres being the west part of the north half of the N.W. Quarter of the S.E. Quarter of Section twenty-eight (28), Township sixty (60), of Range twenty-seven (27)." This land was located in Washington Township, Daviess County, Missouri, and she was living there at the 1900 U.S. Federal Census.

Land inherited by Mary L. Haven from her father, John D. Haven's will in 1891, located in Daviess County, Missouri, as seen in 2013

When we visited Mary Fox's Missouri land in 2013, on a Sunday morning, the area was very quiet with absolutely nobody stirring about. We had to cross a creek on an old iron bridge to get to the location.

We know that in 1903, she purchased a 160-acre piece of land in Hickory Township, Grant County, in the Territory of Oklahoma. She sold this same land in 1909.

At the 1910 U.S. Federal Census, she was living in Grant County, Oklahoma, with husband, James Vernon Fox. She was, apparently, not in the best of health, because we see that her husband sold his farm equipment and they moved to Arkansas City for her health. It's unclear where Arkansas City is, although on a 2013 Arkansas road map, there is a small town by that name along the west shore of the Mississippi River in Southern Arkansas, or another Arkansas City just north of Grant County in Kansas.

Mary passed away around 29 July 1913. She is buried in the Rosemound Cemetery, Medford, Grant County, Oklahoma next to her husband James Vernon Fox.

Read more on Mary L. Haven Fox on page 112.

MRS. FOX DEAD

Passed Away at Arkansas City Tuesday.

Walter Waldie, secretary of the Odd Fellows lodge, received a telegram Wednesday from J. V. Fox, announcing the sudden death of Mrs. J. V. Fox, his wife, at Arkansas City Tuesday. The remains will be brought here today and the funeral services will be held Friday afternoon at 2 o'clock at the M. E. Church of which Mrs. Fox was a member.

Mrs. Fox had been in ill health for some time. Mr. and Mrs. Fox went to Arkansas City recently for Mrs. Fox's health. She is the mother of Mrs. W. H. Kinney on route one.

Announcement of the death of Mary L. Haven Fox which appeared in The Medford Patriot, Medford, Oklahoma, Vol. 20, No. 43, Ed. 1 Thursday, 31 July 1913

Questions

1. When did Mary sell her Daviess County, Missouri land?
2. What was the sex, birthdate, and death date for her unnamed child which she indicated she had given birth to in the 1900 U.S. Federal Census?

A small marker on the grave plot of Mary L. Haven Fox in Rosemound Cemetery, Medford, Grant County, Oklahoma, as it appeared in 2013. A larger Fox marker with both their names was placed at a later time.

The Children of James Vernon Fox and Mary L. Haven

According to the 1900 U.S. Federal Census, Mary L. Haven Fox had given birth to 2 children with 1 surviving at the Census. Nothing is known by the author of the second child: whether it was a boy or girl, born alive or stillborn, where born, cause of death, etc. As birth records were recorded in a random fashion prior to the 1900s, we may never know the answer to these questions. What we do know, however, is that their firstborn child survived, married, had 5 children, and 3 different husbands.

Anna Rachel Fox

1877-1956

Anna Rachel Fox's granddaughter, Valeria La Verne Kinney Stewart, always remarks that "Grandma Anderson had a very hard life." As I learned about Anna's life, I had to agree with my Aunt Valeria—Anna Rachel did indeed have a difficult life.

Anna Rachel Fox was born 16 July 1877 in Platte City, Platte County, Missouri, to James Vernon and Mary L. Haven Fox. She was their first child.

At the 1880 U.S. Federal Census, Anna was listed as a granddaughter in the household of her mother, Mary's, parents, John D. and Margaret A. Harmon Haven.

She married William Homer Kinney at her family's home in Daviess County, Missouri on 20 October 1896 by an elder from the Methodist church. She was just 19 years old.

Marriage license for Anna Rachel Fox and William Homer Kinney, Daviess County, Missouri

MARRIAGE LICENSE.

STATE OF MISSOURI, COUNTY OF Daviess } THIS LICENSE AUTHORIZES any Judge, Justice of the Peace, Licensed or Ordained Preacher of the Gospel, or any other person authorized under the laws of this State, to SOLEMNIZE MARRIAGE between W. H. Kinney of County of Grundy and State of Mo, who is over the age of twenty-one years; and Miss Anna R Fox of Grand River Tp, in the County of Daviess and State of Mo, who is over the age of eighteen years.

(Seal)

WITNESS my hand as Recorder, with the Seal of office hereto affixed, at my office in Gallatin Mo this 20 day of Oct 1896

By Deputy. O.B. Price Recorder.

STATE OF MISSOURI, COUNTY OF Daviess } ss. This is to certify that the undersigned Elder in the Methodist Church did, at Brides fathers in said County, on the 20th day of October A. D. 1896, unite in marriage the above named persons. Thompson Penn

The foregoing Certificate of Marriage was filed for Record in my office on the 31 day of Oct A. D. 1896, at 9 o'clock and 30 minutes A. M.

By Deputy. O.B. Price Recorder.

At the 1900 U.S. Federal Census, the couple was living in Tarkio City, Atchison County, Missouri, and 2 children had already been added to the family: Homer Veigh, 2, born in August 1897 in Gallatin, Daviess County,

Missouri, and daughter, Valeria, 5 months, born in January 1900, presumably in Tarkio City. William Homer had a brother, Jesse A. Kinney, who lived and worked in Tarkio City for a prominent rancher. Perhaps William Homer, who was a farm hand, was also working in a similar situation.

By 1902, the family was living back in Daviess County in the small town of Coffeysberg. In 2013, it was called Coffey. Son, Vernon Haven Kinney, was born here on 21 February 1902.

Around Coffey, Daviess County, Missouri in 2013

When we arrived in Coffey, Missouri, in 2013, the place seemed quiet with no activity around. There were a number of crumbling buildings that were probably more than 100 years old. As this is the town where my grandfather, Vernon Haven Kinney, was born, I was curious to find buildings that may have stood when he was living there in 1902. As soon as we began photographing, someone arrived in an electric golf cart. We took this as a gesture of, "Welcome to our town." The man whom we met was interested to learn about our quest. In fact, he returned to his home and brought us a book detailing the history of the town published for an anniversary celebration of the town of Coffey.

Remains of Coffey, Daviess County, Missouri

The old safe in the former Coffey bank, empty in 2013, but nearly impossible to move

Sometime around 1904, Anna Rachel and William Homer followed her parents, James Vernon and Mary L. Haven Fox, to Oklahoma Territory as evidenced by numerous articles mentioning William Homer in the Grant County newspapers beginning in 1904.

The last child born to Anna Rachel and William Homer was James August Kinney, born 4 August 1908, Medford, Grant County, Oklahoma.

At the 1910 U.S. Federal Census, they had been married 13 years, and Anna had given birth to 5 children with 4 living at Census time. When could this fifth child have been born? At the 1900 Census, Anna stated she had given birth to 2 children and 2 were living. These 2 would have been Veigh and Valeria. Therefore, the unknown child must have been born between 1900 and 1910, most likely between Vernon Haven and James August, December 1902 and October 1907. Alternately, although less likely, it is possible this child could have also been born between November 1900 and April 1901, or July 1909 and April 1910 when the Census was taken. In the Census, William Homer listed his occupation as farmer, working on his own account, and he owned his farm with a mortgage. A check of the 1907 Oklahoma plat maps showed William Homer Kinney's name on a tract of land which his father-in-law, James Vernon Fox, had purchased in 1905.

In 1913, despite not having located any official records to date, family tradition and a very brief notice in a Missouri newspaper, tell us that Anna's husband, William Homer Kinney, died in November. The Missouri newspaper does not give a cause of death. His son, Vernon Haven Kinney's 1918 application for life insurance stated that W. H. Kinney had stomach cancer and had been sick for two years. In another application for life insurance dated around 1930, Vernon stated W. H. Kinney, his father, had died by an "accident with a gun." Anna was left with 4 children, between 5 and 15 years of age, and a farm to operate. Fortunately, her father had only recently returned to Oklahoma following the death of his wife, Mary Haven Fox, Anna Rachel's mother. Perhaps he assisted Anna with the farm.

Presumably, Anna Rachel stayed in Oklahoma as evidenced by newspaper articles mentioning her son, Veigh, and daughter, Valeria. For example, in The Medford Patriot, Medford, Oklahoma, Vol. 20, No. 38, Ed. 1 Thursday 26 June 1913 we see Valeria Kinney listed as a graduate along with the name of her teacher, L. Dervage, from school No. 54.

In the Thursday 22 May 1913 edition of The Medford Patriot, Vol. 20, No. 33, we read that Valeria and brother, Veigh, had both graduated from eighth grade. The paper notes that this was the largest graduating class from the eighth grade in Medford.

In a 1914 edition of The Medford Patriot under a section about school news, it's noted that Valeria had been absent from school because of sickness.

In Medford County court documents dated 3 January 1916, James Vernon Fox sold to Anna Rachel Fox Kinney for $1 and a mortgage of $1,500, the 80 acres of land on which she and her family had been living. In this document, Anna Rachel was identified as being "of Medford, Oklahoma."

We know that Anna Rachel Fox Kinney relocated to Wichita, Sedgwick County, Kansas sometime after January 1916 and before 5 August 1916, as a marriage license was granted to Anna by Sedgwick County, Kansas, to marry Mr. Orley Gregory of Wichita, Kansas. It is unclear if she was already living in Wichita at the time the marriage license was issued because it states "Anna R. Kinney of Medford, Oklahoma." The date of their wedding is unknown because there was no endorsement or "return" to the court stating that the marriage had taken place. The marriage license was issued on 5 August 1916.

STATE OF KANSAS, COUNTY OF SEDGWICK 65779

Office of the Probate Judge of Said County

BE IT REMEMBERED, That on the 5th day of August A. D., 1916, there was issued from the office of said Probate Judge a Marriage License, of which the following is a true copy;

(Seal)

Marriage License

State of Kansas, County of Sedgwick

Wichita, Kansas, August 5th 1916.

To any person authorized by law to perform the Marriage Ceremony, Greeting:

YOU ARE HEREBY AUTHORIZED TO JOIN IN MARRIAGE

Orley Gregory (Groom) of Wichita, Kansas, aged 27

Anna R. Kinney (Bride) of Medford, Okla., aged 38

with the consent of .... (Name of parent or guardian consenting) and of this license, duly endorsed, you will make due return

.... (Name of parent or guardian consenting)

to the office of the State Registrar of Vital Statistics, at Topeka, immediately after performing the ceremony.

(Seal) E. W. C. Jones, Probate Judge

ENDORSEMENT

TO THE STATE REGISTRAR OF VITAL STATISTICS, Topeka, Kansas:

I hereby certify that I performed the ceremony joining in marriage the above-named couple on the ....

day of .... 191..., at ....

Signed ....

Title ....

Address ....

Marriage License for Anna Rachel Fox Kinney and Orley Gregory

Sadly, we do learn the date of the wedding from the divorce files accessed at the Sedgwick County Courthouse in September 2013. Anna and Orley were married 5 August 1916, and separated 3 February 1919. The divorce was granted 25 October 1919. The grounds for divorce were gross neglect and abandonment. There was no alimony and no children. Anna had her Kinney name restored and received her free right to property.

A check of Wichita City Directories gave the following addresses for Anna Gregory:

- 1917 she was boarding at 320 North Seneca Avenue, Wichita, Kansas, along with husband, Orley Gregory, and son, Vernon Kinney. She was working as a helper at Peoples Cleaning and Laundry Works.
- 1919, Anna Gregory was listed as boarding at 209 Mathewson Avenue, along with son, Vernon Haven Kinney. We later learn this was the residence of William Allen Anderson.

At the 1920 U.S. Federal Census, Anna's name had been restored to Kinney and she was listed as a divorced housekeeper in the household of William A. Anderson and his son, William D. Anderson. Also living in the home were Anna's sons, Vernon Haven and James August, who were both listed as lodgers. William was mistakenly identified as divorced, but descendants of his state that he was widowed. The Census was taken in January 1920, and on 2 May 1920, Anna Rachel Fox Kinney married for the third time to William Allen Anderson.

STATE OF KANSAS, Sedgwick County, ss: May 1st, 1920

W. A. Anderson files application and affidavit for Marriage License to be issued to W. A. Anderson and Anna Kinney Affidavit showing that said Parties are legally entitled to License to marry is ordered filed and numbered 66486.

Office of the Probate Judge of Said County

BE IT REMEMBERED, That on the 1st day of May A. D. 1920, there was issued from the office of said Probate Judge a Marriage License, of which the following is a true copy:
[Seal]

MARRIAGE LICENSE

State of Kansas, County of Sedgwick

Wichita, Kansas, May 1st, 1920

To any person authorized by law to perform the Marriage Ceremony, Greeting:

YOU ARE HEREBY AUTHORIZED TO JOIN IN MARRIAGE

W. A. Anderson (Groom) of Wichita, Kansas, aged 48

Anna Kinney (Bride) of Wichita, Kansas, aged 42

with the consent of ____ (Name of Parent or Guardian Consenting) and of this license, duly endorsed, you will make due return

____ (Name of Parent or Guardian Consenting)

to my office at Wichita, Kansas, within ten days after performing the ceremony.
[Seal] G. W. C. Jones, Probate Judge.

ENDORSEMENT

TO WHOM IT MAY CONCERN:

I hereby certify that I performed the ceremony joining in marriage the above-named couple on the 2nd day of May, 1920, at Wichita, Kansas

Signed W. H. Hormel

Title Gospel Preacher

Address Wichita, Kansas

Marriage License for William Allen Anderson and Anna Rachel Fox Kinney

Sometime after that date, probably during 1921, the couple relocated to Goulds, Dade County, Florida, where William Allen's father, Reuben Archibald Anderson, had farmed in the 1910s. Also, Anna's obituary in The Miami Herald of 1956, stated she came to Miami 35 years previously, which would make the year of arrival 1921.

One of the many unanswered questions I have about Anna Rachel Fox is, "How did she meet William Allen Anderson?" There are 2 theories I've settled on.

The first theory involves Anna's son, Vernon Haven, who took a job as a printer for the Western Newspaper Union, owners of the Wichita Daily Eagle newspaper. William Allen's son, William Dimple Anderson, was an 18-year old high school student who had a paper route for the Wichita Daily Eagle, according to his 12 September 1918 World War I Draft Registration Card. On 19 December 1918, Vernon Haven completed an application for life insurance. Under the question, "Where lived in the last 3 years," he answered, "Medford, Oklahoma and Wichita, Kansas; present address, 209 Mathewson Avenue, 2 years." Vernon appeared in the 1917 Wichita City Directory (information collected during the fall of 1916), living with his mother and her husband, Orley Gregory, at 320 North

Seneca Avenue, Wichita, Kansas. Therefore, I theorize that Vernon Haven and William Dimple may have met each other through their jobs and Vernon may have come to room with the Anderson family.

My second theory involves Anna's daughter, Valeria Kinney Winfield, and her husband, Richard Webster Winfield. In the 1910 U.S. Federal Census for Renfrow Village, Grant County, Oklahoma, the family of Richard Winfield, Ransom D. Winfield and wife Emily J., was living on McKinley Street, next door to a couple by the names of William B. Anderson and wife, Sarah A. Anderson. This William's birthplace was Indiana, his father's Kentucky, and mother's was Indiana. The Kentucky and Indiana birthplaces are curious as those are consistent with our William Allen Anderson family history. Perhaps this William B. Anderson is related to the William Allen Anderson family. In addition, William Allen Anderson had a half-brother named James Winfield Anderson. The Winfield middle name was the same as Valeria's husband's last name. Perhaps Valeria met William Allen Anderson through a family connection of her husband's, Richard Winfield.

At the time of Anna Rachel's father, James Vernon Fox's, death in 1923, the obituary stated that he and she were both living in Goulds, Dade County, Florida.

Anna Rachel Anderson does not appear in any of the Miami City Directories, however, until 1926 when she and W. A. Anderson were reportedly living at 62 N.W. 62 Street, Miami. If Anna Rachel was living in Goulds as the obituary for her father, James Vernon Fox, indicated, then she may or may not have been listed in a Miami City Directory as Goulds is a small suburb located closer to Homestead in South Dade County, than to the City of Miami. Therefore, I checked the Homestead City Directories in the Miami Downtown Main Public Library in 2012. The first Homestead City Directory preserved in the Library was the 1926 issue. Anna Rachel does not appear in that directory. In the 1927 and 1928 Miami City Directories, she was located at 54 N.W. 62 Street, Miami.

Anna Rachel Fox Kinney Anderson and William Allen Anderson circa. 1920-27.

Anna lost her third husband, William Allen Anderson, on 23 May 1928 while they were traveling in Smithville, Lee County, Georgia.

Anna returned to Miami as her 2 sons, Vernon Haven and James August, were living there. The 1930 Miami City Directory listed her address as 534 N.W. 31 Street, Miami, which was just around the corner from her son, Vernon. Her grandson, Lawrence Sherman Kinney, recalls her living in an apartment on the north side of N.W. 31 Street, midway between N.W. 6 and 7 Avenues.

The Miami City Directory for 1929 listed Anna Anderson, widow of William A., living at 54 N.W. 62 Street, Miami. The following year, 1930, her residence was 534 N.W. 31 Street, Miami. In 1931, she was back at 54 N.W. 62 Street, Miami. In 1933, she moved to 134 East Flagler Street and was working as a housekeeper at the Ritz Hotel.

In 1934, she was living with her son, Vernon Haven, and his family.

The 1935 Florida State Census recorded Anna's address as 260 N.W. Fourth Street, Miami, Dade County, Florida. There were 6 different family groups listed at the same address. In 2013, this address no longer existed, but perhaps in 1935 it may have been an apartment complex. Anna was a housekeeper and son, James, was a salesman. Anna finished grammar school while James finished high school.

From 1936-1938, she did not appear in the Miami City Directory. Perhaps she was living with her son, Vernon, as family tradition states.

By 1939, she was living with son, James August, at 1441 N.W. 55 Street, Miami. In 1949, she was at 2120 N.W. Flagler Terrace, Miami, and finally at her death in 1956, she was living at 2170 N.W. 93 Street, Miami.

At the end of Anna's life, she had Bell's palsy in addition to cancer of the face. She reportedly lived in a nursing home at the end of her life in Miami. Her obituary in The Miami Herald, 4 March 1956 edition stated: "Mrs. Anna R. Anderson -- Services for Mrs. Anna Rachel Anderson, 79, of 2170 N.W. 93 Street, who died Friday, will be at 2 p.m. Monday in [??] Memorial Mortuary, with burial at Woodlawn Cemetery. She came here 35 years ago from Wichita, Kansas. She was a member of the Stanton Memorial Baptist Church and is survived by 3 sons, Veigh Kinney of Texas, and Vernon and James Kinney, both of Miami, 9 grandchildren and 13 great-grandchildren."

Anna died 3 March 1956 in Miami, Dade County, Florida. She was buried in the Woodlawn Park Cemetery.

Anna Rachel Fox Kinney Anderson, circa 1950s

Ana Rachel Fox Kinney Anderson's grave stone in Woodlawn Park Cemetery, Miami, Dade County, Florida

---

Bell's palsy is defined at Dictionary.com as a noun: suddenly occurring paralysis that distorts one side of the face, caused by a lesion of the facial nerve. The word's origin was 1855-60, named after Charles Bell (1774-1842), a Scottish anatomist, who first described it.

Questions:

1. Anna's obituary states that she had 9 grandchildren. I know of only 8 grandchildren. So, is it possible the child born to Valeria Kinney and Richard Winfield in 1918 survived? If so, who raised this child? Valeria's widower, Richard Winfield, went on to marry again and raise a family in Los Angeles, California. There's no mention of any other child.
2. How did Anna meet William Homer Kinney, her first husband?
3. How did Anna meet Orley Gregory, her second husband?
4. How did Anna meet William Allen Anderson, her third husband?
5. Did Anna inherit property from either William Allen Anderson upon his death in 1928, or from her father, James Vernon Fox, upon his death in 1923? If so, what happened to the property?

The Third Husband of Anna Rachel Fox

William Allen "Billy" Anderson

1872-1928

For a long time, as a child, I always heard Anna Rachel Fox referred to as "Grandma Anderson." She passed away when I was less than 1 year old, so do not remember her first hand. She was a topic of conversation only. It didn't even dawn on me that she was my grandfather, Vernon Haven Kinney's, mother and my great grandmother.

When I began family history research, I wanted to know why Anna Rachel was called Grandma Anderson and not Great Grandmother Kinney. What I discovered was William Allen "Billy" Anderson.

One day I was researching in the local cemetery where Anna Rachel is interred and found a link to William Allen Anderson, or so I thought. It turned out to be his father, Reuben Archibald Anderson, and he was buried in the same cemetery as Anna Rachel and my grandparents. At the bottom of his Find A Grave Memorial No. 52262309, was a little note from a family member wanting to connect with other relatives. So, I e-mailed and a wonderful relationship ensued from which I learned so many things about my step great grandfather, William Allen Anderson, and my 2 times step great grandfather, Reuben Archibald Anderson.

William Allen Anderson was born 4 October 1872, in Curry Township, Sullivan County, Indiana, to Reuben Archibald and Elizabeth "Eliza" Jane Nelson Anderson. He was one of 10 children. After the death of his mother, Eliza, his father, Reuben, married "Lucinda," spelled Lou Cinda, Bowdre, and called "Lou B" by her family. Together they had 3 children; William Allen's step siblings.

By the 1880 U.S. Federal Census, William Allen, was living with his family in Sumner County, Kansas, and by 1905, he was married to Dora Overstreet Anderson, and they had 4 children: Audrey, Reuben, Daisy, and William Dimple. They were living at 341 New York Avenue, Wichita, Kansas according to the Wichita City Directory. They continued in 1908, 1910, and 1911, on New York Avenue, but their house number changed to 335. William was a carpenter and a contractor. By 1916, he had moved to 209 Mathewson Avenue, Wichita, Kansas, possibly because his wife, Dora, had passed away in 1911.

By the 1918 Wichita City Directory, William Allen had 2 boarders in his home: Veigh Alva Kinney and his brother, Vernon Haven Kinney. At the 1920 U.S. Federal Census, William Allen was mistakenly listed as divorced, when in fact he had been widowed. Also living in the household was James August Kinney and Vernon Haven Kinney, plus Anna Rachel Fox Kinney, recently divorced from Orley Gregory. Anna was William Allen's housekeeper. Just 5 short months after the Census was taken, Anna and William Allen married. Shortly thereafter, they relocated to Miami, Dade County, Florida.

Since there was no City Directory published for Wichita, Kansas in 1921, and they do not appear in the 1922 Wichita Directory, it is safe to say they most likely relocated to Miami before 1922.

We know that William Allen's father, Reuben Archibald, had been farming in the Goulds area of Dade County before his death in 1913, and that some of William Allen's siblings were located in Goulds, as well. Perhaps this prompted William Allen and Anna Rachel to relocate to Florida.

To further pin down the date when they relocated to Dade County, we can turn to the obituary for Anna Rachel's father, James Vernon Fox, which was published in The Miami Herald, 23 August 1923 edition. It stated that James Vernon had been living in Goulds for about 2 years, which would have meant he arrived there in 1921. James Vernon's wife, Mary L. Haven Fox, had died in 1913 Medford, Oklahoma, making his daughter, Anna Rachel, his only surviving relative. I imagine he relocated to Dade County to be near his daughter. Therefore, we can assume that Anna Rachel and William Allen Anderson probably relocated to Dade County during 1921.

William Allen Anderson, right, with his stepson, Vernon Haven Kinney and step daughter-in-law, Alberta Anna Bell Culbreath Kinney in front of an orange tree somewhere in Dade County, Florida.

William Allen Anderson's grave stone in the White Chapel Memorial Gardens, Wichita, Kansas

The 1926, 1927, and 1928 Miami City Directories listed William Allen as a carpenter and contractor. In 1928, while staying in a hotel in Smithville, Lee County, Georgia, William Allen Anderson passed away. He is interred in White Chapel Memorial Gardens, Wichita, Sedgwick County, Kansas. His Find A Grave Memorial No. is 77569631.

William Allen's father, Reuben Archibald Anderson, was a soldier in the Civil War drafted to Company B, Indiana 30th Infantry Regiment. He mustered out on 13 October 1865. Shortly thereafter, he married Elizabeth "Eliza" Jane Nelson at the American Hotel in Sullivan, Indiana. Sometime before 1880, he relocated to Sumner County, Kansas. He was quite a successful farmer with a large amount of acreage according to his descendants.

Sometime before 1913, he relocated to Miami, Dade County, Florida, taking some of his children with him including: James Winfield Anderson, who passed away in Dade County sometime before 1928; Isadore Anderson Grenell, who passed away in Homestead, Dade County, Florida 26 October 1960; and Hazel Maude Anderson Pickens, who served as the executor of Reuben Archibald Anderson's estate in 1913, and whose obituary appeared in the 22 May 1916 edition of The Miami Herald.

Reuben Archibald Anderson passed away 21 May 1913 in Miami, Dade County, Florida. His obituary appeared in the 21 March 1913 edition of the Miami Metropolis, a predecessor of The Miami Herald. It stated: "Mr. Reuben Anderson, father of Mrs. Homer O. Pickens, residing at 1011 Avenue G passed away this morning. The funeral services will be held at the King undertaking establishment at 3 p.m." He is interred at the Woodlawn Park Cemetery, Miami, Dade County, Florida, in Grave No. 1, Lot 117, Section 1. He is located in a family plot which also contains Section 1, Lot 116, graves 1 and 2. There is no grave stone. His is one of the earliest burials in this beautiful Miami cemetery. All markers are flat as the frequent hurricanes tend to destroy upright monuments.

Reuben Archibald Anderson's will, a 90 page document which can be viewed on microfilm in the Miami Public Library Main Branch, was probated in Dade County, Florida, and described 2 different tracts of property as follows:

The first area was located in the town of Goulds. It consisted of several smaller parcels all adjacent to each other and totaling 170 acres. The location extended about ¼ mile west and ¼ mile east of 127 Avenue starting at about S.W. 216 Street and going south to S.W. 224 Street.

The second area consisted of 2 parcels of 10 acres each in a town called Leisure City. Apparently, the executor of the will indicated there were debts of $1,500. So, in 1918, a piece of land in the Leisure City area was sold for $45/acre. The sale resulted in $450.

In 1925, the 170 acre section was sold to cover the remainder of the indebtedness from the original $1,500 debt amount. The court ordered the property sold to cover the debts. It sold for $91/acre and brought in $15,000.

In 2013, Roger Kinney located these properties on Google Earth to see what they look like now. The Leisure City property was a combination of a corn field, open land, a day care center, and some houses, while the Goulds property had some average looking houses and some run down houses.

Reuben's daughter, Hazel Maude Pickens, and her husband, William Moore, had 7 children including: Miriam, Howard, James, Willa, who married Jim Wulz, Susan Renee, who died when she was just 2 days old, Richard, and Ronald. It was our privilege to meet Willa and her husband, Jim Wulz, in 2013 after becoming acquainted on the Internet. Willa has supplied most of the information about William Allen Anderson. Willa retired as the Senior Vice President of Human Resources at Union National Bank, Wichita, Kansas, and relocated to her beloved lakeside home in Missouri.

Willa Moore, great granddaughter of Reuben Archibald Anderson and her husband, Jim Wulz, 2013

William Allen Anderson (1872 - 1928)

husband of great grandmother

Anna Rachel Fox (1877 - 1956)

wife of William Allen Anderson

Vernon Haven Kinney (1902 - 1984)

son of Anna Rachel Fox

Lawrence Sherman Kinney (1928 -)

son of Vernon Haven Kinney

Barbara Elaine Kinney

daughter of Lawrence Sherman Kinney

Reuben Archibald Anderson

Some of Reuben Archibald Anderson's descendants

Looking east on 12 Street at Avenue B, Miami, in the 1910s, from *Historic Photos of Greater Miami*, *by Bramson, p. 27. Reuben Archibald Anderson lived on Avenue G.*

The Shores of Biscayne Bay, Miami during the 1910s photos from http://us.yhs4.search.yahoo.com/yhs/search;_ylt=A0oG7pFogqdSd1IA4koPxQt.?p=images+of+miami +florida+1910&fr2=sb-top&hspart=att&hsimp=yhs-att_001&type=att_lego_portal_home

The Parents of James Vernon Fox

William Abner Fox and Sarah Jane Cravens

1814-1891 1823-1858

The only child of James Fox and Lucinda Eskridge was William Abner Fox, born 13 May 1814, in Fauquier County, Virginia. The Annals of Platte County by Paxton, tells us, "He received a superior education. He wrote frequently for the papers. The family came to Howard County, Missouri, in 1836, and to Platte in 1838."

On 27 October 1840, in Daviess County, Missouri, William Abner married Sarah Jane Cravens. In 2013, when researching in the Daviess County Courthouse, I came across his marriage certificate as the first entry in the marriage book. I was surprised to find that he had married in Daviess County, since his family had established themselves in Platte County.

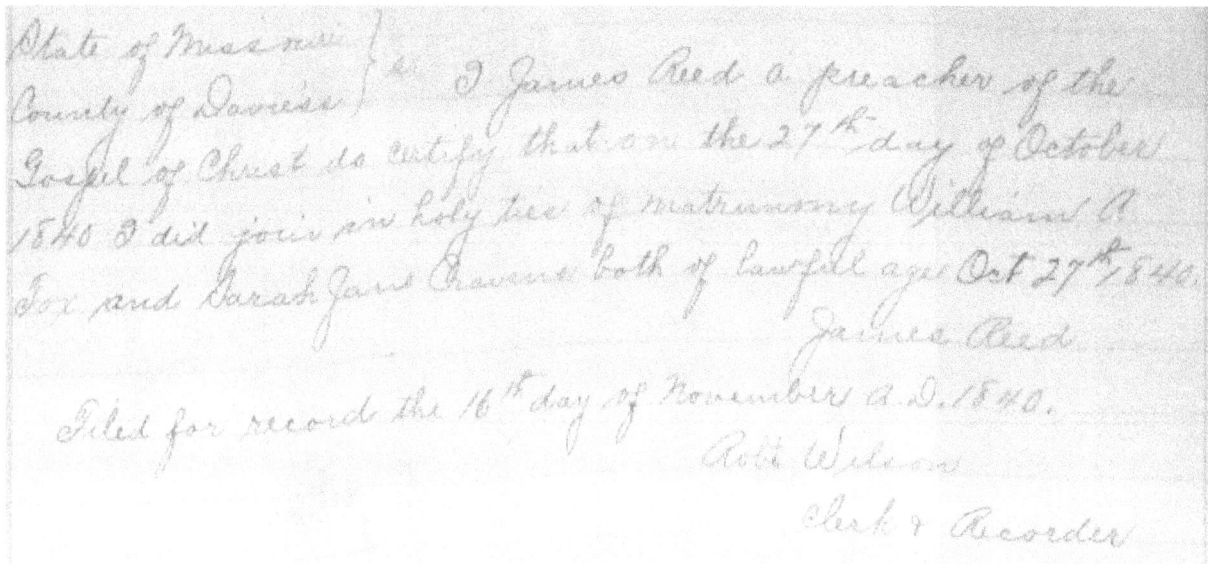

State of Missouri }
County of Daviess } ss I James Reed a preacher of the
Gospel of Christ do certify that on the 27th day of October
1840 I did join in holy ties of matrimony William A
Fox and Sarah Jane Cravens both of lawful age Oct 27th 1840
James Reed

Filed for record the 16th day of November A.D. 1840.
Robt Wilson
Clerk & Recorder

Marriage Certificate for Sarah Jane Cravens and William A. Fox in Daviess County, Missouri, 1840.

Paxton continues, "William A. Fox married 20 October 1840, Sarah Cravens, born 4 January 1823, daughter of John Cravens, of Daviess County, Missouri. She died 25 December 1858."

A check of the Missouri plat map indicates William A. Fox registered land in Carroll Township, Section 17, the S.W. Quarter, on 17 August 1843.

On the 1849 Tax List, William Fox did not pay a poll tax, nor did he have any slaves. He did have other property valued at $150. So, his taxable amount was $150. State tax was 0.300, county tax, 0.450, for a total of 0.750. Wow! Wouldn't that be a great tax amount to pay in 2013.

In the 1850 U.S. Federal Census, William Abner was a merchant with real estate valued at $2,500. He was living in Carroll Township, Platte County, Missouri with his wife, Sarah Jane, daughter Eliza, 9; daughter Mary, 3; and son John, 1. William Abner was living next door to his father, James Fox. The Slave Schedule which was part of the Census showed that William Abner owned one 10 year old slave boy.

At the 1860 U.S. Federal Census, William Abner was now listed as a farmer, with real estate valued at $6,000, and personal property at $3,700. He was also a widower as Sarah Jane had died 2 years earlier. The two youngest sons had been born since the 1850 Census: James Vernon, 7; and George Dorriss, 5. John Edwin, 12, was still listed, though all other children mentioned in previous Census records had passed away, with the exception of Eliza Virginia who had married. These 4 children all lived into adulthood, married, and had children of their own.

The Annals of Platte County, by Paxton, pgs. 606-607, gives us an account of William Abner's activities during the Civil War: "Mr. Fox was an enthusiastic Methodist, a zealous Mason, and a spirited Southerner. He went south with Col. John H. Winston, and, in his absence, his real estate was virtually confiscated for his debts. For a number of years he was a merchant in Platte City, and was a leading partisan in every controversy of church or state."

~~~~~~

Here are some highlights of the military career of Colonel John H. Winston, whom William Abner Fox served under during the Civil War, from the Annals of Platte County, Missouri, by Paxton, p. 205

Col. Winston was long a militia officer. In early days I mustered under him. In military matters he was well informed; and when the war broke out in 1861, his Southern enthusiasm and his soldierly bearing pointed him out as the commander of Southern troops, raised in this county. In August, 1861, a military rendezvous was formed in his neighborhood and called Camp Cain. Here the Southern bands gathered, and a number of companies were organized, under Capts. Chesnut, Chrisman, Chiles, Miller, Mitchell, Rogers, Spratt, and others. Before the regiment was fully organized, the men were hurried to the front. They were in time to take part in the siege and taking of Lexington. They were at Pea Ridge, Corinth, and other important engagements. In the spring of 1864 Col. Winston, by order of Gen. S. Price, returned home to recruit men for the Southern army and to help them on their way to the front. While on this duty he was captured by a troop of Federal soldiers, at his home, three miles southeast of Platte City. For twenty months, until the close of the war, he was confined in military prisons—successively at St. Louis, Alton, and Jefferson City—in apprehension of death by military order, at any time. The return of peace brought him liberty. Col. Winston had long been a favorite of the people of Platte, and on his return he was joyfully received. From 1872 to 1876 he represented the county in the State Legislature, and his name has been frequently suggested for the State Senate. Col. Winston yet lives at his old home, honored and revered by all who meet him. Ch:
~~~~~~

The condition of Platte County at the start of the Civil War is detailed below in ***The Annals of Platte County, Missouri****, p. 312.*

CONDITION IN PLATTE.

Aug. 12—Rebel flags are flying; anarchy prevails; rebel camps are formed at Platte City, at Gooseneck, and at Cain's; a regiment is to be raised for the South. J. H. Winston is to be colonel. Brasfield, Chesnut, Chiles, Carr, Chrisman, Gordon, McKinnis, Miller, Synnamon, and others are enlisting companies. Arms are gathered and provisions collected. The Union men close their eyes in silence; business stands still; merchants dispose of their goods; valuable property disappears; horses are stolen or pressed, and crime goes unpunished.

March 1864, below describes the arrest of Colonel John Winston in ***The Annals of Platte County, Missouri****, p. 360.*

JOHN AND SAMUEL WINSTON.

Early in March Capt. Lewis A. Ford, commanding at Parkville, sent a squad of soldiers into the Winston neighborhood, and Capt. Samuel Winston was arrested. He was an officer of the Southern army, and was placed under a $25,000 bond for his good conduct. Inquiry and search were made, without avail, for his brother, Col. John H. Winston, and it was given out that he was not in the county; but in truth Col. Winston was at home, under orders from Gen. S. Price, to recruit a regiment from northwestern Missouri. His policy was to foment discontent in the militia, and to get them to manifest disloyalty, so that they would have to find safety by going South. Col. Winston, fearing arrest and the summary justice dealt out to spies, dressed in the uniform of a Confederate colonel.

On the 22d of March a squad of United States troops passed through Platte City, going east, and in an hour returned with Col. Winston as their prisoner. They had found him at his home, in his uniform, covered by a bed. He was confined in military prisons until the close of the war. His brother Samuel shared his fate. They were in constant apprehension of death, until the return of peace.

~~~~~

~~~~~~

The 1870 U.S. Federal Census for William Abner Fox, raises many questions. On the grave marker for Sarah Jane Cravens Fox, her date of death is 1858. In addition, there was a Jane Fox, born about 1830, in Virginia listed as" keeping house" in the household of William Abner Fox. Who is this Jane?

We find James Vernon at age 17, as a farm hand; John Edwin, age 21, also a farm hand; and youngest son, George Dorriss, 12, listed as "at home". Family tradition says that George was not in the best of health and was unable to do farm work.

Also in the household was William Abner's father, James, who was 80 years old, his wife, Lucinda, who was 73, and a farm hand named Nealy Sawyers. Perhaps Nealy was either Wesley from the 1850 and 1860 Censuses of James Fox, or related to Wesley.

Finally, we find the following: E. Eskridge, 22, black male, born in Virginia, farm hand; Eliza Fox, 30, black female, born in Virginia, domestic servant; Lewis Fox, 12, black male, born in Missouri, farm hand; and Mary Fox, 9, black female, at home; George Fox, 8, born in Missouri, black male, at home; and the most curious one of all is Laura Fox, 5, born in Missouri, listed as mulatto on the original Census form, but as black on the index for the Census. Perhaps these are the former slaves of James Fox, William Abner's father, who have been granted their freedom, and are now working as farm laborers and servants.

In 1873, William Abner married a widow, Rachel Kinnamon Vanlandingham, who had been married previously to her husband, Austin, since 1847. In the 1870 Census we find that Rachel and William were neighbors. A sad note in The Annals of Platte County, by Paxton, is that Rachel died childless at age 55 on 28 December 1884. She is buried in the Fox Family Cemetery.

The 1880 U.S. Federal Census finds William, 66, still farming, and Rachel, 51, keeping house. None of the children were present in the home. There were 2 laborers and 2 servants, all black males, in the household. These were Lewis and George Edwards, and Thomas and Andrew Spencer.

William Abner's parents, James Fox and Lucinda Eskridge Fox, both died before the 1880 Census.

During the next decade, Rachel died, in 1884, and at the age of 75, William Abner married for the third time on 23 April 1890, to Mrs. Mary E. Little. He enjoyed one year with his bride before his own demise on 24 October 1891, in Platte City, Platte County, Missouri.

~~~~~~

Back in the Day . . . The terms "Southerner", "Southern sympathizer", and "going south" are references to a person's political views during the Civil War. The area of Missouri around where William Abner Fox lived was populated by many former residents of Virginia who had brought their slaves and their Southern way of living with them when they migrated to Missouri. A Southerner or Southern sympathizer was a person who sided with the South during the Civil War. In the case of William Abner, we see that his sentiments ran so deeply that he actually went off to war for the South under the command of Colonel John H. Winston without much thought for his businesses and farms. Paxton's <u>Annals</u> tells that much of his property was confiscated to pay his debts.

~~~~~~

Questions:

1. Are there any articles William Abner Fox wrote for the papers available online?
2. Why does he marry in Daviess County?

3. How did William Abner Fox meet Sarah Jane Cravens?
4. Was she the daughter of the infamous Dr. John Cravens who established Cravensville which later became Pattonsburg, Daviess County, Missouri?
5. What type of merchant was William Abner Fox?
6. Where was his store located?
7. What Methodist church did he belong to?
8. What did he do with Col. John H. Winston during the Civil War?
9. What were his views which were so controversial?
10. Did William Abner set his slaves free before or after the Emancipation Proclamation?
11. What happened to all 6 of the children who didn't live past childhood?
12. Who is Jane Fox in the 1870 U.S. Federal Census?
13. Who is the mother of Lewis Fox, Mary Fox, George Fox, and Laura Fox?
14. Was Laura Fox mulatto or black? If she was mulatto, who was her father?
15. Are these 6 black farm hands the former slaves of father James Fox?

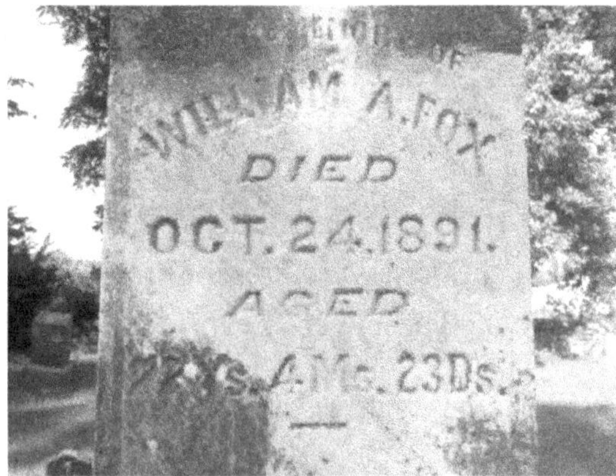

Above, the Fox 4-sided grave marker in Fox Family Cemetery, Platte County, Missouri, 2013

Upper right, William Abner Fox's side of the marker

Lower right, Rachel Fox, second wife of William Abner Fox

Sarah Jane Cravens Fox's grave stone.

These are the children of Sarah Jane Cravens and William Abner Fox who did not survive childhood, and whom are buried with Sarah Jane Cravens Fox in the Fox Family Cemetery:

Eugene Fox, aged 11

William M. Fox, aged 2 years

John J. Fox, aged 3 years

Mary J. Fox, aged 7 years

William H. Fox, aged 7 years

Alvin T. Fox, aged 2 years

James Fox and his wife Lucinda Fox, parents of William A. Fox and grandparents of James Vernon Fox in Fox Family Cemetery, Platte County, Missouri, 2013

William Abner Fox it is said was a writer for the newspapers on every controversial subject. So, we decided to investigate. Here's a segment from my trip journal describing what we did.

"We next found the Landmark Newspaper. They let us come inside and we saw a really old linotype machine that was taking up the whole front window of the shop. There was a lot of lead type everywhere and sitting amid the ancient technology were the workers with a few new computers. It was really interesting. They didn't have any old copies of the paper, though."

Inside the Landmark Newspaper Can you read the lead type word right?

Two pieces of former James Fox farms. Above left, location of the Fox Family Cemetery

Above right, the land he left to Eliza Virginia Fox Eskridge

Left, more of the same land left to Eliza, but now it is the Prairie Creek Greenway which follows the old railroad track bed which cut across the corner of his land.

The Children of William Abner Fox and Sarah Jane Cravens

These are the children which survived into adulthood:

Virginia Eliza Fox, married December 28, 1865, John Eskridge, they had 9 children. In the 1870 U.S. Federal Census, we find these children: Sarah Josephine, 3, born 1867; Lucy E., 2; and John, 1 month old. Also living with the family is Lucy F., 19, born in Virginia in 1851. Perhaps she is a sister of John Eskridge.

In the 1880 U.S. Federal Census, the family has grown. Children joining Sarah J., 13; and Lucy M., 12, are James W., 10, born 1870, Martha E., 8, born 1872, George T., 6, born 1874, John E., 4, born 1876, Henry L., 2, born 1878, and Loula Frances, 1, born 1879. The son John, who was 1 month old in the 1870 Census is absent in this Census. Also living with the family was John's father, Sidney, who was an 80-year-old widower.

At the 1900 U.S. Federal Census, 20 years had passed, and the family was still living in Carroll Township, Platte County, Missouri. John was 55, Eliza Virginia, 58, and the children still in the home included sons James W. and John E., both single, son Giles, 19, born 1881, also single, and daughter

Lou, single, 22 years old, born in 1879, who was probably Loula, from the 1880 Census. Eliza Virginia was mother to 9 children with 9 living at the Census.

The 1910 U.S. Federal Census finds John and Eliza Virginia with an empty nest. Within the year, Eliza Virginia Fox Eskridge would die on 29 June 1910. John E. Eskridge lived another 7 years and joined his wife in death on 12 June 1917. Both are interred in the Fox Family Cemetery, Platte County, Missouri.

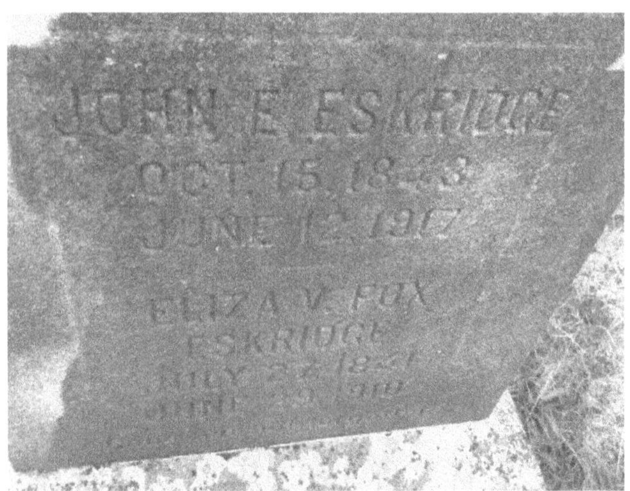

Left, John E. Eskridge and Eliza Virginia Fox Eskridge, Fox Family Cemetery, Platte County, Missouri
Right, Eliza Virginia Fox Eskridge, who married her cousin, John E. Eskridge, Fox Family Cemetery, Platte County, Missouri, 2013

<u>John Edwin Fox</u>, born 2 April 1849, married 9 November 1871, Virginia E. Phillips, born July 1855. They lived in Carroll Township, Platte County, Missouri, on land inherited from his grandfather, James Fox's will. Children included Sarah, birthdate unknown; Mattie (Martha A.), born January, 1879; Howard Clayton, born October 1882; and Walter, born January 1885.

According to the 1900 U.S. Federal Census, Virginia gave birth to 5 children with 4 surviving at Census time.

At the time of the 1920 U.S. Federal Census, John was 70, Virginia 64, and son Walter, 34, was living with them. Walter was single and working as a mechanical engineer.

John Edwin Fox died 8 February 1927 and was buried in the Fox Family Cemetery. Virginia also was buried in the Fox Family Cemetery when she died 10 August 1952. Howard Clayton Fox is also buried in Fox Family Cemetery. His grave marker is inscribed with a death date of 1914, yet he is listed in the 1920 U.S. Federal Census. So, this is a mystery.

Howard C. Fox, youngest son of John Edwin Fox and Virginia E. Phillips Fox in Fox Family Cemetery, Platte County, Missouri

James Vernon Fox, born in September 25, 1853, married September, 1876, Mary Haven, of Daviess County, Missouri. Children: Anna Rachel, born July 17, 1877. At the 1900 U.S. Federal Census, Mary L. Haven Fox stated she was mother of 2 children with 1 living. For more on James Vernon Fox, see page 73.

George Dorriss Fox, born June 24, 1858, married March 29, 1877, Ida O. Winn of Daviess County, Missouri. Children include Sarah, Laura, William H. Fox, James Fox, Charles, and Mary E.

In the 1880 U.S. Federal Census, daughter Sarah was 2 years old, and Laura was 7 months. Also living with the family was Wesley Sawyer, the long-time farm hand of George's father, James Fox.

The 1900 U.S. Federal Census reveals that Ida gave birth to 10 children with 8 surviving by the Census time. Listed in the Census were: Harry, 19, born August 1881; James, 14, born July 1886; Donnie, 12 year old son, born April 1888; Charles, 10, born November 1889, Hettie, 7, a daughter born May 1893, and John, 5, born February 1895.

In the 1910 U.S. Federal Census, James, Charles, and John were living in the home along with Walter, 22, who seems to be missing from the 1900 Census. It is curious that Ida stated in this Census that she was the mother of 9 children born with 8 surviving when she answered 10 children born with 8 surviving in the previous Census of 1900.

George Dorriss Fox died 18 August 1911 from a protracted illness of several months in which he was able to be up and about according to his obituary which appeared in The Medford Patriot (Medford, Oklahoma), Vol. 18, No. 46, Ed. 1 Thursday 24 August 1911.

.

George Dorriss Fox and wife Ida O. Winn Fox, Fox Family Cemetery, Platte County, Missouri, 2013

The Parents of William Abner Fox
James Fox and Lucinda Eskridge
1790-1875 1797-1876

We are introduced to James Fox by this account in The Annals of Platte County by Paxton, pgs. 606-607, "He was born in Virginia 11 November 1790, came to Platte in 1839, and settled 4 miles southeast of Platte City. He married 29 December 1812, Lucinda Eskridge, born 14 August 1797, died 27 October 1876. Their only child, William A. Fox, was born in Fauquier County, Virginia, 13 May 1814."

The rich farmlands of Virginia that had sustained families since the 1600s had been divided and subdivided among families with many children so that by the early 1800s, many descendants of early settlers were spreading out and pushing westward in search of newly opened lands. Overland trails and the advent of river travel, particularly by steamboat, made it easier to seek new opportunities.

In 1836, the family made the trek west settling in Howard County, Missouri. They didn't stay long here, however, for in 1838, they went further west to Platte County settling near the Mississippi River.

James Fox appeared on the 1839 Tax List for Platte County, as well as his son William Abner Fox.

In the 1840 U.S. Federal Census, James' household consisted of 1 white male 15-20 years of age; 1 white male 20-30; and 1 white male 40-50. There was 1 white female 40-50. There were 4 female slaves including 2 under 10 years old, and 2 between 10 and 24. Also, there's a notation that he registered land in Carroll Township in 1842-43. A check of the plat map shows this was Section 19, the N.W. Quarter, registered 17 August 1843.

The 1849 Platte County Tax List included a poll tax for men, number of slaves and value of same, other property which could have included horses, mules both jacks and jennies, cattle, clocks and watches, and carriages as these were listed separately in the 1847 tax list, but combined under the category of "other property" in 1849, money, salary, taxable amount, state tax amount, and county tax amount. James Fox for some reason wasn't charged a poll. He had 5 slaves valued at $1,000, and $125 of other property. He had $200 in cash, no salary, and a total taxable amount of $2,125. He paid 4.25 in state tax, 6.375 in county tax, for a total tax of 10.63.

At the 1850 U.S. Federal Census, James Fox's middle initial was listed as "A." He was 65 years old and his wife, Lucinda, was 50. He was still farming. They had the same farm hand living with them, Wesley Sawyers, who was 30. James' real estate was valued at $3,500. He and Lucinda were both born in Virginia, while Wesley was born in Missouri.

The Census also listed separately in the Slave Schedule, 6 slaves ranging in age from 1 to 20. There were 5 females and 1 male. The 4-year old male was listed as mulatto, while the other 5 were black.

Another addendum to the 1850 Census was the Productions of Agriculture. We find William A. Fox and James Fox both listed. James Fox reported about his land in Carroll Township and a second tract of land in Pettis Township. The Pettis land contained a total of 320 acres and was valued at $3,200, while the Carroll land contained 315 acres. William Abner's land totaled 200 acres. Although tobacco was a popular crop, and still was in 2013, in this 1850 Productions of Agriculture report, there doesn't appear to be hardly anyone producing tobacco in Pettis Township.

At the 1860 U.S. Federal Census, just before the start of the Civil War, James was still farming and valued his property at $9,600, and his personal property at $7,000. Lucinda , age 63, and Wesley Sawyers, 45, were still in the household.

By the 1870 U.S. Federal Census, James and Lucinda were listed in the household of son, William Abner. This is curious, because they apparently retained their land through the death of Lucinda as per James Fox's will. So, were they living with son William, or was William living with them?

In an issue of The Platte City Landmark about 20 August 1875, we read an account of the death of James Fox:

"A Pioneer Dead:

Death of James Fox, one of the very Oldest Citizens of Platte County

James Fox died at his residence, 4 miles south of Platte City, last Saturday 14 August 1875. The death of such a man deserves more than a passing notice, for the history of his life is a history of Platte County and the Platte Purchase.

The subject of this notice was born in Farquier County, Virginia, 11 November 1790. He was raised and lived in Virginia until 1836, when imbibing the spirit of adventure, he joined the vast tide of emigration that was wetting in toward the great west. He removed to Howard County, Missouri with his wife Miss Lucinda Eskridge. He remained in Howard County only one year. Attracted by the wonderful stories of the fertility of the then noted Platte Purchase, he came to Platte County and settled upon and preempted the farm, 15 October 1837, upon which he lived the remainder of his life. His only child, Mr. William A. Fox, one of our oldest and best citizens and his aged wife alone survive him, the latter a hopeless invalid. Mr. Fox literally died of old age, having been confined to his room since last December. Although a pious, God-fearing man, he only publicly made a profession of religion about one year ago when he joined the Methodist Episcopal Church, South. His remains were buried at the family burying ground upon the farm where he had lived and died.

Such, in brief, is an epitome of the history of James Fox, familiarly known as "Uncle Jimmy", a [??] history that must remain incomplete, for it is beyond our power to record the thrilling events that made up his romantic career. He came to Platte County when it was home of the Indians and was a wilderness. He lived to see it grow from its [??] pioneer population to its present populous condition—the very finest agricultural county in Missouri.

Mr. Fox was emphatically a hard worker, and it is said that he performed more hard physical labor than any other man in the county. He was restless and discontented unless he was actively engaged in his farm duties. He was essentially honest and during all his long life he never was engaged directly or indirectly in a law-suit. He was a kind neighbor and a great citizen, respected by all who knew him…"

James Fox's will left his lands to his grandchildren rather than to his son, William Abner Fox. In the case of James Vernon Fox, the sum of $2,000 was to be used to purchase land for him. James Fox also operated a still and distillery which he left for his grandchildren to use, but if they did not wish to operate the distillery, then the land would revert to George Dorriss Fox. He wanted the Fox family graveyard to remain forever as a burial yard. Also, he granted road access to the land on the west side of him. He also granted road access to the Hickory Grove Church

Lucinda Eskridge Fox, lived just over 1 year after James' death when she joined him on 27 October 1876. Both lie in the Fox Family Cemetery on one side of the 4-sided tower monument which dominates the cemetery.

The Annals of Platte County by Paxton, gives a brief biography on Lucinda: "The Eskridges. Mrs. James Fox was an ESKRIDGE. Her mother was a MOXLEY, who was descended from the Lee family, of Virginia. Three of Mrs. Fox's brothers were killed in the Revolutionary War, on the Patriot side, and two others fought throughout the bloody struggle."

An issue of The Platte City Landmark newspaper around 17 August 1877 states: "Funeral: The funeral of Mrs. Lucinda Fox, mother of Mr. William A. Fox, will be preached by the Rev. C. I. Vandeventer at Hickory Grove Church, on the first Sunday in September."

Periodically, the government would take an accounting of agricultural productivity in the U.S. These Productions of Agriculture reports were usually taken along with a Census record, either a State Census or the U.S. Federal Census. Following is the Production of Agriculture for James Fox and son, William A. Fox, for 1850.

Productions of Agriculture

1850 U.S. Federal Census

Carroll Township, Platte County, Missouri

Item	James Fox	William A. Fox
Improved Acres	70	70
Unimproved Acres	245	130
Cash Value of Farm	$3,200	$2,400
Value of Implements	$150	$150
Horses	6	4
Asses and Mules	4	3
Milch Cows	4	3
Working Oxen	--	4
Other Cattle	10	6
Sheep	60	--
Swine	50	15
Value of Live Stock	$845	$385
Wheat bushels	150	150
Indian Corn bushels	750	750
Wool pounds	180	--
Irish Potatoes [?]	20	10
Value of Orchard Products	$75	$25
Butter pounds	728	546
Hay tons	5	5
Dew Rotted Hemp [?]	--	3
Bees and Honey [?]	648	648
Value Homemade Manuf.	$100	$70
Value Animals Slaughtered	$110	$60

~~~~~~

Back in the Day . . . The Platte Purchase bought 3,149 square miles of land from the Indians and added it to Northwest Missouri. The area was comparable in size to Delaware and Rhode Island combined. Platte County was all Indian Territory prior to early 1836 when the land became the County of Platte belonging to the State of Missouri. In 1839, Platte was divided into townships including: Preston, Carroll, Pettis, Lee, Green, and Marshall. James Fox and William Abner Fox had land in Carroll and Pettis Townships.

~~~~~~

Two tracts of James Fox's land in Pettis Township Section 19, accessed at: http://digital.library.umsystem.edu/cgi/i/image/image-idx?sid=b8d3c09cbf4744058736189137ede461;page=index;c=platic

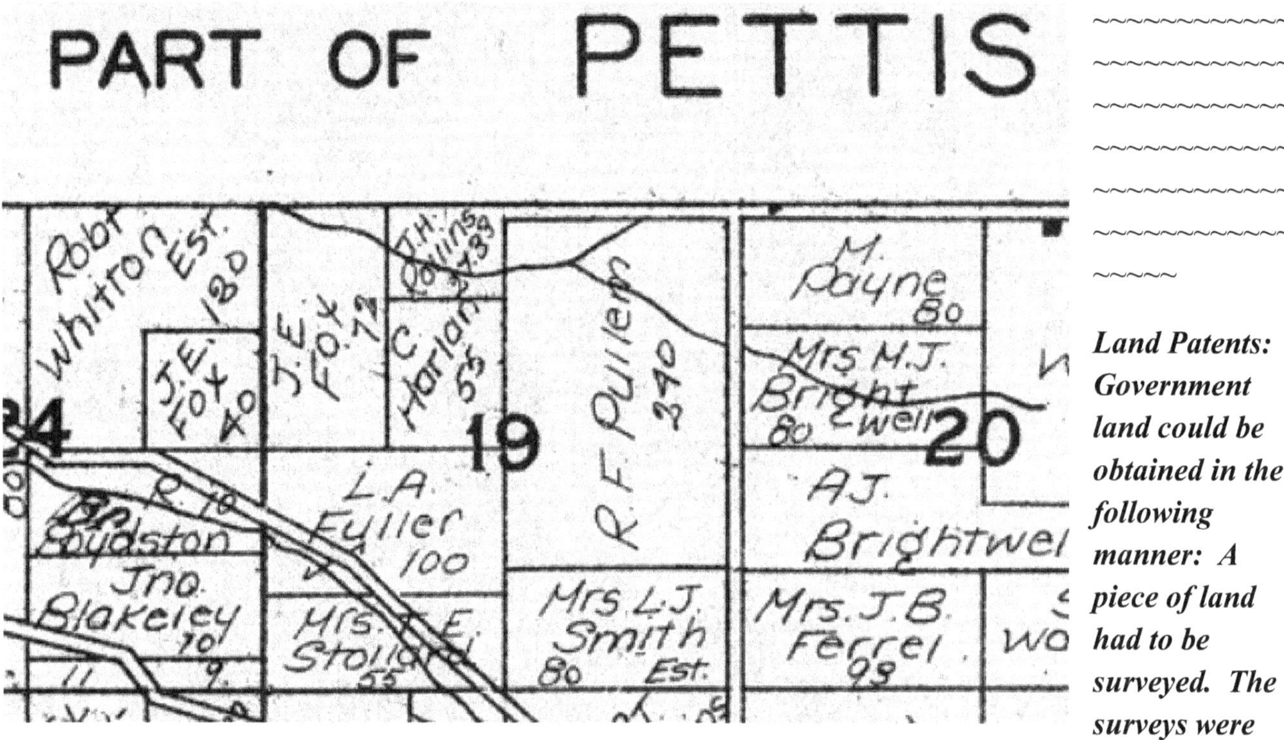

~~~~~~~~~~~~~~~~~~~~

Land Patents: Government land could be obtained in the following manner: A piece of land had to be surveyed. The surveys were measured with east and west base lines and north and south meridians. Parallel to the meridians were ranges of townships. A township was 6 square miles with 36 sections. A section had 640 acres and was divided into 4 quarter sections each with 160 acres. A tract of land was normally described in terms of quarter section, section, township, and range. For example, James Fox's land description was: "The N.W. Quarter of Section nineteen, in Township 52, of Range thirty four in the District of Lunas subject to sale at Plattsburg, Missouri, containing two hundred and fifty six acres and forty seven hundredths of an acre."

~~~~~~

Following is a larger segment of the plat map showing where James Fox's lands were located in Section 19 and Section 24.

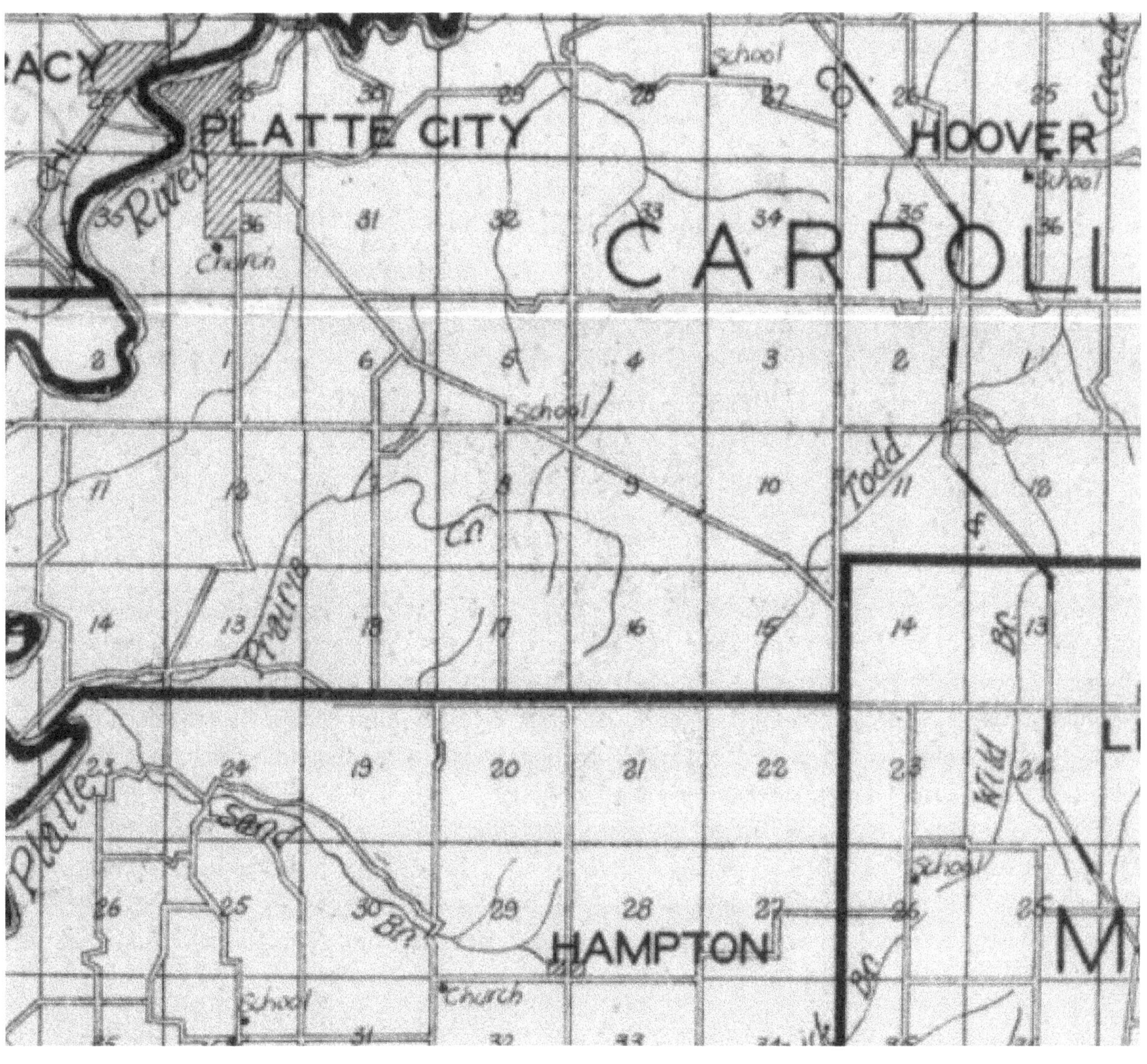
PLATTE CITY
HOOVER
CARROLL
HAMPTON
River
Platte
School
Church
Todd
Prairie
Cr.
Sand
Br.
Wild
Br.
Creek

4

The Wife of James Vernon Fox

Mary L. Haven

1852-1913

Mary L. Haven first appeared in the 1860 U.S. Federal Census for her father John D. Haven. She was born in July of 1852 in Virginia, apparently the last child of John D. and Margaret Ann Peggy Harman Haven. Some records indicate she was born in West Virginia. It is unclear exactly where she was born, because the area of Virginia where her family lived at her birth later on became the dividing line between Virginia and the new state of West Virginia. Most records show she was born in Virginia, though in later Census records, she indicated West Virginia.

Sometime after her birth and before 1860, her family migrated from Virginia to Daviess County, Missouri, where she lived until her marriage to James Vernon Fox. Thereafter, they lived in Daviess County, Platte County, and Grant County in Oklahoma Territory.

Mary L. Haven would give birth to 2 children, but only her first-born, Anna Rachel Fox Kinney Anderson, would survive.

See more on Mary beginning on page 82.

The Parents of Mary L. Haven

John D. Haven and Margaret Ann "Peggy" Harman

1814-1891 1819-1900

John D. Haven was born 27 January 1814, in Tazewell County, Virginia, to Howard H. Havin and Martha "Matty" Davidson. In 1833, John's father, Howard Havin, died. John D. was left lands and property in his father's will. So, when he married Margaret Ann "Peggy" Harman on 14 December 1837, he was already a successful farmer. At the death of his grandfather, Joseph Davidson, the father of John D.'s mother Martha Davidson, he received additional land, about 200 acres, situated near lands owned by William Witten and James Dillon.

In the 1850 U.S. Federal Census, John had real estate valued at $2,000. John and Margaret were enumerated in the Western District of Tazewell County, Virginia. John was 36 years old and wife, Margaret, was 30. They had the following 5 children: Martha Jane, 10; Sarah A., 7; William H., 5; Ballard P., 2; and Jonothan W., 11 months. A farmer by the name of Jeremiah Goodwin, 27, was living in the household. Perhaps he was a laborer or possibly a servant.

It is unclear exactly when John D. Haven migrated to Missouri from Virginia. We do know that it had to have been sometime between 1852 after Mary's birth, and 1860, when they were enumerated in the Missouri Census. Also, how they migrated is unknown.

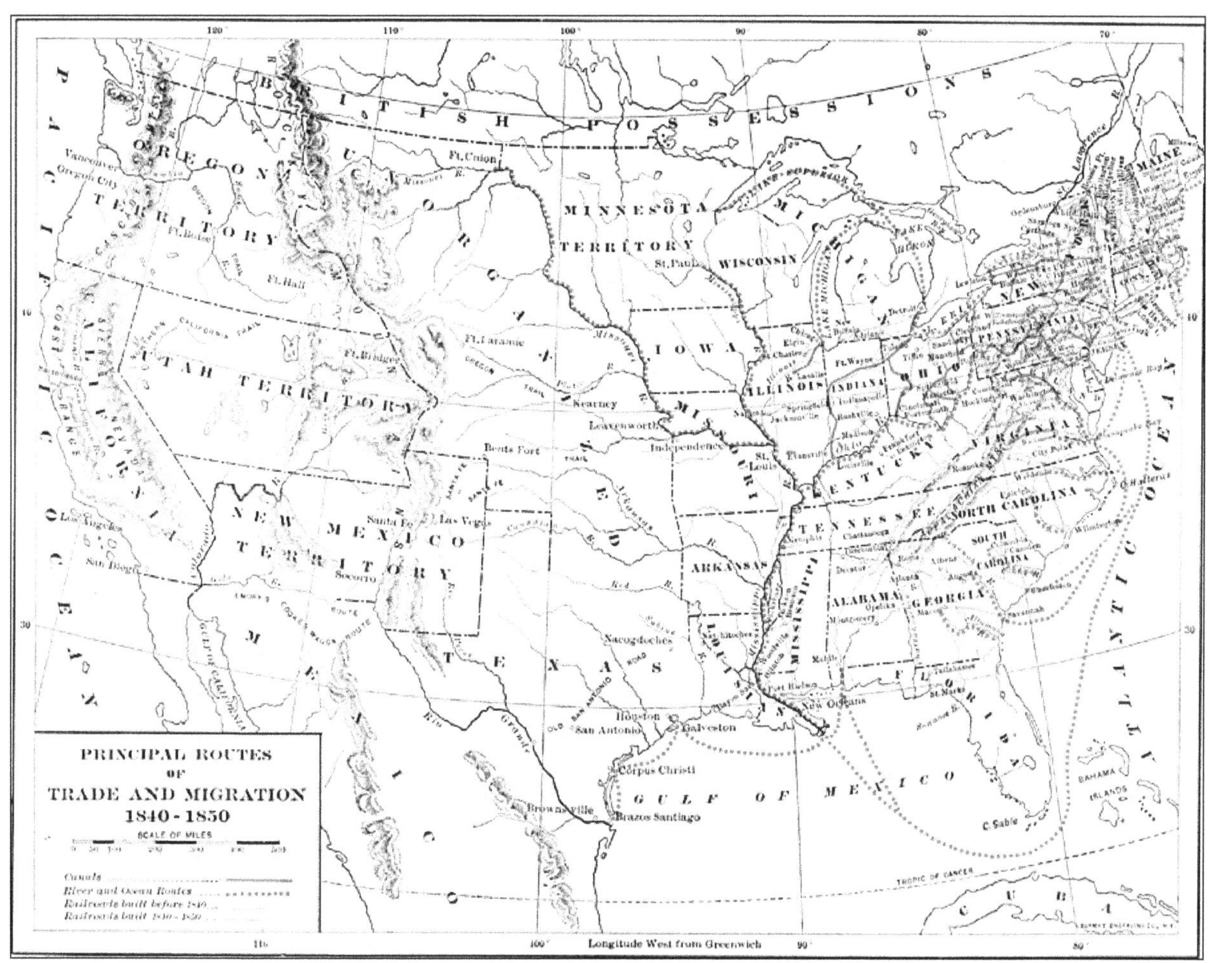

Principle migration routes 1840-1850 accessed from http://etc.usf.edu/maps/pages/3300/3328/3328.htm. In addition, the Cumberland Road had been extended to the Mississippi River.

The 1860 U.S. Federal Census incorrectly listed John D. Haven as "Haver". The family had relocated to Grand River Township, Daviess County, Missouri. Martha was then 19, Sarah, 17, and the child who was listed as William H., 5, in the 1850 Census seems to be named Howard in the 1860 Census and he was 15 years old. Bullard P. is probably Ballard P. of the 1850 Census, and he was then 14. The youngest was John W., 10, who was listed as Jonothan W. in the 1850 Census.

Also, in 1860, there was a Slave Schedule for John D. Haven which listed the following:

1 black female, 23; 1 mulatto male, 19; 1 black female, 7; 1 black female, 5; and 1 mulatto male, 2 months. This totals 5 slaves owned by John D. Haven. Of interest is that there were 2 mulattos. Masters impregnating their female slaves was not an uncommon practice, however, I have no information about this on the part of John D. Haven. Perhaps this is a good question to research.

Of interest is the next slave owner listed under John on the schedule: Charles A. Cravens. The surname of Cravens was one of the family names in James Vernon Fox's ancestry. Perhaps this Charles Cravens may be a lead to research a possible Cravens connection to James Vernon Fox.

~~~~~~

Back in the Day. . . It's said that the Civil War really began between Kansas and Missouri, with the border conflict as described at Wikipedia, accessed 12.13.13: http://en.wikipedia.org/wiki/Bleeding_Kansas

Bleeding Kansas, Bloody Kansas or the Border War was a series of violent political confrontations involving anti-slavery Free-Staters and pro-slavery "Border Ruffian" elements, that took place in the Kansas Territory and the neighboring towns of Missouri between 1854 and 1861. At the heart of the conflict was the question of whether Kansas would enter the Union as a free state or slave state. As such, Bleeding Kansas was a proxy war between Northerners and Southerners over the issue of slavery in the United States. The term "Bleeding Kansas" was coined by Horace Greeley of the New York Tribune; the events it encompasses directly presaged the American Civil War, as well as the future relationship between Kansas and Missouri.

Congress had long struggled to balance the interests of pro- and anti-slavery forces. The events later known as Bleeding Kansas were set into motion by the Kansas–Nebraska Act of 1854, which nullified the Missouri Compromise and instead implemented the concept of popular sovereignty. An ostensibly democratic idea, popular sovereignty stated that the inhabitants of each territory or state should decide whether it would be a free or slave state; however, this resulted in immigration en masse to Kansas by activists from both sides. At one point, Kansas had two separate governments, each with its own constitution, although only one was federally recognized. On January 29, 1861, Kansas was admitted to the Union as a free state, less than 3 months before the Battle of Fort Sumter, which began the Civil War.

~~~~~~

By the year 1861, the Civil War issues had already been brewing in Northwestern Missouri for almost a decade. In this part of Missouri there lived a number of Southern sympathizers—families who had migrated from Virginia and had brought their slaves with them to continue farming in the traditional way of the South. John D. Haven was among those who migrated from Virginia, accompanied by his slaves.

We see that in 1861, he joined the Confederate Army as a private in Company C of the 11th Regiment of the Missouri Infantry. Just what his feelings were towards slavery and what his treatment of his own slaves was, I have found no records. Nor have I found records of him granting freedom to the slaves enumerated with him in the 1860 Slave Schedule. Later on, we do not see any slaves enumerated in future Census records, so the likely conclusion is that he probably granted them their freedom.

The 1870 U.S. Federal Census for John D. Haven eluded my research for quite some time. When it was finally located, the Haven name had been misspelled as John B. Hareens. The family was living in Gallatin, Grand River Township, Daviess County, Missouri. John D. was 56 years old, and Margaret was 50. The oldest daughter, Martha Jane, had married Joseph Speaker, so was not enumerated with John D. Haven. The other children enumerated included: Sarah, 20, John, 19; Mary, 17; and Preston, 23, whom I believe is Ballard P. of the 1850 and 1860 Censuses. John and Preston are farm laborers with their father, John D., whose real estate was valued at $3,500 and personal property at $1,000.

The Missouri State Census of 1876, lists John D., Margaret, Preston, John, Lavalette, who was John's new bride, Mary L., and James V. Fox, who was Mary's husband. A part of this Census was a record of animals and farm production for each farm. We find in the same household with John D. Haven, his son, John, son, Preston, who is probably Ballard of earlier Census records, and his son-in-law, James Vernon Fox.

John D. Haven had the following animals and products recorded in the Census: horses, 2; mules, 9; cattle, 8; sheep, 76; hogs, 7; bushels of corn, 500; bushels of oats, 116; pounds of tobacco, 147; pounds of wool, 200; pounds of hay, 4; gallons of molasses, 15. Son, John Haven, had 2 horses. Son, Preston, had 11 hogs. Son-in-law, James Vernon Fox, had 2 mules and 1 cow. Notice there was no mention of son, Howard, at this time.

By the 1880 U.S. Federal Census, only John D. Haven's daughter, Mary, and son-in-law, James Vernon Fox, were still a part of the household. They had added a daughter, Anna Rachel, to their family. Sons, John, Preston, and Howard, are not enumerated with John D. Haven. In the Census record on the next line, which usually indicates a neighbor, there was a listing for Presley and Kate Haven. It is unclear who these two are. Perhaps it could be Preston and a wife, or another relative. They do not appear in later Census records.

Records indicate they were members at the Gallatin Methodist Church. This was apparently the oldest established church in Daviess County, and it was still holding services in 2013. The first building was erected in 1859 at a cost of $1,500. If John and Margaret's daughter, Martha Jane, was married inside the church, it was most likely the first building erected in 1859.

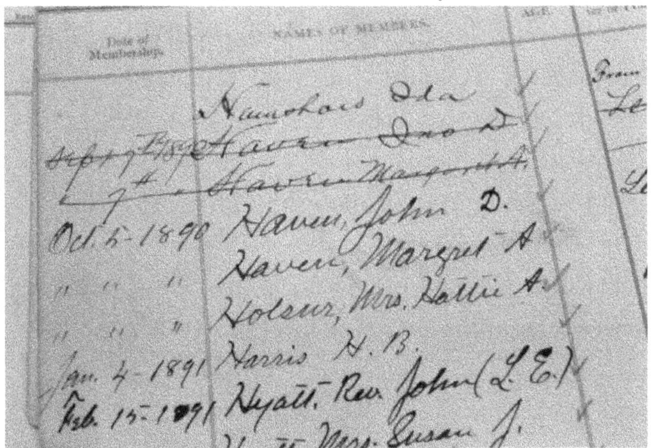
Date of Membership
NAMES OF MEMBERS
Oct. 5-1890 Haven, John D.
" " " Haven, Margret A
" " " Mrs. Hattie A.
Jan. 4-1891 Harris H. B.
Feb. 15-1891 Hyatt, Rev. John (L. E.)

John D. and Margaret Haven's names on the membership roll of the Gallatin Methodist Church, Gallatin, Daviess County, Missouri, for 1890

Left, Pipe organ inside the Gallatin Methodist Church
Right, Gallatin Methodist Church, Daviess County, Missouri, as it appeared in 2013

By 21 August 1890, Margaret A. Haven had applied for a Civil War Pension stating that John D. was an invalid. Just 1 year later, 25 August 1891, the status of "widow" was entered on the pension card. John D. Haven passed away about 18 August 1891. He was interred in Brown Cemetery, Union Township, Daviess County, Missouri. The Brown Cemetery is located north of Gallatin, Missouri, and is part of a "cemetery complex" of 3 different named cemeteries in one location.

Some of the interesting receipts from John D. Haven's will include: a receipt for wire from Mann & Miller, Dr., Dealers in Hardware, Stoves, Tin Ware, Farm Implements, Etc.; $26.50 for a coffin and box from Selby & Boggs, Dealers in Furniture and Undertaking; $2 from Wes. L. Robertson, Dr., Editor and Publisher of the Gallatin Democrat; $4 to J. A. Myers, Dr. Proprietor of The City Call, Bus and Carriage Line, for buses to the funeral; $6.95 to William Chamberlain, Dealer in Drugs and Patent Medicines for medicines from late July through late August.

In John D. Haven's will, he left land to his daughters, Martha Jane Speaker, Sarah A. Gentry, and Mary L. Fox. He left to his sons, Ballard P. Haven and John W. Haven, the sum of one dollar each, in addition to what he had given them before writing the will. His will was signed 1886. We know that the 2 older daughters accepted $300 each in lieu of the land, so it's unclear if they got land in the end or not. Some of the items from the appraisal of his estate included: several horses, 8 stands of bees, Certificates of Deposit in the Farmer's Exchange Bank of Gallatin, 3 tons of hay, 6 acres of growing corn, and the income from pasturing stock belonging to 11 different people including James Fox and James Vernon Fox.

Margaret A. Haven petitioned the court to be able to sell some land to pay the debts of her husband, John D. Haven. James Vernon Fox purchased a tract of land from the estate of John D. Haven for $200. This was very near to the edge of Gallatin.

Questions:

1. When exactly did John D. Haven migrate to Missouri from Virginia?

2. What does the middle initial "D" in his name stand for? Is it "Davidson" as some researchers have indicated?
3. What happened to his son, William Howard, who was present in the 1850 and 1860 U.S. Federal Census records, but absent in any other Census records and not mentioned in his will?
4. Why did he spell his name "Haven" with an "e" when his father, Howard H. Havin, spelled his name with an "i" as per his father's will?

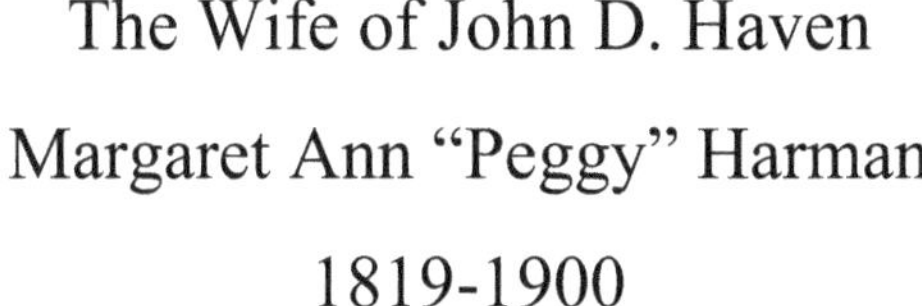
Right, John D. Haven grave stone in Brown Cemetery,
Gallatin, Daviess County, Missouri

The Wife of John D. Haven
Margaret Ann "Peggy" Harman
1819-1900

From the Annals of Tazewell County, Virginia, by Harman, we find these genealogies for Margaret:

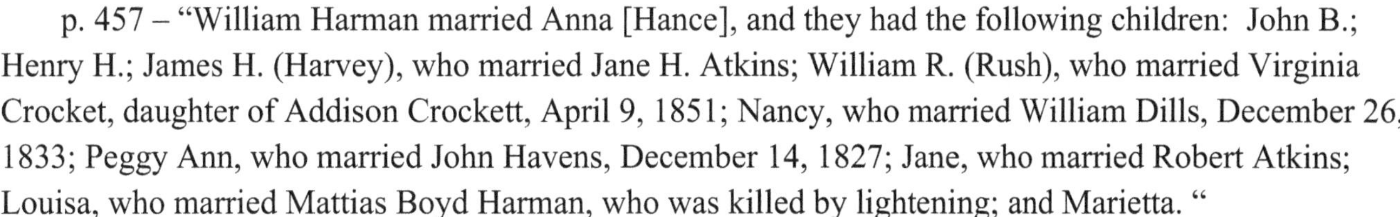
p. 457 – "William Harman married Anna [Hance], and they had the following children: John B.; Henry H.; James H. (Harvey), who married Jane H. Atkins; William R. (Rush), who married Virginia Crocket, daughter of Addison Crockett, April 9, 1851; Nancy, who married William Dills, December 26, 1833; Peggy Ann, who married John Havens, December 14, 1827; Jane, who married Robert Atkins; Louisa, who married Mattias Boyd Harman, who was killed by lightening; and Marietta. "

p. 280 – William Harman and Anna Hance were Margaret's parents. "William's will was probated November, 1843 in Will Book No. 2, p. 266. He devised his property as follows: To his son, John B., to his wife Anna, to his son Henry H., to his daughter Nancy Dills, wife of William Dills; Peggy Havin, wife of John D. Havin; to his sons James H., and William R., to his daughters, Jane, Louisa, and Marietta Harman."

Margaret's grandparents were some of the first settlers in the New River area of Virginia. A brief biography of her grandparents, Daniel Harman and Anna Bughsen, is detailed in the Annals of Tazewell County, Virginia, by Harman, pgs. 456-557: "DANIEL HARMAN, SR. Daniel Harman, Sr., son of Adam, was born in Pennsylvania about 1729. He came with his father to the Valley of Virginia about 1735, thence to New River, in the present Giles County, Virginia, in 1744 or 1745. In 1746 he was with George Draper and others exploring the country along the headwaters of the Sandy and Clinch Rivers when Draper and a man by the name of McGary were killed by a party of Indians. The death of Draper deferred the founding of Drapers Meadow for about 2 years. Daniel Harman was also an explorer of the country and a famous Indian fighter, being 1 of the "Long Hunters." He was captured by the Indians in 1757, at the time his brother, Valentine, was killed by them, but he succeeded in making his escape. In

1760 accompanied by his brother, Mathias, on a hunting and exploring expedition, he visited Abbs Valley and Ingles Crab Orchard, near Pisgah Station. April 21, 1764, he married Anna Bughsen, in Rowan County, North Carolina. It appears that he took up his residence there until 1778, when he moved to the head of Clinch River, in Tazewell County where he died in 1820. In his will he names his children as follows: Mathias, William Daniel, Henry, Adam, Buse, Pheby Davidson, Christina Harman, Rebecca Wright, Nancy Milam, Levicey Harman, and his son-in-law Adam Harman."

Margaret A. Harman Haven died 17 March 1900, in Gallatin, Daviess County, Missouri. She was interred in Brown Cemetery alongside her husband, John D. Haven.

Her land that remained at her death was sold on the court house steps to the highest bidder which was James Vernon Fox, her son-in-law, for $35. This land was by that time within the City of Gallatin. In 2013, I had opportunity to visit Gallatin and locate the last land which she had owned. There were houses along the perimeter of the land. One house looked old enough and of the architectural type to possibly had been standing at the end of her life, leading me to speculate whether or not it had been her dwelling place. I was told by the court house that it would be a lengthy process to discover if that house were the one in which Margaret had lived, so have not pursued that action. At any rate, I've included a picture of the house in question.

Margaret Harman Haven grave stone in Brown Cemetery, Daviess County, Missouri

House on Margaret Haven's former land which looks as if it could have dated to the time she was last alive, in the late 1890s. There is no proof that this was her dwelling, but it is intriguing that a house of this age sits on her former land in 2013.

Questions:

1. How many children did Margaret have?
2. What happened to child William Howard after the 1870 U.S. Federal Census?

3. Was there an 1865 Missouri State Census?
4. Was there an 1895 Missouri State Census?

The Children of John D. Haven and Margaret Ann "Peggy" Harman

Martha Jane Haven, 1840-??, married Joseph Speaker, 1824-1895, in the Gallatin Methodist Church, Gallatin, Davies County, Missouri, just before the Civil War began. In fact, her marriage entry in the church's books was the last one recorded before the war. The church didn't record marriages again until after the war ended.

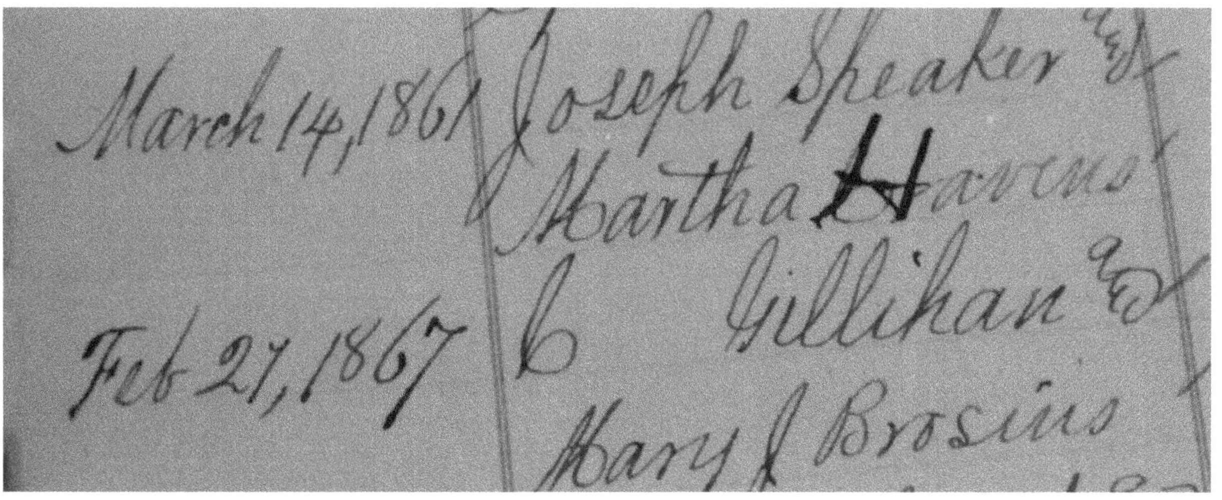
March 14, 1861 Joseph Speaker &
Martha Havens
Feb 27, 1867 [illegible] Gillihan &
Mary J Brosius

Marriage entry for Joseph Speaker and Martha Haven in the record books of Gallatin Methodist Church, Gallatin, Daviess County, Missouri. Note the lack of marriages recorded during the Civil War.

Martha Jane, sometimes called "Matt" or "Mattie" and Joseph Speaker had 3 children: John Dexter, Mary, and William P. Speaker. Joseph Speaker was born in Columbiana County, Ohio in 1824. He came to Daviess County in 1851 to settle an estate and stayed. He began farming in 1861, the same year he was married to Martha Jane. They were married in the Gallatin Methodist Church. A newer church building still stands in Gallatin in 2013.

Joseph Speaker died in 1895 and was interred in the Everly Cemetery located in Daviess County, Missouri. Martha Jane received of her father $300 in lieu of 20 acres of property as heir to his estate on 12 February 1887

Questions:

1. Where is Martha Jane buried as she is not listed on the grave marker with her husband Joseph Speaker?
2. Where was she in the 1900 U.S. Federal Census?
3. When did she die?
4. What happened to her children?
5. How did she meet Joseph Speaker?

6. Although they were married in the Methodist church, did they remain Methodist?
7. Was Joseph Speaker a Methodist or other faith?

We visited the Everly Cemetery early in the morning. The sunshine was strong and the place was quiet and peaceful. After walking the whole cemetery, we hadn't found Joseph's grave. As we got into our car to leave, I looked out the window, and there it was. Joseph's grave sat just beside the road, so close we had overlooked it.

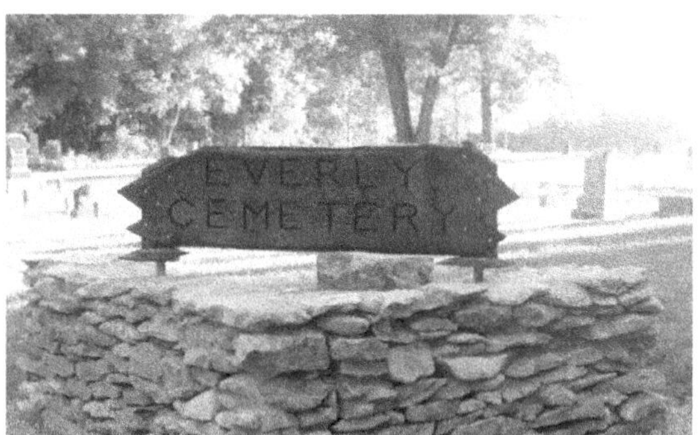

Joseph Speaker's grave stone in Everly Cemetery, Daviess County, Missouri

Sarah A. Haven, 1842-??, married Isaiah J. Gentry on 24 February 1876, at her father's home. Sarah and Isaiah had at least 4 children: Charles E., Della A., Stella, and Leonard E. Gentry. Sarah received $300 cash from her father in lieu of 20 acres of property as heir to his estate on 19 July 1888. However, at his death, it appeared she still inherited land in his will. I have yet to uncover information on where she spent the rest of her life and where she is interred.

CERTIFICATE OF MARRIAGE.

U. S. Revenue Stamp
5 Cents.

STATE OF MISSOURI,
County of Daviess.

This certifies, that on the 24" day of Feby. A. D. 1876, at J. D. Haven's in said County, according to law, and by authority, I duly Joined in Marriage Isaiah J. Gentry. and Sarah A. Haven

Given under my hand the 26" day of Feby. A. D. 1876

Filed for record this 3rd Mch. 76. Wm. T. Abell R. J. A. Munford Min.

Marriage Certificate for Sarah A. Haven and Isaiah J. Gentry. Some researcher claim he was married to another. It bears research.

Questions:

1. Where is Sarah Haven Gentry buried?
2. When did she die?
3. Where is her husband Isaiah Gentry buried?
4. Did she inherit land in addition to the $300 cash?
5. How many children did she have and what happened to them?

Ballard P. Haven, 1847-1922 married Mary H. Casey and had one daughter, Vivian Haven. In the 1900 U.S. Federal Census, he had been married to Mary for 5 years. He would have been 48 years when he married. It is curious that in the 1880 U.S. Federal Census for Grand River Township, Daviess County, Missouri, there was a Presley Haven and Kate Haven living next door to John D. and Margaret Haven. I wonder if this may be Ballard P. Haven and a first wife. There are no other records for Presley and Kate that I've been able to locate.

Ballard is mentioned in his father John D. Haven's will of 1891. I have no further information about Ballard aside from his place of burial which, according to the website billiongraves.com, is located in Oakley Chapel Cemetery, Rogers, Arkansas.

Questions:

1. Was Ballard married before Mary to Kate Haven or another?
2. Did Ballard's middle initial "P" stand for Preston or Presley?
3. How did he end up in Arkansas?
4. What happened to his daughter, Vivian?

William Howard Haven was listed in both the 1850 and 1860 U.S. Federal Census records, but was absent from the 1870 U.S. Federal Census and the 1876 Missouri Productions of Agriculture report. He was not named in his father, John D.'s will in 1891, therefore, I presume he may have died.

Questions:

1. Did William Howard Haven die before his father did in 1891?
2. If he didn't die before 1891, why isn't he listed in his father's will?
3. If he did die before 1891, where is he buried?
4. When did he die?
5. Was he married?
6. Did he migrate to Oregon as one researcher suggests?

Jonothan W. Haven, 1850-??, married Lavalette Harmon Haven in 1875. They had 2 children: Maude Haven Ewing and John Clarence Haven. The last record for Jonothan W. Haven and Lavalette, was the U.S. Federal Census for 1920 where they were living with their son, John C.; daughter Maude Ewing, and her 2 children: Lavalette and Elmer Ewing. Jonothan was mentioned in his father, John D. Haven's will of 1891.

Questions:

1. Was Jonothan's wife, Lavalette Harmon related to his mother, Margaret Harmon Haven? If so, how?
2. Where are Jonothan and Lavalette buried?
3. When did they die?
4. What happened to their children?
5. What did Jonothan do with the land his father, John D. Haven, left him?

Mary L. Haven, 1852-1913, married James Vernon Fox and had 1 child: Anna Rachel Fox.

CERTIFICATE OF MARRIAGE.

U. S. Revenue Stamp
5 Cents.

STATE OF MISSOURI,
County of Daviess.

This certifies, that on the 19th day of September A. D. 1876, at ________ in said County, according to law, and by authority, I duly Joined in Marriage Mr James Fox of Platte Co. and Miss Mary Havens

Given under my hand the 16th day of October A. D. 1876

Filed for Record this 21 day Oct. 1876
Wm S Abell
Recorder

J. H. Sharp (seal)

Marriage Certificate for Mary L. Haven and James Vernon Fox

After farming for many years in Daviess County, Missouri, they relocated to Oklahoma Territory around 1902 or 1903. Mary L. Haven Fox died in 1913, and is interred in Rosemound Cemetery in Medford, Grant County, Oklahoma, along with her husband, James Vernon Fox. For more on Mary L. Haven, see pgs. 83 and 112.

The Parents of John D. Haven,
Howard Havin and Martha "Matty" Davidson
1780's-1833 1794-1873

In 2011, I had just started researching the family history and really didn't know just how far I was going to go with it. One weekend we went to visit a cousin who was dying of cancer. I shared some of my research with her and she immediately jumped up from her sick bed, rummaged in the closet, and produced an envelope crammed with some really old documents. I gingerly unfolded the ancient parchment paper, and read the name "Howard Haven" on the first document. As I studied the document, I learned it was an original land grant signed by the governor of Virginia. Being fairly new to family history research, I didn't even know exactly what a land grant was. What intrigued me the most was the name Howard Haven. My cousin asked me who the names on the land grants were. I recognized the surname Haven as being the middle name of my grandfather and my cousin's uncle: Vernon Haven Kinney. So, I surmised correctly that Howard Haven must be an ancestor of Vernon Haven Kinney.

Thank goodness for Google! By the end of the weekend, I'd discovered not only who Howard Haven was, but was able to link him into my tree as my fourth great grandfather.

Two land grants down; two to go. The third land grant bore the name of Davidson. I started with the assumption that this was probably a family name as well. Sure enough. Davidson was the maiden name of Howard's wife, Martha "Matty" Davidson, daughter of Joseph Davidson and Matilda Amanda Patton. The discovery of this name blazed a trail back through my family history which took me back to my sixth great grandfather John G. "Goolman" Davidson.

The final land grant was in the name of Heaven. It wasn't difficult to surmise that this was an earlier spelling of Heavin. Research along this line has bogged down somewhat so I have put it on hold for now and will return to searching when I can concentrate more fully on this line only.

So, who was Howard Havin? He was born 1 September 1788, in Tazewell County, Virginia, the son of, I believe, F. John Heavin and Mary Pepper. I've not made this connection beyond all doubt at this point, so will not research back any further until I can have more definitive proof of this connection. When I started researching Howard Havin, I was warned that there had been several persons by the name of Howard Havin in and around Tazewell County and I should be very careful with my research to be sure and connect with the correct ancestor. I have kept this warning ringing in my head while researching, and it's paid off well.

According to The Annals of Tazewell County, Virginia from 1800 to 1922 in two volumes, by Harman, p. 53, on 30 March 1809 Howard Havins and Mattey Davidson were married by David Ward, an officer of the court.

At the 1820 U.S. Federal Census, Howard Haven's household contained the following persons: 1 white male under age 10 (John D.); 1 white male between 26 and 44 (Howard); 2 white females under age 10 (Matilda and Nancy); 1 white female between 26 and 44 (Martha); 2 male slaves under age 14; 1 male slave between 14 and 25, for a total of 8 persons in the household.

The Lutheran Church in Tazewell County was organized in 1828 in Burke's Garden, Virginia according to The Annals of Tazewell County, Virginia from 1800 to 1922 in two volumes, by Harman, p. 813-815. A subscription arrangement was undertaken where those who wished to share in the use of the facility would contribute to the building of it. Everyone's pledge of labor, materials, and time was recorded including Howard Haven: 4 day's work. Howard Haven would have been in his 40s at this time.

At the 1830 U.S. Federal Census, Howard and Martha's household consisted of the following: 1 white male 15-20 (John D); 1 white female 15-20 (Nancy); 1 white male 40-49 (Howard); 1 white female 30-39 (Martha), 1 female slave under age 10; 1 female slave between 10-23; 1 female slave 24-35, for a total of 7 persons. The oldest daughter, Matilda, had married David Whitley in 1829, therefore, she was not enumerated in her father, Howard's, household.

This was the last Census record for Howard Havin as he passed away in January 1833.

There are family trees on the Internet which attribute 10 children to Howard and Matty. While it was probably biologically possible for them to have had 10 children between 1809 and 1833, there were only 3 children listed in the 1820 and 1830 U.S. Federal Census records, and Howard's will leaves his property to just 3 children in addition to his wife. Therefore, I am fairly confident that he was the father of just 3 children.

Howard Havin's will was recorded in Will Book 2, Page 19 and following and filed in the Tazewell County Circuit Court, Tazewell, Virginia, January of 1833. The appraisal of his estate was also recorded in Will Book 2, page 24 and following. The will is summarized below as well as selected items from the appraisal of his estate.

"I Howard H. Havin of Blue Stone, Tazewell County, Virginia, being in a bad state of health but of sound and disposing mind, do make this my last will and testament hereby revoking all former wills."

He wishes his funeral expenses to be paid and that none of his property be subjected to a public sale. He divided his slaves among his wife and 3 children.

To his wife, Martha, he left his slave woman, Amey, and her 3 sons, plus the house, orchard, garden, outhouses, part of the hides in the tan yard, and as much of the improved land as she may want to cultivate, up to the widow's one-third allotted by law. On her demise, all of this was to go to his son, John.

Next, he divided some lands along the Bluestone River and Cove Creek between his two married daughters, Matilda and Nancy, plus gave each some farming and tanning equipment, livestock, horses and horse tack, and furniture.

To his son, John, he left horses, livestock, furniture, a tract of land on which he was living at his death, and the hides in the tan yard. He also received the use of the tan yard. Upon his mother's death, everything left to her would revert to him.

Finally, he gave to his 2 sons-in-law, David Whitley and Russell Bane, the sum of $1.00 each. He appointed his wife, Martha Davidson, to be the executrix of his last will and testament.

Some of his belongings included lands, a tan yard, slaves, horses, cattle, furniture, cooking equipment, dishes, spinning wheels, farming equipment, harvesting equipment, guns, books, etc.

From the will I surmise that he must have been both a farmer and a tanner. I wonder if he wasn't also a hunter. There were many hunters in the area during the 1700s, so it would not have been unusual for him to have been a hunter.

From the land descriptions in his will, he owned considerable holdings. Here are some of the legal descriptions from his will: "I give to my daughter Matilda Whitley the east end of my tan yard tract of land, beginning at a knotty white oak east of Cove Creek, near a small spring by a path. Northwardly in a line passing a large spring near the tan yard one rod to the east to the back line of said tract and with the lines and courses thereof round the east end of said tract to the beginning."

"I also give to my daughter Nancy Bane all my outlands lying north and south of the tan yard tract from the lines herein described. On the north, the beginning to be at the mouth of Cove Creek and to run with Bluestone River the extent of my lands to Cumpton's lands from thence to run in such manner as to include all the lands belonging to me on the east side of Bluestone and north of the tan yard tract. On the south, the beginning to be at a sycamore corner to my two old tracts of land on the north side of Bluestone to run a straight line southwardly to John B. George's land, from thence to run in such manner so as to include all my lands on the south side of the tan yard tract and east of said line the two last described tracts of land to be equally divided between my two daughters named, Matilda getting the east end and Nancy the west end of each tract, which land I give to them and their heirs forever."

The original land grants which have remained in the family's possession are described as follows:

- In the name of John Davidson, 13 May 1802, 113 acres, Tazewell, Virginia
- No. 6765, in the name of Howard Havens, 16 December 1819, 220 acres
- Warrant No. 18572, in the name of William Heaven, 1783, 16 acres

- No. 4855, in the name of Howard Havens, 21 February 1812, 50 acres

The mouth of the Bluestone River, 2013. Howard Havin had property along the Bluestone River per his will. He also had land along Cove Creek.

Questions:

1. Who did Howard Havin leave his tan yard to?
2. Who were his parents?
3. Was he descended from F. John Heavin and Ruth Hall?
4. Did he live in the Haven house on Plum Creek that still stood in the 1900s?
5. Where is he buried?
6. Which year was he born in?
7. What was the total land holdings he had?
8. Was he a Lutheran as he helped to build the Lutheran church?
9. How did he die?
10. Did he have an illness?
11. Of the 4 land grants in my family's possessions, who was William Heaven on one grant in relationship to Howard Havin? Who was John Davidson on another grant in relationship to Howard Havin?
12. What does Howard Havin's middle initial "H" stand for?

The Wife of Howard H. Havin
Martha "Matty" Davidson
1794-1873

Martha Davidson was born in 1794 in Montgomery County, Virginia. In 2013, this was Tazewell County. Her parents were Joseph Davidson and Matilda Amanda Patton. She was 1 of at least 8 children. She married Howard Havin in 1809. Together they had 3 children before Howard's death in 1833.

She remarried in 1837 to Howard Bane. Matty died 30 December 1873 in Clear Ford, Tazewell County, Virginia. Her place of burial is unknown to me.

The Parents of Martha "Matty" Davidson
Joseph Davidson and Matilda Amanda Patton
about 1755-1851 1769-sometime after1851

` Joseph Davidson was born about 1755, according to some records, or 1762 according to other records, probably in Pennsylvania, to John Goolman Davidson and Martha. Some researchers believe Martha's maiden name to be Draper, while others are unsure. Joseph had at least two siblings: Martha and Andrew Davidson. There are a number of local history books with accounts on Joseph Davidson, each varying slightly from the other.

In 1785, he is listed among the court records for Montgomery County as claiming "2 old wolf heads" for which he received 350 each. Searching back in the court records to the first entry for wolf heads, we see the 350 figure represented pounds of tobacco, according to the Annals of Southwest Virginia, Montgomery County, Virginia, Minutes of the County Court, pgs. 803-806.

The Annals of Southwest Virginia, 1769-1800, p. 903, record that on 14 June 1789, Joseph Davidson married Matilda Amanda Patton in Montgomery County, Virginia. She was the daughter of Henry Patton and Martha Randolph. Together Joseph and Matilda had the following children: Henry Preston, 1790-1849; Jane George, 1792-1830; John, 1794-1848, Martha "Matty", 1794-1873; William G., 1795-1870; James Cartmill, 1797-1868; Samuel Patton, 1800-1854; and Robert Wallace, 1801-1868.

Know all men by these presents that we Joseph Davidson & Samuel Patton are held & firmly bound unto his Excellency the governour of Virginia for the time being & his succefsors in the just & full sum of £50. current Money. to the which payment well & truly to be made, we bind ourselves our heirs Executor's & administrator's jointly & severally & firmly by these presents as witness our hands & seals this 10th Day of June 1789.

The Condition of the above obligation is such that whereas the above bound Joseph Davidson, hath this day obtained a Licence for his marriage with Mathilda Patton Daughter of Henry Patton of this County now if there should be no legal cause to obstruct the said then the above Obligation to be void. or otherwise to remain in full force & Virtue

Test
Abram Trigg

J Davidson (Seal)
Samuel Patton (Seal)

A Copy Teste:
ALLAN C. BURKE
Circuit Court Montgomery County, Virginia
By: ______, Deputy Clerk

The Marriage Bond for Joseph Davidson and Mathilda Patton

In 1796, Joseph Davidson constructed a two-story log home with an attic above. A new stone chimney was added in 1812. This home was in continuous use by Davidson descendants until 1936 when the City of Bluefield, West Virginia, bought the property to construct a school. Knowing the significance of the structure on the property which they had purchased, that it had been built by one of the pioneers of Tazewell County, it was decided to move the cabin and preserve it in the City Park in Bluefield, West Virginia. In 2012, I had the opportunity to visit the cabin and have a tour so graciously provided by the local chapter of the Daughters of the American Revolution, under the direction of Phyllias Smith and Carolyn Demopoulas, who are preserving the cabin.

During our visit in August 2012, the editor of the Bluefield Daily Telegraph, Bill Archer, interviewed us for the paper, then asked if we'd like to meet a direct descendant of the cabin builder. Of course we were thrilled at the prospect of meeting a distant cousin. So, we were introduced to Joe P. Davidson, Jr. We are fourth cousins twice removed, and both of us descended from Joseph Davidson, the cabin builder. Joe P. Davidson, Jr. is the 3 times great grandson of Joseph Davidson, and I am the 5 times great granddaughter of Joseph Davidson.

Left, Joe P. Davidson, Jr. and Barbara Kinney Black fourth cousins twice removed common ancestor Joseph Davidson, Bluefield, West Virginia, 2012
Right, Stone with plaque identifying the cabin as being built by Joseph Davidson

Left, Joseph Davidson Cabin in its original location. Photo from: A New River Heritage, Volume IV, by William Sanders, McClain Printing, Parsons, WV, 1994, p. 348. Here is the photo caption from the book: The Davidson settlement cabin, which is now preserved at the Bluefield City Park and formerly sat in the present rail yard between Valley and Stony Ridges.
Right, Joseph Davidson Cabin as it stood in 2013, in the Bluefield , West Virginia City Park

In October 1800, Joseph Davidson was appointed a justice of the peace for Tazewell County as per the History of Tazewell County and Southwest Virginia, 1748-1920, p. 477.

In January 1801, Joseph Davidson, among others, was "appointed to fill the following offices: Joseph Davidson, to act as Colonel Commandant for the 112th Regiment…..and Andrew Davidson [Joseph's brother] to act as Captain tin the 1st Battalion of said Regiment; John Davidson…..to act as Lieutenant in the 1st Battalion….." as recorded in the Annals of Southwest Virginia, 1769-1800.

In July 1817, according to The Annals of Tazewell County, Virginia from 1800 to 1922 in two volumes, by Harman, p. 192, Joseph Davidson and others were "recommended to his Excellency, the Governor as fit persons to execute the office of Sheriff of this County, for the ensuing year."

At the 1830 U.S. Federal Census, Joseph Davidson's household included: 1 white male aged between 60-69; 1 white male aged between 70-79; 1 white female aged between 60-69; 1 male slave under 10; 3 males slaves between 10-23; 1 male slave between 24-35; 1 male slave between 36-54; 2 female slaves between 24-35; for a total of 10 slaves and 3 white persons.

In the 1840 U.S. Federal Census, Joseph Davidson listed the following members of his household: 1 white male 80-89 years of age; 1 white female 70-79 years of age; 1 male slave under 10; 3 male slaves 10-23 years of age; 1 male slave 55-99 years of age; 1 females slave under 10; 1 female slave 10-23 years of age. This totaled 7 slaves and 2 white people.

According to the American Revolutionary War Rejected Pensions, accessed on Ancestry.com, Joseph Davidson applied for a pension on 8 January 1844, in the Mercer County Court. He was 87 years old. He gave details of his Revolutionary War involvement as an Indian spy in the company of Captain Moore over the course of 4 years. In addition, he performed guard duty in a fort on the headwaters of Clinch River. Unfortunately, his application for a Revolutionary War Pension was denied because he was supposedly never called out to perform any military duty by any officer of the Militia.

Joseph Davidson wrote his Will in 1846, and added two codicils in 1849. His Will was proved in court in 1851 and he was deceased at that time. It is unknown to me where he is interred.

The Will of Joseph Davidson

"I, Joseph Davidson of the County of Tazewell and Commonwealth of Virginia being of sound mind and memory, do constitute this my last will and testament in the words and manner following to wit (Viz) I direct that after my decease all my just debts be paid.

I give of my real estate to Martha Bane adjoining of Howard Havens all that portion of land beginning west of Baileys Mill Creek about 80 yards and running a south east course 20 poles thence east crossing the Creek and running with the top of a ridge known as the Valley Ridge until nearly opposite the Meeting House so as to leave it upon the land recently owned and occupied by Robert Davidson, thence a northwest course to the lands deeded by me to Howard Havens.

I give unto my Son Robert Davidson all that tract or parcel of Land on which he recently resided lying in the County of Mercer and being within the following boundary to wit. Beginning on the top of the Valley Ridge and running east to the division line between him and the land of Henry Davidson and with that division line a straight line barely crossing the Stony Ridge, thence a west course to a line made as a division line between Robert and Samuel Davidson of the land known as the Waldron Place -- and with that division line to a ridge dividing the waters of the Brush Fork from Bluestone and with the south side of said ridge a west course to a corner dividing the land between me and Howard Havens and with that line to the top of the Stony Ridge and to the beginning to him and his heirs forever.

I give unto my son Henry Davidson all that tract or parcel of land on which he recently resided lying in the County of Mercer and within the following boundary to wit. Beginning on the top of the Valley Ridge and running east to the division line between Henry Davidson and William Davidson and with that division line a straight line to the line of a survey made latterly for John Davidson and with the lines of said survey so as not to intrude upon the survey owned by Samuel Davidson and with the division line between Robert & Henry Davidson crossing the Valley to the beginning -- to him and his heirs forever.

I give unto my Son William Davidson all that tract or parcel of land lying in the County of Mercer and within the boundaries herein specified and adjoining Henry Davidson. Beginning on the top of the Valley Ridge and running east to a corner made between me and Joseph Clarke and with that line to the top of the Stony Ridge and over the same 70 poles thence a straight line to the division line between Henry and William Davidson and with that line to the beginning -- to him and his heirs forever.

I give unto my Son Samuel Davidson the one half of the land known as the Waldron Place -- including the addition made to it in the survey made by Robert H. Boltin and Hezekiah Harman -- lying between the lines of Robert Davidson and the lines run and marked as the division by said Boltin between Robert and Samuel Davidson to him and his heirs forever.

I give unto my Grandsons Joseph Davidson the eldest son of Henry Davidson and Samuel Richardson to the first named the sum of eight hundred dollars and the last the sum of four hundred dollars to be paid to each of them out of the proceeds of the sale of the Lorton Lick tract of land lying in the County of Mercer and on which I formerly lived to them and their heirs forever.

I give unto my Grandson Joseph Davidson eldest son of William Davidson and Samuel Richardson -- their heirs forever all that tract or parcel of land lying within the boundary hereafter named to wit. Beginning at the blazed corner at the stone lick and running out at the head of the branch a north course to Lorton's Lick Creek and with the Creek a west course to John Coleman's line and with his lines to Coleman's beginning corner and thence to the line dividing me and William Witten Senior and with it to that boundary Joseph Davidson son of Henry as above mentioned to the blazed corner at the stone lick.

I give unto John Havens all that portion of land lying within the following boundary to wit. Beginning at the Stone Lick and running a North East corner to the path leading to William Witten's and running so as to include the land on both sides of the path leading to James Dillon's being part of a survey made for Samuel Flumoner the quantity to be not less than 200 acres.

I give unto my son Henry Davidson 200 acres of land lying on the Hurricane Ridge in the County of Mercer -- to him and his heirs forever the above being an entry made by Jessie Belsher, Senior -- and lying between the Brush Fork of Blue Stone and Brush Creek -- and further I give unto my son Henry Davidson 200 acres of land beginning on the survey lately made for John Davidson and running up the Brush Fork for quantity as he may direct -- to him and his heirs forever.

I give unto my Son John Davidson all that tract or parcel of land in which he now lives and included within the metes and bounds of a survey of 1,395 acres be the same more or less made for said Davidson by Robert Hall -- except where it may intrude upon the land laid off upon the south east side by William H. Boltin for Samuel Davidson -- to him and his heirs forever.

And further I give unto my sons John, Henry, Robert, William, James and Samuel Davidson all my right title and interest in and to the following Slaves -- namely Elias Isaac -- also one female slave named Dido, one other named Biddy, and a third Charlotte -- being desirous that they should remain with them -- the division to be made by themselves or such person or persons as they may mutually agree upon with view to arrive at their value each legatee to give bond and security to the other for his share and that sum only payable at the end of two years from such division without interest. But on the division of said slaves giving to the two first named, John and Henry, One Hundred Dollars more than an equal proportion of such slaves or their value.

And further I direct that Joseph Davidson son of William Davidson pay to Samuel Richardson the sum of One Hundred Dollars in consideration of the land here given him.
And that all the remainder of my real estate not otherwise disposed of shall be equally divided between my son Henry Davidson and William Davidson's last three children to them and their heirs forever.

And that the slaves Hiram and Quinn remain in the possession of my wife Matilda Davidson, the last mentioned, Quinn, not to be separated from his father until he shall arrive at the age of sixteen years, then at that time it is my wish that whomsoever of the family Hiram may be desirous of his living with shall buy him.

I give unto my grandchildren Havens, Matilda, Hannah, and Jane Richardson, children of my daughter Jane Davidson and their heirs forever, one female slave named Mariah and her increase to be equally divided amongst them.

I further charge my Executor that in the event of Samuel Davidson producing any claim or claims against my estate for money at any time paid to me or to any other person for me, he shall be charged with the following slaves, namely, Smith, George, and Lovey, the sum of Seven Hundred and Fifty Dollars, together with a bond transferred by me to him on Zachariah Muncey for $40 as an offset. And should none be presented, then no further account is to be taken of them.

I moreover appoint my friend John B. George of the County of Tazewell Executor of this my last will and testament hereby revoking all others and in testimony whereof have hereunto subscribed my hand and affixed my seal this 30th day of May 1846.

Witnesses his
Robert Hall Joseph X Davidson {seal}
Wm. H. French mark
Wm. Houchins
Alexander Johnston

Whereas I, Joseph Davidson, of the County of Mercer having made and duly executed my last will and testament in writing bearing date on the 30th day of May 1846 by which last will and testament I gave and bequeathed to my grandson Joseph Davidson the sum of Eight Hundred Dollars to be paid out of money arising from the sale of my land on Lorton's Lick. Also the sum of Four hundred Dollars to my grandson Samuel Richardson to be paid out of the sale of said land. I also gave and bequeathed in said will to each of my sons Henry Davidson and John Davidson the sum of One Hundred Dollars. Now I, the said Joseph Davidson, being desirous of altering my said will in respect to the said legacies do therefore make the present writing, which I will and direct to be annexed as a codicil to my said will and taken as part thereof, and I do hereby revoke the said legacy by my said will to my grandson Joseph Davidson as I have (since I made said will) conveyed in fee simple to him by deed a portion of my land lying upon Lorton's Lick which I regard as fully equivalent in value to the said legacy and I do hereby also revoke the said legacies by my said will given to each of my sons John Davidson and Henry Davidson as both of my said sons are now dead and I consider that I have otherwise given to them & their families their just proportion of my estate. I do hereby also revoke the said legacy by my said will given to my grandson Samuel Richardson and I do give to him the sum of Five Hundred Dollars to be paid to him by my Executors as soon as possible after my death. The legacies above mentioned of One Hundred Dollars given in my said will to each of my sons Henry & John Davidson and which I wish revoked is embraced in that portion of my said will which gives to each of my said sons $100 more than their equal proportion of certain slaves to be decided between them and others.

And I ratify and confirm my said will in everything except when the same is hereby revoked and altered as aforesaid. In witness whereof, I, Joseph Davidson the testator have to this a codicil to my will written on one piece of paper set my hand and seal this 12th day of March 1849.

his
Signed, sealed, and published by the said Joseph X Davidson {Seal}
Joseph Davidson of the County of Mercer mark
and for a codicil to be added to and be considered part of his last will and testament in the presence of us who have subscribed our names in his presence.
Alex Mahood
Robert B. McNutt

I, Joseph Davidson, Senior, now of the County of Mercer and State of Virginia in order to obviate any difficulty which might possibly arise in reference to sale of my slave Hiram to Nancy Sullender, (a free woman of color), on the 14th day of May 1849 as will more fully appear by reference to a Bill of Sale of the aforesaid slave, Hiram. I have thought proper in this Codicil to my Last Will and Testament to declare it to be my intention that the aforesaid slave Hiram shall be held as the property of the aforesaid Nancy provided the terms of the contract aforesaid be complied with and provided, moreover the said Nancy can according to the laws of Virginia hold the aforesaid Hiram as her property. But if it shall appear that the said Nancy cannot hold legally the said Hiram as her property then it is my wish as soon as the said Nancy complies with the conditions of the aforesaid contract that the aforesaid slave Hiram shall be free forever from the claim of myself or my heirs provided he complies with the requirements of the laws of the Commonwealth of Virginia. It is my wish that the rents of the farm now in the occupancy of Nancy Sullender and which has been rented to her until the 1st of March 1851 shall be paid to my wife Matilda. In testimony whereof, I hereunto affix my name and seal this 14th day of March 1849.

his
Joseph X Davidson {seal}
mark

Witness
Thos. G. Witten
Johnston Bane

Virginia In Tazewell County Court Nov. 28th 1849

The Last Will and Testament of Joseph Davidson dec'd with the two codicils thereto appended was presented in Court and one of the codicils to said will was proved according to law by the oath of Thomas G. Witten and Johnson Bane subscribing witnesses thereto.
Teste
Geo. W. G. Browne Clerk
And in the same Court July 31st 1850
The Last Will and Testament of Joseph Davidson dec'd was proved according to law by the oaths of William H. French, William Houchins, & Alexander Johnson subscribing witnesses thereto

Teste Geo. W. G. Browne Clerk

And in the same Court July 30 1851.
One of the codicils to the will Jospeh Davidson Dec'd was proved by the oath of Robert B. McNutt, a subscribing witness thereto.

Teste Geo. W. G. Browne Clerk

And in the same Court Oct. 29 1851
The Last Will and Testament of Joseph Davidson dec'd with two codicils thereto appended was again produced in Court and further proven by the oath of Alexander Mahood a subscribing witness to one of the codicils aforesaid, and the said Will and Codicils are ordered to be recorded.

Teste Geo. W. G. Browne Clerk

In obedience to an order of the County Court of Mercer made at the June Term 1849 appointing the undersigned appraisers of the personal Estate of Joseph Davidson Sr. dec'd having been duly sworn for that purpose we proceeded on the 10th and 11th of August 1849 to appraise the following property shown to us as belonging to said Estate Viz.

1 roan horse	$20.00	Sarah (girl)	300.00
1 small wheat stack	5.00	Quinn	550.00
12 harrow teeth	1.80	1 bedstead bed, furniture	8.00
1/3 of 8 acres growing corn	10.00	1 " " "	7.00
1/3 of 7 acres " oats	6.00	1 large Bible	1.00
2 hand stacks of wheat	2.00	1 lot old books	.50
Dinah (Negro woman)	75.00	1 side saddle	4.00
Charlotte (Negro woman)	400.00	1 blind bay horse	5.00
James Pearis (Negro boy)	200.00	8 head geese 1/6	2.00
Isaac (old man)	50.00	1 small mare & colt	40.00
Biddah (Negro woman)	300.00		

Given under our hands this 11th day of August 1849
James Calfee
Elias Hale Johnston Bane

A Copy
Teste C. W. Calfee C. C.
Virginia: In Tazewell County Court Nov 26th 1851
This appraisement was returned to Court and ordered to be recorded.

Teste Geo. W. G. Browne Clerk

A late bill of the personal property of Col. Joseph Davidson, Deceased, made on the 5th day of January 1850 by John B. George Executor at Lorton's Lick in the County of Mercer the late residence of the deceased:

```
Nancy Sullender one Roan horse          $2.50
Same      12 harrow teeth                1.12½
Same      1 small oats stack             1.12½
James W. Davidson, corn in the crib
being the third appraised growing      $10.00
Zachariah W. Davidson, the wheat
That was appraised                       8.12½
Riley Hambrick, one mare and colt       41.38
Robert W. Davidson, one blind bay horse 3.38
Two bedsteads and furniture, one large
Bible, one lot of old books,
one side saddle and 8 head of geese
the whole being appraised to the sum   $22.50 cents
of was by consent of the heirs present
given up to the Widow of Col. Davidson
```

John B. George, Exec.

Virginia in Tazewell County Court Nov. 26th 1851
This account of sales was presented in Court and ordered to be recorded.
Teste Geo. W. G. Browne Clerk"

A curious point is raised by reading the will: Who exactly was Nancy Sullender, (a free woman of color), named in the codicil of the will? A reading of the codicil seems to indicate that Joseph Davidson had sold a slave, Hiram, to Nancy Sullender, but that there may have been some question as to whether or not she can legally own Hiram under the laws of the Commonwealth of Virginia.

In The Annals of Tazewell County, Virginia from 1800 to 1922 in two volumes, by Harman, p. 284, we read the following: "Joseph Davidson. Will probated October ,1851. Will Book 3, p. 32. Devises his property as follows: to his wife, Matilda; to his sons, John, Henry, Robert, William, James and Samuel; to his grandsons, Joseph Davidson (son of Henry), Samuel Richardson, Joseph Davidson (son of William), and to John Haven; to his granddaughters, Matilda, Hannah, and Irene Richardson, children of his daughter Jane; to his daughter, Nancy Sullender; and to Martha Bane." In this reference, we see Nancy Sullender named as his daughter.

In the 1850 U.S. Federal Census, after Joseph Davidson has died, we find the following record for Hiram Davidson and Nancy Sullender. Hiram appears to be the slave sold to Nancy Sullender mentioned in Joseph Davidson's codicil. In the following record, it appears that Hiram and Nancy are married:

Name:	**Hiram Davidson**
Age:	35
Birth Year:	abt 1815
Birthplace:	Virginia
Home in 1850:	District 42, Mercer, Virginia
Race:	Mulatto
Gender:	Male
Family Number:	409

Household Members:

Name	Age
Hiram Davidson	35
Mancy Sullender	26
Charlotte Sullender	9
Christina Sullender	7
Joseph D Sullender	5
John D Sullender	4
Mary J Sullender	2
Cristina Sullender	26

The date of his wife, Matilda's, demise and the place where she is interred, is unknown to me, but she received the following from her late husband, Joseph Davidson's, estate on 26 November 1851, when she was about 82 years of age. Therefore, we can assume she passed away some time after that date. Matilda received from the estate: "2 bedsteads and furniture, 1 large Bible, 1 lot of old books, 1 side saddle, 8 head of geese; the whole being appraised at $22.50."

Questions:

1. Where exactly was Joseph Davidson born?
2. What other siblings may he have had?
3. Where exactly is Joseph Davidson buried?
4. Was Nancy Sullender his daughter as <u>The Annals of Tazewell County, Virginia from 1800 to 1922 in two volumes</u>, by Harman, p. 284, states?

Cabin of Joseph Davidson as it appeared along the railroad track circa late 1890s. It was said by the representatives of the local chapter of the Daughters of the American Revolution, who are preserving the cabin, that the original cabin had been preserved inside a more modern structure which was built right around the original. That is what helped to preserve the original in such good condition all these years.

The Parents of Joseph Davidson

John Goolman "Cooper" Davidson and Martha Draper

about 1729-1793 1718-1898

As one of the pioneer families of Tazewell County, Virginia, the John Goolman Davidson Family is written about in several local history accounts including, Summers History of Southwest Virginia, 1746-1786, Washington County 1777-1870, and Annals of Southwest Virginia 1769-1800, Vol. I, II; Annals of Tazewell County, Virginia from 1800-1922 in 2 Volumes, by Harman; and History of Tazewell County and Southwest Virginia, 1748-1920, by Pendlton.

The U.S. and International Marriage Records, 1560-1900 collection from Ancestry.com has a record for John Goolman Davidson in which it lists his birth year as 1729 in Ireland and his spouse's name as Martha Draper. Some researchers claim he married Martha Draper in Ireland and that she was a relative to the Draper Family who established Draper's Meadows, present day Blacksburg, Virginia.

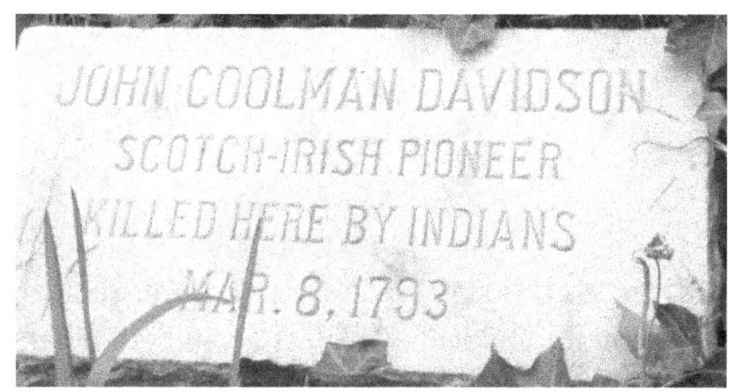

Left, Barbara Kinney Black at the grave marker of John Goolman Davidson, her sixth great grandfather
Right, Grave marker inscription of John Goolman Davidson

A brief bio of the Davidson Family appears in A History of Middle New River Settlements and Contiguous Territories, by David Emmons Johnston, p. 401: "John Goolman Davidson, born in Dublin, Ireland, a cooper by trade, came to America about 1755, and settled in Beverly Manor, in what was then Augusta County. [Previously, he had settled in Pennsylvania where son Joseph Davidson was born before making his way to Virginia. In addition, his ancestors moved between Scotland and Ireland before immigrating to the New World.] Subsequently, he removed with his family to the Draper Meadow's settlement [present day Blacksburg, Virginia], and from thence in the year of 1780, he removed and located at the head of Beaver Pond Creek, in what was then Montgomery County, Virginia, now Mercer County, West Virginia. During the same year, he was joined by Richard Bailey and family, and they erected a block house, or fort, a short distance below the head of Beaver Pond Springs. From John Goolman Davidson has descended all of the people of that name now in this and the adjoining counties. A portion of the City of Bluefield is built on lands formerly the property of Mr. Davidson. His descendants, or quite a number of them, have been prominent in civil affairs in the Counties of Mercer and Tazewell. Honorable A. C. Davidson, of Mercer County, is a great, great grandson of John Goolman Davidson."

One of the history books which contains several entries on John Goolman Davidson is the Annals of Southwest Virginia, 1769-1800. Page numbers appear before each entry which is reprinted here:

p. 884, lists 2 tracts of land belonging to John Davidson:

- 2 January 1783, 138 acres, on the Brush Creek Branch of the Bluestone Branch of the New River
- 4 January 1783, 330 acres on a branch of the Bluestone, named Cove Spring

p. 940, 1 October 1800, Daniel & Rachel Neal sold 146 acres to John Davidson for 100 pounds in Montgomery County.

p. 936, 13 March 1799, Henry Long sold 240 acres to John Davidson for 70 pounds on Walker's Creek Branch of New River. This transaction would later end up in court where Henry Long would claim that 18 pounds was still owed by John Goolman Davidson and he wanted the heirs of John Goolman Davidson to pay.

p. 1483 gives a list of persons who served in the War of 1812-14 and names John Davidson. Whether this is John Goolman Davidson or not is unclear. He would have been in his 50s at the time.

p. 1508-1509 -- "John Davidson Killed—At what precise time this occurrence took place I have not been able to learn. It is supposed to have occurred sometime in 1789-90. Mr. Davidson was on his way home from a trip to Rockingham County, whither he had been on business, and had got as far back as to where John D. Peery now lives when he was killed by a band of Indians. The circumstances of his murder, were told to some prisoners who had been taken from this County, and who were then among the Indians. It seems that Mr. Davidson had stopped at an old cabin to feed his horse and rest himself, when the Indians fired on him. The Indians say, a white man was with them, and that they found in his saddlebags a considerable sum of specie.

A few days after his son, Colonel Davidson, became uneasy on account of his absence, and raising a small company, went in search of him. Luckily, when they got to the cabin, they found a hatband, which, being of peculiar structure, was recognized as that worn by Mr. Davidson. After considerable search, his body was found striped of clothing, and somewhat disfigured by birds.

As the Indians had been too long gone to be overtaken, Mr. Davidson was taken home and buried."

This story is one of a number of accounts of the same event. Most other accounts, however, state that because his body was so disfigured by the birds, that he was buried near the spot he was located. In fact, we visited the grave marker in 2012 as seen on pg. 139.

Here's the story of how the grave was located and a grave marker placed as detailed in the Annals of Tazewell County, Volume II, by Harman, p. 329.

"Erect Monument After 130 Years"

"Grave of John Goolman Davidson, Killed by Indians and a Renegade White Man in 1783, Only Recently Marked.

"Recently a simple monument was erected over the desolate grave of John Goolman Davidson, a pioneer citizen of this section, who was killed by Indians and a renagade white man by the name of Rice more than 130 years ago.

The monument bearing the description of his death marks the grave of the man who was buried where he was found by friends and neighbors long years ago, after his murderers had left him to go back to the elements. In the years to come, thousands of Americans will see the monument and comment on the life in this section in the days of the frontiersmen's great battle in driving back the Indians, for the Lakes-to-Florida Highway runs within twenty feet from where the tragedy was enacted. The grave is about 2 miles this side of Rocky Gap, on the new road, and sets back from the highway about twenty feet.

W. H. Gibson of Rocky Gap, was the last man alive who remembered the spot where the man was buried. Some forty-nine years ago he was taken to the Davidson grave by John A. Davidson and Joseph Terry, and the story of the shooting was related. John Davidson at the time was more than eighty years old.

It was the intention of John Davidson to erect the monument, as the murdered man was his great-grandfather. The desire has been continued until Dr. J. J. Davidson and his brothers finally erected it recently.

John Goolman Davidson was riding from Rocky Gap to his home, near Beaver Pond, in the spring of 1783, and taking several horses with him. It is related he encountered a few Indians, and as he stopped to talk to them he was shot from ambush by a white man named Rice. A tomahawk was found in a tree nearby, where neighbors think the white man rested his gun while taking aim. The dead man was stripped of everything and left near the bank of Laurel Creek, where he was found several days later by a party of friends. The condition of his body did not permit removal to his home, and the grave was dug on the spot where the monument now stands, marked by a huge tree. The party followed the trail of the murdering party and reclaimed the horses after a bitter fight.

The location of the grave was lost sight of for many years, and then it was located on the farm of T. G. Dangerfield by Joseph Terry, an early citizen, who later moved to McDowell county. Mr. Terry was back in Rocky Gap visiting when he showed the grave to John Davidson. It was the desire of the Davidson family for generations to erect the monument, but each man died without fulfilling his wish. With the opening of the road, however, the present family of Davidsons, living in Rocky Gap, completed the task".

I find it ironic that he spent time and effort defending the community from Indian attack, and still he met his own demise at the hands of Indians.

And his is not the only Indian attack story in the Davidson family, for the tragic events which occurred to his daughter-in-law, Rebecca Burke, wife of Andrew Davidson, which follow, are truly shocking.

From The Annals of Southwest Virginia, by Lewis Preston Summers, 1903, pgs. 1502-1503:

"Andrew Davidson left his house one day in April of 1791 on business of importance, which would keep him from home several days. The family consisted of Mrs. Davidson (Rebecca Burke), 2 daughters, 1 son (all small) and a bound boy and girl, orphans, whose parents were Broomfields. The latter 2 children were between 7 and 10 years of age.

Several days had elapsed since the departure of her husband, when Mrs. Davidson found her doors suddenly darkened by the swarthy forms of several Indians, who, speaking English, told her she must go with them to their towns in the west.

There remained no alternative to her, though her situation was such as almost to prevent the possibility of her performing such a trip. (She was pregnant). She took up her youngest child, the Indians taking the others, and left the house to try the realities of Indian captivity, of which she had heard much said. They had not proceeded far when they relieved her of her burden; 1 of the Indians taking her child, and unexpectedly to her, carried it on in safety.

The exertions and anxiety of mind undergone by Mrs. Davidson, was the cause of an addition of numbers to the captives. Two hours relaxation from the march, was sufficient rest, in the estimation of the Indians, and again they pushed on, 1 of the Indians carrying the stranger, which after a day's time, was drowned, on account of apparent or real indisposition.

The Indians who captured Mrs. Davidson were more humane than she expected. They seemed to pity her, and showed every leniency that could be asked for, under the circumstances.

But, when they arrived at the Indian towns, quite a different fate awaited them. The 2 girl children were tied to trees, and shot before her eyes. The boy, her son, was given to an old squaw, who, in passing over a river, upset her canoe, and he was drowned. What became of the bound boy and girl was never known.

Mr. Davidson, 2 years after, it being a time of peace, went to the Shawanoe towns to look for his wife, who had been sold to a French gentleman. Mr. Davidson made inquiries after her, but could learn nothing of her fate. An old Indian, who no doubt pitied him, told him that if any Indian in the town knew of her whereabouts, he could not be told, as they would have to refund the price paid for her in case she had to be given up. But, that if he would go home, that he would find out where his wife was, and inform him. Mr. Davidson returned, little thinking that the Indian would keep his promise.

In a short time after Mr. Davidson returned, the old Indian conveyed the necessary intelligence to him, and he set out a second time, but now toward Canada, where he had been informed she was. When he had got into the Canada settlements, he stopped at the house of a wealthy French farmer, to get a meal and to inquire the way to some place where he had heard she was.

He noticed a woman passing him, as he entered the house, but merely bowed to her and went on. Asking for his dinner, he seated himself, and was, perhaps, running over in his mind, the chances of finding his wife, when again the woman entered. She laid down her wood, and looked at the stranger steadily for a moment, when she turned to her mistress, and said: "I know that man." "Well, who is he," said the French lady. "It is my husband! Andrew Davidson, I am your wife." Mr. Davidson could scarcely believe his senses. When he last saw her, she was a fine, healthy-looking woman; her hair was black as coal; but now, her head was gray, and she looked many years older than she should have looked. Yet it was her, though he declared nothing but her voice seemed to say she was Rebecca Davidson.

Soon the French gentleman returned, and being a humane man, gave up Rebecca to her husband, also a considerable sum of money, and next morning sent them on their way rejoicing."

The Will of John Goolman Davidson is reprinted below complete with the "interesting" spelling of words.

"In the name of God, Amen. July 1791. I John Davidson of Wythe Co., and state of Virginia being very sick and weak in body but in and of perfect mind and memory thanks be given God calling unto mind the mortality of my body and knowing that it is appointed for all men once to die do make and ordain this my last will and testament that is to say principally and first of all I give and recommend my sole unto the hand of almighty God that gave it and my body I recommend to the earth to be buried in decent Christian burial at the discretion of my executors nothing doubting but at the general resurrection I shall receive the same again by the mighty power of God and a touching such world by estate wherewith it hath pleased God to bless me in this life I give and devise and dispose of the same in the following manner and from first I give and bequeath to my sons Andrew, John, and George Davidson my land at the mouth of Absolam Wells counting 400 akers to be devided betwixt them as follows George Corner to stand at the medow and run ther a long the old line to the corner at the pounding Mill brench and then to the creek to be the line from that through and the remainder part of said land to be divided betixt Andrew and John in quantity and quantity. Likewise I bequeath a tract of myne lying on the Brushey Fork known by the name of the Quekers Cabans to John Burk. Likewise I bequeth to my dought Betse a tract of myne lying on the head waters of Lortons Lick Creek. Likewise I do bequeath to Marthew my beloved wife the plantation on which I now reside which I bought of my son William Davidson to be for her seport if shee thinks proper to keep house upon it if not to disspose of the same to George Peery or John Bele for or at its vallue and to take his mentanens out of the same land. Likewise I do bequeth my two sons John and George my still and my wife the thirds of the profits maid by hir while shee lives. Likewise I bequeth to my sons Wm and Jossph Davidson one English Crown Starling apees. To George Peery, Lo Brown and John Belle to eatch of them I bequeath one Crown Starling to be leved out of my astat and I dow hair by utterly disallow, revoke and disavowel all and every other other former testaments, will, Legacies, bequest, and executors by me in any wise before naimed weill and bequethed ratifying and confirming this and no other to be my last will and testament. In witness thereof I have hair unto set my hand and seal this 22nd day of July in the year of our Lord 1791.

(signed) John Davidson

Signed Sealed published pronounced and declared by the said John Davidson as his last will and testament in the presence of us who in his presence and the presence of each other have hair until subscribed our names.
Robert Wallace, David Wallace

At a Court held for the Co., of Wythe on Tuesday the 3rd day of June 1795. This the last will and Testament of John Davidson, Dec'd, was exhibited in Court and proven by the oaths of Robert Wallace and David Wallace, the witnesses thereto, and ordered to be recorded. Testee:
Samuel Crockett, D.C."

For a nice compilation of information about John Goolman Davidson, check out his Find A Grave Memorial No. 15054737 at http://www.findagrave.com/cgi-bin/fg.cgi?page=gr&GSln=DAVI&GSfn=J&GSpartial=1&GSbyrel=all&GSst=48&GScntry=4&GSsr=121&GRid=15054737&

5

Leroy C. Culbreath

1835-1919

Leroy C. Culbreath (1835 - 1919)

is your 2nd great grandfather

Thomas Sherman Culbreath (1866 - 1962)

son of Leroy C. Culbreath

Alberta Anna Bell Culbreath (1903 - 1970)

daughter of Thomas Sherman Culbreath

Lawrence Sherman Kinney (1928 -)

son of Alberta Anna Bell Culbreath

Barbara Elaine Kinney

daughter of Lawrence Sherman Kinney

Leroy C. Culbreath was born 1 January 1835, in Wilson County, Tennessee, to Thomas and Sarah Gregory Culbreath. He joined older brother, Stephen Henderson Culbreath. Sometime shortly after his birth, the family relocated to Williamson County, Illinois. Court records show clearly that the family was in Williamson County by 8 October 1839. His family bought an 80-acre farm. Typical crops of the time included corn and tobacco.

By 1850, Leroy had at least 3 brothers and 2 sisters. His oldest brother, Stephen Henderson, had married and was farming his own land. It's likely that Leroy was running his family's farm, particularly since his father, Thomas Culbreath, had died that year.

~~~~~~

Williamson County was still a wilderness when the Culbreath and Fulk families migrated from Tennessee. For example, there were still deer, bear, elk, wildcat, otter, mink, rattlesnake, copperhead, moccasin, buzzard, crane, eagle, wild geese, golden oriole, blue jay, and martin in abundance. Just before they migrated, there were bison everywhere. From <u>The History of Williamson County, Illinois</u> by Milo Erwin, Marion, Illinois 1876, accessed 8.19.13 from Ancestry.com, page numbers precede quotes:

p. 39 -- The early settlers came in wagons. They made all their furniture upon arrival. Their bed was a fork driven into the ground and poles laid on, then into the cabin wall. All was covered with boards, straw, and bear or deer skins. Table ware was pewter dishes or wooden bowls, trenchers and noggins. Or gourds were used. Iron pots were brought with them. Almost every woman was a
~~~~~~

weaver with a loom. By 1840, two turning lathes were available so they made round bed posts.

p. 40 -- For food they ate wild meat and corn bread, but there was a lot of grit in the bread. Hoe-cake and gravy, Johnny-cakes and pones were for breakfast and dinner. Milk and mush was supper. Fish and all kinds of greens were eaten. Pumpkins, beans, squash, and potatoes were made into a pot pie. They had wild fruits such as grapes, cherries, plums, paw-paws, persimmons, crab apples, red and black haws, and berries.

p. 40 -- Even though there was no law or church, there was a set of morals which everyone lived by. Everyone was expected to fight Indians, help raise houses, use no deadly weapon in a fight, and avoid theft or "carry the United States flag on his back, to-wit: thirteen stripes."

p. 77 -- In the summer from 1850 to 1872, teamsters hauled products to the railroads and river. Before then anything that went to market had to walk. Ox teams were used through 1866; then horses.

p. 236 -- Taxes were 25 cents for 100 dollars-worth of property. One could pay with wolf scalps, bear, deer, or coon skins.

p. 241-- "On the same day, October 8th [1839], John Davis reported as Justice of the Peace, of having fined Thos. Culbreath $3.00 for an assault and battery on Michael Shanks, which is the first criminal case recorded in the county."

~~~~~~

Leroy's life course was set when on 29 November 1857, he married Mary Ann Fulk, whose family also migrated from Tennessee to Williamson County, Illinois. Leroy and Mary Ann would continue migrating further west during the 62 years of their married life together, but for now, they settled into farm life in Illinois.

At the 1860 U.S. Federal Census, the couple has added son, George W., to their family. At 10 months old, life must have held such promise, but a firestorm was heating up.

In July 1863, Provost Marshal Captain Isaac A. Phillips came to Crab Orchard and recruited 27 year old Leroy, for military duty. Leroy's registration listed his occupation as a farmer.

At the 1865 Illinois State Census, Leroy was enumerated with 3 males and 6 females in his household. Records are ink blotted so they are unreadable in part. It is unclear the identity of the persons in his household. Of interest is that this time, sister Caroline Culbreath was enumerated next door. She had 3 males and 5 females in her household. There is no indication that she had married, so the identities of these members of her household are unknown.

Shortly after this Census, the family moved further west near Grand Tower, which is in Jackson County. Son, Thomas Sherman Culbreath, was born in 1866.

~~~~~~

At the 1870 U.S. Federal Census, Leroy and Mary Ann were living west of Marion, Illinois, in Jackson County, near Carbondale. Children listed in the Census were: George, 10; Andrew, 8, (was incorrectly recorded as 18); Sarah, 6; Thomas, 3; and Otis, 1 year old. Leroy was a day laborer, which may mean that he didn't own the land on which they were working. He did list personal property valued at $100. Also of interest, Leroy and wife, Mary Ann, did not read or write.

1845

Map of Williamson County. Note Grand Tower in Jackson County to the west.
Map accessed from http://www.ilgenealogy101.com/williamson-county/

When we visited the Grand Tower, it was early morning and there was light rain falling. The tower was barely visible on the opposite shore of the river next to the Missouri bank. I thought about my family and wondered where they might have lived, whether actually in Grand Tower, or just nearby. At this point, the river didn't seem too wide, but this river changes dramatically.

Bernie Black next to Mississippi River in Grand Tower. The tower rock formation is barely visible.

~~~~~~

Back in the Day . . . Grand Tower is a rock formation in the Mississippi River after which the small town of Grand Tower is named. In the 1800s, there were dangerous rapids near the Tower and boats were often wrecked and passengers killed. The town was a busy port where all manner of goods were shipped and received. Two iron furnaces operated around the time of T. S. Culbreath's birth.

~~~~~~

Tower Rock, Illinois, rock tower along the shore of the Mississippi River Accessed at: http://www.southernmostillinoishistory.net/tower-rock.html

Court records for 1879 Williamson County indicate that Leroy Culbreath was the administrator of Andrew J. Fulk's estate. It is unclear if this estate belonged to his father-in-law, Andrew J. Fulk, who died in 1861, or to his brother-in-law, Andrew J. Fulk, as the date of his brother-in-law's death is unknown. At any rate, regardless of which person's estate he administered, shortly after the conclusion of this business, the family relocated to El Dorado, Butler County, Kansas; a booming oil town. Although George apparently stayed in El Dorado, Leroy and Mary didn't, because in 1881, their youngest children, twins Oscar and Arthur, were born in Marvel, Arkansas. Presumably, sons Logan and Thomas accompanied the family to Arkansas. At this time, there were 2 more sons in the family: Henry, 7; and Edgar, 1. Neither of these survived past the 1900 U.S. Federal Census.

Not much is known about the family between 1881 and 1900. At the U.S. Federal Census of 1900, Leroy showed up in Joplin City, Jasper County, Missouri. Leroy, 65, was still working as a day laborer, along with the twins. A family portrait of Leroy and Mary Ann with their 5 surviving sons was made by a photography studio named Letour in Joplin, Missouri, presumably around this time.

We do know from the Bureau of Land Management records that Leroy, George, and Logan all owned land in Pratt County around 1888 and 1890. Here are the land descriptions.

Accession	Names	Date	Doc #	State	Meridian	Twp - Rng	Aliquots	Sec. #	County
KS2440__.424	CULBREATH, GEORGE W	12/2/1890	7553	KS	6th PM	026S - 015W	Lot/Trct 1	30	Pratt
						026S - 015W	SE¼NE¼	30	Pratt
						026S - 015W	E½SE¼	30	Pratt
KS2270__.450	CULBREATH, LEROY C	8/5/1890	5488	KS	6th PM	026S - 015W	E½SE¼	19	Pratt
						026S - 015W	W½SW¼	20	Pratt
KS2120__.411	CULBREATH, SNEED L	12/29/1888	2433	KS	6th PM	026S - 015W	E½NE¼	19	Pratt
						026S - 015W	W½NW¼	20	Pratt

In 2013, I drove by these Pratt County lands. They were located along a sandy farm road which necessitated driving at 35 m.p.h., or risk becoming stuck in the sand. As I whizzed along, surfing as it were, the sandy road dodging gigantic harvesting vehicles, I was only able to view the lands and take a rather poor video. The land belonging to Leroy was, in 2013, the Pratt Sand Hills Wildlife Area. Leroy and sons, George and Logan's lands, were adjacent each other. The intersection of farm road N.W. 110 Street and 80 Street marks the northern boundary of their lands in Sections 19 and 20. Section 30 was further south. It is unknown whether they actually lived on these lands. Here's some info about the Pratt Sand Hills Wildlife Area from their website http://www.stateparks.com/pratt_sandhills.html.

"Most of the 5,715-acre area is sand hill prairie with moderate to steep dune topography. There are also several miles of multi-row shelterbelts throughout the area, as well as windmills, solar wells, and hydrants that provide water for wildlife.

In spring, summer, and early fall, Pratt Sand Hills Wildlife Area is an excellent place for wildlife watching. Songbirds, furbearers, crows, and a variety of other species may be found by the patient observer.

Township roads through Pratt Sand Hills Wildlife Area are loose sand, so good judgment must be used to avoid getting stuck. Vehicle traffic is prohibited within the Sand Hills, so a walk of up to 2 miles may be necessary to reach some of the more remote spots."

Topography of the Pratt Sand Hills

In 1906, according to Leroy's obituary, they moved to Stafford County, Kansas. Sometime about 1911, they moved into the town of Saint John.

Leroy's obituary appeared in the 20 March 1919 issue of The Saint John News: "**GRANDPA CULBREATH DEAD – He Passed Away Last Saturday at 10:30 a.m., After Several Years of Suffering From the Terrible Cancer – Burial Monday**. – "Grandpa" Culbreath is dead. He passed away at 10:30 o'clock last Saturday forenoon, after suffering from cancer for several years.

Funeral services were conducted from the home at 2:30 o'clock Monday afternoon by Rev. S. A. Chappell, pastor of the Methodist church. Burial was in Fairview cemetery. Veterans of the World War acted as pall-bearers, all but one having seen service overseas.

The following sketch of the life of the deceased was read during the ceremony by Rev. Chappell:

"LeRoy C. Culbreath was born in Wilson County, Tennessee, 1 January 1835 and died at his home in St. John, Kansas, 15 March 1919.

On 29 November 1857, he was married to Mary Fulk, and to this union ten children were born, five of whom are living: George and Logan of St. John; Thomas of Hutchinson; Oscar of Pittsburgh, Kansas; and Arthur, who has just returned from the war. Besides these five sons and the wife, there is a sister, Mrs. Bowers, of Kinsley, Kansas.

Mr. Culbreath was converted and joined the Baptist church when a boy and has sought to follow the Master all these years.

The family came from Illinois to Kansas in 1879 and to Stafford County in 1906. The family has resided in St. John about eight years. He was a man of even temper and quiet, retiring ways. For about five years he had been afflicted with cancer, which finally caused his death."

Questions:

1. How did Leroy and Mary Ann meet?
2. Did Leroy ever live on his Pratt County, Kansas land?
3. Where did he live between 1881 and 1900?
4. What was his occupation between 1881 and 1900?
5. Where are his five children, which didn't survive, buried?
6. What type of cancer did Leroy die from?
7. Did Leroy belong to a Baptist church in St. John at the end of his life? If so, which one, and is it still functioning in 2013?

The Parents of Leroy C. Culbreath

Thomas Culbreath and Sarah Gregory

1801-1850 1802 - after 1860

Thomas Culbreath was born 1801 in Virginia. In August of 1820 in Mecklenburg, Virginia, he was enumerated in the 1820 U.S. Federal Census. He owned a farm and 3 slaves: 2 male and 1 female.

On 12 January 1822, at age 21, he married Sarah Gregory. The couple did not stay in Virginia because by the 1830 U.S. Federal Census, we find they were living in Smith County, Tennessee. There were 2 male children under 5 years of age; 1 male between 5 and 9; 1 male 20 to 29; and 1 female 20 to 29. The 2 males under 5 years of age are unknown to me. The male between 5 and 9 is probably Stephen H. Culbreath, 1823-1860. The male and female between 20-29 were probably Thomas and Sarah.

In 1935, son, Leroy C. Culbreath, was born. Shortly thereafter, the family made the trek to Williamson County, Illinois. We know they were living in Williamson County on 8 October 1839, because that is the date Williamson County split from its neighbor, Franklin County, to the north and became their own county. Thomas had the unfortunate distinction of being recorded as the newly formed Williamson County's first criminal case when he was fined $3 for an assault and battery on Michael Shanks.

On 25 October 1839, Thomas purchased land from the Shawneetown, Illinois land office as recorded in the Illinois Public Land Purchase Records, 1800-1990 database accessed online at Ancestry.com. He received 80 acres described as, "The east half of the N.W. Quarter of Section 13, Township 9 South, Range 3 East." He paid just $100. The price per acre was $1.25.

Thomas received his land grant signed by President John Tyler in 1841.
Thomas didn't have very long to improve his land, because we see that he was listed in the Mortality Schedule of the 1850 U.S. Federal Census. He died in May just before the 1 June 1850 enumeration date for the Census. In fact, his death entry was the last one in the record book. He reportedly died from apoplexy which was defined as: "A sudden loss of consciousness followed by paralysis, due to cerebral hemorrhage or blocking of an artery of the brain by an embolus or thrombus (stroke); and effusion of blood into the lungs or other organs."

Given under my hand, at the City of Washington, the first day of July in the year of our Lord one thousand eight hundred and forty one and of the Independence of the United States the sixty fifth

By the President: John Tyler

By R. Tyler Sec'y

J. Williamson Recorder Commissioner of the General Land Office.

Sarah Gregory Culbreath was then left with at least 5 children to raise. The oldest child which I know about, Stephen Henderson Culbreath, had married in 1845, and established his own farm nearby. Sarah had in her household: son, Leroy, 15; daughter, Caroline; son, Levi Marion, about 13; daughter, Arena M. (Rena), about 11; and son, Jefferson, about 6 years old. There may have been other children which I do not know about.

In the 1855 Illinois State Census, Sarah was enumerated in Township 10 with her 2 youngest sons and 2 daughters. Her oldest son, Stephen Henderson, had his own land, and Leroy was not listed here either. Sarah was recorded in the 1860 U.S. Federal Census back on her original land in Township 9, with son, Leroy, next door. Perhaps in 1855, as Leroy would have been a man of 20 years at that time, he may have been farming the family land, while Sarah was farming elsewhere, perhaps assisting her widowed daughter-in-law with her 8 children. Although no record has yet to be discovered, it is highly possible the family owned more than 1 farm, as that was quite a common practice.

As mentioned, in the 1860 U.S. Federal Census, Sarah was back in Township 9, Range 3 East with her daughter, Arena, while Leroy was farming next door.

Part of the 1860 Census was a separate report called "Productions of Agriculture." These reports are detailed below for both Sarah and Leroy. The report details number of acres improved, unimproved, and numbers of livestock and also crops that had been grown that year.

Improved Acres:	Sarah - 50	Leroy - 10
Unimproved Acres:	Sarah - 110	Leroy - 0
Cash value of farm:	Sarah - 1600	Leroy - 100
Cash value of implements:	Sarah - 25	Leroy - 70
Horses:	Sarah – 3	Leroy - 1
Asses or Mules:	Sarah – 1	Leroy - 0
Milk Cows:	Sarah – 3	Leroy - 1
Working Oxen	Sarah – 3	Leroy - 3
Cattle	Sarah – 6	Leroy - 1
Sheep	Sarah – 10	Leroy - 0
Swine	Sarah - 28	Leroy - 13

Value of Livestock	Sarah - 330	Leroy - 150
Wheat	Sarah - 86	Leroy - 15
Indian corn	Sarah - 520	Leroy - 250
Tobacco	Sarah - 1000	Leroy - 600
Wool	Sarah - 22	Leroy - 0

Left, Thomas and Sarah Gregory Culbreath's former land in Williamson County, Illinois, as seen in 2013
Right, Culbreath Road near Crab Orchard, Williamson County, Illinois

In the 1865 Illinois State Census, there is a Sarah Gregory enumerated in Township 9 Range. It is unclear whether this is the same Sarah Gregory. There are no further records which I've uncovered as of 2013 regarding Sarah.

While visiting the Williamson County Historical Society in September 2013, I learned of the existence of a Culbreath family cemetery. It is thought that Sarah is buried there. I was unable to locate the cemetery during my visit to Williamson County in 2013, however, Helen Lind of the Williamson County Historical Society graciously gave me some photographs from the time when she personally read the cemetery. According to cemetery records in the Williamson County Historical Society, the Culbreath Cemetery is located in the N.W. Quarter of Section 13, East Marion Township. Those buried there include:

1. Thomas Culbreath, died 9 May 1850, 49 years, 8 months, 13 days. Born in Virginia, died in May of apoplexy. He appeared in the 1850 Williamson County Mortality Schedule.
2. Permelia Culbreath, daughter of Stephen Henderson and Louis Jane Keaster Culbreath, died 21 June 1864, 6 years, 3 months, 10 days. Her grave stone is broken. Her parents were Stephen Henderson Culbreath who married Louisa Jane Keaster, 25 September 1845 according to the Williamson County Marriage Record.

3. Stephen H. Culbreath (stone is broken), died 1 January 1860, 36 years, 5 months, 23 days, died January of typhoid pneumonia according to the 1860 Williamson County, Illinois Mortality Schedule.
4. In addition, there is supposed to be a burial without a marker: "S. L. Culbreath, died the 19th of consumption, buried in family graveyard, 2 miles northwest of Crab Orchard." This is the text as it was reported in The Leader, 26 July 1897 edition.

A note of thanks to the Williamson County Historical Society is in order for these pictures. Helen Lind, who photographed the cemetery, graciously gave them to me.

Left, grave stone for Thomas Culbreath, in Culbreath Family Cemetery, Crab Orchard, Williamson County, Illinois
Right, grave stone for Stephen Henderson Culbreath, Culbreath Family Cemetery, Crab Orchard, Williamson County, Illinois

Questions:

1. When did Thomas and Sarah migrate to Illinois?
2. How many children did they actually have?
3. Who are the parents of Sarah Gregory?
4. What happened to the land they got in 1841?
5. Is Sarah buried in the Culbreath Cemetery with Thomas and son, Stephen Henderson Culbreath? whose death is reported in The Leader edition 26 July 1897? Could it possibly be Sarah Gregory Culbreath? If it is, then she would have been almost 100 years old at her death. It is possible there is another S. L. Culbreath.

Thomas Culbreath's former land in Williamson County, Illinois, 1839, described as the east half of N.E. Quarter of Section 13, Township 9S, Range 3E, 80 acres. Shown above in 2013 Google Earth.

The Wife of Leroy C. Culbreath

Mary Ann Fulk

1839-1919

Mary Ann Fulk was born in 1839 in Wilson County, Tennessee, to Andrew J. and Jane Caplinger Fulk. She was 1 of up to 8 children. She apparently named 2 of her own children after at least 3 of her siblings including: Sneed Andrew Logan Culbreath, who was probably named for her father and 2 brothers, Sneed H. Fulk and father and brother, both named Andrew J. Fulk; and George W. Culbreath, who is probably named for her brother, George W. Fulk. Other siblings included Parmenus Fulk, Elizabeth Fulk, and Samantha Frances Fulk.

Sometime between 1850 and 1855, her family relocated to Williamson County, Illinois.

~~~~~~

Back in the Day . . . The move to Illinois from Tennessee necessitated crossing the Ohio River. Most pioneers traveled by ox drawn cart. The 3 most common crossings from Kentucky into Illinois were at Golconda, Cave-in-Rock, and Shawneetown. Either of these crossings could have been likely for both the Fulk and Culbreath families, as all 3 were located southeast of the destination at which they settled near Crab Orchard, Williamson County, Illinois.

~~~~~~

Ohio River at Golconda, Illinois, one of three popular river crossings in the 1830s

On 29 November 1857, Mary Ann Fulk married Leroy C. Culbreath in Williamson County, Illinois.

By the 1860 U.S. Federal Census, the couple was living near Marion, Williamson County, Illinois, and she had given birth to their first son, George W. Culbreath, who was 10 months old at Census time.

Mary Ann would give birth to a total of 10 children, 5 of whom survived to adulthood. The family would live in El Dorado, Butler County, Kansas; in Marvel, Arkansas; in Joplin, Jasper County, Missouri, in Pratt County, Kansas; and St. John, Stafford County, Kansas.

Mary Ann Fulk Culbreath passed away on 22 May 1919, in St. John, Stafford County, Kansas. Her obituary appeared in The Saint John Weekly News, Stafford County, Kansas, Thursday, 26 May 1919.

"Mrs. Culbreath Passes Away – She Was Found Dead in Her Bed Sunday Morning – Was Apparently in Her Usual Health Upon Retiring Saturday Night.

The city of St. John was greatly shocked Sunday morning, upon learning that Grandma Culbreath had been found dead in bed at her home on North Broadway. The only person in the home with her Saturday night was her son, T. S. Culbreath of Hutchinson. Mr. Culbreath stated to a News reporter that he went to his mother's home about ten o'clock Saturday night and not seeing her in the sitting room he went into her bedroom. She was in bed and apparently sleeping, but he now believes she was dead at that time. The next morning Mr. Culbreath went into her room and found his mother dead.

Mrs. Culbreath, on Saturday, was apparently in her usual health. She visited at the home of her son, George, and took dinner there. Later in the day she walked to the home of her son, Logan, and from there she was taken in an auto to her own home. The death of Grandma Culbreath was a real shock, not only to the relatives, but all the people.

The funeral services were conducted from the home at ten o'clock yesterday forenoon by Rev. S. A. Chappell, pastor of the Methodist church. Interment was in Fairview cemetery.

Mary J. Faulk was born in Tennessee and was eighty years of age at the time of her death. She was married to L. C. Culbreath in the state of Illinois sixty-two years ago. To the union ten children were born, of whom five sons survive their parents. They are: George W., S. L. and Arthur, of St. John, Kansas; T. S. of Hutchinson, Kansas; and Oscar of Pittsburg, Kansas. Arthur, the youngest, recently returned from the World War. He was making his home with his mother at the time of her death, but had gone on a visit to Joplin, Missouri. He and his brother Oscar, were notified and arrived in St. John Tuesday night. Grandma Culbreath is also survived by nineteen grandchildren, and all except four were present at the funeral. She is also survived by a sister, Mrs. Samantha Jackson, of Marion, Illinois.

Deceased had been a member of the Baptist Church for a great many years and was a member of that organization at the time of her death.

The family came from Illinois to Kansas in the year 1879 and located in Butler County, near El Dorado. The family moved to Pratt County in the year 1885. Deceased and her husband (who just died two months and two days before) moved to Stafford County about twelve years ago, residing all or the greater part of the time in St. John."

Mary Ann Fulk and Leroy C. Culbreath grave marker in Fairview Cemetery, St. John, Stafford County, Kansas

Questions:

1. What happened to Mary Ann Fulk Culbreath's siblings?
2. What is Mary Ann's exact birth date?
3. How did Mary Ann meet Leroy Culbreath?
4. Which Baptist church did she belong to at her death?
5. Did she live any other places besides Williamson County,

Illinois; El Dorado, Kansas; Marvel, Arkansas; Joplin, Jasper County, Missouri; Pratt County, Kansas; and Stafford County, Kansas?

6. How did her children, who did not survive, die? Where are they buried?
7. What was the sex, birthdate, and cause of death for her tenth child?
8. Does her former home in 1919 on North Broadway in St. John, Kansas still stand in 2013?

Cave-in-Rock, Illinois, a cavern along the Ohio River's edge, which is well-hidden from sight of passing boats. Robbers would hide in the cave and attack unsuspecting river boats. Cave-in-Rock, the town by the same name, was a popular river crossing for 1830s pioneers.

Left, Foot traffic only in 2013 inside the Sandy Creek Covered Bridge off of Missouri State highway 21, northeast of Hillsboro.
Right, The Sandy Creek Covered Bridge, built in 1872, utilized the Howe-truss construction method.

For more than 100 years now, bridges have spanned these mighty rivers, making crossings a relatively simple process. This bridge on U.S. highway 45 in Paducah, Kentucky, built in 1929, spans the Ohio River. It has a steel deck and an impressive sky blue steel structure. Speed limit is a mere 25 miles per hour over this extremely narrow expanse.

Even though bridges over our great rivers abound, there are still some ferries that operate in less populated areas as we experienced when crossing the Mississippi River on this small passenger car ferry operating between Modoc, Illinois, and St. Genevieve, Missouri, in 2013.

The Parents of Mary Ann Fulk

Andrew J. Fulk and Jane Caplinger

1805-1861 1812-1874

Mary Ann Fulk's father, Andrew J. Fulk, was born in North Carolina about 1805. He moved with his family to Wilson County, Tennessee, where he married Jane Caplinger on 30 July 1831. Jane was born in Wilson County, Tennessee on 1 March 1812.

Around 1854, they moved to Williamson County, Illinois, where Andrew filed on a piece of land located in Section 12, of Township 10 South, and Range 3 East. He paid just 13 cents per acre for 40 acres, totaling just $5.

In 2013, we went to see this piece of land. We met the current owner who graciously escorted us to the site where he believed a homestead may have stood. There was a level spot in front of a beautiful pond. We also observed the remains of a rutted wagon trail leading away from the property. While standing at the pond outlet, a large deer bounded into view, and once he caught sight of me, sprung across the pond outlet and away into the woods in just 2 leaps. It was a magnificent sight to see.

Andrew and Jane lived the rest of their lives in the Crab Orchard area of Williamson County, Illinois. They are both buried in the Mt. Pleasant Church Cemetery. The church was also known as Shed Church. Local long-time resident and local historian, Helen Davis, explained that church members would come from far and wide for "brush arbor" meetings at the Mt. Pleasant Church. These camp meetings often would last for several weeks. Men would hunt game and women would provide meals. Church services were held continually. The Shed Church, built in 1839, was a Presbyterian church which had the distinction of being the oldest church in continuous use in Illinois until it ceased meeting sometime after 2000.

Left, Pond outlet. Note far right side of pond is a possible former homestead site of Andrew J. and Jane Caplinger Fulk, in Williamson County, Illinois, as seen in 2013
Right, Looking back over the pond from a level spot possibly used as a home site for Andrew and Jane Fulk during the mid-1800s.

If indeed this was the former homestead site of Andrew and Jane, I can see why they would have chosen it. Wildlife abounds, the pond is serene, and there was obviously a trail to the place.

Faint rutted wagon trails lead away from the home site above

Questions:

1. What happened to the siblings of Mary Ann Fulk Culbreath?
2. Who were the parents of Jane Caplinger?
3. Who were the parents of Andrew J. Fulk?
4. How did they meet each other?
5. Did they own other land besides this one tract in Williamson County? If so, where was it and how many acres did it contain?
6. Did Jane Caplinger's family also migrate to Illinois? There was a road sign off of Highway 166 called Caplinger Pond. It was very near to the Shed Church road.

Left, Andrew J. Fulk, died June 22, 1861, aged 56 years, Shed Church Cemetery, Crab Orchard, Williamson County, Illinois, 2013.
Right, Jane Caplinger Fulk, wife of Andrew J. Fulk, died May 5, 1874, aged 62 years, in the Shed Church Cemetery, Williamson County, Illinois, 2013

Left, Mt. Pleasant Presbyterian Church, also known as The Shed Church, Williamson County, Illinois, 2013
Right, A line of Fulk graves in the cemetery behind Shed Church in Crab Orchard, Williamson County, Illinois, 2013

Andrew and Jane's graves are in line with other Fulk and Caplinger graves including Sneed Fulk who died in the Civil War, and Sneed Caplinger, who died 1 September 1896. Their daughter, Samantha, who married Leonidas P. Askew, is also buried in Shed Church Cemetery, along with several of their children.

The Children of Mary Ann Fulk and Leroy Culbreath

The following children did not survive to adulthood, according to the 1900 U.S. Federal Census, where Mary Ann stated she had given birth to 10 children with 5 children surviving at the Census time.

- Sarah Culbreath, born 1864, in Illinois, and died sometime before the 1880 Census or possibly was married by the 1880 Census and not enumerated with the family and then died sometime before the 1900 Census.
- Otis Culbreath, born in 1869, in Illinois, and died sometime before the 1880 Census.
- Henry L. Culbreath, born in 1873, in Illinois, and died sometime before the 1880 Census.
- Edgar A. Culbreath, born 1879, probably in El Dorado, Butler, Kansas, or possibly Williamson County or Jackson County, Illinois, and died sometime before the 1900 Census.
- A fifth child, sex unknown, birthdate unknown, death date unknown, was also born, perhaps during one of these time frames:
    1. Born August-October 1858, and died before the 1860 Census
    2. Born during 1865, and died by the 1870 Census
    3. Born between September, 1867-February 1868, and died by the 1880 Census
    4. Born between 1874-1878, and died by the 1880 Census
    5. Born between April 1879-June 1880, and died by the June 1880 enumeration of the Census
    6. Born in January 1880, and died by the June 1880 enumeration of the Census
    7. Born between June 1882-1885, and died by the 1900 Census
    8. After 1885, it is highly unlikely that Martha Ann could have given birth because she would have been 46 years old.

The following children were born and did survive to adulthood:

- George W. Culbreath, born 24 September 1859, in Williamson County, Illinois
- Sneed Andrew Logan Culbreath, born 15 February 1862, in Marion, Williamson County, Illinois
- Thomas Sherman Culbreath, born 18 November 1866, near Grand Tower, Jackson County, Illinois
- Arthur Main "Pete" Culbreath, twin to Oscar, born 22 August 1881, in Marvel, Arkansas
- Oscar Miles Culbreath, twin to Arthur, born 22 August 1881, in Marvel, Arkansas

Leroy C. Culbreath, center left, and his wife, Mary Ann Fulk Culbreath, with their 5 surviving sons: Sneed Andrew Logan, front left. George W., front right. Thomas Sherman, back left. Twins Oscar Miles and Arthur Main Culbreath, center and right back. Photo taken in Joplin, Missouri, circa late 1890s or early 1900s. The family lived in Joplin at the 1900 U.S. Federal Census.

George W. Culbreath

1859-1919

George W. Culbreath was the first of 10 children to be born to Mary Ann Fulk and Leroy C. Culbreath. He entered the world on 24 September 1859, in Williamson County, Illinois.

At the 1860 U.S. Federal Census, George was living at the family farm in Township 9, Range 3 East, Williamson County. By the 1870 U.S. Federal Census, he was in Carbondale, Jackson County, Illinois, and 4 siblings had joined the family. For a time, it was difficult to locate this Census record because the name was completely misspelled as "Colbrebreth"

At the 1880 U.S. Federal Census, George had relocated to El Dorado, Butler County, Kansas with his family. It was here at age 20, that George began his adulthood. His occupation was listed as "farm". His parents must have left him here, as in 1881, they were living in Arkansas where George's brothers, twins Oscar and Arthur, were born.

George married Rosa Matilda Peggs of El Dorado, Butler County, Kansas on 20 September 1883. In the 1885 Kansas State Census, the couple was living in Towanda, Butler County, Kansas, and their first child, Etta Mary, who married Thomas Ackley, was 7 months old. George was farming.

George and his family must have relocated to Joplin, Missouri, because his wife, Rosa Matilda, died there 30 December 1894. According to George's obituary, see below, Rosa and George had 5 children, 3 of which survived to adulthood. These 3 were: Etta Mary;
Charles W. who married Edna Gann; and Grace Pearl, who married Ervin Winkler.

Left, Charles Culbreath and Edna Gann taken in Gray's Photographic Studio, St. John, Stafford County, Kansas
Right, George Culbreath Family in 1912, with 3 of his children, possibly Etta, Charles, and Grace from his first wife, Matilda Rosa Peggs

George moved to Stafford County, Kansas in 1895. He had land dated 1890 described as: "Lot 1 S.E. Quarter of N.E. Quarter and East ½ of S.E. Quarter of Section 30, Township 26 South, Range 15 West, 156 acres." This land was located in Rose Valley Township, Stafford County, and was very near to D. S. Carnahan's land.

In 1896, George married one of D. S. Carnahan's daughters, Ella Arminda, called Minnie. They gave birth to 6 children before she died in 1907. These 6 were: Lenna May Culbreath, who married James E. Burke; Aletta Mabel Culbreath, who married Dr. Harry A. West; Mark Carnahan Culbreath, who married Elsie Mae Lawless; Ethel Beatrice Culbreath, who married Herbert Berger; Goldia Anna Culbreath, who married Dean Burleigh; and Helen Eliza Culbreath, who married Willard Dunagan. Helen Eliza probably never knew her mother, as Ella Arminda Carnahan Culbreath died the same year that Helen was born.

In the 1900 U.S. Federal Census, George and Ella were living in Albano Township, Stafford County, Kansas. George was 40 and Ella 35. Two of George's children from his first marriage, Charles, 19, born in Kansas, and Grace, 10, born in Arkansas, lived with them, as well as 3 children born of Ella Arminda, including Lenna Mae; Mark C.; and Mabel Aletta. Two farm hands completed the household. The Census was enumerated by Ella's father, D. S. Carnahan.

Grace Culbreath, 1909, taken in Gray's Studio, St. John, Kansas

George W. and Arta B. Niver Culbreath, January 1911, possibly taken in Gray's Studio,

In the 1905 Kansas State Census for Albano Township, Stafford County, George's family was living next door to brother, Sneed Andrew Logan Culbreath. Logan's land was kitty-corner from the land belonging to Ella's parents, the Carnahans, while George's land was due west of Logan's.

The untimely death of Ella occurred in 1907. George was left with 2 children from his first wife and 6 children from Ella. It's no wonder that in 1909 on the fifth of August, he married for the third time to Arta B. Niver from Iowa. The marriage, however, took place in Jackson County, Missouri, which is in the area of Kansas City in 2013. I wonder how the couple met and why they married in this place. George's signature from the Marriage License appears below:

At the 1910 U.S. Federal Census, again enumerated by his former father-in-law, D. S. Carnahan, George was 50 and his wife, Arta, was 41. They had 8 of George's children, and Arta's 11 year old son, Claude A. Niver, living in the household, for a total of 11 people. Arta had another child who was not living with the family. George was still farming and they were living on a farm. His parents, Leroy and Mary Ann Fulk Culbreath, were living next door, but the Census indicates they were living in a rented house; not a farm.

In the 1915 Kansas State Census, George and Arta were living in St. John, Stafford County, in a rented house. Six of George's children ranging from age 8-18, remained with the family.

George Culbreath departed this life in an unexpected fashion as the following obituary will detail. He left behind his third wife, Arta B., and 3 of his children still under age 18. I have no knowledge of how the family sustained themselves after his untimely demise. Perhaps a check for a will would be profitable.

George died suddenly and tragically as reported in the 13 November 1919 issue of The Saint John News: "George W. Culbreath Dead – He Died Saturday Afternoon From Injuries Received Last Thursday in a Runaway – Funeral Monday Afternoon – George W. Culbreath died Saturday afternoon from injuries received in a runaway two days before. It seems that no one knows just how the accident occurred, more than that, Mr. Culbreath was found by team near the corner of Main Street and First Avenue. It is believed that the team became frightened and that Mr. Culbreath was either out or got out of the wagon and undertook to check them by going in front of them and that the tongue of the wagon hit him.

Mr. Culbreath was soon found and taken to his home, where he died late Saturday afternoon.

The funeral services were conducted from the Methodist church at two o'clock Monday afternoon by the pastor, Rev. Chappell. Interment was in Fairview Cemetery. The I.O.O.F. and Modern Woodman lodges participated in the services.

The following regarding the life of Mr. Culbreath was furnished The News for publication:

George W. Culbreath was born 24 September 1859, in Williamson County, Illinois. In 1879, he moved with his parents to Butler County, Kansas. On 20 September 1883, he was united in marriage to Rosa Matilda Peggs of El Dorado, Kansas. To this union five children were born: Mrs. Thomas Ackley of St. John, Kansas; Charles W. Culbreath of Garden City, Kansas; Mrs. Ervin Winkler of St. John, Kansas; and two children who died in infancy. The mother of these children died 30 December 1894, at Joplin, Missouri.

In 1895, Mr. Culbreath moved to Stafford County, Kansas, and on 10 March 1896, he married Ella Arminda Carnahan of this County. Six children were born to this union: Mrs. James Burke of Wichita, Kansas; and Mark, Alletta, Ethel, Goldia, and Helen. The mother of these children died 9 November 1907, at St. John.

On 5 August 1909, he married Arta Belle Niver of Iowa.

Besides the wife, he leaves four brothers, Logan and Arthur of St. John; Thomas and Oscar of Wichita; and five grandchildren to mourn his loss. He had lived in this County 24 years and in St. John about seven years. He was 60 years, 1 month, and 14 days of age. He was a member of the Odd Fellows and Woodman lodges, and of the M. E. Church, having been a Christian for many years."

~~~~~~

Back in the Day . . . The Modern Woodmen of America was founded by Joseph Cullen Root on January 5, 1883. He had operated a number of businesses, including a mercantile establishment, a grain elevator, and 2 flour mills, sold insurance and real estate, taught bookkeeping classes, managed a lecture bureau, and practiced law. Root was a member of several fraternal societies through the years. He wanted to create an organization that would protect families following the death of a breadwinner. See Wikipedia for more information at http://en.wikipedia.org/wiki/Modern_Woodmen_of_America

~~~~~~

Questions:

1. After George died, did Arta Niver Culbreath continue to raise his youngest children?
2. What became of his children?
3. Is George's second wife, Ella Arminda "Minnie" Carnahan Culbreath buried next to him as his grave marker indicates, or is she buried in Neelands Cemetery as her obituary states?

4. What happened to Arta Niver Culbreath? When did she die and where is she buried?
5. Did George W. Culbreath die with a will?
6. What happened to his lands after his death?

Lena Mae Culbreath, 1917, taken in Gray's Studio, St. John, Kansas

George W. Culbreath and Ella Arminda Carnahan grave site in Fairview Cemetery, St. John, Stafford County, Kansas

George's land in Stafford County was described as, "The S.E. corner of Section 28, Township 25 South, Range 14 West, 160 acres."

We know that George owned multiple properties as a newspaper article about one of his daughter's weddings stated that the married couple would live on one of George's farms. A check of court records shows numerous land transactions.

Logan's land (S. A. Culbreath) is "The S.W. corner of Section 27, Township 25 South, Range 14 West, 160 acres."

Left, Intersection of S.W. 60 and S.W. 80 Street is the dividing line between the former lands of brothers George W. Culbreath and Sneed Andrew Logan Culbreath in Stafford County, Kansas. Logan's land was to the right side of the road and George's land was to the left side.
Right, The sand roads in Stafford County, Kansas, usually run along the land Section boundaries. This road going straight, runs along the south side of the former lands of George W. Culbreath and brother, Logan Culbreath. The road turning right divides George and Logan's former lands.

The Second Wife of George W. Culbreath

Ella Arminda "Minnie" Carnahan

1865-1907

Ella Arminda was born the third child of Susan Stevenson and David Smith Carnahan, in 1865 Illinois. She joined 2 older sisters: Mary Celestia and Margaret Anna. She married the brother of her sister, Martha Emma Carnahan Culbreath's husband, Thomas Sherman Culbreath. So, 2 Carnahan girls married 2 Culbreath boys.

Ella Arminda's married life is detailed on page 279.

Ella's obituary in the 15 November 1907 issue of The Saint John News, informs the reader: "**DIED OF CONSUMPTION** – Mrs. George W. Culbreath of Albano Township, died at 12:15 a.m. Sunday, of consumption, at the home of her brother-in-law, T. S. Culbreath, in the south part of this city. Deceased had been in very poor health for some time past. The funeral services were conducted by Rev. H. S. Beach, pastor of the Emerson Presbyterian Church of Albano Township, of which organization we understand deceased was a member, and the remains gently laid to rest Sunday evening in the Neeland Cemetery. [There is a grave marker for Ella in the Fairview Cemetery where she supposedly lies next to George Culbreath.]

Deceased was the mother of six children. She was married to G. W. Culbreath in 1886 [incorrectly stated, as she married 1896] on March 10th.

The family has resided in Albano Township for a great many years and Mrs. Culbreath was known as one of the many good women of that township. Not only the family, but the entire community, feel keenly the great loss."

Sneed Andrew Logan Culbreath
1862-1934

The second child of Mary Ann Fulk and Leroy C. Culbreath was Sneed Andrew Logan Culbreath, born 15 February 1862, in Marion, Williamson County, Illinois. He was named after 2 of his mother's siblings and her father: Sneed and Andrew. He grew up in both Williamson and Jackson Counties of Southern Illinois until 1979, when his family relocated to El Dorado, Butler County, Kansas. Shortly afterwards, about 1881, the family moved to Arkansas and Logan probably went along.

Sometime before 1892, Logan was living in Bentonville, Benton County, Arkansas, as he was married in that town to Margaret E. Foster on 30 October 1892.

During his time in Arkansas, Logan worked at least 12 years for the railroad, per his obituary. In what capacity, it is not known. He also worked as a section foreman on the road.

~~~~~~

Back in the Day . . . Road building and maintenance in the early days of our county was done by local citizens. Often the courts would appoint workers and foremen. A road crew's job was to scout out the best route for a road to take, clear the right of way, and actually construct, and then maintain the road.

~~~~~~

By 1904, Logan owned land in Albano Township, Stafford County, Kansas.
Once Logan relocated to Stafford County, he worked as a thresher man. A thresher would contract to harvest other farmer's fields.

By the time of the 1910 U.S. Federal Census, Logan and Margaret had been blessed with 6 children. A seventh child would also be born. Logan was working as a laborer doing odd jobs. Logan's sister-in-law, Irene Foster, was living with the family. She had been married 2 times and had 1 child.

In 1911, tragedy struck the household when daughter, Eunice, passed away. The sad account was told in The Saint John News, 22 June 1911: "Little Girl Dead – Miss Eunice Elizabeth Culbreath, the thirteen-year-old daughter of Mr. and Mrs. Logan Culbreath, of St. John, died at the family home last Thursday afternoon at 3:30 o'clock, after a short illness. Rheumatism of the heart, we understand, was the cause of her untimely death.

The funeral services were held at the home Friday afternoon at 2:30 and were conducted by Rev. J. R. Rairden, pastor of the First Baptist Church. The little one was laid [??] in Fairview Cemetery.

The bereaved ones have the most profound sympathy of the entire community.

The following short sketch of the life of the deceased was given The News for publication:

"Eunice Culbreath was born in Arkansas, 13 December 1898, and died in St. John, Kansas 15 June 1911, aged 13 years, 6 months, and 2 days. Her life, though short, was full of untoward experiences with much of sickness and pain. Pneumonia, scarlet fever, and small pox followed each other closely at a very tender age and left her constitution weakened. A kick from a horse later and then the measles, and that by rheumatism of the heart which proved fatal.

She was a dutiful daughter and was universally beloved. She belonged to the Golden Ruler class in the First Baptist Sunday School and was an appreciated member, which was proven by the attendance of the entire class at her funeral. She gave careful and sympathetic attention to the teaching of Holy Truth which she heard from her faithful teacher, Miss Lillie Tanner, and always seemed thoughtful and earnest in their consideration. She will be greatly missed by her classmates and a large circle of friends."

After the difficult loss of Eunice, within the year, Logan and Margaret welcomed the birth of their final child, son Andrew Leroy, named after his father and grandfather.

In the 1915 Kansas State Census, the family was living in St. John, Stafford County, and Logan's brother, Arthur, was living with them.

In 1917, on the 26 of April, daughter, Neta, was married to Chester L. Green. The ceremony was performed by Elder J. S. Moore, the pastor of the First Missionary Baptist Church. She was described in the newspaper as a "fine little lady with many friends." The groom was said to be the proprietor of the West Side Meat Market and was called Codge by his friends. The couple planned to live in St. John.

By the 1920 U.S. Federal Census, Logan and Margaret were still living in St. John and Arthur continued living with them.

In the 1925 Kansas State Census, Logan's wife, Margaret, was referred to as Eva. Perhaps this was her middle name. Also in 1925, on the 4 of June, their youngest daughter, Anna, wed Wayne E. Sidman. According to The Saint John News, the couple was planning to live in Gray County where Wayne would work for Frank Toland, who was living near Cimarron.

An issue of The Saint John News, 4 June 1925, reported the St. John market prices: "Below are prices paid for the various farm products by the buyers in St. John.

The prices are for today—Thursday:

Wheat, per bushel	$1.48
Corn, per bushel (white	.96
Corn, per bushel (yellow)	.96
Corn, per bushel (mixed)	.94
Heavy Hens, per pound	.16
Light Hens, per pound	.12
Broilers, 1 ½ to 2 lbs.	.23
Leghorns and Blacks	.18
Roosters, per pound	.06
Cream, per pound	.33
Eggs, per doze	.21"

Left, Wouldn't it be great to go back to these prices? In 2013, there was hardly anything less than one dollar.

Right, Neta Culbreath Green, left, with Edith Culbreath Kint, right, and Edith's grandchildren Barbara Hollowell and Kent Hollowell

For the 1930 U.S. Federal Census, Logan and Margaret were still living in St. John. Sons, Ted and Le Roy, remained in the home, and brother, Arthur, also. Logan owned his home and it was valued at $3,000. It was not a farm. In addition, Logan had acquired a new occupation as a house plumber. Son, Ted, was a mechanic helper in a garage, while Le Roy didn't have an occupation. Next door we see daughter, Anna, and her husband, Wayne Sidman, and their son, Bobbie O. Sidman, were living. A daughter, Patsy A., had been born within the year. Wayne was a house carpenter.

Logan's son, Ted, was married on 21 July 1932, to Thelma Henry. They planned to live in St. John.

~~~~~~

Back in the Day . . . Threshing crews went from farm to farm to thresh the wheat. The men did the work while the women cooked meals and did farm chores for each other. A steam engine pulled the separator behind the wheat stacks. Men on each stack would put the wheat onto a big belt between the engine and the separator. The wheat was then fed into the separator and threshed. The threshed wheat was delivered into a farm wagon through a spout and the straw was put out another spout. This straw was used for cattle feed during the winter.

The invention of the combiner machine combined the separate operations of cutting and threshing the wheat into one operation.

~~~~~~

Wheat threshing crew, Stafford County, Kansas, circa 1900s

One never knows the day of his or her demise. Logan Culbreath surely didn't anticipate his. We read of the unfortunate event in the 5 July 1934 edition of The Saint John News, page 8: "**CULBREATH DIED FROM INJURIES – Logan Culbreath Fell From Tree At His Home Saturday Evening Sustaining Injuries From Which He Died About 9:00 O'Clock Sunday**. –The people of St. John and vicinity were greatly shocked Sunday upon learning that Logan Culbreath, highly respected citizen of St. John, was dead.

Mr. Culbreath, as the report comes to The News, was trimming the dead limbs from a high tree at his home Saturday evening. He was supposedly standing upon a ladder and was using a pruning knife in cutting off the dead limbs, and that he fell from the ladder, the fall rendering him unconscious. He was rushed to St. Rose hospital in Great Bend, but died Saturday morning at 9:00 o'clock without regaining consciousness.

Funeral services were conducted from the Christian Church at 10:00 o'clock Tuesday forenoon by Rev. Fred R. Seely of the Plano church, with the Odd Fellows in charge. Interment followed in Fairview Cemetery.

The following sketch of the life of Mr. Culbreath was read during the funeral service:

S. L. Culbreath was born on 15 February 1862, at Marion, Illinois. He died in the hospital at Great Bend, Sunday morning, 1 July 1934, at the age of 72 years.

When about twenty-one years of age, Logan Culbreath came, with his father's family, from Illinois to Butler County, Kansas. Later , he went to Arkansas, and it was there, at Bentonville, that he married Margaret E. Foster, on 30 October 1892. Twelve of the years in Arkansas were given to railroad work, and for a good part of that time Mr. Culbreath was a section foreman on the road.

About thirty years ago, Mr. and Mrs. Culbreath came to our County, locating on the farm sixteen miles southwest of St. John. Logan Culbreath was a thresher man for a number of years after coming to Stafford County.

For the last 28 years, Mr. and Mrs. Culbreath have lived in St. John where Mr. Culbreath has been a general 'helper' around town.

To Mr. and Mrs. Culbreath 7 children were born. One of these, Eunice, died in her girlhood. The 6 others are here with their mother, today. They are: Mrs. Ollie Hantla, of Meade; Mrs. Neta Green, Mrs. Leona Sutton, and Mrs. Anna Sidman, of St. John; Ted and Leroy Culbreath, of St. John. Mr. Culbreath is survived, also by 12 grandchildren, and by 2 brothers, Thomas, of Miami, Florida, and Arthur, of St. John.

Mr. Culbreath had become a member of the Baptist church in his youth. For 7 years after coming to Kansas, he attended Ottawa University. He had been a member of the I.O.O.F. for the last forty-two years."

Stafford County Historical Society

A wheat threshing crew in Stafford County, Kansas

Questions:

1. Where is Logan in the 1900 and 1930 U.S. Federal Census?
2. What did he do in Arkansas for employment?
3. Where did he meet his wife?

4. When exactly did he come to Stafford County?
5. When did he buy/sell his land in Pratt County?
6. How many farms did he own?
7. What other types of jobs did he do as per the obituary?
8. Where was the Ottawa University Logan attended and what did he study?

Wheat in Stafford County

~~~~~~

Back in the Day . . . Ottawa University was a Baptist school. Perhaps it was located in Ottawa, Franklin County, Kansas. In 2013 Ottawa was located southwest of Kansas City.

~~~~~~

Life went on for Margaret. In the 1940 U.S. Federal Census, she was living at 312 Westcoats Avenue in St. John, and her daughter and son-in-law, Anna and Wayne Sidman, were living next door. Margaret was working in a restaurant as a café cook.

During the early 1940s, every mother hoped to never get the dreaded telegram from the War Department bearing horrible news. Unfortunately, Margaret would not be spared that awful experience, because according to the 9 July 1942 issue of The Saint John News, we learn: "Le Roy Culbreath Reported Missing – Mother Receives Notification From Navy – It looks as though Le Roy Culbreath is among the missing sailors of the U.S. Navy. A message was received by his mother Wednesday from the Navy Department in Washington. The service Le Roy has given his country since he enlisted for duty in the Navy almost three years ago has brought many acts of heroism. He has seen service in both the Atlantic and Pacific oceans, his letters telling very little of combat service, however, he told much of the beauty of countries that he had seen.

His mother, Mrs. Logan Culbreath, received a Mother's Day letter from him, her last direct word being the last of May.

Le Roy grew up in St. John, graduating from the St. John high school with the class of 1932. It is to be hoped that he may be returned to his many school friends, his relatives, and mother, safe and sound.

Following is the letter Mrs. Culbreath received:

Washington, 8 July 1942

Evaline Culbreath,

St. John Kansas.

The Navy Department deeply regrets to inform you that your son, Andrew Le Roy Culbreath, Machinist's Mate Second Class U.S.N. is missing following action in the performance of his duty in the service of his country. The department appreciates your great anxiety and will furnish you further information promptly when received. To prevent possible aid to our enemies, please do not divulge the [?] of his ship or station.

Rear Admiral Randall Jacobs,

Chief of the Bureau of Navigation"

Andrew Le Roy Culbreath's name is inscribed in the National Memorial Cemetery of the Pacific also called Punchbowl. He was lost at sea from the U.S.S. Yorktown at the Battle of Midway.

Andrew Le Roy Culbreath; gone, but not forgotten. According to the 22 June 1944 issue of The Saint John News an organization called Mothers World War II agreed to name their unit in memory of Andrew Le Roy Culbreath as he was the first boy from St. John to die in the war.

In addition, Andrew was also honored as 1 of the 3 veterans that the St. John VFW was named after, Post 7519 Metz-Harter-Culbreath, 402 North Santa Fe Street, St. John, KS 67576.

Andrew LeRoy Culbreath's name inscribed in the National Memorial Cemetery of the Pacific, also called Punchbowl, located in Honolulu, Hawaii

CULBREATH, Andrew LeRoy, Machinist's Mate 2c, USN. Mother, Mrs. Evaline Culbreath, St. John.

From the World War II Navy, Marine Corps, and Coast Guard Casualties, 1941-1945 Index.

As the Lord takes away, He also gives. And He did give life again when just months before her death, Margaret's son, Ted, and his wife, gave birth to a baby boy named Clyde Le Roy, born in May 1946.

The end had come for Margaret as we read in the 14 January 1947 edition of The John News: "**MARGARET E. CULBREATH GONE – Margaret E. Culbreath** died Monday, 13 January, at 6:25 a.m. at the Stafford hospital, following an illness of three years. She was taken to the hospital Sunday evening.

Mrs. Culbreath was born in Neosho, Missouri, and would have been 71 years of age on 14 January. She had been a resident of this community 43 years. She was preceded in death by her husband, Logan Culbreath, who died in 1934.

She is survived by three daughters, Ollie Hantla of Meade, Kansas; Neta Green and Mrs. Wayne Sidman of St. John; one son, Ted Culbreath of St. John; and one sister, Mrs. W. M. Bremmer of Edna, Kansas.

Funeral arrangements have not been made at this time."

Right, Eunice Culbreath, the 13-year-old daughter of Margaret and Logan Culbreath, in Fairview Cemetery, St. John, Kansas
Left, Andrew Le Roy Culbreath, lost at sea from the U.S.S. Yorktown, in 1942. His name is inscribed at the Punchbowl Cemetery in Hawaii.

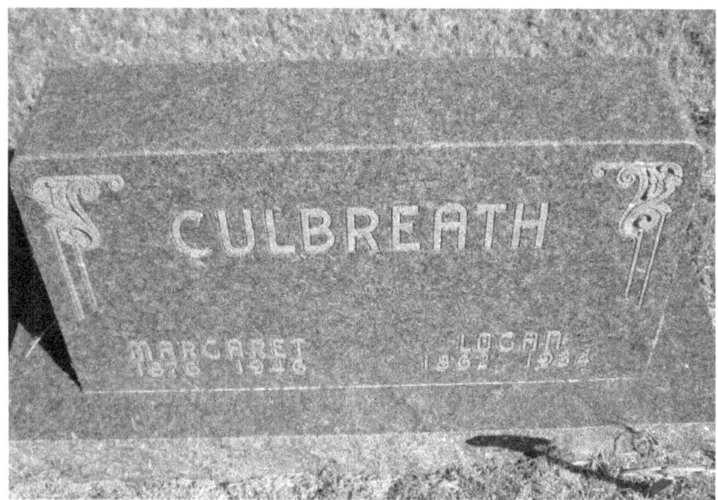

Margaret Evaline Foster and Sneed Andrew Logan Culbreath's grave marker in Fairview Cemetery, St. John, Kansas

Thomas Sherman Culbreath

1866-1962

Thomas Sherman Culbreath was either the fourth or fifth child born to Mary Ann Fulk and Leroy C. Culbreath. He was, undoubtedly, the longest living, as he died in 1962 at 95½ years of age.

He was born near Grand Tower, Illinois in 1866. His family was recorded in the Illinois State Census of 1865 as living in the Crab Orchard area of Williamson County. They must have relocated to the next county to the west, Jackson, between the Census time in 1865 and November of 1866.

During the 1870 U.S. Federal Census, his family was recorded at Carbondale, Jackson County. It appears they lived in and around Jackson County until 1879 when they migrated to Butler County, Kansas. Thomas was 13 at that time. The family didn't stay long in Butler County, but moved on to Marvel, Arkansas.

Between 1880 and 1890, I've not located any records to indicate where Thomas Sherman was. He next showed up in 1890, 7 August, when he married Martha Emma Carnahan in Stafford County, Kansas. Their first daughter, Edith Ardella, was born 21 March 1892, in Stafford County, Kansas. According to his son, Chalmer's, 1917 Draft Registration Card, Chalmers was born in 1893 in St. John, so we assume that Thomas Sherman and Martha Emma were living in St. John after their wedding. The next child to be born was Hobart William Culbreath, born 18 March 1897 in Stafford County. He was followed by Charles Harlan Culbreath in 1902, and Alberta Anna Bell Culbreath on 11 August 1903. The last child was Wilma Dorothy Culbreath, born in 1906 and died 21 May 1907. Family tradition states that Wilma took a fall from a high chair while her sister, Alberta, was the only one in the room. Although Wilma died from an illness, Alberta thought for much of her life that she was the cause of her sister's death, thinking it was a result of the fall from the high chair.

In 1895, the family was enumerated in Rose Valley Township, Stafford County, Kansas. This is located south of St. John and was farming county. Two of Thomas Sherman's brothers, George and Logan, had farms there, as well as Martha Emma's family, David Smith and Susan Stevenson Carnahan.

The 1900 U.S. Federal Census finds the family still living in Rose Valley Township. Thomas was a farmer.

At the 1905 Kansas State Census, the family was living in St. John in a house which they owned. Family tradition says that Alberta was born in Pratt in 1903, so I wonder just where they did live. There is a photograph in my possession of a house labeled "Grand View St. John, Kansas" and family state this is the house where Alberta was born.

There is a 13 October 1905 article in The Saint John News, (see page 192) which announces a business being opened by Thomas and his brothers, "And still the new enterprises come! This time it is a new steam laundry…" The use of the conjunction, "And," to begin the article leads me to believe that this business was just one among several that had been established by Thomas Sherman Culbreath.

A curious statement in the 1905 article referenced above, "The new laundry will be located on the east side of the public square, adjoining Culbreath's opera house on the south." It was the reference to an opera house with the Culbreath name in possessive form associated with it that caught my attention. The staff at St. John City Hall informed me the opera house was also the Convention Auditorium and was the same building that the City was using for their offices in 2013. What was T. S. Culbreath's true connection, if any, with this building remains a mystery. At any rate, here are some pictures of the building in use as an auditorium.

The Convention Hall in 1910

The Convention Hall in use November 1914

We do know from family tradition that T. S. owned a roller skating rink. Whether it was in St. John, Pratt, or Hutchinson is unclear. Some believe it was in Pratt. There is a photograph among the family heirlooms of T. S. with possibly Chal, on roller skates inside the rink. Later, we will see that he was an inventor of various machinery, particularly contraptions designed for farming and harvesting.

Left, Thomas Sherman Culbreath and son, Chalmers Culbreath, on roller skates inside T. S.'s roller skating rink. Daughter, Edith, supposedly could skate faster backwards than other people could skate forwards. Some family believe the rink was located in Pratt.
Right, Highchair in the Stafford County Historical Society Museum; the type common when Wilma Dorothy took her fall from one.

Tragedy struck the family in 1907 with the loss of their youngest child. The issue dated 24 May 1907, of The Saint John News, bore the sad details, "**THEIR BABY DEAD**. – Wilma Dorothy, the infant daughter of Mr. and Mrs. T. S. Culbreath, died Tuesday evening at 5:30. The little one had been seriously ill for the past month or so. The funeral services were conducted Wednesday afternoon at 3:00 o'clock by Rev. Richardson from the First Baptist Church. Interment was had in Fairview cemetery."

The 1910 U.S. Federal Census put Thomas and family in Pratt, Kansas, living at 106 South Pine, Center Township, Pratt City, Pratt County. Thomas and Martha had been married 19 years and she had given birth to 6 children with 5 living. Thomas was a house carpenter and none of the older children were yet working.

In 1915, the Kansas State Census recorded the family living in Pratt and Thomas was working as a carpenter.

It is said that he owned a steam operated tractor, and whenever the trains would come into the station and be stopped on "dead center" the station would call T. S. to use his steam tractor to pull them off of dead center so they could get going again. There were 3 major train stops during the time when he lived in Stafford County: St. John, Stafford, and Macksville. Of course, there was also Pratt in Pratt County to the south. Any one of these train stations could have been the one which relied on T. S.'s steam tractor when locomotive engines were stuck on dead center.

Left, A steam tractor was a powerful machine, as we can see here, where the steam tractor is moving a grain elevator.
Right, Pratt, Kansas Train Station

Sometime between 1915 and 1919, they relocated northeastward to Hutchinson, Reno County, Kansas. They lived at 322 Third Avenue West, as per the 1919 Hutchinson City Directory. Son, Harlan, was working as a mechanic for Taylor Motor Company. Daughter, Edith, and her husband, Melvin Kint, lived at 604 Seventh Avenue East. Melvin worked as a car repairman.

Left, Former home of T. S. Culbreath in Hutchinson, Kansas, 1919, as seen in 2013
Right, Alberta Anna Bell, Harlan, Martha Emma, and Thomas Sherman Culbreath, circa 1919

As mentioned, Thomas Sherman was an inventor. One of his inventions was a road-grading machine. Family tradition states that his wife, Martha Emma, was tired of bouncing all over the wagon while riding through the countryside of Stafford County, so she challenged her husband to do something about the rutted sandy farm roads. His solution was the ingenious road-grader. It was steam powered and had "arms" that lowered to the sides to allow grading of road surfaces, and were raised whenever a vehicle needed to pass by the road grader.

It apparently was quite a useful piece of machinery as evidenced by the following notice in the 14 July 1919 issue of The Hutchinson News: "T. S. Culbreath has sold one of the road-grading machines which he has invented to the township board of Ohio Township, in Stafford County."

The Real Road Maker road grader invention of Thomas Sherman Culbreath, used to grade the rutted farm roads of Stafford County, Kansas. Alberta Anna Bell Culbreath, daughter of T.S. Culbreath, sits at the controls.

In addition to the road grader, he invented a distinctive combiner as described in the 16 July 1920, issue of the Hutchinson News, p. 16: "**A NEW ONE INVENTED – T. S. Culbreath Has a "Combine" That's a Little Different From Others** – A "Combine" header and thresher driven by a 14-28 [??] horse power tractor which makes three miles per hour, cuts a swath of 14 feet and which will cut 50 acres of grain in a ten-hour day has been built here. The machine was built by T. S. Culbreath, formerly of Hutchinson and Irvin J. Marriage of Mullinville.

Work was started on the "combine" over a month ago when patents on the parts which they designed had been obtained. It was finished too late to try out for the harvest here so they tested the machine with bundled grain. It worked perfectly, they said. It was shipped to Mullinville, to the John Marriage ranch where there are 2,000 acres of wheat yet to be harvested. This "combine" is distinctive from all others made in that it possesses features which are found in no other machine. By removing five bolts on either side of the frame, the tractor may be removed and used for fall plowing. The header and thresher, being small, can be housed until the following harvest, the inventors say. The machine is driven by motor power and more wheat can be cut in a day than if horsepower was used, they said."

T. S. Culbreath was thinking about the entire grain harvesting process, right down to the details of shipment to market via the railroads. His next invention dealt with train car doors, as we read in the 20 August 1920, issue of The Hutchinson News: "**INVENTS MEANS FOR SAVING GRAIN CARS – T. S. Culbreath Has Device which Will Prevent Destruction of the Doors** -- T. S. Culbreath, of Wichita, and H. A. Kint, of Hutchinson, are the inventors of a new lifting jack for removing doors from cars loaded with grain without destroying the door. The jack is being built by the Hutchinson Foundry and Machine Works here [Hutchinson] and will probably be given its first tryout this evening.

Mr. Culbreath has been here for the past week supervising the construction of the machine by which he hopes to eliminate destruction of grain car doors. He also has been negotiating for a plant for the manufacturer of this and two other pieces of machinery he has invented. The Wichita man, who, until two years ago resided here, is the inventor of a road-making machine which he believes will revolutionize road construction.

He also has invented a three-in-one harvester and thresher combine, which was given a trial with considerable success on the Marriage ranch, near Mullinville this year. He is expecting to show all three of his inventions here at the State Fair. If he can get the financial backing, Mr. Culbreath said today he would manufacture the machines in Hutchinson."

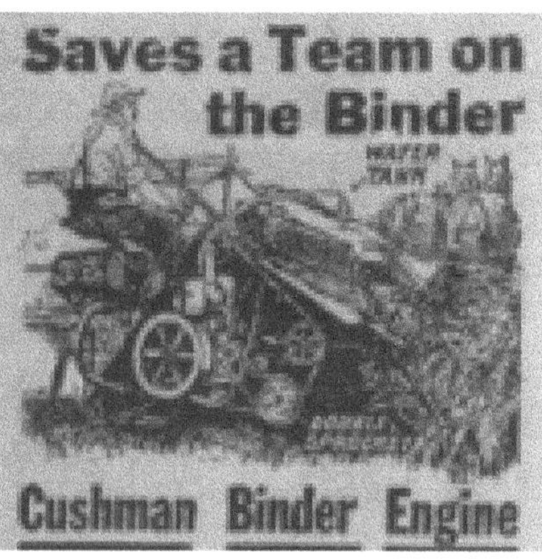

Advertisements in The Saint John News for a combine harvester thresher and binder.

According to the article above, Thomas Sherman moved to Wichita sometime in 1919, however, we have a listing for him in the 1919 Hutchinson City Directory at 322 Third Avenue, East. Presumably, the data for the directory may have been collected during the fall of 1918, as was the practice in Wichita. In addition, in his parents' obituaries of March and May 1919, he was listed as being from Hutchinson. So, perhaps some time after May 1919, he moved permanently to Wichita. He doesn't appear in the Wichita City Directory until 1920 where he is listed as the President of the Read Road Machine Company with offices at 208 Bitting Building. Additionally, the 1920 U.S. Federal Census listed him as an inventor of machinery working on his own account. The family consisted of Thomas and Martha, son Harlan, and daughter, Alberta, and they were living at 223 North St. Francis Street in Wichita.

Family tradition says he sold the patent for the road grader to the Allis-Chalmers Company for $10,000. Others in the family believe his patent was stolen.

Back in the Day . . . The Allis-Chalmers Company was a producer of industrial equipment and one of the largest steam engine producers in the U.S. During the 1910s, they developed farm equipment. Their tractors, painted in a California poppy orange color, were distinctive and set a trend among farm equipment manufacturers who followed Allis-Chalmers' lead and selected bright color schemes for their own equipment lines. The company acquired a number of other industrial equipment manufacturing companies and thereby continually kept themselves on the cutting edge of industrial equipment manufacturing. During the mid-20th century, they manufactured tanks and other heavy military equipment for the U.S. war effort. And in the 21th century, Allis-Chalmers has evolved into a multi-faceted oil field services company.

Former Bitting Building, Wichita, Kansas, where T. S. Culbreath had his Real Road Machine Company offices in suite 208 around 1920. In 2013, the building was awaiting redevelopment.

According to the Wichita City Directories for 1922-1925, Thomas Sherman and Martha Emma continued living in the city, but at various addresses including 154½ North Market and 1832 South Washington Avenue. His occupation was listed as machinist and carpenter. We have already seen he was an entrepreneur, inventor, and a farmer. In future we will read of his skill as a builder, auto mechanic, and laborer as well. We can see that he was a man of infinite creative abilities.

T. S. and Martha Emma would have migrated to Miami sometime between the fall of 1924, when they would have submitted their entry for the 1925 Wichita City Directory, the last directory they appeared in, and the summer of 1926 when the devastating hurricane wiped out half of Miami, as they were present for that catastrophic event. They moved to Miami for a number of reasons, primarily, because there had been a construction and building boom there all through the 1920s, and T. S. needed work. Secondly, his youngest daughter, Alberta Anna Bell Culbreath Kinney, was living there with her husband. Probably, the warm weather attracted them as well. Here are his addresses along with occupations as listed in the 1926-1936 Miami City Directories:

- 1927, 1928, 1929, 1930, carpenter, 1131 N.W. 37 Street
- 1931, 1932, general mechanic, 1884 N.W. 47 Street
- 1933, laborer, 1884 N.W. 47 Street
- 1934, 1935, auto mechanic, 1884 N.W. 47 Street
- 1936, carpenter, 1650 N.W. 50 Street

- 1937-1938 T. S. Culbreath does not appear in the Miami City Directory, nor the Los Angeles City Directory. He relocated sometime during this time period to Los Angeles where he lived out the rest of his life.

Butts Building, Wichita, Kansas. Sometime during the 1920-25 time period, T. S. and Martha Emma Culbreath lived above this building. It was turned into a car dealership. Notice the garage door at the far right end of the building. During remodeling of the building when the tile floor was taken up, Martha Emma collected the tiles and brought them upstairs for the children to play with according to her niece, Julia Kint Rice Connell.

Left, 1832 South Washington Avenue, Wichita, Kansas, as seen in 2013. This address was the residence of T. S. and Martha Emma Culbreath around 1925 before they relocated to Miami, Florida. It may have been a different structure from the one shown above. The house shown at right is the one which was on Washington Avenue in 1925.

Right, Martha Emma and the flowers Alberta made; T. S. Culbreath, right

In 1926, a devastating hurricane hit Miami. It is still referred to and discussed in 2013 during almost every hurricane season. Thomas Sherman and Martha Emma experienced this hurricane shortly after their move to Miami. It's a wonder they didn't pack up and return to Wichita.

Miami after the 1926 Hurricane

~~~~~~

Back in the Day . . . The 1926 hurricane was a Category 4 hurricane with sustained winds of 145 m.p.h. The science of hurricane prediction was basically nonexistent then, so the storm caught Miami by surprise. Boats ended up several blocks inland, houses lost their roofs, Miami Beach was filled with sand, bridges were washed away, downtown streets were littered with all sorts of debris, and a number of people lost their lives.

~~~~~~

Sometime during the 10 years Thomas Sherman and Martha Emma lived in Miami, their oldest granddaughter, Julia Kint, recalled seeing Thomas making bricks by a river where Indians were wrestling alligators. Julia would have been around 10-15 years old at the time. Perhaps she saw T. S. working along the Miami River near the Musa Isle Indian Village.

Musa Isle Indian Village operated as a tourist attraction in Miami. During its heyday in the 1950s, visitors to the site could observe Indians wrestling alligators. The Indians wore colorful clothing of intricate patchwork design. The Musa Isle Indian Village, one of Miami's earliest tourist attractions, was located along the banks of the Miami River. Supposedly, Indians lived there as well as put on shows for tourists.

Indian wrestling an alligator at the Musa Isle Indian Village, Miami, Florida, circa 1950s

In the 1935 Florida State Census, we learn that Thomas Sherman only had a fifth grade education, and wife, Martha Emma, a high school education. It is my opinion that Thomas Sherman was a brilliant man to have accomplished so many things including inventions and operating businesses with just a fifth grade education.

A family photograph entitled "Chal and Dad C. in Cuba 1935," was quite a shock to discover. For me, growing up during the Cuban Missile Crisis and knowing that travel to Cuba was restricted, to have had a great grandfather and a grand uncle actually vacation there was intriguing. I only wish that I'd been old enough to have asked questions of them about their experiences.

According to Barbara Hollowell Block, great granddaughter of Thomas Sherman, Chal had been working in Los Angeles selling Philco radios. He had apparently sold quite a lot of radios; enough to win a contest. The prize was a trip to Havana, Cuba, for a sales convention. He elected to take his Dad on that journey. My ESL students, many of whom are from Cuba, are very excited to see my 1935 photograph. In 2013, they can still identify the location in Havana where the photo was taken by the landmark monuments in the background.

By 1939, T. S. and Martha Emma had relocated again, this time to the other side of the country, to Los Angeles. While their youngest daughter, Alberta Anna Bell Culbreath, had moved to Miami for her husband, Vernon Haven Kinney's, job, Chal, Hobart, and Edith had all moved to California. Son, Harlan, would also migrate there sometime after the Second World War. T. S. was located in the 1939 Los Angeles City Directory living at 126 South Kingsley Drive, Los Angeles. This is the first Los Angeles City Directory in which T. S. appeared. In 1940-1942, he was at 1042½ Kingsley Drive. In 2013 when I visited Los Angeles, I was unable to locate either of these addresses.

During 1944, both T. S. and Martha Emma joined the Bell Gardens Baptist Church on profession of faith. According to their great granddaughter, Barbara Hollowell Block, they had been involved with another church—the International Church of the Four Square Gospel--founded and led by Aimee Semple McPherson in Los Angeles. She held Pentecostal revival meetings all over the country. Angelus Temple was built with the gold which was a gift from a Romani tribe king who had been healed by Aimee. Perhaps T. S. and Martha Emma first saw her in Wichita when, in 1922, her prayers supposedly held back a rain storm. The Angelus Temple was located in the Echo Park area of Los Angeles. Reportedly, her sermons integrated drama, theater-like productions, speaking in tongues, and faith healings. Barbara Hollowell Block said that when T. S. and Martha Emma moved out to Bell Gardens, son, Chal, decided he wouldn't drive them back into town to attend the Four Square church services. So, they joined the Baptist church near their house. In 2013, I had opportunity to visit the First Baptist Church of Bell Gardens and see their names on the membership rolls dated April 1944. T. S. was listed as inactive from 1957 onward. According to Julia Kint, T. S. built the communion table which still stands in the church in 2013.

Chall and Dad C. in Cuba 1935

After the end of World War II, the extended family all shared a house together. Housing was scarce and the economy was still suffering. Many military personnel returning from the Pacific landed in Los Angeles, and rather than return to their former homes, elected to begin a new life in Southern California. Thomas and Martha's granddaughter, Pauline Kint Hollowell, worked at a laundry on the military base in Los Angeles during the war while her husband entered the Navy near the end of the war. Pauline's mother, Edith Culbreath Kint and husband, Melvin Kint, retired and relocated from Wichita to Los Angeles to care for T. S.

Martha Emma had had a stroke sometime near the end of the war, and she couldn't sleep at night afterwards. As a result, she often wandered outside in the yard, or she'd play the piano in the middle of the night.

At the age of 76, on 8 October 1946, T. S. lost his soul mate, Martha Emma, whom he was married to for 56 years. She died in her granddaughter's home and was interred at Inglewood Park Cemetery, Los Angeles. Her grave has a grave marker, but Thomas' next to hers, does not.

[illegible]	[illegible]-1944	Baptism	
Culbreath, Martha	[illegible]-1944	Baptism	IA-86
Culbreath, T. S.	[illegible]-1944	Baptism	

T. S. and Martha Emma's names on the membership roll at Bell Gardens Baptist Church, Bell Gardens, California, 1944.

Bell Gardens Baptist Church, 2013

T. S. and Martha Emma in their yard in Bell Gardens. Martha Emma always had a dog.

Grave stone for Martha Emma Carnahan Culbreath, Inglewood Park Cemetery, Los Angeles, California, 2013

Great granddaughter, Barbara Hollowell Block, recalled some memories of T. S. and his life in the Bell Gardens house at 6653 Loveland. For example:

- He kept rabbits and chickens.
- Martha Emma had a vegetable garden, a rose garden, and a dahlia garden.
- There was a windmill which operated a doll-sized merry-go-round.
- T. S. built a glider for the yard.
- The most impressive thing Barbara recalls was the cement swimming pool that he built in the back yard. Neighborhood children enjoyed swimming in this unusual structure.
- T. S. also had a violin that he would play while the dog, Curley, danced and howled.
- He grew peach trees in his yard and his son, Chal, brought over some bee hives to encourage pollination of the peach blossoms.

Barbara Hollowell Block and the windmill T. S. Culbreath made for his yard in Bell Gardens, California

Barbara Hollowell Block on the glider T. S. Culbreath made for his yard in Bell Gardens, California

Cement swimming pool built by T. S. Culbreath in the back yard of his house in Bell Gardens

After Martha Emma's death, Thomas continued to keep busy. For example, he used to stand in front of Chal's appliance store everyday soliciting people to sign petitions to get old age pensions. He also continued with his inventions and house building. Even in his 80s and into his 90s, he built houses. He supposedly was a developer for houses in the Bell Gardens neighborhood where he resided. Julia recalled that he made violins from shoe boxes. Also, he sometimes stood on his head to relieve leg pain.

It was during this phase of his life that he created one of his most innovative, cutting-edge inventions: a smogless electric car. The exhaust system ran through water, thus eliminating the emissions. He appeared on The Art Linkletter Show with his invention sometime between 1956 and 1959, though efforts to obtain a video archive to date have proven unsuccessful. I know that he appeared between these dates, as I was old enough to remember my mother going to a neighbor's house to watch the episode on television as we didn't have a television of our own. We moved from that neighborhood where she had viewed the television in the neighbor's house in early 1959. Another of Thomas's granddaughters, Valeria Kinney, recalled that he wouldn't stop talking about the car even though the show's host was trying to go to commercial break! I don't know whatever happened to the car, but believe that if he had been born just 50 years later in time, he undoubtedly could have had an illustrious career in the field of automobile design.

Dear Friend:

SMOG is a manufactured article, and must be refined before it is admitted to the air.

Come over and see how this can be done.

Sincerely,

T. S. Culbreath
6653 Loveland St.
Bell Gardens, Calif.

T. S. and his invention, the smogless electric car, circa 1958

Sometime after Martha Emma's death, T. S. married Anna DeShane whom he supposedly met during one of his petition name-gathering campaigns. There's a picture of her and him on the front porch of daughter, Alberta's, house in Miami where they had come for a visit. Once, Alberta took a trip to Los Angeles, and while there discovered that Ann probably needed to move to a residential care facility. According to Barbara Hollowell Block, Alberta arranged for Ann to move into a nursing home. Thereafter, T. S. would get all dressed up in his best clothing and go into town on a street car to visit Ann in the nursing facility. They would walk the grounds of the nursing home together. She passed away 23 May 1961 and is interred at Inglewood Park Cemetery, though I was unable to locate a grave marker in 2013.

From time to time, Thomas Sherman would return to Miami for a visit to daughter, Alberta Anna Bell Culbreath Kinney. One such visit was detailed in the 25 December 1957 issue of The Miami News, "**Grandpa Culbreath Visits Kin – Ex-Miami Builder, 91, Returns For Holidays**" "How come you don't have a train set up near the tree? What's Christmas without a train to play with?"

Ninety-one-year-old T. S. Culbreath, of Bell Gardens, California, asked these questions as he walked into the home of his daughter, Mrs. Alberta Kinney, of 3051 N.W. Sixth Avenue, to spend the holidays with her and other relatives.

As Mr. Culbreath was introduced to a photographer and reporter of The Miami News, it was explained by Mrs. Kinney that "father doesn't hear so well out of one ear." **But He Hears Enough** But he heard enough of the remark to say, "That's nothing, I don't hear so well out of the other ear either."

When the amenities were completed, into his bedroom went Mr. Culbreath and out he came with a homemade "git-fiddle" and a mouth organ and proceeded to dance and sing as he played.

"Made this git-fiddle from a cigar box and a few piano string wires," he explained. "Turned out to be mighty profitable one time, too."

Paid For His Trip "I was traveling from Los Angeles to Miami a few years ago and started playing just for my own amusement. The people took up a collection which amounted to enough to pay for my train trip."

Mr. Culbreath traveled by train this time, also. Took him four days. But he did not enjoy it too much. "I rode in one of those double-decker cars and when it swayed I swore it was going to turn over."

Grampa Culbreath used to live in Miami and was a carpenter and builder. To kill time while visiting 10 years ago – when he was 81 – he added an extra room onto his daughter's home here.

Buys Pool Table On his 91st birthday – November 18 – he bought himself a pool table so he could get some exercise. He carries a hollow cane which can be taken apart and then joined into a regulation sized pool cue stick.

His piercing blue eyes and thick shock of hair match his wonderful humor and energy.

Principal reason for coming here, he said, was to make sure his grandchildren have a Merry Christmas.

I can't vouch for the grandchildren, but after visiting with Mr. Culbreath, it is certain he is going to have one whale of a time during the holidays."

During Thomas Sherman's latter years, his daughter, Edith, and family would take him to Hollywood Park to see the horse races. He liked to be around the action and excitement.

The following obituaries appeared in a Los Angeles paper: "CULBREATH, Thomas Sherman, 95 of 6653 LOVELAND Street, Bell Gardens, died Friday. Services 11 a.m. tomorrow, Chapel of the Chimes, Inglewood Park Cemetery; burial to follow."

"Thomas Culbreath Dies at Age 95 – Memorial services for Thomas Sherman Culbreath, 95, of 6653 Loveland Street, Bell Gardens, were held Monday in the Chapel of the Chimes in Inglewood Park Cemetery; burial followed.

Mr. Culbreath, who died Friday, was born in Illinois and had lived in Bell Gardens 21 years. He was a member of the Baptist Church.

Surviving are three sons, David, of Chatsworth; William, of Davis, and Charles, of Los Angeles; two daughters, Edith Kint, of Bell Gardens; and Alberta Kinney, of Florida; seven grand children and 14 great-grandchildren. Rev. Harry Hobby officiated at the services."

Thomas Sherman Culbreath lived a very full life of 95½ years before his death, 30 March 1962. He was born just 15 years after gold was discovered in California. He grew up in the aftermath of the Civil War, experienced the westward migration first hand, was a part of the industrial revolution, survived the Great Depression and the Dust Bowl, participated in the building boom of Miami during the 1920s, lived through the Spanish American War, both World Wars, the Korean War, and the early days of what would become the Vietnam War. He witnessed the invention of radio, television, the automobile, and telephone. He watched the airline industry grow from its first days of the Wright Brothers experiments on Kitty Hawk Beach to seeing astronauts orbit the earth. He witnessed the revolution in transportation from the ox drawn wagon of his youth, to steam driven farm equipment, to gasoline powered cars and trucks. He learned to write with paper and pencil, and by the end of his life witnessed the dawn of the computer age. What an exciting age to have been alive.

He lived more than 20 years longer than any of his siblings. He lived in more places than one can shake a stick at. When he finally died, 30 March 1962, our family lost a truly great man. Although his body is interred in Inglewood Park Cemetery, Los Angeles, California, his soul lives among us, his family, but his spirit is with his Heavenly Father. Until we meet again!

Two of the houses occupied by T. S. and Martha Emma in Miami between 1926 and 1936, as seen in 2012

Questions:

1. Was he living with his parents in Arkansas between 1880 and 1890?

2. Did he build his house in Bell Gardens and when did he move in to it? Did Martha Emma live in that house?
3. When did he live in the apartment behind Julia's house?
4. What other inventions were created by Thomas Sherman Culbreath other than those outlined in this book?
5. Which Kansas train station would call him to move the train off dead center?
6. In the 1905 Kansas State Census for St. John, Stafford County, Kansas, there is a family No. 238 named John Faulk, the same surname as Thomas Sherman's maternal grandparents. Is it possible this family is related?
7. Where did Thomas Sherman and Martha Emma marry? Is there a marriage certificate somewhere?
8. Where was Marvel, Arkansas? Was it actually Marble, which is located in the northwest part of the state?
9. Did T. S. live in Arkansas with his parents, or did he move with one of his older brothers?
10. How did he meet wife, Martha Emma Carnahan? We know that brothers, George and Logan, both owned land adjacent to Martha Emma's family's land in Stafford County, Kansas, but where was Thomas living which would have allowed him the opportunity to meet Martha Emma?
11. Per the article in The Saint John News, see pg. 192, about T. S. opening a steam laundry in St. John, what other enterprises did T. S. and his brothers introduce in St. John before 1905?
13. Where was the laundry located on the square?
14. Did the laundry have other branches in other cities as was intimated in the article?
15. What was the name of the laundry?
16. How long was the laundry in business?
17. What was meant by "Culbreath's opera house"? Did T. S. have something to do with the construction, operation, or ownership of the opera house in St. John which was inside the Convention Hall? In 2013, we visited the former Convention Hall which was being used as the City of Saint John offices. We were escorted back into the former opera house and shown the old stage and lighting rigs and the famous hand painted curtain which was rolled up for preservation. The area of the opera house was being used as a garage for City vehicles. None of the current employees knew anything of the past ownership or construction of the building.
18. Where did T. S. work while in Miami? Julia Kint Rice Connell recalls seeing him making cement brick near a river and being able to see Indians living nearby.
19. The Hutchinson Foundry and Machine Works Company was stated as being the manufacturers of the jack that opened grain railroad car doors without damaging them. Does this company still exist, and if so, do they have old blueprints of the jack?
20. The Reschke Machine Works Company of Wichita, Kansas was supposedly the manufacturer of the road grader as painted on the machine in the picture. Does the company still exist and if so, do they have old blueprints of the road grader?
21. Does the road grader sold to the Ohio Township of Stafford County, Kansas, still exist lying around somewhere in a junk yard or other location?

Oscar Miles Culbreath

1881-1924

Oscar Miles Culbreath was born 22 August. He was a twin to Arthur Culbreath. On Oscar's World War I Draft Registration Card, he wrote that he was born in 1882, and his grave marker in the Mount Olive Cemetery, Pittsburg, Crawford County, Kansas, also is inscribed with a birth year of 1882, but, his twin brother, Arthur Culbreath's grave marker was inscribed with 1881 as his birth date. So, which brother's record is correct? One thing I'm sure of is that twins are born on the same day. If they were not twins, and the 22 August birthdate is correct for both of them, what is the possibility that they were both born on 22 August, one in 1881 and one in 1882? I find that probability extremely unlikely. At any rate, family tradition states that they were twins. What is known is that Oscar was born in Marvel, Arkansas, though no Marvel appears on a 2013 Arkansas highway map. The closest town to Marvel seems to be Marble, Arkansas, located nearby where his parents and brother, Logan, were known to have lived in the late 1890s.

Oscar first appeared in the 1900 U.S. Federal Census along with brother, Arthur, and parents, Leroy and Mary Ann. They were living in Joplin City, Jasper County, Missouri. Oscar and Arthur were 17 years old. Father, Leroy, was a day laborer, as well as Oscar and Arthur. The family was living at 403 Kentucky Avenue.

In the 13 October 1905 issue of The St. John News, we read, "**A NEW STEAM LAUNDRY** – T. S. Culbreath and Brothers Will Have One in Operation in St. John within Sixty Days And still the new enterprises come! This time it is a new steam laundry, one of the things St. John has been needing for years. Messrs. T. S., S. L., and O. M. Culbreath will put in a nice laundry here. They have already ordered the necessary machinery and the laundry building is under course of construction. The new laundry will be located on the east side of the public square, adjoining Culbreath's opera house on the south. The building will be a two-story frame structure. The lower rooms will be used for the new laundry and the upper rooms will be used for bath rooms. The building will be 32x60 feet.

Mr. T. S. Culbreath informs us that the very best laundry machinery has been ordered and that the business will be in charge of Mr. O. M. Culbreath, an experienced laundryman, who has worked eight years as head laundryman in some of the larger cities of the country. They will also fit up for cleaning and pressing clothes and expect to do as good work in all the branches of their business as is done in Hutchinson, Wichita, Topeka, or any of the larger cities of the state.

The new enterprise will be ready for operation within sixty days. St. John should liberally patronize it."

At the 1910 U.S. Federal Census, Oscar was 27 and had been married for 8 years to Leona Culbreath who was 24. They had 2 daughters: Cleo, 6; and Loraine, 2. Oscar's brother-in-law, Samuel Grace, 18, was living with them in Albano Township, Stafford County, Kansas. Presumably, they were living near brothers, George and Logan, who both had farms in Albano Township. He was born in Texas, though Leona was born in Missouri. They were renting a farm and Oscar indicated his occupation was farmer.

In the 1915 Kansas State Census, they were living in Pratt Township, Pratt County, Kansas. Oscar's wife's name is unclear in the record. It is listed by initials of "V. J." or "U. J." rather than

Leona, as in the 1910 Census. The daughter, Cleo, is listed as "E. C.", aged 11; and daughter, Loraine, was 7.

By the time Oscar completed his 1918 World War I Draft Registration Card, he was living in Pittsburg, Kansas, and working as a self-employed mechanic. The family was living at 809 West Third in Pittsburg. His wife was listed as Leona J. Culbreath. Oscar was described as being medium height and build, with blue eyes and light brown hair.

For the 1920 U.S. Federal Census, we find Oscar and Leona were living at 209 West Third Street, Pittsburg, Crawford County, Kansas. Daughter, Cleo, was 16, and Loraine was 11. Oscar was working on his own account as an auto mechanic in a garage.

There is an entry in the 1924 Tulsa, Oklahoma City Directory for Oscar M. Culbreath and wife, Leona, residing at 1631 East Admiral Boulevard. Oscar was a foreman, but it doesn't indicate in what type of business. Later that same year, Oscar died. There was a record of his death in the Fraternal Order Death Index, 1873-1969, listing his date death as 26 November 1924. He apparently was a member of the International Order of Odd Fellows Rescue Lodge No. 393. His residence was listed as Pittsburg, Crawford County, Kansas. There is also a Find A Grave Memorial No. 87812119 for Oscar Miles Culbreath, located in Mount Olive Cemetery, Pittsburg, Crawford County, Kansas.

Grave marker for Oscar Miles Culbreath, located in Mount Olive Cemetery, Pittsburg, Crawford County, Kansas

Questions:

1. Which year was Oscar born: 1881 or 1882?
2. When and where did he get married?
3. Is the 32x60' wooden 2-story building supposedly constructed on the St. John, Kansas square for the steam laundry still standing in 2013? If so, which building was it and what business is in it now?
4. In what other cities did Oscar work as a laundryman?
5. What happened to the laundry? Did it succeed? By the 1910 U.S. Federal Census, Oscar is working as a farmer.
6. What work was Oscar doing in 1915 Pratt?
7. Did Oscar really work in Tulsa in 1924 as the City Directory suggests?
8. How did he die?
9. What happened to his wife and children after his death?

10. Is there a death certificate or obituary somewhere?
11. There was a letter from an "Aunt Leona" located in Bell Gardens, California, to Alberta Anna Bell Culbreath Kinney in the late 1960s from Los Angeles. Could Oscar's widow be that Aunt Leona?

Arthur Main "Pete" Culbreath

1881-1944

Arthur Main Culbreath, known as Pete, was born with twin brother, Oscar, on 22 August 1881 in Marvel, Arkansas. A check of the 2013 Arkansas highway map does not list a Marvel, but there is a Marble, Arkansas, along the Kings River in Madison County on U.S. highway 412 west of Huntsville. Since his brother, Logan, lived for a while in Bentonville, and his parents, Leroy and Mary Ann Culbreath, lived in Jasper County, near Joplin, Missouri, and both these locations are near to Marble, I'm inclined to think that Marvel may be actually Marble.

Nothing is known about the twins as they were born just 1 year after the 1880 U.S. Federal Census so that the first Census they appear in is 1900, and they were already grown up at that time. Arthur was living in Joplin, Jasper County, Missouri and working as a day laborer. He was living with his family in their own house.

There is a family photograph of Leroy and Mary Ann with their 5 surviving sons taken in Joplin, Missouri. There are no 2 siblings in the photo that look identical, so I'm assuming they were paternal twins.

In an article in The Saint John News, 19 April 1917, we learn that, "St. John Boys to the War – Recruiting Officers From Great Bend Here Monday and Secured Four Recruits for Company C – St. John is likely to be represented at the front by four of her young men—George Bright, Mack Gooing, Joe Walker and Pete (Arthur) Culbreath. Five recruiting officers from Company C, at Great Bend, were here on Monday to secure recruits and they succeeded in getting the 4 young men above mentioned to "sign up". Other young men of the town and vicinity are thinking seriously of enlisting, besides Gilbert Rudge and Chris Swartz, who, we understand, expect to leave Saturday night for Kansas City to make application to join the Marine Corps. They will be accompanied by Harry Youst and another Cimarron boy.

Bright, Culbreath, Walker and Gooing are awaiting orders to appear in Great Bend to be examined. If the boys succeed in getting accepted, they will take with them the very best wishes of the entire community."

We know that Arthur M. Culbreath was successful in being recruited because of the Application for Headstone which details his military service: Private first class, Company C, 137 Infantry. He enlisted 10 April 1917 and was honorably discharged 13 March 1919.

For the 1920 U.S. Federal Census, Arthur was enumerated in the household of his brother, Logan Culbreath, in St. John, Stafford County, Kansas. He was 38, single, and working as a laborer. The industry was unreadable. It appears the family was living at 314 N.W. Fourth.

1925 Kansas State Census showed that Arthur and Ferne were living at 420 North Exchange in St. John, Stafford County, Kansas along with a daughter named Ione. Family records, and his obituary, state his wife was Katherine Massoni. Perhaps "Ferne" is a nickname, a middle name, or an error on the Census record. Arthur listed his occupation as a steam engineer. Perhaps this is in a steam laundry.

In the 1930 U.S. Federal Census, he was again enumerated as living with his brother, Logan, in St. John, Stafford County, Kansas. They were living on either Third Avenue or Second Avenue. The Census record is unclear. Also unclear is Arthur's marital status. The transcribed index states he is widowed, but it also appears he may have been divorced. He was supposedly 26 years old at his first marriage. If that information is true, then he would have married in 1907. He was working as a waiter in a restaurant.

During 1930, there was an "Enrollment of Ex-Service Men of the World War or His Widow and Orphans" taken. Arthur was enrolled with the following information:

Rank at discharge Pravite First Class

Organization Army 35 Divison 137 Inf Co-c

Wounded or injured (in service) or deceased? Gassed, shot, machine gun bullet.
(State fully)

Member of the American Legion? Yes
(Yes or no)

If so, name and number of post Courtney M. Long Post No. 53

It appears Arthur's wounds included being gassed and shot, and perhaps from the wording above, a machine gun bullet remained in his body.

The next information available for Arthur Main Culbreath is his obituary which appeared in The Saint John News 28 December 1944: "**Obituary – Arthur Main Culbreath** – Arthur Main Culbreath, son of Leroy and Mary Culbreath, was born in Marvel, Arkansas, 22 August 1881, and died while at work in St. John, Kansas, 21 December 1944. He was 68 years, 3 months, and 29 days of age at the time of his death.

Pete, as he was known to all of his friends, grew to manhood in Arkansas, coming to St. John, before the First World War and has made this his home since then. He enlisted in the First World War and served two years in Company C, 137 Infantry, 35th Division, in France. While in the service he was seriously injured by being gassed and has never been a well man since that time.

Upon his return from the Army he was later married to Katherine Massoni on 17 December 1934, at Great Bend.

Pete was an obliging friend and used what strength he possessed in serving the community where he lived. He joined heartily in the task of building and equipping the present American Legion Hall in St. John. He was a charter member of the Courtney M. Long Post No. 53 of St. John.

He is survived by his widow, Mrs. Katherine Culbreath; one step-son, Sgt. Edwin Massoni, now in England; one step-daughter, Lt. Iona Wise, of the Army Nurse Corps, believed to be on the Atlantic enroute overseas; one brother, Tom Culbreath, of Garden Plains, California, other relatives and wide circle of friends.

Funeral services were conducted Sunday afternoon, December 24, in the Peacock & Soice Memorial Chapel at Stafford, with Rev. H. C. Atkins in charge. Interment in Fairview Cemetery, St. John."

Back in the Day . . . Chemical weapons in World War I were primarily used to demoralize, injure, and kill entrenched defenders, against whom the indiscriminate and generally slow-moving or static nature of gas clouds would be most effective. The types of weapons employed ranged from disabling chemicals, such as tear gas and the severe mustard gas, to lethal agents like phosgene and chlorine. This chemical warfare was a major component of the first global war and first total war of the 20th century. The killing capacity of gas, however, was limited – only 4 percent of combat deaths were caused by gas. See Wikipedia http://en.wikipedia.org/wiki/Chemical_weapons_in_World_War_I

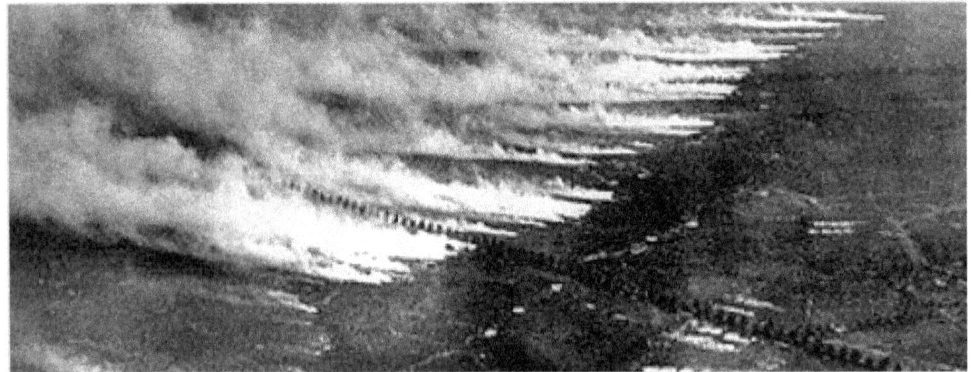

Poison gas attack using cylinders in World War I

Back in the Day . . . The American Legion is a social and mutual-aid veterans' organization including members of the United States Armed Forces. The organization was founded in 1919 by veterans returning from Europe after World War I, and was later chartered as an official American patriotic society under Title 36 of the United States Code. See Wikipedia http://en.wikipedia.org/wiki/American_Legion

The Seal of the American Legion

There's a newspaper announcement of a dismissal from a Great Bend hospital on 15 December 1967: Katherine Culbreath. Could this be the wife of Arthur? After all, she was apparently from Great Bend. If it is her, then she was likely in her 80s at the time of this hospitalization.

Arthur Main Culbreath grave marker in Fairview Cemetery, St. John, Kansas.
Although Arthur died in 1944, he was a veteran of the First World War

Questions:

1. Where exactly was Arthur Main Culbreath born?
2. When exactly did he get married?
3. Did he marry 2 times? One census says he was 26 at his first marriage which would be 1907.
4. Where is he in the 1910 U.S. Federal Census?
5. Why is he shown as single or divorced in the 1930 U.S. Federal Census, when his obituary states he is survived by his wife and step-children?
6. What did he do for a living? One census says he was a waiter in a restaurant.
7. How did he die?

This horse drawn hearse belonged to the Peacock and Soice Funeral Home of Stafford, Stafford County, Kansas. Since they handled the funeral arrangements for Arthur Main Culbreath, there is a slight chance that this hearse was used to transport him to Fairview Cemetery.

Back in the Day . . . How would you like to go back to 1944's food prices? Advertised in <u>The Saint John News</u> for the week of 28 December 1944 we see: Campbell's tomato soup 3 cans for 27 cents; Wheaties were 11 cents a package. Pillsbury mincemeat, a 30 ounce jar, was just 44 cents, and Pillsbury pancake flour was 28 cents for a 3½ pound package.

The Wife of Thomas Sherman Culbreath

Martha Emma Carnahan

1868-1946

Martha Emma Carnahan Culbreath must have had an adventurous spirit to have been married to Thomas Sherman Culbreath. Certainly life was a constant challenge and full of change and creativity. One of her granddaughters, Valeria La Verne Kinney, after looking at a picture of one of the houses that Thomas built for Martha Emma in Miami, remarked that this particular house had been Martha Emma's favorite one and she never wanted to leave it. Surely, she must have loved South Florida as we see by the following poem she wrote about it.

Florida as is:
There is a spot
Way down in Dixie
Where most all the
Winter tourists go
A pleasant spot where velvet breezes blow,
The place where all good sensible people go.
The winters are so fine and for her I pine, on Biscayne Bay she doth recline
Like an amethyst shinning in the sun.
If you go there, she will have your [??] won
Miami under the southlands,
Lonesome Sun.
Mrs. T. S. Culbreath

Life wasn't always easy in Miami, though. For example, during the 1926 hurricane, Martha Emma's oldest daughter, Edith's children tell a story about how Edith, who operated a type of boarding house for single working men, endured the hurricane. During the eye of the hurricane, Martha Emma came walking down the street with her little dog on a leash to see how Edith had fared in the hurricane. Martha Emma didn't have any idea that she was out walking during the eye of the hurricane, which is a lull time with no wind and often accompanied by sunshine. She reached Edith's boarding house, and was there just a short time when the second half of the killer storm hit. Edith and Martha Emma ended up holding the door shut to keep from being blown away. As it was, Edith broke her neck during this monster storm.

Martha Emma sure moved around a lot. She was born in Viola, Illinois, migrated to Kansas with her family and settled in Clear Creek Township, Stafford County, on her family's farmstead. Once she married T. S. she lived in St. John Township, Rose Valley Township, Pratt, Hutchinson, at least 4 places in Wichita, 3 places in Miami, and at least 3 places in Los Angeles making for a total of at least 15 different places. Here she is in her home called Grand View in St. John, Stafford County, Kansas.

Martha Emma Carnahan Culbreath with 3 of her children in front of her house in St. John, Stafford County, Kansas, known as Grand View. Perhaps the children may be Hobart, Harlan, and Alberta.

The following is a one page letter written by Martha Emma Carnahan Culbreath and was in the possession of her youngest daughter, Alberta Anna Bell Culbreath Kinney.

"Bell Gardens, Thursday morning. Dear ones. All today I am too nervous to write. I think everyone everywhere has an ailment, mostly by doctor it is pronounced high blood pressure, but they have lots of other ailments like myself. I am too tired to even pray. Dad Culbreath is out this morn with a life payment petition to try to be a plan perfected like the one Townsend got put

in jail at W.D.C. I don't think it will come to pass. This place needs is where we are is money to pay their bills when they bring in water meters, gas, etc. our electric was turned up yesterday. The electric clock went out ???. We have no clock now. Dad has his old silver watch yet. I look at that if I need time. My nerves are in such a state that I can't write you any more letter and I think the other Culbreath children should send Edith some money to pay her for caring for me. They [??]

When they get to be my age and over Edith said she would get [??]

God has blessed you. We have to dig for what we have this world. So good bye. Mother. You will probably find what became of me if you read the papers. So good bye
Mother"

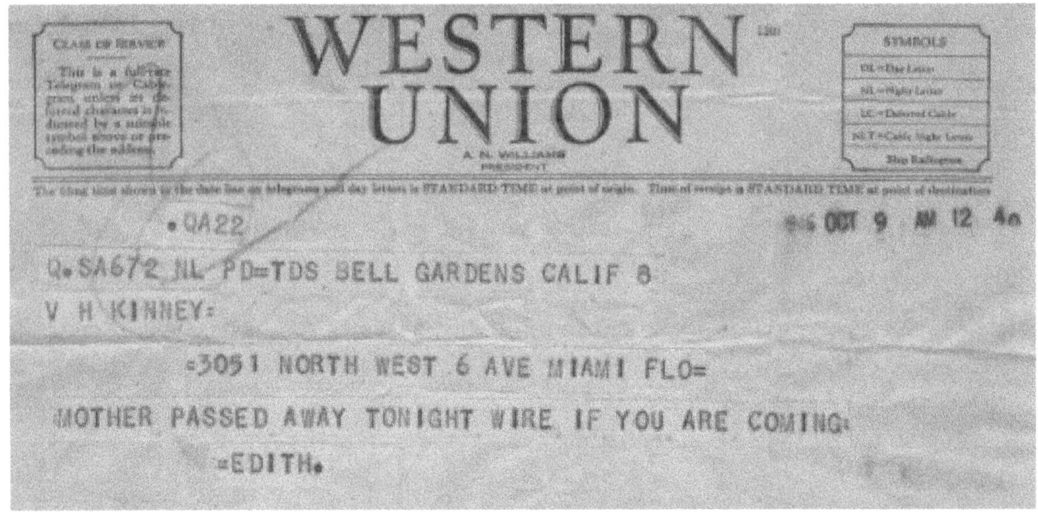

WESTERN UNION

•QA22 1946 OCT 9 AM 12 4n

Q.SA672 NL PD=TDS BELL GARDENS CALIF 8

V H KINNEY:

=3051 NORTH WEST 6 AVE MIAMI FLO=

MOTHER PASSED AWAY TONIGHT WIRE IF YOU ARE COMING:

=EDITH.

Before we had computers, cell phones, or land lines our ancestors communicated quickly with a Western Union telegram. Here's one about the death of Martha Emma Carnahan Culbreath sent to Alberta Culbreath Kinney, 1946.

The following obituary appeared in a Los Angeles paper: "CULBREATH, Martha E., beloved wife of Thomas S. Culbreath; mother of Edith Kint, Alberta Kinney, William H., David C., and Harlan Culbreath; sister of Ruby Davidson, Mabel Stevens and Rev. R. A. Carnahan. Services Saturday, 11 a.m. at Edwards Brothers Colonial Mortuary."

Read more on Martha Emma Carnahan Culbreath on page 282.

The Children of Martha Emma Carnahan and Thomas Sherman Culbreath

Edith Ardella Culbreath

1892-1984

Just 2 years after the marriage of Martha Emma Carnahan and Thomas Sherman Culbreath, their first child was born, Edith Ardella, 21 March 1892, in Stafford County, Kansas.
Her younger brother, Chal, was born in 1893. According to Chal's World War I Draft Registration Card, he was born in St. John, so perhaps Edith was born there as well.

In 1895 and 1900, Edith's family was enumerated in Rose Valley, Stafford County, which was the location of both of her parents' family farms.

In 1910, they were living in Pratt, Pratt County, Kansas. Sometime during her childhood, Edith learned to roller skate according to her daughter, Julia. Her father, T .S. Culbreath, owned a roller skating rink in Pratt. Edith was known to be one of the most frequent skaters. She could skate faster backwards than the others could skate frontwards.

As a teenager, Edith was responsible for cooking for her father's wheat threshing crew out in the fields. She had a portable cook oven and prepared breakfast, then washed up, and started cooking beans for the noon meal. When she wasn't working, she'd rest up on the table in the cook shack.

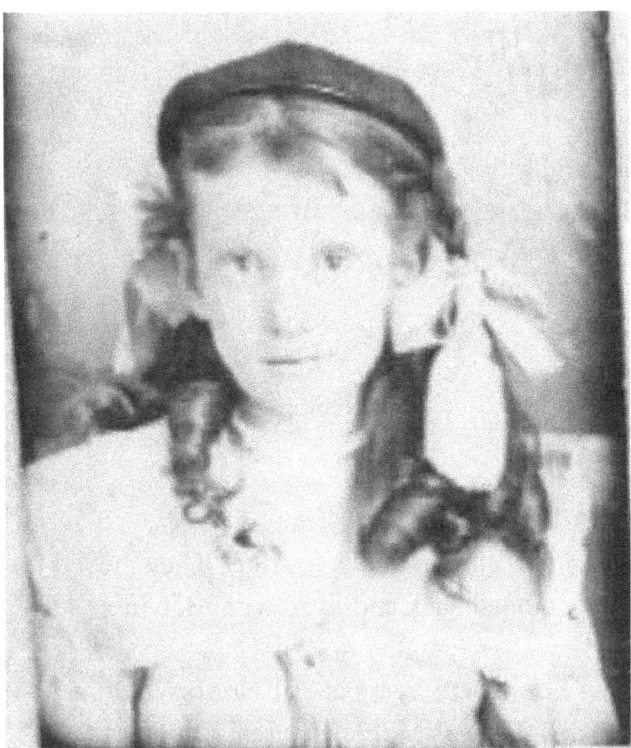

Edith Culbreath, circa 1900

This house, in 2013, was located across the street from the former 122 South Pine Street location of the Culbreath family farmhouse in Pratt.

At the 1915 Kansas State Census, Edith was no longer listed with her family because she had married Melvin Hubert Kint, who was originally from Sewall, Iowa. Melvin's father was Adam Kint. He is buried in Greer Cemetery, Allerton, Iowa. He was known for not taking oaths due to his religious practices. In the 1910 U.S. Federal Census, he was enumerated with his family, aged 21, in Pratt, Pratt County, Kansas. He was a car repairer for the railroad. This is probably where Edith and Melvin met as they both lived in Pratt at 1910 Census time. Edith and Melvin were married on 21 July 1913, before Probate Judge Hudson at the courthouse in Hutchinson, Kansas.

On 1 October 1916, their first child, Julia Lois, was born in the Culbreath family farmhouse in Pratt. Melvin's 1917 World War I Draft Registration Card placed the family at 122 South Pine Street, Pratt. This address was the family home of Edith's parents. Melvin was working as some sort of inspector, either bar or car (the writing is unclear), for the Anthony and Northern Railroad Company. I believe this is the same railroad that Chal worked for as a motorman.

By 1919, the family had moved to Hutchinson, Reno County, Kansas, and were living at 604 7th Avenue East. They stayed here for the 1920 U.S. Federal Census. They had 2 daughters: Julia, 3½ years old; and Pauline 1½ years old. Melvin's job was car repairer for the railroad.

In 1921, while living in Hutchinson, Edith's sister, Alberta Anna Bell Culbreath, returned from Wichita to watch Julia and Pauline while Edith went to the hospital for the birth of her son, Leslie Marvin Kint, 9 September 1921.

Left, Leslie, the baby, Julia, and Pauline Kint, circa 1921
Right, Julia and Pauline Kint, circa 1920

Sometime after Leslie's birth, Melvin lost his job on the railroad due to a strike. They moved to Chicago to work on the railroad, but it was so cold that they moved back and lived with Melvin's parents.

In the 1923 Hutchinson City Directory, Melvin and Edith were living at 301 North Waldron. This was probably after they returned from Chicago. Perhaps this was Melvin's parents' address.

Edith Culbreath and Melvin Kint

The rest of Edith's family had already moved on to Wichita, and they would follow. In 1924, they were living with T. S. and Martha Emma at 1832 South Washington Avenue, Wichita.

The family was listed in the 1925 Kansas State Census living in Wichita. Melvin was working at the Union Stockyards, and Edith was a starcher at a laundry. Their residence was 213 Minneapolis Street, Wichita.

Since they were absent from the 1925-27 Wichita City Directories, and family tradition says they were in Miami, Dade County, Florida during the killer hurricane of 1926, I assume they were probably living in Miami from sometime in 1925 through late 1927. Their daughter, Julia Kint, in a 2010 interview stated that they operated a dormitory for working men in Miami. They were there when the hurricane of 1926 hit. Edith broke her neck holding the door closed against the storm. Also while in Miami, Melvin worked as a night watchman on the skyscrapers that were being built in Miami during the building boom of the 1920s.

At 1928, the family was back in Wichita and Melvin was working as a janitor for the Union Stock Yards Company in Wichita. Their home address was 1812 Arkansas Avenue.

By 1930, Melvin had moved up at the stock yards and was now a painter. Edith had begun to work at the American Laundry. The 1930 U.S. Federal Census noted that she was a starcher. A curious thing is that in the 1930 Wichita City Directory, Melvin's residence was 1840 Arkansas Avenue, while Edith's was 930 North St. Paul Avenue. Perhaps this was the year they moved to the St. Paul address which we know they were at in later years.

In both the 1936 and 1937 Wichita City Directories, Edith was a presser at American Laundry and Dry Cleaning Company. Julia was a housekeeper, and Melvin was a laborer for the Wichita Union Stock Yards and Company. They were living at 930 North Saint Paul Avenue.

In the 1938 Directory, Melvin continued at his previous address and job, but daughter, Julia was at a different residence: 3424 East Waterman. Perhaps this is the time when Julia returned to Wichita from working in her Uncle Hobart's restaurant in Sacramento, to complete her high school education. Julia stated in a 2010 interview that after her return from Sacramento, around age 20 or 22, she lived with a woman named Virginia for whom she had previously babysat for. Julia went to East High School, then North High School to finish up. Later, Julia would name her son, David, after Virginia's son that she babysat for in Wichita.

In the 1940 U.S. Federal Census, Melvin was a painter at the Wichita Stock Yards, Edith a press lady at American Laundry, and Leslie was painting.

By 1941, Melvin was working in construction for the W.U.S.Y. Company, and he continued there in 1943, as per the Wichita City Directory.

In the 1943 Wichita City Directory, son, Leslie, was living with Melvin and Edith, but he was married to Gwen. He was working at Beechcraft. As this was the middle of World War II, it was common for families to live together as the economy was difficult.

Near the end of World War II, Edith and Melvin moved to California. After the war, in October 1945, Melvin and Edith moved in with Edith's father, Thomas Sherman Culbreath. Her mother, Martha Emma, had suffered a stroke and T. S. needed help. So, they lived in the Bell Gardens house at 6653 Loveland. Melvin worked as a roofer.

Edith's daughter, Pauline, and great granddaughter, Barbara Hollowell, moved to the Bell Gardens house. Thomas Sherman had a chicken coop with an incubator for baby chicks. He converted this into a bedroom for Pauline and Barbara. Now, 4 generations were living at the same address. They all continued living together after Martha Emma's death in October 1946.

When Pauline's husband was discharged from the Navy, they moved to Venice where a detached garage was converted into a bedroom for Edith and Melvin. Soon, they moved from the garage into a house in Mar Vista. They decided they needed to be closer to T. S. as he needed someone to look after him. So, Edith and Melvin rented out their Mar Vista house and then rented a house for themselves on Suva Street near T. S. in Bell Gardens.

Once Melvin and Edith stopped driving, they built an apartment on the back of Edith's daughter, Julia's, house. Melvin and Edith lived in the apartment until their deaths.

Melvin passed away at 84 years old. His last residence was in Maywood, Los Angeles County, California.

Edith lived 12 years longer and died in Los Angeles, 3 January 1984. She is interred at a small cemetery in Bell Gardens, perhaps known as Park Lawn Memorial Park.

Daughter, Julia Kint, married Jack Amonds Rice. They had 2 children: David Rice, born 1948, and Julia Karen, born 1941.

After the family moved to Los Angeles, Jack died. After Jack's death, Julia married Hubert W. Connell, in 1962.

David married Susan and had 2 children: Corrina Maria, who in 2010 had a Ph.D. in holistic medicine, and practiced acupuncture. His second child was Graham Leslie Rice, who, in 2010, worked as a forest ranger fire fighter in Truckee, California.

2013, Los Angeles, California, Julia Karen Rice and brother, David Rice, daughter and son of Julia Kint Rice Connell, with cousin, Barbara Kinney Black

Left, Barbara Hollowell Block, grand niece of Julia Kint Rice Connell, 2013, Los Angeles, California
Right, Julia Kint Rice Connell, age 97, in 2013, at her home in Los Angeles, California

Julia was still living at the time of this writing. She turned 97 years old on 1 October 2013. She is officially the longest living Culbreath since the 1800s.

During a 2010 interview with Julia, I took shorthand notes of the many stories and memories that seemed to gush out of her like a flood. Rather than try to put these into chronological order, I've elected to list them in bullet point fashion, grouping them under geographical locations where they supposedly occurred. I invite further clarification from readers more informed than myself.

St. John, Stafford County

- Once Julia went with her grandmother, Martha Emma, to St. John. They were out by the Carnahan homestead and Martha Emma said, "One day I held all those trees in my apron. I planted all those trees." I believe she was referring to the Carnahan timber claim.
- Once, Julia was out in a field in the countryside and she and her grandmother, Martha Emma, had to go under a barbed wire fence to get at the wild plums that were growing there. They were somewhere near the former Carnahan homestead.

Hutchinson

- Julia's aunt, Alberta Culbreath, gave Julia money to buy her first violin for Christmas when Julia was 7 years old.

Possibly the Carnahan timber claim

- When Alberta came to babysit Julia and Pauline while Edith was in the hospital giving birth to Leslie, Julia and a friend went down into some culverts beside the railroad tracks. Alberta went after her with a switch.
- Julia's Grandmother Kint lived in Hutchinson. Once a rooster tried to attack Julia through the fence. He had ahold of

her skirt. This incident occurred near the Brethren Church which they attended as children.

- When she was 5 years old, she recalled Thomas brought a model to their house of a piece of machinery he planned to build or had already built. It was electric. She remembered he plugged it in to the wall in her house. This would have been around 1921. Thomas had invented the road grader a few years previously and was at that time marketing it from Wichita. Perhaps this is the model she saw. It is unclear whether the road grader was operated by electricity or not. We do know that the smogless car he invented later in life was electric. It is possible that earlier inventions were also electric.

Chicago

- Julia said she lived in Chicago for 3 months while her father, Melvin Kint, was out of work. The school she attended would put saw horses up at either end of the street when it was time for recess.
- They lived in an apartment and they had to have an empty milk bottle in order to get another bottle of milk. Julia broke the bottle when she stepped on the porch, but the milk distributor delivered her milk in spite of the loss of the bottle.
- Once, Edith and her sister-in-law, went to see an evangelist named Billy Sunday preach in Chicago. The evangelist was a friend from their church.

Wichita

- Julia served as the flower girl for Alberta Anna Bell Culbreath and Vernon Haven Kinney's wedding. Alberta had a special doll she had treasured from her childhood. Julia believed she would get the doll if she did a good job in the wedding. When the doll was not given to Julia, she concluded that she hadn't done a good job as flower girl. In reality, the doll was being saved to be passed on to Alberta's daughter.
- Julia referred to a place where they lived in Wichita, possibly 930 North St. Paul Street, as the "½ acre". The family grew a vegetable garden. Also, someone willed another ½ acre to them. It sounded like this made for a full acre in the city.
- She described the property as having cottonwood trees in the yard between which they strung a hammock.
- Once, Julia had a ukulele or a banjo and she would not stop playing it, so Pauline busted it over Julia's head because she was tired of hearing it.
- During the fall, Julia would "cold pack" vegetables. This involved putting canned fruit into a cellar located on the "½ acre."
- The house on Washington Boulevard where Martha Emma and T. S. lived right before leaving for Florida, had large trees in the front yard.
- Julia recalled that her family lived over the Butts Building in Wichita. A hot tamale vendor would come by at night. The foyer of the building was all tiled and when they tore it up, Martha Emma put the tiles into a box and the children all played with them. In 2013 when we visited Wichita, we saw the Butts Building. It had a garage door in the right front side of the building. An article in The Wichita Daily Eagle noted that Mr. Butts had turned the first floor of his

building into the first Buick car dealership in Wichita. Perhaps he replaced the tile floor with something more appropriate for the cars to park upon.

- The street froze over and Julia and friends would then ice skate on the street.
- At night, she remembered Thomas would go out of the house and clap wood together to get the crows out of the trees which were in front of the Washington Boulevard house.
- Once when she was on the porch of the Washington Boulevard house before going to Florida, it was thundering and raining. T. S. told her that God was moving furniture around in heaven.
- Julia could hear the ice cream truck from the back of the house on Washington Boulevard. She'd go out the back door and T. S. would come around the side with an ice cream cone for her.

Miami

- In the spring of 1923, or there about, Julia traveled to Florida with her family. Julia thought that Martha Emma and Thomas Sherman went to Florida first; then Julia and Edith both followed. Census and City Directory records indicate that T. S. and Martha Emma moved to Florida around 1925. Perhaps there was a trip there before they moved.
- When Julia went to Miami for the first time, there was a submarine in Biscayne Bay and she was allowed to go onboard.
- On the way to Florida, they had to cross the Mississippi River at Vicksburg, Mississippi on a barge being used as a ferry. On the return trip to Kansas, a bridge had been built.
- This first trip to Florida was made in an old Ford with side curtains. When a storm came up in Georgia, Melvin struggled to get the curtains in place; but the storm stopped before he was successful.
- On this same trip, Julia was hanging over the side and watching him change a flat tire when she heard him utter a bad word.
- She recalled they ran over a cow in Georgia. Also, it seemed that every time Edith got in the back seat, something bad happened.
- On one trip, the water they drank had alum in it, so they all bought sodas to counteract the alum.
- Once she remembered being in the Florida Everglades on U.S. Highway 41.
- At one time, she lived in the apartments located across the street from Alberta and Vernon Kinney's house on N.W. 6th Avenue. Son, David, threw rocks at the giant rats that were all over the place. They then moved into the tenement apartments, possibly the ones next door to Alberta.
- She remembers a tragic experience when a neighbor of Alberta's backed up his car over his own child and killed it.
- After a hurricane had come through Miami, Vernon took her to Key West over the causeway. Perhaps during the same trip to Key West, she recalled being on a glass bottom boat.
- Again, after a hurricane had passed, Alberta told her to go look for a house with its roof still on. She recalled living in a Miami subdivision known as West Little River near 79 Street. Her house number was 2233. That was about August 1951. They lived there until they left for Los Angeles, 2 weeks before Christmas.
- She recalled Martha Emma and Thomas living in or near an orange grove in their Miami home. She also said they grew tomatoes.

- She remembered living in an apartment near Biscayne Bay about 60 Street and N.E. Second Avenue. This was near the end of World War II. She lived there with her husband, Jack.

Los Angeles

- At Christmas 1951, Julia and her family moved to California.
- On her first visit to Los Angeles, sometime during the late 1920s, Uncle Chal treated her to her first elevator ride.
- At one time, her family lived in Culver City across from a Hollywood studio. She thought it was called MGM.

Daughter, Pauline Kint, married George Arthur Hollowell and gave birth to 2 children: Barbara Hollowell Block and Kent Hollowell. Son, Kent, born in 1947, suffered a high fever at a tender age which left him in a delicate state. He still lives in Sunnyvale, California.

Left, George Hollowell, Pauline Kint Hollowell, and Barbara Hollowell
Right, Paula (Pauline) Culbreath Kint Dyer, and her 2 grandsons, children of Barbara Hollowell and Carl Block: left, David Block, and right, Darren Block, Christmas 2010, Los Angeles, California

After a divorce, Pauline later married Roland Dyer. She worked at Lockheed, soldering and cutting fiberglass. She officially changed her name from Pauline to Paula Dyer.

She is pictured here with two of her grandsons at Christmas 2010. She passed away in 2013.

Pauline's daughter, Barbara, married Carleton Block. They had 2 sons, Pauline's grandsons.

In a 2010 interview, Julia recalled that when her brother, Leslie, moved to Arizona, he lived in Tuscon at one time and sold Singer sewing machines. Although he spoke Spanish, he still used an interpreter who was a Mexican American, when selling the sewing machines to customers. He learned Spanish in Mexico by the total emersion in the culture method.

In Leslie's obituary of 21 April 2011, originally published on the Internet at www.melcherchapelofroses.com we read: "Les, 89, of Mesa Arizona, passed away 21 April 2011. He was born in Hutchinson, Kansas on 9 September 1921. He married his childhood sweetheart Gwendolyn (deceased) on 12 April 1942, and moved to Arizona in 1947. Les was the proud father of three daughters: Andrea Gibson, Leslie Mangino (deceased), and Karen Smith. He welcomed in 9 grandchildren, 18 great-grandchildren, and 8 great-great-grandchildren to his clan. He was a World War II Navy veteran, Beech aircraft radio electronics expert, businessman, contractor, realtor, inventor, and much more. Les provided love and encouragement to all of his family and will be missed by everyone he touched in life."

Questions:

1. What things did Leslie invent?
2. Where did he do his Navy military service?
3. Where was Edith born: in St. John or on the farm in Rose Valley?
4. When did Edith and Melvin live in Miami? Was it 1925-1928? Family tradition says they were there during the 1926 killer hurricane and that Edith broke her neck during the storm.

David Chalmers Culbreath

1893-1987

The first-born son of Martha Emma Carnahan and Thomas Sherman Culbreath was David Chalmers Culbreath. It has been suggested he also had the middle name of Sherman. He was born 25 May 1893, in St. John, Stafford County, Kansas.

His family was enumerated in both the 1895 Kansas State Census and the 1900 U.S. Federal Census in Rose Valley Township, Stafford County, Kansas. Thomas' brothers, George W. and Sneed Andrew Logan Culbreath, both had farms in Rose Valley Township. It's unclear where T. S. and Martha Emma lived.

By the 1905 Kansas State Census, the family was living in St. John, Stafford County, and Chal was aged 11. In the 1910 U.S. Federal Census, they had relocated to Pratt Township, Pratt County, Kansas. It was here in Pratt that Chal married Irmah M. Heaton, on 6 January 1916. Chal was 22 years old.

The Hutchinson News ran an article in an edition dated Friday, 11 July 191[??] which announced: "Chal Culbreath has taken a position on the Anthony and Northern. He has been assigned to a run on the motor passenger car between Pratt and Kinsley." Although the date is unreadable in the copy, we know from his 1917 World War I Draft Registration Card, that he was already a motorman on the Kinsley to Pratt line for A.P.N. Railroad. His residence at that time was in Kinsley, Edwards County, Kansas. He was described as medium height and build with gray eyes and brown hair

Left, In a small museum in Kinsley, sits this train engine of the era and from the line that Chal worked for. Perhaps he even drove this particular engine.
Right, a prairie chicken

The 1920 U.S. Federal Census indicated that Chal and Irmah had a son named Jack who was 2 years old. They were living in Kinsley on Moss Avenue. Chal was a conductor.

May 9, 19[??] Edition of The Hutchinson News, in an article entitled "**Pheasants So Numerous Are Destroying Crops – Pratt State Fish Hatchery Started Game and Now Sportsmen are Using Guns --** ….. Chal Culbreath, motorman on the motor car plying on the Anthony and Northern between Pratt and Kinsley, reports great droves of prairie chickens and pheasants seen in the sand hills every day. They are much more numerous than ever known in that vicinity."

Sometime before 1930, Chal relocated to Los Angeles, California. He was the first of the Culbreaths to move to Los Angeles. According to his niece, Julia Kint, he went to Wichita to say good-bye to the family and announce that he was moving to Los Angeles. As T. S. and Martha Emma were still living in Wichita as late as 1925, we can imagine that Chal moved to Los Angeles sometime between 1920 when he was enumerated in the Census living in Kinsley, and 1925 before T. S. and Martha Emma moved to Florida.

According to Chal's grandniece, Barbara Hollowell Block, he first had slot machines in casinos located in Los Angeles. One of the mayors elected in Los Angeles went on a campaign to clean up the City's casinos and most of the owners then moved their operations to Las Vegas. Apparently, Chal didn't move to Las Vegas, rather he began repairing something: most likely radios.

In the 1930 U.S. Federal Census, he was living in his own home valued at $7,000. Of course he had a radio since he either owned or worked in a store which sold them. He was a radio salesman. His son, Jack, was then 12 years old. No other children were listed. Chal's grandniece, Julia Kint Rice Connell, stated that Chal worked for Philco Appliances. It's unclear if this was a company name, or if the appliance store which Chal owned known as D. C. Appliances was a Philco representative.

In the 1933 Los Angeles City Directory, D. C. Culbreath's address was 4573 West Pico Boulevard.

There is a family photo that is entitled "Chal and Dad C. [Culbreath], Cuba, 1935". According to Barbara Hollowell Block, this trip to Cuba for a sales convention was a reward from the company Chal worked at for having sold the most Philco radios.

In the 1938 Los Angeles City Directory, David Chalmers Culbreath's address was 1210 Mullen Avenue. His employment was listed as electric appliances at 4137 West Pico Boulevard. A separate entry appeared for his wife, Irmah Culbreath, who was working at Sears Roebuck and Company, while her home address was 1210 Mullen Avenue. Of interest, there is a Mrs. Leona Culbreath, living at 1830 East 71st listed. In a letter from Alberta Culbreath Kinney to her family members informing them of their brother, Hobart's death in 1965, she refers to "Aunt Leona whom she corresponds with". I wonder who Aunt Leona is and if this Mrs. Leona Culbreath in the phone directory is the same as Aunt Leona Alberta references. Perhaps she is the widow of Oscar Culbreath.

At the 1939 Los Angeles City Directory, David's occupation was radio, and his address was the work location at 4137 West Pico Boulevard. Irmah, on the other hand, had a separate entry with a residence of 1822 Crenshaw Boulevard.

In the 1940 U.S. Federal Census, we find David C. Culbreath was the respondent to the Census taker, and we find he was living at 1316½ Sixth Avenue, Los Angeles, California and married to Ida B. Culbreath with a step daughter of Jimmie Eberly and a brother-in-law of Homer D. Walton. It stated that he lived in Los Angeles in 1935 as well. Ida B. was born in Texas as well as the stepdaughter and brother-in-law. David's work was manager and owner of a radio shop, and Ida's was assistant manager of the radio shop. Jimmie was a seamstress finisher for a department store, and Homer D. Walton was a sales clerk in the radio shop.

In a separate entry for the 1940 U.S. Federal Census, Irmah M. Heaton Culbreath, and son Jack C. Culbreath, were living in the household of Irmah's mother, Clara E. Heaton, at 1822 Crenshaw Boulevard, Los Angeles, California. Irmah was divorced from David Sherman Chalmers Culbreath. Also living in the house were various sons and daughters of Clara Heaton along with their families. Irmah was a clerical clerk for a department store, while Jack was a porter for the National Park.

So, David and Irmah probably divorced about 1939. David then married Ida Bea who was also divorced. Ida was listed in the 1935 Houston, Texas City Directory with former husband, William E. Eberly and was living at 724 East 11th. Her husband was a sanitary inspector.

Later, Barbara Hollowell Block stated that Irmah took Jack to Wichita and they lived with Chal's sister, Edith, and her husband, Melvin Kint. Edith's children, Julia and Pauline, reported that Jack wore silk underwear while they had to wear flour sack underwear. Oh the observations children make and how they remember such inconsequential facts for so long!

David's son, Jack, enlisted in the Army on 30 November 1942, in Alameda, California. He was a private in the Infantry. His enlistment indicated he had completed 4 years of college and was single.

According to Chal's grandniece, Barbara Hollowell Block. Jack became a forest ranger and lived in Washington State.

Meanwhile, back in Los Angeles, Chal and Bea had moved to Chatsworth and lived on Comanche Trail.

We see that Chal and Ida Bea probably treated themselves to a Hawaiian cruise as they are listed on a Honolulu, Hawaii, Passenger and Crew List for the ship, Lurline. It departed Honolulu on 3 June 1951.

In 1970, Chal was mentioned in the obituary of sister, Alberta Anna Bell Culbreath Kinney, as residing in Chatsworth, Los Angeles County, California.

Barbara Hollowell Block recalled that at Ida's death in 1971, her daughter, Jimmie, came for the funeral. She told Chal that if he could get out of bed and walk over to her, then she would take him to live in her house in Texas.

According to the U.S. Social Security Death Index, Chal died at age 94 in Walker County, Texas. His last residence was in the zip code area of 77340 Huntsville.

He is interred in Forest Lawn Memorial Park, 6300 Forest Lawn Drive, Los Angeles, California. This branch of Forest Lawn is actually located at Griffith Park. He's lying in the Eternal Love section of the cemetery next to his second wife, Ida Bea Culbreath.

Left, David Chal Culbreath grave marker in the Eternal Love section of Forest Lawn Cemetery, Los Angeles, 2013
Right, Ida Bea Culbreath grave marker

Questions:

1 What was the exact name of the train line which Chal worked for?
2. Did Chal have an additional middle name of Sherman?
3. Where did he live in Kinsley?
4. Where was Chal during the 1915 and 1925 Kansas State Censuses?
5. When did David and Irmah get divorced?
6. What happened to Irmah after the divorce?

Hobart William Culbreath

1897-1964

Hobart William Culbreath was the third child born to Thomas Sherman and Martha Emma Carnahan Culbreath, 18 March 1897, in Stafford County, Kansas.

Hobart in the early 1900s, photo taken at Mrs. O'Neal's Studio, St. John, Stafford County, Kansas

In 1900, he lived with his family in Rose Valley Township, Stafford County, Kansas. In the 1905 Kansas State Census, his family was located in St. John, Stafford County, and from 1910-1915, the family was in Pratt Township, Pratt County, Kansas.

His 17 June 1917 World War I Draft Registration Card stated he was of medium build and height, with blue eyes and red hair. His address was Rt. 1, Cullison, Kansas.

His grave marker lists his World War I military service as Private, 164 Depot Brigade, Kansas.

At the 1920 U.S. Federal Census, he was working as a laborer and living in the household of Harry Rose in Richland Township, Pratt County, Kansas.

In 1925, the 28-year-old Hobart appeared in the Sacramento, California City Directory as an apprentice. In the 1926 Sacramento Directory, we see he was still an apprentice at S. P. Company. His home address was 804 G. Of interest, there was a wife named Alice listed, though family history tells us his wife's name was Dessie. In the 1927 Sacramento Directory, he was a mechanic living at 2330 24th. He continued to be listed at the same address and working as either a mechanic or machinist through the 1933 directory. In 1934, he was listed at the same home address, but his occupation was now "restaurant". They owned a restaurant which Dessie managed, while Hobart did farming. The address of the restaurant was 2433 21st in the 1940 Sacramento City Directory.

Hobart sent for his nieces, Pauline and Julia Kint, and said that he would pay for their college education. Hobart and his wife, Dessie, did not have children. They owned a road-side restaurant, and after the lunch crowd left each day, according to Julia, Dessie would sit on the counter and drink and smoke. Hobart did combining or other agricultural work on a farm outside of town. After a while, when it became apparent that Julia and Pauline weren't going to go to college, rather they were working in the restaurant, Martha Emma asked Hobart to send Julia back to Wichita so she could complete her high school education. Julia was already 20 years old by that time which would have been around 1936.

The Sacramento City Directory entries for Hobart from 1936-1941 continue to list his occupation as restaurant. In 1943, he was listed as a farmer.

Sometime during the late 1940s or 1950s, Hobart's sister, Alberta Anna Bell Culbreath, got a small travel trailer and made a trip out to California to see Hobart. She commented that the restaurant made delicious pies.

Apparently, Hobart and Dessie never had any children. Hobart met a violent death on 26 August 1964 in Yolo County, California. This transcript of the following letter explained the circumstances.

"Miami, Florida, February 5, 1965 – To those that receive this letter, I hope you will forgive me for making carbon copies. I received a letter today in answer to one that I wrote and I am copying it to send to you. I want to send one to Chal, Edith and Harlan, also Aunt Leona, as she writes to me. This letter is from F. D. Monroe, Sheriff, County of Yolo, Woodland, California. He is also the Coroner of that County. The letter is as follows:

Dear Mrs. Kinney:

In regards to your letter of 26 Janaury 1965, requesting information about the death of your brother, Hobart William Culbreath. Your brother was hit by a train on his way to work, on the morning of Wednesday, 26 August 1964, approximately two blocks from his home, at the Southern Pacific Railroad crossing. The pick-up in which he was the driver went through the signal arm and onto the track in the path of the coming train.

It was thought by witnesses and the Dixon Police Department, that your brother did not hear the signals and that the sun was in his eyes.

Your brother was taken by ambulance to the Woodland Memorial Hospital in Woodland, California, where he was x-rayed and treated for various injuries, but his condition became more severe and he was pronounced dead at 10:40 a.m., 26 August 1964.

Burial for your brother was at Dixon Cemetery on 28 August 1964, the Milton Carpenter Funeral Home, Dixon, California.

We are sorry you were not notified sooner about your brother's death, but it is the responsibility of this office to notify the next of kin, which was his wife.

If this office can be of any further assistance in the future, please let us know.

Yours truly, F. D. Monroe, Sheriff-Coroner, Yolo County, Roger G. Smith, Deputy Coroner."

Hobart's grandniece, Barbara Hollowell Block, said he was a very sweet man and that he was hard of hearing. Perhaps his hearing loss is what caused him to move across the tracks in the path of the oncoming train. We may never know.

Hobart is interred in Dixon Cemetery, Dixon, Solano County, California. His Find A Grave Memorial No. is 46697934. The cemetery is also known as Silveyville Cemetery District.

Left, Hobart Culbreath's grave marker in Dixon Cemetery, Dixon, Solano County, California. Right, Dessie Marie Musgrove Culbreath's grave marker in Dixon Cemetery, Dixon, Solano County, California

Dessie Culbreath herself lived just 13 months after Hobart's death. She, too, is interred in the Dixon Cemetery. Her Find A Grave Memorial No. is 46697933.

Questions:

1. Where did he meet Dessie and when were they married?
2. Did Hobart have an obituary in a local newspaper or funeral card?
3. Did Hobart attend his father, Thomas Sherman Culbreath's, funeral in 1962 Los Angeles? If so, there's no indication in the guest book.
4. Why did he apparently give up the auto mechanic business to return to farming?
5. What did he do in World War I and where did he serve?
6. Who was Aunt Leona that Alberta referenced in the letter she sent to her siblings regarding Hobart's death? Is she possibly the widow of Alberta's Uncle Oscar Culbreath? If so, Leona would have probably been in her 80s at the time the letter was written in 1965. In the 1938 Los Angeles City Directory, there is a listing for Mrs. Leona Culbreath, living at 1830 East 71st listed. In a letter from Alberta Culbreath Kinney to her family members informing them of their brother, Hobart's death, she refers to "Aunt Leona whom she corresponds with". Who is Aunt Leona? Is Mrs. Leona Culbreath in the 1938 phone directory the same as Aunt Leona whom Alberta references in her letter?

Charles Harlan Culbreath

1902-??

Born in Stafford County, Kansas in 1902, Charles Harlan Culbreath, was the last son born to Martha Emma Carnahan and Thomas Sherman Culbreath. According to his niece, Julia Kint Rice Connell, as a child, Harlan, and younger sister, Alberta, were buddies. One day when they were living in an upstairs place, Martha Emma shouted that they were making noise, but Harlan blamed his sister, Alberta, claiming she was making the noise behind the piano.

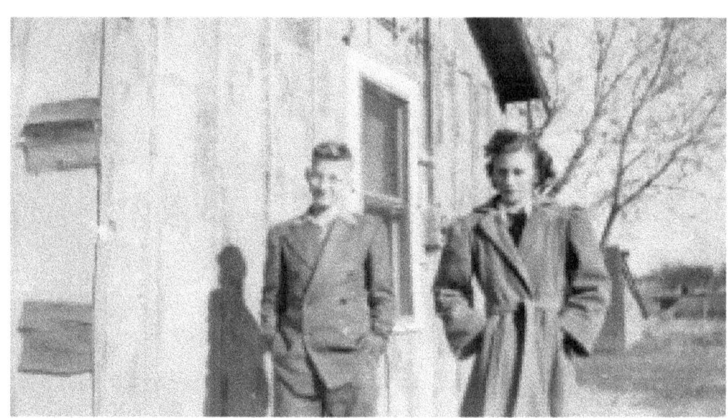

Harlan and wife Dollie Culbreath

Harlan Culbreath

He grew up in St. John and Pratt, and relocated to Hutchinson, Reno County, Kansas around 1919 where he worked as an auto mechanic for the Taylor Motor Company. He lived with his family at 322 Third Avenue East in Hutchinson.

At age 18, he again followed his family to Wichita, Sedgwick County, Kansas, where he became a machinist in the auto industry.

In the 1924 Topeka City Directory, we find that Harlan was living in the capitol of Topeka then, and had married Dolly Elliott. They were renting their residence at 2027 Lincoln.

In the 1926 Topeka City Directory, Harland had become a department manager for Badders Motor Company. His residence was on RFD 27 at 1147.

Left, Harlan was a department manager for Badders Motor Company, 1926 Topeka, Kansas
Right, One of the cars that Harlan painted

Niece, Julia, recalled Harlan living in a small house in Topeka which had a garage with 3 vertical doors each with 4-pane windows in the top. She also recalled he had pick-up trucks. In 1927, he was listed residing at 19th & Bowman.

In the 1929 Wichita City Directory, Harlan was still a service manager, but for H. H. Edsall.

Now at the 1930 U.S. Federal Census, the stock market crash had occurred, but Harlan seems to have been unaffected. At 28 years old, he was still living at 1901 Bowman Court, in his own home valued at $2,000. He had a radio, a job as an auto mechanic, and 2 children had joined the family: Dorothy L., 5; and Charles, 3.

In 1931, there was a change in his employment. He became a mechanic for the Capital Gas and Electric Company, a job he apparently kept through at least 1935, even though his address changed in 1933 to 3415 West 19th.

At the 1940 U.S. Federal Census, Harlan was living at 1266 Medford Avenue in his own house which was valued at $5,000. We see that Harlan completed 1 year of high school, while his wife had completed 3 years. They lived in the same house in 1935. Daughter, Dorothy, was 15, while son, Charles Harlan, was 13. Harlan was now a furnace repairman at Capital Gas. The Topeka City Directory, however, stated his occupation was a pipe fitter for the Gas Service Company. I wonder if he had 2 jobs, or 2 different descriptions of the same job.

By 1942, he had become a city inspector. After the Second World War, in 1946, he was a "splty mn," whatever that stood for. The index of abbreviations in the Topeka City Directory said that "spl" was "special." There wasn't any listing for "splty" or for "ty". The abbreviation "mn" was for "man."

Family tradition says that he relocated to Los Angeles and worked with his brother, Chal, in his appliance store.

By his sister, Alberta Anna Bell Culbreath Kinney's, death in 1970, Harlan, and wife Dollie, were living in Arizona. He would have been 68 at that time.

Harlan's grandchildren

Questions:

1. What did Harlan do after he moved to Los Angeles? Some family members say he worked with Chal. If so, what was he doing?

2. When did he move to Arizona? Where did he live there?

3. When did Harlan and Dollie die and where are they buried?

4. Were there obituaries about their deaths?

5. Are any of their children or grandchildren still living? If so, who and where?

Alberta Anna Bell Culbreath

1903-1970

The youngest child to survive of Martha Emma Carnahan and Thomas Sherman Culbreath was Alberta Anna Bell Culbreath, born 11 August 1903, in St. John, Stafford County, Kansas. The birth took place in a large Victorian farmhouse the family called Grandview.

The house in St. John, Stafford County, Kansas, where Alberta was born, called Grand View, 1903

Blonde-haired Alberta was recorded with her family in the 1905 Kansas State Census living in St. John. Here's the 1905 Productions of Agriculture compiled as part of the Kansas State Census.

As part of the 1905 Kansas State Census there was a Schedule of Agriculture: General Statistics relating to Farms, Productions of Agriculture, etc. There are 4 families for whom this data was collected.

Column 1 - D.S. Carnahan (grandfather of Alberta) and W.H. Stevens (uncle of Alberta)
Column 2 - G.W. Culbreath (uncle of Alberta)
Column 3 - S.L. Culbreath (uncle of Alberta)
Column 4 - E.S. Davison (uncle of Alberta)

	1	2	3	4
2. Total number of acres in farm, whether owned or rented (including all outlying or separate meadow, pasture, woodlots, etc., pertaining thereto)	320	320	160	480
3. Number of acres of unimproved land March 1, 1905; i.e., land which has never been plowed or mown, and land now grown up to trees and shrubs.	95	52	60	80
4. Number of acres of improved land March 1, 1905, including all	225	268	100	400

	1	2	3	4
not reported as unimproved.				
5. Number of acres under irrigation.	--	--	--	--
6. Source of water-supply: Stream, well, or storm-water reservoir.	--	--	--	--
7. Depth of well.	--	--	--	--
8. Power used in lifting water.	--	--	--	-
Number of acres of land under fence and not under fence				
9. Acres under fence	160	160	160	280
10. Acres not under fence	160	160	--	200
11. Total number of acres	320	320	160	480
Fences – Number of rods and cost per rod				
12.-15. = Stone, Rail, Board, or Hedge	--	--	--	--
16. Wire Fence	480-20	640-18	800-16	1530-17
17. Value of entire farm (including all owned or leased land contained therein, together with the value of the buildings and other permanent improvements).	8,000	3,000	3,500	8,000
18. Value, March 1, 1905, of all the buildings on the farm.	500	1,000	400	2,000
19. Value, March 1, 1905, of all implements and machinery belonging to the farm (including all ordinary implements, wagons, carriages, harness, etc., apparatus for making butter, cheese, syrup, etc.).	400	800	100	800
Numbers of Acres Sown in the Fall of 1904				
20. Winter wheat	157	210	65	200
21. Spring wheat	--	--	--	--
22. Corn	20	40	35	60
23. Oats	2	--	--	--
24. Rye	25	--	--	??
25. Barley	--	--	--	--
26. Buckwheat	--	--	--	--
27. Irish potatoes	1	½	½	--
28.-36. = sweet potatoes, sugar beets, castor beans, cotton, flax, hemp, tobacco, broom corn, sorghum for syrup or sugar:	--	--	--	--

	1	2	3	4
37. Sorghum for forage or grain	--	--	--	20
38.-39. – millet and Hungarian; milo maize	--	--	--	--
40. kafir corn	10	5	2	--
41. Jerusalem corn	--	--	--	--
42. Bushels of corn on hand March 1, 1905	400	800	150	600
43. Bushels of wheat on hand March 1, 1905	--	--	--	??
44.-49. = Aggregate acres of grasses under cultivation: timothy, clover, blue-grass, alfalfa, orchard-grass, other tame grasses	--	--	--	--
Hay				
50. Uncultivated land under fence for meadow or pasture	93	22	60	60
51. Number of tons of tame hay cut in 1904	25	--	--	--
52. Number of tons of prairie-hay cut in 1904	--	--	--	--

Read and Heed – Whenever factories, large or small, for the manufacture of butter or cheese, or both, are located and operated in any township, city, or ward, the respective assessors thereof are earnestly urged to secure such information concerning the name (except when adjuncts to central establishments) as is contemplated in schedule 5 of this book, especially statistics as to quantity and value of finished product, and record it therein where such data rightly belongs.

	1	2	3	4
Dairy Products for year ending March 1, 1905				
53. Made in Family Cheese Number of pounds made	--	--	--	--
54. Made in Family Butter Number of pounds made	400	400	600	600
55. Value of milk and cream sold during the year to cheese factories, creamries, and skim stations	--	--	--	60
56. Value of milk and cream sold during the year other than that sold To cheese factories, creameries, and skim stations	--	--	--	--
57.-59. Bees: Number of stands of. Number of pounds of honey	--	--	--	--
Produced in 1904. Number of pounds of wax produced in 1904.				
60. Value of poultry & eggs sold during the year ending March 1, 1905	--	--	--	--
61. Value of animals fattened and slaughtered or sold for slaughter During the year ending March 1, 1905	203	150	40	700
62. Number of pounds of wool clip of 1904	--	--	--	--
63. Value of wood marketed during the year ending March 1, 1905	--	--	--	--
Livestock on hand March 1, 1905				
64. Horses	10	6	4	3
65. Mules and asses	--	--	3	6
66. Milch cows	6	5	2	6
67. Other cattle	22	4	2	55
68. Sheep	--	--	--	--
69. Swine	33	12	??	25
Number that have died of disease during the year ending March 1, 1905				
70. Horses	1	--	--	--
71. Mules and asses	--	--	--	--
72. Milch cows	1	--	--	--
73. Other cattle	--	--	---	3

	1	2	3	4
74. Sheep	--	--	--	--
75. Swine	--	--	--	7
76.-77. = Sheep killed by dogs or wolves	--	--	--	--
78. Number of dogs	--	--	--	--

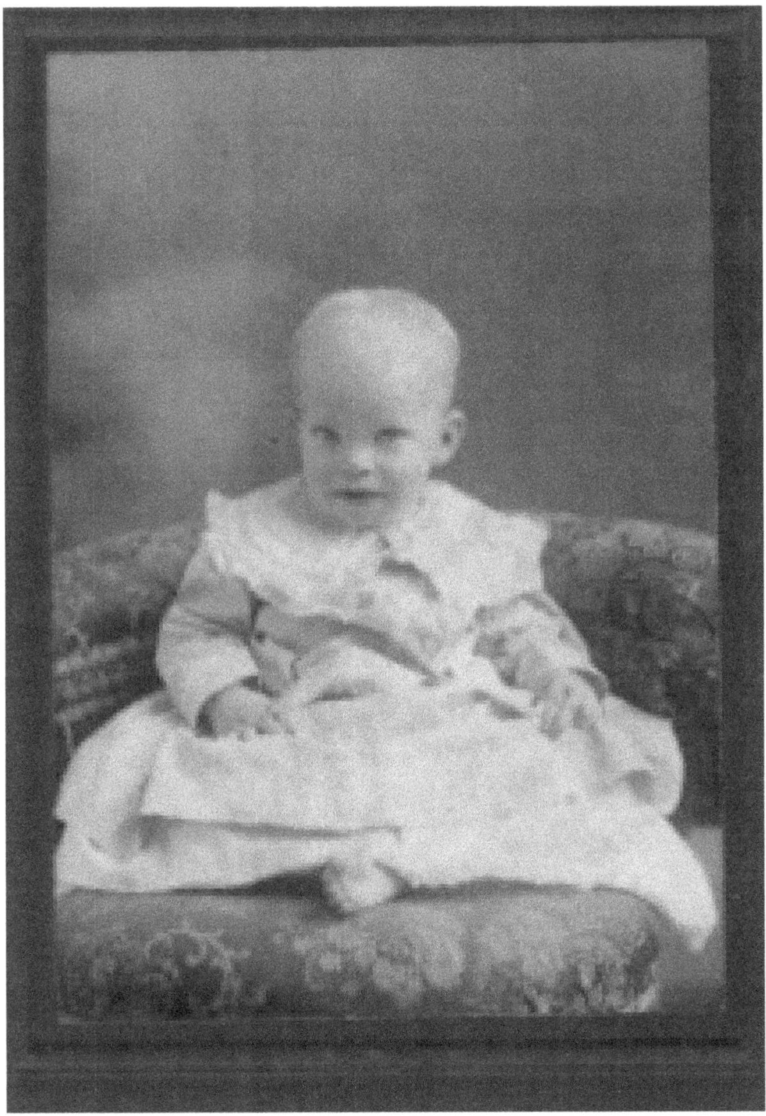

Alberta Anna Bell Culbreath, 1 year old

One of the stories I recall Alberta telling me about her childhood was that she had to wear underwear made from potato sacks stamped with the name of the town on them, "Pratt." I seem to recall a story about the underwear falling down one time, but that's a fuzzy memory. The Pratt potatoes underwear story is probably why I always thought she was born in Pratt. It wasn't until I saw the pictures of the house called Grandview and saw the inscription on the back stating it was located in St. John, Kansas, that I realized she was born in St. John, and not Pratt. Just when the family moved to Pratt is unclear.

In the 1910 U.S. Federal Census and the 1915 Kansas State Census, at age 12, Alberta was residing in Pratt. During a 2013 visit to Pratt, I found the address of their farmhouse, 106 South Pine. It was located right along the main highway through Pratt. Of course, the original Victorian farmhouse was no longer there. In its place were modern Ranch style houses.

Her niece, Julia Kint Rice Connell, recalled that about this age, Alberta invited her entire school class to her house for her birthday party. Afterwards, she told her mother the class was coming, and Martha Emma then had to milk the cow and make the homemade ice cream.

As an adult, Alberta was known for her ice cream. I recall many holidays and summer weekend celebrations at her house in Miami where the ice cream machine was always sitting in the kitchen doorway packed with ice. I loved to eat ice, so once, before anyone could stop me, I had grabbed an ice cube from the side of the freezer and popped it into my mouth. Everyone laughed at my screwed up face when I spit it out quickly. That was when I learned the secret ingredient for making ice cream freeze was rock salt!

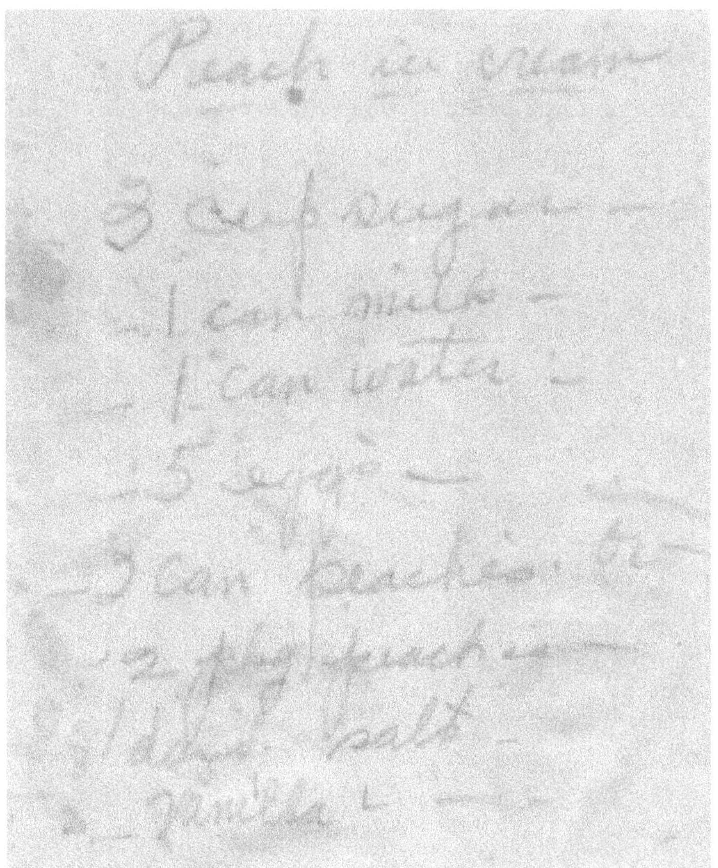
Peach ice cream

3 cup sugar
1 can milk
1 can water
5 eggs
3 can peaches
2 pkg peaches
1 dash salt
vanilla

Alberta's peach ice cream ingredient list. She served this to her family on Mother's Day, 1970—the last time she cooked for them before she passed away.

Her family worked as harvesters, also called threshers. They would go from farm to farm during the wheat harvest with their combiner which her father, Thomas Sherman, had invented. Mother, Martha Emma, along with her sister, Edith, and she would go out to the fields and cook for the workers. It was said that Alberta often cooked for 16 farmhands a day. Her specialties were fried chicken and cherry pie, among others. They cooked on a portable stove set on a wagon which was pulled by a team of horses. Her daughter, Valeria, stated that when she was learning to make pie dough, she would throw the dough that didn't turn out well behind the blackberry bush in their yard.

Alberta always cooked by eye. She'd throw together a little of this and a pinch of that until it looked and felt right. Family who came after her would often get frustrated when asking her for recipes because she'd just respond with a list of the ingredients—no measurements or directions to make. Once, my mother asked for Alberta's chocolate cake recipe. Alberta listed the ingredients, but no measurements or directions. My mother, Betty Mae Williams Kinney, then took her Betty Crocker

Cookbook and looked for cake recipes which had similar ingredients. Then she created her own version of Alberta's cake and named it Grandma's Hot Water Devil's Food Chocolate Cake. We enjoy this cake at family gatherings still, although Alberta has been gone for more than 40 years now.

Grandma's Hot Water Devil's Food Chocolate Cake
By Alberta Anna Bell Culbreath Kinney c. 1922

Two Layers:

½ c. shortening	2 c. sugar	2 eggs
3 heaping Tablespoons cocoa	½ c. sour milk*	¼ tsp salt
2 tsp. soda	2 c. flour	
1 c. boiling water		

Three Layers:

¾ c. shortening	3 c. sugar	3 eggs
4-5 Tbs. cocoa	¾ c. sour milk	
1/3 tsp. salt	3 tsp. soda	3 c. flour
1 ½ c. boiling water		

1. With an electric mixer, beat shortening & sugar; add eggs.
2. In separate bowl, mix flour, salt, soda, and cocoa.
3. Add flour to sugar mix, alternately with sour (*evaporated) milk.
4. Add boiling water; beat well; mixture will be thin like pancake batter.
5. Bake 350 degrees in greased and floured tube pan 30-40 minutes; or 20 minutes in two pans.

Chocolate Icing
Obtained somewhere by Betty Mae Williams Kinney c. 1970

1. Mix in 2 quart saucepan: 1 c. white sugar; 4 Tbs. flour; and ¼ c. heaping cocoa powder.
2. Slowly add 1 c. canned evaporated milk.
3. Add ½ tsp. vanilla; 2 Tbs. butter.
4. Cook and stir until desired thickness
5. Spread on layers and top of cake.

When I began researching family documents in preparation for writing this book, I came across a familiar recipe for strawberry pie in Alberta's hand. I had always believed my mother, Betty Mae, had invented this recipe. Perhaps she did, as there were specific ingredient measurements listed in Alberta's hand as if she had taken the recipe from my mother. Of course, Alberta added her own touch—nuts and mints—to the completed pie!

Here is the list as she wrote it:

"2 cups sugar – 2 cups water – 4 tbl corn starch – cook until clear. Add 1 small box – strawberry Jello – slice berries – regular crust. Cream for pies – nuts & mints"

Alberta's cakes were widely celebrated. She made such elaborate decorations for them. For example, for her son, Lawrence's, wedding cake she recreated the entire wedding party in 4" tall dolls which were placed on a spiral staircase which wound around the perimeter of the cake to the top where the bride and groom proudly stood, complete with his flame-red hair and her turquoise taffeta dress.

For daughter, Valeria's wedding, there was no time to prepare the cake, so they had bought one from a bakery. I recall being told that Alberta didn't think much of the decorations on the bakery bought cake so she went over them with her own creations. Therefore, the icing was doubly thick.

Lawrence's wedding cake made by Alberta. All the members of the wedding party were recreated in miniature dolls.

When I was about 11 years old, she taught me how to make Boiled Icing. This is the kind of hard icing which covers cakes and is smooth like glass. I recall sitting in front of a blowing fan on a very hot day in her sweltering dining room hand-beating the icing and holding the fork aloft in front of the fan and letting the icing drip back into the bowl to see if the consistency was correct. I did succeed in making some miniature decorated cakes. The little cakes were Easter baskets baked in small 4" pie plates. They were decorated with flowers made from the boiled icing. For the handles on the baskets, I made handle forms from poster board and covered the forms with the delicately shaped flowers. Alberta must have prepared the recipe for me because there are ingredient measurements included. My only regret today is that she died shortly after she had begun to teach me how to bake. Lessons in sewing also would have been a wonderful experience.

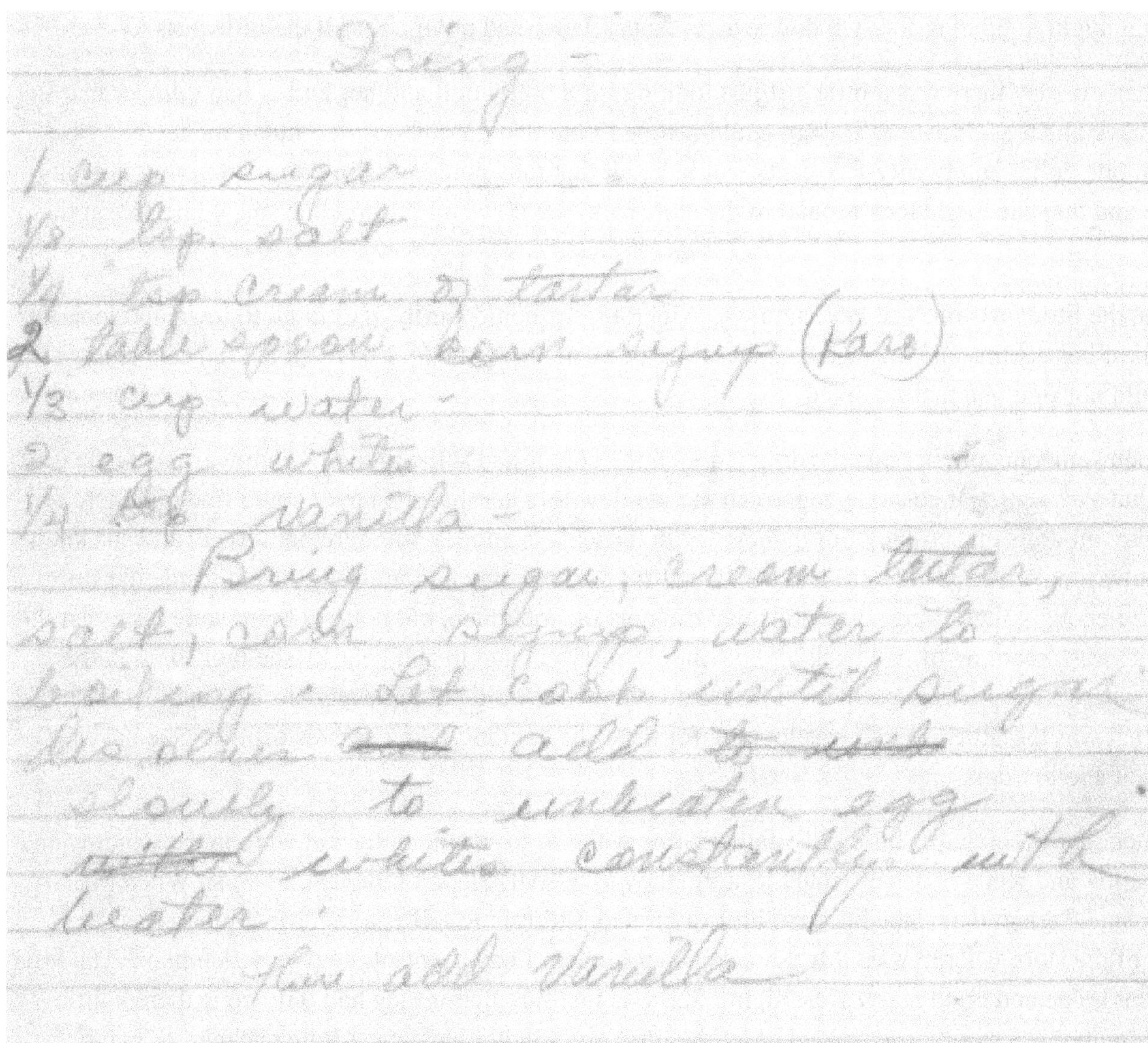

Icing –

1 cup sugar
1/8 tsp. salt
1/4 tsp cream of tartar
2 table spoon corn syrup (Karo)
1/3 cup water –
2 egg whites
1/4 tsp vanilla –

Bring sugar, cream tartar, salt, corn syrup, water to boiling & let cook until sugar dissolves add slowly to unbeaten egg whites constantly with beater.

Then add vanilla –

Alberta's Boiled Icing recipe for cakes. She taught granddaughter Barbara Kinney Black to make this icing when she was about 11 years old.

Not only could Alberta cook and bake well, she also excelled at sewing. The story of how she learned is a delightful one retold here in her own words:

Mary Anna

CHRISTMAS 1913

This story began many years ago and it is all about me. Oh yes, I know you are wondering who I am and why I want to write this story.

First, I must tell you that my name is Mary Anna. That is the name my first mistress gave me. Of course I called her Mother.

I was a very lonely doll and wanting so much for someone to adopt me, and the first thing I knew I was hanging high up in a store window where Santy Clause had put me for all the little girls to see.

Then one day there was a little girl just looking for a pretty doll and her Father had told her that she might have one that Christmas if there could be one found that did not cost too much money and he thought one dollar and twenty-five cents would be all that they could possibly think of giving to Santy Clause and that she might look around in the stores and see if she might find one she would like at that price.

So, the little girl--oh, yes, her name was Alberta—she could hardly wait to go to town and look for the doll of her dreams and the next day she went to town. First, she looked in all the ten cent stores and she could not find one that she liked.

Then someone told her that the drug store on the corner had some in their window. This is the next place that she went. Of course, one look in the window told her that she never could find one there for they were all dolls that cost a lot of money, for in those days, money was sure hard to get and she knew that she was only a poor little girl and her father did not have much money. She went inside the store and, sure enough, there were some dolls that did not cost too much, but none of them were just what the little girl was dreaming of. So back to the window she went and lo and behold, she looked up in the corner where I was. I was so ashamed for her to see me for I did not have any clothes, but in a flash, I knew that was the little girl that was looking for me. She couldn't take her eyes off me. She never looked at another doll.

Then that evening, the little girl's father came with her to see the dolls that were in the window and in the store, and when they went into the store, they asked Mr. Shrack how much I was. When Mr. Shrack said, "ten dollars," the little girl almost fainted. I forgot to tell you that Mr. Shrack was the owner of the store where I was. Mr. Shrack also told them I had been sold to a very rich man. The little girl went home and cried most of the night. She was just sure that if they had only gone there a little sooner, maybe the store owner would of let the little girl's father have me a little cheaper, or maybe he could have had me on time, and her father might of paid for me a little at a time.

What the little girl did not know was after they left the store, the little girl's father made arrangements for Santy Clause to take me to the little girl on Christmas Eve.

Several weeks passed after that before Christmas, and I was still hanging in the store window, but I had a tag on that said, "sold." That did not keep the little girl from coming to town and looking in the window at me, but each time I could see that she had been crying, and, of course, I wanted to tell her not to cry, that I was really coming to her home, but that was the way we had to stay until Santy Clause was ready to take me home.

CHRISTMAS EVE came at last. That night the little girl was to take part in a Christmas play at the church, and when the play was over and she came home and opened the front door, there I was big as life sitting in a rocking chair in the living room with just a towel wrapped around me. I just did not want her to see me without any clothes. You will never know how happy we both were as I had a new mother and she named me Mary Anna.

After I went to live with Alberta, she told me how each day after she first saw me, she would cry and tell her mother how much she had wanted me. Her mother couldn't stand to see her cry and as she was milking a cow and the little girl was crying, her mother told her if she did not stop crying, she would not get the doll her father had laid away for her. Of course she had no way of knowing that Santy was going to bring me, but she knew she was going to get some kind of doll.

When I went to live with her, I found she had a lot of other little dolls. Of course, they were just little kids beside me, and Alberta was so glad to get me that she decided if she could find some other little girls that did not have a doll that she would give them all away and that is just what she did. The next day, Alberta started to sew and made me pretty clothes, and, believe me, I had a lot of pretty ones, too. She really learned to sew making my clothes. She got many a whipping because when she was sewing for me, she would forget to help her mother, and her mother would whip her. One time I remember real well her mother was so mad as she had told her several times to wash the dishes. Each time Alberta would pay no attention to her mother so at last her mother whipped her with a highly polished yard stick and it was a real thick one. She broke it on Alberta. After that, when she told her to do something, Alberta would do it real quick so she could get back to sewing for me.

I lived with Alberta for many years, but when she got married, she almost forgot about me and I just sat around with a couple of cats that liked to sharpen their claws on my legs, and they still show the scars. Alberta was too busy with her new life to pay much attention to me, and the first thing I knew, I was in a trunk and I thought my time was sure up. But one day, she took me out of the trunk and made me the prettiest dress you ever saw. It was blue satin trimmed with lace, and I had some long pink panties that covered my scars on my legs. I wondered what she was going to do with me. I did not have much time to wait for she gave me to her beautiful daughter. She was just ten years old. She had big blue eyes and a head full of curls. I really started to live all over again. My new mother's name was Valeria, but everyone called her Dee Dee and I called her that too.

After I went to live with Dee Dee, I had two little sister dolls that looked like me. I am still living with them.

Dee Dee liked to play with dolls, but she never did like to sew. So, I would always have to have my grandmother make me my clothes. She made many for me and Dee Dee would like to dress me and put me to bed. That she like to do best, as I had a lot of pretty gowns and pajamies.

Sometimes she would take me for long walks in a beautiful doll carriage. Of course, the two other little dolls would go with me. Sometimes we would all go dressed alike.

Dee Dee kept me with her until Jimmy came along and then it was the same thing. He loved her so very much and made her so very happy that she forgot all about me. In fact, she forgot to take me with her when she went to her new home with Jimmy, so my first mother put me back in the trunk. A lot of time has passed since then, and Dee Dee and Jimmy have had four lovely children; only one of these was a girl. Soon, she will be ten years old. At that time, I am told I will go to live with her. She knows I am coming and is looking for me. I only hope she likes me like my first mother did. After all, she ought to be able to take good care of me, for after all, she will be just the same age as my first mother when she got me. She will be ten years old June 14, 1966.

My goodness. That time is almost here and I am just sick. I must have an operation and get me a new body. I was taken to a doll hospital and they wanted forty dollars for the operation, but my first mother still knows a lot about sewing, and I am sure there are to be a lot of stitches as I am to be made well again. She volunteered to do the operation, and in about two weeks, I was as good as new again. Now I am ready to go to my new mother. This time I will be dressed in blue embroidered silk and I can hardly wait.

My new mother's name is Sandra. I do hope she will be good to me and keep me for another mother in about twenty some more years.

I will be given to her on her tenth birthday at a party which I am sure I will be the guest of honor.

--Story by Alberta Anna Bell Culbreath Kinney

Sandra Stewart, 10, and Mary Anna ... doll was a birthday present

Sandy Stewart and the doll, Mary Anna, passed down from Alberta to Valeria La Verne Kinney Stewart, to Sandy.

Sometime between 1915 and 1919, the family relocated to Hutchinson, Reno County, Kansas. Alberta completed the 11th grade, but it's unclear where she went to school—Pratt or Hutchinson or another place. While living in Hutchinson, Alberta was quite the popular girl with many friends as evidenced by the following articles about her social life from The Hutchinson News.

In the 14 August 1919 edition of The Hutchinson News, we read that, "Miss Bianche Grogan and Miss Thelma Wilson entertained last evening for Miss Alberta Culbreath at the home of Mrs. Walter Mead on Third Avenue East. The evening was spent informally with games, and later a luncheon was served to the following guests: Miss Bertha Peterson, Miss Dorothy Stauffer, Miss Opal Wilson, Miss Helen Chabin, Miss Ota Burgess, Miss Bernice Bunton, Mr. Harold Wilson, Mr. Chester Dewhurst, Mr. Darrel Mend, Mr. Milton Burgess, Mr. Donald Stauffer, Mr. Orville Todd, Mr. Harland Culbreath."

In the 20 October 1919 edition of The Hutchinson News, "Miss Alberta Culbreath, Miss Helen Chabin, and Mr. Harlan Culbreath gave a delightful surprise party last Saturday evening for Miss Thelma Wilson, in honor of her sixteenth birthday. The house was most cleverly decorated with Halloween suggestions and the evening was spent with games, appropriate to Halloween. The center of the table was adorned with one large birthday cake, and a delicious lunch was served to about twenty-five guests."

In the 12 August 1920 edition of The Hutchinson News, we read that "Miss Thelma May Wilson entertained some of her friends last evening at her home on Fifth Avenue east, in honor of the birthday of her guest, Miss Alberta Culbreath of Wichita. The evening was spent informally and Miss Erma Lupardas gave 2 splendid readings: "The Green-Eyed Monster" and "Redhead." The guests included:

Mrs. Wilson, Mrs. M. H. Kint [Alberta's sister, Edith], Miss Esther Cooley of Haven, Miss Harriet Fayette and Miss Ruth Fayette of Pratt, Miss Pamela Conner, Miss Ruby Adkinson, Miss Opal Wilson, Miss Lupardus, Miss Bianche Grogan, Miss Pauline Kint and Miss Julia Kint [Alberta's nieces], Miss Charlyne Folby, Mr. Harold Shephard, Mr. Emort Richards, Mr. Darrel Mead, Mr. Milton Burgess, Mr. Guy Farrell, and Mr. T. S. Culbreath."

By the 1920 U.S. Federal Census, Alberta had moved once again with her family; this time to Wichita. Alberta was 16 and did not list an occupation. They lived at 223 North St. Francis Avenue. In 2013, this address was an empty lot in the downtown area which looked as if it were being prepared for construction.

In the 1922 Wichita City Directory, Alberta's address was 154 North Market. In 2013, this was a parking lot in the downtown business district. Alberta was a machine operator for Johnston and Larimer Dry Goods Company. Family tradition says she sewed overalls for farm wear. She was especially talented at installing fly button holes in men's overalls.

Family tradition states she lived above her place of employment in the Butts Building. In the 1922 Wichita City Directory, this advertisement appeared: J. Arch Butts –Distributor Buick Automobiles, Phone M 593 located at 205-213 Lawrence Avenue. In 2013, with street name changes, the building was located on the S.W. corner of First and Broadway. Since we have no record of where she lived in 1921 because there was no City Directory published, it is possible she lived in the Butts Building. I don't believe, however, that this was above her place of employment as the Johnston and Larimer Dry Goods Company was located along the railroad track, and the Butts Building was not.

Many family members believe that Alberta met Vernon when he came to visit family or friends in Wichita. Since he had also lived in Wichita from about 1916-1920, I find it curious that he should "go to Wichita to visit friends". Alberta's niece, Julia Kint, thought Vernon had been living in Miami before 1922 when he and Alberta moved there after their wedding. It is my opinion that when Vernon's mother, Anna Rachel Fox Kinney, married her third husband, William Allen Anderson, and went to Florida, that Vernon went with them. This was thought to be sometime in late 1920 or 1921. Neither Anna Rachel nor her husband, William Allen Anderson, were listed in the 1922 Wichita City Directory which leads me to believe they moved during 1920-21. Neither was there an entry for Vernon in the Wichita City Directory for 1922, and there had been entries for him every year from 1917-1920. Incidentally, Wichita did not publish a directory for 1921. Perhaps if they had, a lot of questions would have been answered.

The fact that is generally agreed upon, is that Alberta and Vernon met at a dance. She had been dating another man at the time. Alberta quickly fell for Vernon. They had a nice church wedding planned with invitations already mailed out, but a job for Vernon in Miami came through. They had to move the wedding up by 3 weeks in order to make the move to Miami in time for Vernon to begin the job. This incident gives further evidence for the idea that Vernon had already moved to Miami before their 1922 wedding. Otherwise, why would a job for him in Miami suddenly become available if he hadn't already applied for positions there?

Alberta and Vernon were married 5 August 1922, in Wichita, Kansas.

STATE OF KANSAS, Sedgwick County, ss: Aug. 5, 1922

Vernon H. Kinney files application and affidavit for Marriage License to be issued to Vernon H. Kinney and Alberta Culbreath Affidavit showing that said Parties are legally entitled to License to marry is ordered filed and numbered 4445

Office of the Probate Judge of Said County

BE IT REMEMBERED, That on the 5th day of Aug. A. D. 1922, there was issued from the office of said Probate Judge a Marriage License, of which the following is a true copy:

(Seal)

MARRIAGE LICENSE

State of Kansas, County of Sedgwick

Wichita, Kansas, Aug. 5, 1922

To any person authorized by law to perform the Marriage Ceremony, Greeting:

YOU ARE HEREBY AUTHORIZED TO JOIN IN MARRIAGE

Vernon H Kinney (Groom) of Wichita, Kansas, aged 20

Alberta Culbreath (Bride) of Wichita, Kansas, aged 19

with the consent of Anna Anderson Mother of Vernon H. Kinney (Name of Parent or Guardian Consenting) and of this license, duly endorsed, you will make due return to

(Name of Parent or Guardian Consenting)

my office at Wichita, Kansas, within ten days after performing the ceremony.

(Seal) G. W. C. Jones, Probate Judge.

ENDORSEMENT

TO WHOM IT MAY CONCERN:

I hereby certify that I performed the ceremony joining in marriage the above-named couple on the 5th day of August, 1922, at Wichita, Kansas.

Signed W. L. Priest

Title Minister

Address Wichita, Kansas

Vernon Haven Kinney and Alberta Anna Bell Culbreath Kinney on their wedding day 5 August 1922

Left, Vernon Haven Kinney, Wichita, Kansas, 1922
Right, Alberta Anna Bell Culbreath, Wichita, Kansas, 1922. I believe these pictures to have been taken on their wedding day.

How they travelled to Miami is unknown to me, but they must have had a glorious honeymoon full of adventure. When they arrived in Miami, they bought a house with the money that Vernon had saved since he had begun working. They first appeared in the 1924 Miami City Directory at 3051 N.W. 6th Avenue. They would live at this address until the late 1960s when the School Board forced them from their home.

Vernon's employment in 1924 was at the Real Estate Journal Publishing Company. He was a press man.

The first job was located in Hollywood, Florida. Both Vernon and Alberta worked—he did printing, and she bookbinding. They had to travel from Miami each day up Dixie Highway, which was then just an unpaved rock road with white dust flying everywhere. I'm sure it was really hot in the summer. Perhaps this was partly why he got a new car with glass all around.

At the 1930 U.S. Federal Census, their home was valued at $3,000. Alberta did not have an occupation, but her first child had been born, Lawrence, 28 September 1928. He had carrot red hair. Although Alberta herself did not have red hair, she carried the gene. Several of her aunts and uncles, plus her sister, Edith, had red hair.

In the 1933 Miami City Directory, Alberta was working at the Ritz Hotel, Miami, Dade County, Florida. Her mother-in-law also worked there as a housekeeper.

Miami in the 1920s from Historic Photos of Greater Miami, by Bramson, p. 88

At the 1935 Florida State Census, daughter, Valeria La Verne Kinney, was 5 years. About this time, Alberta's father and brother, Thomas Sherman and Chal Culbreath, departed from Miami on a boat to Cuba. Valeria recalled seeing a man on the deck of a ship waving his hat vigorously in her direction. At the time she didn't realize it was her grandfather.

Alberta continued sewing and spreading her creative skills around the community. She sewed a couple of ambitious projects for each of her children's school classes as shown on pgs. 233 and 234.

Lawrence's class band. All costumes made by Alberta

Towards the end of the Depression, Vernon had been out of work for some time when his union got a temporary job for him in St. Augustine. Vernon went there alone. Once Alberta and Anna Rachel loaded the kids into the Whippet car and made the trek to St. Augustine via Dixie Highway, a long journey of at least one day. In 2013, one can take the journey in 5½ hours from Miami via the interstate highway. On the way back, Alberta was nervous about driving on 2-lane roads with 2 young children and her mother-in-law in the back seat. Suddenly, Dee Dee shouted, "Stop the car! Stop the car!" Nobody knew why she wanted them to stop, so Anna Rachel began to question Dee Dee. Her reply was, "I want to pick some pretty yellow flowers."

Alberta worked for a time in a mattress rebuilding company which was owned by one of the neighbors. One could get their mattress torn apart and the cotton would be run through a cotton gin, then the mattress would be retied and new ticking added. The mattress would then be returned to the owners as a rebuilt mattress. One time an employee got angry at the boss and threw a mattress needle at him. This tool was about the size of a pencil and about a foot in length. Shortly after this incident, Alberta decided to leave this position.

Dee Dee's class dressed like pumpkins. Alberta made all the costumes.

In the 1940 U.S. Federal Census, we find that Vernon's mother, Anna Rachel Fox Kinney Anderson, a widow, was living with the family.

During World War II, Vernon lost his job in Miami because the government declared it nonessential to the war effort, but his union located him a position in Chattanooga. He went there alone, initially, to work. It took a year for Alberta to save enough money for her to go with the children to visit. Once in Chattanooga, Alberta decided they would all stay. Valeria was in the sixth grade and Lawrence was probably in the eighth grade. At any rate, they attended different schools.

In 2013, I went to visit Chattanooga in hopes of finding some of the houses and sites where they had lived, worked, worshipped, gone to school, and played. During the trip, I stayed on the phone much of the time with Alberta's son, Lawrence, my father. He described locations from his memory of 60 years previous, while I looked around and described what I was seeing in 2013. Between the 2 of us, we managed to located several sites. Here's an excerpt from my travel journal describing our day in Chattanooga:

"Tuesday, September 17, 2013 -- We explored Chattanooga today. First up was the second house in which Dad lived in 1943 or1944 in the area of town called East Lake. It was a small house across from a lake at 3104 East 36 Street. In front of the house, 36 Street starts up the hill in front of the house which was Missionary Ridge. Dad used to ride his bike up and then coast down. He could go all the way down into Rossville, Georgia by riding his bicycle south on Dodd Avenue.

Next was the little church which Aunt Dee Dee described as white while Dad described as brick. When we found the former East Lake Baptist Church, it was both brick and white. They were both saved and baptized there.

After photographing the old middle school one block away from the house and behind the new elementary school, we began to think that may have been the old school where Aunt Dee Dee had gone, or else the old school she went to may have been replaced by the newer and current one which is an elementary school located on the corner from the block in which they lived.

Then we went into town to find their first apartment at 1405 Bailey Avenue. It was just an empty lot now. Dad was on the phone and said that Vernon worked exactly behind the house 3 blocks north on McCollie Avenue and across the avenue. We saws 2 building on that street – 1 single story and one 2-story. The older 2-story building was brick and was occupied by a business, while the single story was concrete, maybe. It was painted cream and gray and was abandoned at this time, 2013.

We went around and around the neighborhood until we found the street that Dad was mentioning as Vance Avenue which he thought was running perpendicular to the house. It was actually 3 blocks away and running parallel to Bailey Avenue. Then Dad remembered said that he meant the street perpendicular to the house was Chamberlaine and that was where the street car named "Vance" was caught.

While they were living on Bailey Avenue, Lawrence attended the East Side Junior High School located on Main Street about 8-9 blocks from their house. He would ride his bicycle to and from school.

He also mentioned attending Sunday School at the old First Baptist Church of Chattanooga which was downtown near their apartment. We called the current First Baptist Church and the downtown church building had become a parking lot and their educational building some other thing.

He also talked about working at a Comet Restaurant which was like a White Castle type restaurant. That was located on the north end of Market Street, but nothing like a restaurant of that name showed itself to us today."

Probable house in East Lake suburb of Chattanooga where Alberta and Vernon lived in early 1940s, as seen in 2013

Possible school where Valeria La Verne Kinney attended sixth grade in East Lake, Chattanooga, Tennessee, 1943

East Lake Baptist Church, Chattanooga, Tennessee, where Valeria and Lawrence both got saved and baptized, 1943

At the 1945 Florida State Census, they have returned from Chattanooga.

Lawrence Sherman Kinney, circa 1945

Valeria La Verne Kinney, circa 1945

Lawrence said that Opa Locka Air Station had been closed down after WWII and a hospital had been built. Alberta was in that hospital. He didn't remember what she was in the hospital for, but her niece, Julia, was living in Miami at the time.

Alberta and Vernon took a trip to California in a little trailer during the late 1940s according to Alberta's niece, Julia. They visited Vernon's brother, Veigh, in Texas, then on to California to see Alberta's brothers, Chal and Harlan, and her parents, T. S. and Martha Emma, and her sister, Edith, in Los Angeles. Finally, she saw her other brother, Hobart, in Sacramento.

Alberta's daughter, Valeria La Verne Kinney, married James Stewart in 1950. Lawrence married Betty Mae Williams, 18 May 1951. Just 4 short months later, he left for Air Force basic training in Texas. Alberta experienced her first Christmas without her son. As one who always had the entire family in her home for celebrations, this must have been a difficult experience.

Alberta and Vernon's first grandchild was born to Valeria and James in July, 1952. Jimmy Junior was joined just 1 year later in July, 1953, by brother, Johnny Stewart. Together these 2 caused their mother, Dee Dee, a lot of stress! They were mischievous youngsters, and Dee Dee was often asking Alberta for her advice on how to handle them.

James Stewart, Jr.

John Kinney Stewart

Sandra Leigh Stewart

The next grandchild was Barbara Elaine Kinney, Lawrence and Betty's first daughter. She had the place of "only granddaughter" for just 6 months, and then Sandra Leigh Stewart joined Barbara. Sandy was the daughter of Dee Dee and Jim.

Barbara Kinney Black, 1963

Alberta Kinney preparing a solo

Grandson, Roger Vernon Kinney, came next, followed by David Stewart, and finally, Thomas Stewart, who was named after his great grandfather, Thomas Sherman Culbreath, was the last grandchild born for Alberta Culbreath and Vernon Kinney.

Alberta was an active member of her church Stanton Memorial Baptist, located at 2948 N.W. Second Avenue, Miami, Dade County, Florida. She was a soprano soloist in the choir. She also taught her adult ladies Sunday School class for more than 20 years. At Stanton Memorial Baptist Church, Lawrence met his first wife, Betty Mae Williams, on the staircase to the second floor of the educational building. In 2013, this building was being used by the City of Miami. I was able to stand on the staircase and muse about what may have occurred the first time they met. Coincidentally, Lawrence's second wife, Joyce, met her first husband, Walter Rozier, at the same church.

I have many memories at this church building, even though I was only 4 years old when our family went to help plant Stanton's newest branch church in North Miami called North Shore Baptist. Stanton had that old, creaky sound. It had been added on to over the years and newer additions were connected by sloped ramps which, even though they were carpeted, creaked underfoot. The sanctuary had wooden theater type seating where everyone had arm rests. The smell of the place stays with me to this day. My grandfather, Vernon, greeted the congregation inside the breezeway on the north entrance by giving them a bulletin of the morning's program. My grandmother, Alberta, would then come in to the sanctuary in her flowing satin cream colored choir robe with burgundy sash. On those occasions when a baptism occurred, the beautiful Holy Land scene painted on the back wall of the baptistery transported me to Israel. I can still hear the splash of the baptismal waters as people were immersed as an outward sign of the inward conversion of their lives. Stanton was the first place I went after coming home from the hospital as a baby. At 3 weeks old, I was enrolled in the Cradle Department of the Sunday School and Mrs. Irene Blocker became my first caregiver. When the church was torn down in the early 1970s, a sadness filled all of our family.

of God
EMORIAL BAPTIST CHURCH, BUILT IN 1923, TOOK PLACE OF OLD EDIFICE WHICH NOW SERVES AS A SUNDAY SCHOOL CLASSROOM.

Stanton Memorial Baptist Church, Miami, Dade County, Florida

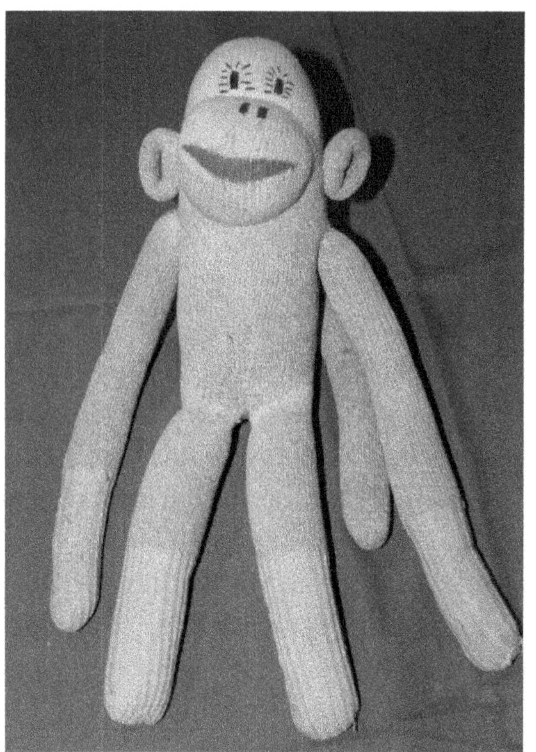

Replacement sock monkey, with tail intact, made by Alberta Anna Bell Culbreath Kinney for 5 of her grandchildren, circa 1958

If I had to sum up Alberta in one word, that word would have to be creative. She was probably the most creative woman I've ever known. As a baby, I'd received a stuffed monkey made from a sock as a gift from a friend of my mother's. I'm told that I never sucked my thumb as other children. Probably I was too busy sucking the monkey's tail as I chewed the thing clean off the monkey. Well, Alberta took pity and made new sock monkeys for all 5 grandchildren.

Being one of the first 5 grandchildren, I benefited from Alberta's many gifts created for us. Later grand kids were spaced out in age and didn't receive exactly the same things we older ones did.

Barbara Kinney Black and Sandy Stewart Dolan wearing the blue wool coats and bonnets with rabbit fur trim made by Alberta, 1959

Barbara Kinney Black wearing dress made by Alberta, 1962 Roger Vernon Kinney

Among the first items she made for me was a blue wool coat and bonnet with an embroidered brim trimmed with rabbit fur. And even though we lived in South Florida where it was rarely cold enough to wear a wool coat, we loved our new duds. We were the envy of every little girl around.

Since I and my cousin, Sandy Stewart Dolan, and our second cousin, Helen Myles Henning, were just 6 months apart in age from each other, Alberta always had lots of fun making matching outfits for us. Usually on Easter we could count on frilly dresses, all handmade. Once we had matching yellow flocked Swiss polka dotted dresses with yellow satin under slips. There were ribbon roses at the waist and on the matching draw string pocketbooks made from cottage cheese containers. A ribbon rose decorated headband completed the ensemble.

In the Santa picture on pg. 242, Roger Kinney is wearing the suit into which Alberta installed an inside pocket into the lining. Roger wanted an inside pocket just like his Dad's suit, so he cut a slit into the lining, inserted his pencil, and, of course, it disappeared down between the lining and outer fabric. Alberta thought this was really cute, so came to Roger's rescue by making him a genuine, working inside pocket.

One day Alberta was clearing out her closets and came across her son's silk parachute left over from his flying days. Alberta went to work transforming that parachute into a silk and lace dress. Of course I still have the dress. About 2 years ago, at a family gathering, Sandy, Helen, and I discovered that Alberta had made dresses for all 3 of us, and we all 3 still had them. So, a photo session was called for.

Helen Myles Henning, Sandy Stewart Dolan, and Barbara Kinney Black with the silk and lace dresses Alberta made for us from Lawrence's parachute

She sewed for the grandsons, too. Jimmy and Johnny Stewart both got cowboy suits. Their sister, Sandy, was jealous, so asked for a cowgirl suit. The result was skirts and blouses trimmed with vinyl leather fringe for Sandy and me. We were in the 5th grade already, but not too old to enjoy our Grandma's special gifts.

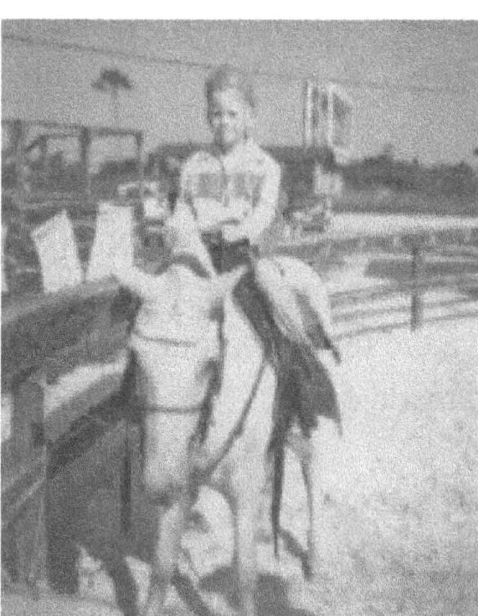

Left, Cowgirl outfit made by Alberta for Barbara Kinney Black and Sandy Stewart Dolan
Right, Cowboy suit made by Alberta worn by David Stewart

It wasn't always just dresses she made for us. Once she sewed some orange and yellow flowered short sets for Sandy and me. We put them on and promptly went out to the nearby junior high school where there were cement bannisters on either side of the steps up to the second floor entrance. We slid down the bannisters as if they were sliding boards. When we got back to Grandma's house, she saw the holes in our shorts. We were "rewarded" with the pancake turner on our back sides. I seem to recall that was maybe the last thing she sewed for us!

Then when I was about 7 and learning the importance of saving money Alberta presented me with my own unique piggy bank. It was a head made from 2 coconuts. The money was deposited into a hole in the top of the head which was concealed by a conical hat. My own blonde hair glued to the coconut head gave my bank personality. Button eyes and a red felt tongue and a candy striped neck tie completed the look. In 2013, I'm the only grandchild to still have my coconut head bank.

Coconut head bank made by Alberta for 5 of her grandchildren, circa 1960. During the Depression, Alberta would make these banks from coconuts to sell as a source of income. She'd pay her son, Lawrence, a few pennies for each coconut he would remove from the stubborn outer husk.

Alberta was very close to her brother, Hobart Culbreath, who lived in Sacramento, California with his wife, Dessie. They owned a restaurant in town which Dessie managed, and Hobart worked outside of town on a farm. Hobart met a tragic death when he was hit by a train. Here are excerpts from a letter Alberta sent to Dessie to console her.

"Miami, Florida, February 1965

Dear Dessie:

I have received from the Sheriff's Office of Yolo County the details about the accident which caused my brother's death. I cannot say this comforted me, but it did relieve the anxiety of my mind—I could not but wonder how as well as why?.....I find that my Christian faith affords me much comfort and strength in this dark hour, and I pray that you too may come to know the comfort and peace that Christ can give.

Although it has been many years since I remember Mother training us in family worship, I know that no matter what has happened in the time that has gone between then and the time of Hobart's death, that he, too, remembered that training, and even now he is receiving his reward for the life he lived on this earth, and I am sure in my heart, that Hobart was a good man and surely a Christian, and he will take his place in God's kingdom.....I am sure this is a terrible loss to you; one that you will never get over, but time and time alone will ease some of the sorrow and loneliness you will have to go through. I wish I could help in some way, but God alone can help, and he says if we will call on him, he will answer us.

I do hope this letter finds you well. I do not have any words that will relieve your sorrow, but do hope God will help you in your sorrow. Yours with Love, Alberta"

During the late 1960s, Alberta contracted lung cancer. She never smoked a day in her life, but she did work with upholstery and book binding—2 activities today associated with mesothelioma. She lived with the disease for about 2-3 years. During this time, the house that she and Vernon had lived in since 1922 was to be taken from them by the School Board of Dade County. They wanted to expand the sports field for the junior high school where Sandy and I had slid down the bannisters. Of course, Alberta wrote a protest letter to the School Board.

In the end the School Board won and they had to leave. Their new residence was at 372 La Villa Drive, Miami Springs, Dade County, Florida. This was a Spanish style home with a large yard with great soil for Alberta's gardening and a large eat in kitchen. Unfortunately, she was too weak to really enjoy it. The cancer was taking its toll.

Alberta's obituary appeared in the 21 September 1970 edition of The Miami Herald: "**KINNEY – MRS. ALBERTA C.**, 67, of 372 La Villa Drive, Miami Springs, September 19. Came to Miami in 1922 from Wichita, Kansas. Mrs. Kinney was an active member of the Stanton Memorial Baptist Church. Survivors include husband Vernon H., Miami Springs; son Lawrence S., Miami; daughter Mrs. Valeria Stewart, Hollywood, Florida; 7 grandchildren; 2 brothers Harlan Culbreath, Tuscon, Arizona; Chal Culbreath, Chatesworth, California; sister Edith Kint, Maywood, California. Repose 6-9:00 p.m. Monday, Van Orsdel Hialeah-Miami Springs Chapel. Services 3:30 p.m. Tuesday at the Stanton Memorial Baptist Church 2948 N.W. Second Avenue. Interment Woodlawn Park Cemetery. In lieu of flowers family requests donations be made to the Cancer Society."

I find the obituary reads with no feeling or insight as to who she was at all. Alberta's life touched so many, and her influence is still felt today in 2013. When I first met Alberta's niece, Julia Kint Rice Connell, in 2010, at age 94, she ran down the sidewalk in front of her house to greet me shouting, "Alberta!" I've always been told I look a lot like her, and that experience helped to reinforce that idea. Whenever I drive past the site of her original house in Miami, I look for the city street light which still stands and is the only reminder of the location of her former residence. When I use my meat thermometer or cheese grater or the "rabbit" footed dessert dishes, my thoughts return to her. The rabbit dishes are a collection of pressed glassware which was her first set of dishes. She assembled the set piece by piece as they were bonuses included in the sacks of rabbit feed they bought for the rabbits they raised when they first arrived in Miami. Funny, only the dessert dishes survived! Still, dessert is the best part of any meal and something we always look forward to. Hardly a day passes without a thought of her and her many influences in my own life. She is missed greatly, but I know we will meet again.

Alberta is interred at Woodlawn Park Cemetery, Miami, Dade County, Florida. Her Find A Grave Memorial No. is 66770093

Wilma Dorothy Culbreath
1906-1907

Wilma died at less than 2 years old. The obituary appeared in the 24 May 1907 edition of The Saint John News: "**THEIR BABY DEAD** – Wilma Dorothy, the infant daughter of Mr. and Mrs. T. S. Culbreath, died Tuesday evening at 5:30. The little one had been seriously ill for the past month or so. The funeral services were conducted Wednesday afternoon at 3:00 o'clock by Rev. Richardson from the First Baptist Church. Interment was had in Fairview Cemetery."

I can't help but wonder what Wilma would have become, had she lived past her young 2 years. Would she have inherited the same spirit of creativity her sister, Alberta had? Would she have some of her father's inventive genes? Who knows what promise her life would have held.

This photograph is the only known one of Wilma Dorothy, the youngest daughter of Thomas Sherman and Martha Emma Carnahan Culbreath. Wilma is the baby being held by her oldest sister, Edith, and her closest-in-age sister, Alberta, aged 3, is sitting on Wilma's left.

Questions:

1. Are there any other pictures of Wilma Dorothy?
2. Did her fall from the high chair as a young baby contribute to her early demise?
3. What was the cause of death?
4. Is there a grave marker for her in the Fairview Cemetery?

6

David Smith Carnahan

1839-1917

David Smith Carnahan (1839 - 1917)

is your 2nd great grandfather

Martha Emma Carnahan (1868 - 1946)

Daughter of David Smith Carnahan

Alberta Anna Bell Culbreath (1903 - 1970)

daughter of Martha Emma Carnahan

Lawrence Sherman Kinney (1928 -)

Son of Alberta Anna Bell Culbreath

Barbara Elaine Kinney

daughter of Lawrence Sherman Kinney

Born the only son in a household full of sisters, David Smith Carnahan entered the world on 6 March 1839, in Mahoning, Mercer County, Pennsylvania. He was the son of Margaret Laughlin and Joseph Carnahan. He had at least 6 sisters including: Agnes Jane, Mary Elizabeth, Martha Ann, Nancy Morehead, Sarah Margaret, and Isabella Josephine. His father, Joseph, died in 1847 in New Bedford, Mercer County, Pennsylvania, leaving young David Smith at age 8, the only male. I wonder if he felt pressure to provide for his family.

In the 1860 U.S. Federal Census, David Smith Carnahan and his new bride, Susan Stevenson, had been married just one month, and they had living in the household with them David's youngest sisters, Sarah and Isabell, plus his widowed mother, Margaret. David was working as a farmer. In the Census record, his name was misspelled as "Karnahan".

In 1863, David Carnahan was registered for the military during the Civil War as evidenced by the document below. To date, in 2013, I have not been able to uncover any Civil War service. He was listed as part of the 24th Congressional District in Pulaski Township, Lawrence County, Pennsylvania.

SCHEDULE 1.—CONSOLIDATED LIST of all persons of CLASS I, subject to do military duty in the twenty fourth Lawrence Greene and Washington State of Pennsylvania, enumerated Capt John Cuthbertson, Provost Marshal.

RESIDENCE.	NAME.	AGE 1st July, 1863.	WHITE OR COLORED.	PROFESSION, OCCUPATION, OR TRADE.	MARRIED OR UNMARRIED.	PLACE OF BIRTH. (Naming the State, Territory, or Country.)
Lawrence Co. Pa						
Pulaski Tp.	Carnahan David	24	White	Farmer	married	Penn^a^

In the 1865 Illinois State Census, he was enumerated in Green Township, Mercer County, Illinois. There were other Carnahan names in the same township including Joseph, William, and 2 different entries for John. Green Township does not appear on a 2013 Illinois highway map. Perhaps the boundaries of Mercer County have changed since 1865. There is a town near Roseville, (the place they later left Illinois from when they migrated to Kansas), in Warren County called Greenbush. I wonder if this could have been Green Township? This is one question for research.

It's unclear to me why they migrated to Illinois. The Census records indicate that he was a carpenter. There were a number of Carnahan family names who were farming in Mercer County, Illinois. Perhaps they were relatives of David's, and the reason he elected to go to Illinois.

In the 1870 U.S. Federal Census, the family had relocated to Viola in Mercer County, Illinois. On a 2013 Illinois highway map, Viola was located at the intersection of U.S. highway 67 and State highway 17, due south of Rock Island, Illinois. David and Susan had 5 children living at that time: Mary Celestia, Anna Margaret, Ella Arminda "Minnie", Martha Emma, and Robert Audley. David was working as a carpenter. His real estate was valued at $400 and personal property at $300. He was born in Pennsylvania, as well as Susan, and his first 2 daughters. Ella Arminda, the third daughter, born in 1865, was born in Illinois. Therefore, it seems the family relocated to Illinois probably between 1863 and 1865. Some researchers also attribute a son, William, who was born and died in 1866, but I've not found records of such as of 2013.

Sometime before 1878, David Smith ventured out of Illinois to Kansas and filed a claim at the land office in Larned, Kansas, on a piece of land located in Stafford County. The family followed in September of 1878. Mabel Pearl's journal stated the family left from Roseville, Illinois, which was 35 or so miles south of Viola in Warren County. So, it seems that sometime after the 1870 U.S. Federal Census, and before David Smith went to Kansas, the family relocated again to Roseville. On a 2013 Illinois highway map, Roseville was located on U.S. highway 67, at the intersection of State highway 116.

Sunflowers abound in Kansas, 2002

Unlike the earlier pioneers who had to travel by oxen drawn wagon, Susan and the children migrated by train. They took various household items with them including a Seth Thomas clock, charter oak cook stove, and a looking glass. The end of the line for them was Sterling, Kansas, about 60 miles from their homestead.

At the 1880 U.S. Federal Census, we find them in Clear Creek Township, Stafford County, Kansas. Local Stafford County history references indicate that David Smith was one of the earliest settlers in this part of Stafford County. We see that the oldest daughter, Mary Celestia, was not listed in the Census as she had died in 1879 on Thanksgiving Day. David was listed as a carpenter. Albano Township was located in the southwest part of Stafford County on the dividing line with Pratt County to the south. In 1875, Stafford County was reorganized and parts given to neighboring counties. In 1879, it was re-established, but Albano Township was given to Clear Creek Township, the township to the west of Albano. Eventually, the Clear Creek Township area was divided, and Albano Township became the eastern part known as Township 25, Range 14. This explains why in the 1880 U.S. Federal Census, D. S. Carnahan was enumerated in Clear Creek Township.

When David Smith Carnahan migrated to Stafford County, permanent settlers had only been there for less than 4 years. He was truly one of the first pioneers in the area. Buffalo still roamed freely. Hunters left their carcasses to rot in the sun.

The square in St. John, Kansas, 1880. A buffalo wallow filled with water was in the center.

In addition to being a carpenter, family tradition and court records indicate he was also a farmer and had a timber claim. David's timber claim was located in the S.E. Quarter of Section 22, Township 25, Range 14 West. His homestead was the N.E. Quarter of Section 27, Township 25, Range 14. Although the plat map shows just 40 acres for a timber claim, the court documents indicate he had the full 160 acres comprising the quarter section for a timber claim.

The 1885 Kansas State Census actually listed D. S. as a farmer and a carpenter. They were again enumerated in Clear Creek Township of Stafford County.

This Census also recorded for the township the following productions of agriculture: peach orchards were the most popular followed by apple. Cherry, pear, and plum were also represented, but by a much smaller number. Peach trees numbered 2,439; apple, 816; cherry, 19; plum, 17; and pear, 9. There was a horse-powered sorghum factory which employed 7 men, a steam-powered "flouring" mill which employed 3 men, and a wind-powered feed mill. Under the heading "Artificial Forest," there were 157 acres of cottonwood trees and 6 acres of walnut. There was $1,370 worth of animals fattened and slaughtered. There were 6 sheep killed by dogs. Wool clip amounted to 12,116 pounds. There were 16 swine which died of disease, plus 3 cows, 1 mule, and 1 horse. Livestock was counted as well totaling 215 swine, 2,152 sheep, 1,983 cattle, 109 milk cows (spelled milch), 14 mules, and 107 horses. Butter production on the family farmstead was very high totaling 6,160 pounds. That's a lot of churning for someone! Poultry and eggs were sold totaling $321, and $216 worth of garden produce. There were 893 tons of prairie-cut hay, and 372 tons of tame-cut hay. Perhaps "tame-cut" was cultivated and "prairie-cut" was wild? We see that corn was still the more important crop as there were 4,210 bushels on hand at Census time, as compared to just 2,334 bushels of wheat. Acres of millet sown were 333. This was to be harvested after the Census. Acres planted of sorghum were 96; sweet potatoes, 4; and Irish potatoes, 29. There were 203 acres of oats in the ground, 1,474 acres of corn in the ground, 191 acres of rye, and 909 acres of winter wheat. There were 3,335 rods of wire fencing installed.

~~~~~~

Back in the Day . . . What's a rod equal? According to Wikipedia.org, accessed 12.5.13, "The rod or perch or pole is a surveyor's tool and unit of length equal to 5½ yards, 16½ feet, or 1/320th of a statute mile and one-fourth of a surveyor's chain. The rod is useful as a unit of length because whole number multiples of it can equal one acre of square measure. The perfect acre is a rectangular area of 43,560 square feet, bounded by sides 660 feet by 66 feet long, or 220 yards by 22 yards long, or 40 rods by 4 rods long. Thus, an acre is 160 square rods. Since adoption of the international yard on 1 July 1959, the rod has been equal to exactly 5.0292 meters…..the rod is still in use in rough terrains with heavy overgrowth where lazar or other optical measurements are difficult or impossible to use."

~~~~~~

Here's the numbers for D. S. Carnahan's farm: He owned his farm and he had 320 acres not under fence. His total value of farm implements was $44, and he did not pay any wages or board, so he may have been farming with just the family for labor. In the ground he had 60 acres of winter wheat, 30 acres of rye, 12 acres of corn, and 1 acre of Irish potatoes. He had 10 acres of millet in the ground, plus 25 bushels of corn on hand, and 50 bushels of wheat on hand. He had 6 tons of tame hay cut and 6 tons of wild prairie hay cut. His farm produced 150 pounds of butter. For livestock, he had the following: 2 horses, 3 milk cows, 8 other cattle, 6 sheep, and 7 swine. He slaughtered $55 worth of animals, and had

1,550 pounds of wool clip. Somehow, this number for wool clip doesn't seem right as he only recorded 6 sheep. I believe this number is possibly an error, although, he could have had a lot more sheep to produce the wool clip and then slaughtered or sold them. He had 100 peach trees and 1 plum tree. Also, he had 10 acres of cottonwood trees that were over 3 years old. Honey locust and walnut trees were not counted because he only had a few of each according to family tradition, and the Census was counting acres of tree type; not individual trees. He owned 2 dogs, as well. Of interest, the report did not record the number of working oxen. We know that D. S. had a team of oxen as they were purchased to help with the planting of the timber claim. They even had names.

Back in the Day . . . Oxen were the animals used to tame the prairie. Oxen liked to follow in a straight line and they preferred level land. They also provided transportation across the prairie. The first roads followed former oxen trails.

Oxen in a team, photo from Wikipedia http://en.wikipedia.org/wiki/File:Bullock_yokes.jpg

Back in the Day . . . The Herd Law was passed in 1879. The herd law required animals to be fenced in rather than roam free. In contrast, the fence law required crops to be fenced in. Barbed wire fencing came to Kansas in 1875.

David's timber claim was planted in 1881 according to Mabel Pearl's journal when she stated that David came home to plant the timber claim. He had been working as a carpenter in Topeka, constructing the staircases in the west wing of the capitol building. In 2002, I had opportunity to visit Topeka and see the staircases that my great-great grandfather, David Smith Carnahan, helped to construct.

Timber claims had to prove up by the owner planting and maintaining 10 acres of trees. They had to find the saplings themselves. Some of the trees that he planted, with the help of a yoke of oxen named Duke and John, were second year cuttings of cottonwood, box elder, ailanthus, walnut, and a thorny tree called honey locust. Peach seeds were also planted to start an orchard. Having a peach orchard may explain why peach ice cream was a favorite of David's granddaughter, Alberta. Perhaps she ate quite a bit of it as a child.

Left, Staircase in the west wing of the Kansas State Capitol, Topeka, Kansas
Right, West wing of Kansas State Capitol, Topeka, 2002

The timber claim did prove up as evidenced by the following copy of the Final Receipt:

Final Receipt.

David S. Carnahan. Final Receivers Receipt No 146.
Application No 1998. Timber Culture
Acts of March 13. 1874. and June 14. 1878.
Receivers Office Larned Ks. Aug 12th 1886.
Received of David S. Carnahan the sum of Four
dollars — cents being the balance of payment required by law
for the timber culture entry of the NE¼ of Section 27, in Town
ship 25 S of range 14 W. 6. P meridian containing
160. 00 acres under the acts of March 13. 1874 and the
act of June 14, 1878 amendatory thereof entitled,
An act to amend the act entitled, An act to
encourage the growth of timber on the western
prairies
$4.00

H. M. Bickel.
Receiver.

Filed for Record. 13. Aug. 1886. 1. P.M
[illegible]
Reg of Deeds.
[illegible]

Sometime after David received the final receipt for his timber claim from the government, he granted to Rev. Samuel Wylie and 3 others a mortgage on that timber claim. I'm not sure how to interpret this action. Perhaps a church was to be built on the property?

S. E. QUARTER NAME OF INSTRUMENT.	NAME OF GRANTOR.	NAME OF GRANTEE.	DESCRIPTION OF PROPERTY	CONSIDERATION. DOLLARS.	RECORDED. VOL.	RECORDED. PAGE.
...l Receipt	United States	David S Carnahan	NE 9	Cash with L	2	381
...tgage	David S Carnahan & wife	Rev Samuel Wylie	" "	250.00	9	12
"	" " " " "	R H Lockwood & J H Blundin	" "	25.00	8	[illegible]
"	" " " " "	James H Tallman	" "	1200.00	16	534
"	" " " " "	Brown & Caffman	" "	120.00	16	544
...ceipt	Samuel Wylie	David S Carnahan	" "	—	9	12
...ease	Lockwood & Blundin	" "	" "	—	8	226
...ent	United States		" "	Cash Entry	4	374

Left, Honey locust trees had horrible thorns according to Mabel Pearl
Right, This sod house was built in 1877 southeast of St. John on the Gray farm. Notice the gable end roof construction

~~~~~~

Back in the Day . . . Sod houses: The sod house was constructed literally from the prairie turf. The virgin prairie was covered with grasses such as buffalo grass, little blue stem, and wire grass. These grasses had roots that often extended deeper underground than the height of the grass above ground. When D. S. was building his sod house, bricks were cut one at a time by hand. They measured about 4" thick and about 12" wide by 3' length. They would be stacked so as to make walls that were 2' thick. Doors and windows would be encased by wooden frames. Sometimes 1½ story sod houses would be constructed. Ridge poles supported the roof. Cedar ridge poles were preferred because they were very strong. The better roof was a shingled gable end roof. If one could afford lumber, this made a better roof with less leaking.

~~~~~~

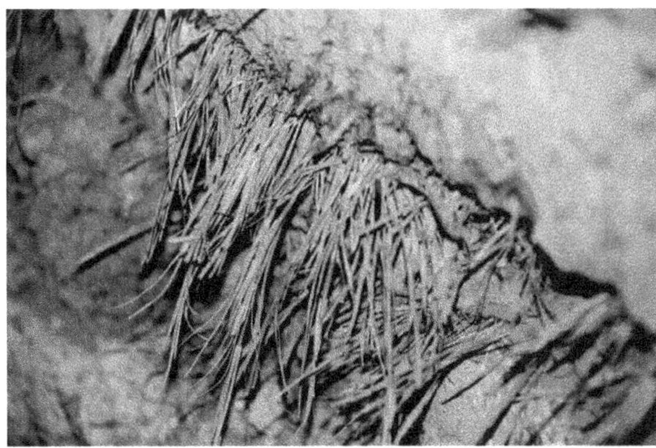

Left, Interior of a sod house showing how a framed window is inserted into the wall

Above, Interior wall of a sod house chinked with mortar to keep out the cold elements

Outside of a typical sod house, 2002

The Carnahan homestead began with a single room sod house with a sod roof, and a sod fireplace. This structure housed the family of 7.

This served the family until D. S.—a carpenter by trade—could build a larger sod structure, 12x24' inside with a shingled gable roof, 3 windows, 2 doors, and a dirt floor. This sod house had a sleeping room with 2 small windows, so it was probably a 1½ story. A rag carpet divided the space for privacy.

According to Mabel Pearl's journal, in 1887, D. S. built a new 5-room house on a hill. One part was 1½ stories high with 2 bedrooms upstairs. The old sod house was abandoned. It seems the family lived in sod houses for the first 8 years they were on the prairie.

David Smith used his carpentry skills to help build the community. For example, in 1883, David helped William Goodman construct a 5-room house for Will's widowed mother and her children. Then together, Will Goodman and David Smith Carnahan, built a school house which Ruby and Mabel Pearl attended. It possibly was the Emerson School building which was located just 2 miles west of the homestead.

D. S. also involved himself with community affairs. He was the commissioner for Albano Township in 1904 as mentioned in the newspaper article about Mabel Pearl's wedding.

According to Mabel Pearl's journal, there were a number of school houses in the vicinity from which the family could choose. One school house was located in a sod house near to their farmstead. Another was built at Livingston 7 miles away to which Audley and Martha Emma walked. This one was about 2 miles, Emerson School House, 1916. Possibly it's the one D. S. Carnahan and Will Goodman built.

In the 1905 Kansas State Census, we see that Mabel Pearl and her husband, W. H. Stevens, were both living with David and Susan. This was the year the productions of agriculture report listed both men working on the Carnahan farm output.

In 1908, David's wife of 48 years, Susan Stevenson, passed away. She was interred in the Neelands Cemetery. In 1909, David married again to Mary Roseann Duff. It was his second marriage and her third according to the 1910 U.S. Federal Census. At the Census time, they were living in St. John City.

At the 1915 Kansas State Census, they were still living in St. John. David was 76 years old and Mary 75. They owned their home.

A look at a 1916 atlas for Albano Township indicates that Enoch Sylvester Davison owned the farmstead that had been David Smith Carnahan's. This prompted a search of court documents which produced the following:

E. QUARTER. NUMERICAL INDEX, Section 27, Township 25, Range 14 W.

[Date] of Instrument.			Name of Instrument.	Name of Grantor.	Name of Grantee.	Description of Property.	Consideration. Dollars.	Recorded. Vol.	Recorded. Page.
6	22	1911	Release	The First National Bank	David S Carnahan	NE¼		38	63
	19	1911	Warranty Deed	David S Carnahan	Enoch S Davison	" "	7760	40	266

D. S. Carnahan sold his 160 acre homestead to his son-in-law, Enoch Sylvester Davison, husband of Ruby Isabel Carnahan Davison.

Throughout the years, D. S. Carnahan conducted a number of transactions involving his homestead, the N.E. Quarter of Section 27, Township 25, Range 14 West. In one of the rentals of his homestead, he specified that he wanted wheat, corn, oats, rye and barley to be the only crops that his tenant could grow.

These transactions were recorded in the Stafford County Courthouse in St. John as follows:

Quarter. NUMERICAL INDEX, Sec. 27 Town 25 Range 14 W.

Date of Instrument	Name of Instrument	Name of Grantor	Name of Grantee	Description of Property	Consideration Dollars	Recorded Vol	Recorded Pg
10 1893	Mortgage	D. S. Carnahan et ux	M. A. Littlefield	NE 1/4	900 00	2	33
20 1888	Assignment	The Showalter Mortgage Co.	Geo. H. Burr	NE 1/4	1100 00	15	9
[illegible] 1897	Release	Geo. H. Burr	David S. Carnahan et ux	NE 1/4		15	9
[illegible]	"	[illegible] M. A. Littlefield	[illegible]	[illegible]	[illegible]	[illegible]	33
[illegible]	Mortgage	[illegible]	[illegible] Bank	[illegible]	[illegible]	[illegible]	[illegible]
[illegible]	Release	The First National Bank	David S. Carnahan [illegible]	[illegible]		[illegible]	[illegible]
[illegible]	Mortgage	David S. Carnahan et ux	W. H. Thompson	[illegible]	2700.	[illegible]	[illegible]
[illegible]	Assignment	R. H. Thompson	The First National Bank	NE 1/4		[illegible]	[illegible]

In a 1894 transaction, D. S. Carnahan leased his timber claim in Section 22 to L. J. Tobias.

On 24 January 1917, David Smith Carnahan passed away and joined Susan Stevenson Carnahan in the Neelands Cemetery. He was 77 years old. His Find A Grave Memorial No. is 89944610. Neelands Cemetery is located in Albano Township, in the S.E. Quarter of Section 4,Township 25 South, Range 14 West, on the original homestead of James Neelands.

David Smith Carnahan and Susan Stevenson Carnahan grave stone in Neelands Cemetery, Stafford County, Kansas

According to the Stafford County History 1870-1990, p. 15, "There are a few unmarked graves in the area. These have become such a distant memory, the names are lost." As several of David Smith Carnahan's grandchildren were buried in Neelands Cemetery, perhaps his daughter, Mary Celestia, may also be there in an unmarked grave. The cemetery was filed for record on January 12, 1884, but it is unknown when it was first opened as a cemetery. We may never know where Mary's grave is located.

In 2013, I had opportunity to visit Stafford County. While attending services at the Antrim Methodist Church, I met the men who are farming the former Carnahan homestead and timber claim: Rick (last name unknown to me) and Roger Russell.

I attended a wonderful service at the Antrim Methodist Church. The congregation was warm and fellowship sweet. Everyone was so helpful when they learned of my family history search, 2013.

Left, Roger Russell and wife, Virginia, who in 2013, were farming the former Carnahan timber claim in Albano Township, Stafford County, Kansas, pictured here by some of Roger's stained glass work inside the Antrim Methodist Church.

Right, Barbara Kinney Black with Rick at the Antrim Methodist Church, Stafford County, Kansas. Rick was farming in 2013 the former Carnahan homestead land for its current owner

Left, Former Carnahan timber claim as seen in 2013. Martha Emma Carnahan stated she planted all the trees on their timber claim, holding them in her apron before they went into the ground.

Right, This "fruit" was found growing on the former Carnahan timber claim. Who knows what it is.

Here is a photo of David with his second wife, Mary Rosanne Duff.

David Smith Carnahan and Mary Rosanne Duff

In 2013, I visited the former Carnahan family homestead and timber claim. As I stood looking at those mature cottonwood trees, I was reminded that Martha Emma once described to her niece, Julia Kint, how she held all those trees as saplings in her apron. More than 100 years later, the fruit of her labor still stood as a testament to the hardiness and tenacity of our pioneer ancestors.

Standing in the super fine sugar sand of the rutted farm roads, I was reminded that their sod house floor was composed of the same fine sand. Before every meal, David Smith Carnahan knelt down in that sand and gave thanks to God for all he had been granted. That picture in my mind is a humbling one. It reminds me of the Scripture which tells us that one day every knee will bow and every tongue will confess that Jesus Christ is Lord. D. S. had a head start in practicing his kneeling before God.

Questions:

1. Why did the David Smith Carnahan family migrate to Illinois?
2. Where did they live in Illinois? Various Census records put them in Green Township, Mercer County; Viola, Mercer County; and family records put them in Roseville, which is in Warren County.
3. When did D. S. go to Kansas to file on a homestead claim?
4. Was there an 1875 or thereabouts Illinois State Census that he would have appeared in?
5. What caused them to migrate on to Kansas?
6. Did they have a son named William born in 1866?
7. Where was Mary Celestia living when she died on Thanksgiving Day?
8. Where is Mary Celestia Carnahan buried?

9. What was the sex, birthdate, death date, and name of the child which Susan Carnahan indicated on the 1900 U.S. Federal Census that she had given birth to, but was not surviving at the 1900 Census?
10. What is the "fruit" in the picture on page 259?

The Parents of David Smith Carnahan

Joseph Carnahan and Margaret Laughlin

1801-1847 1804-1876

Joseph Carnahan was born in 1801 in St. Clair Township, Allegheny County, Pennsylvania, the youngest child of David Carnahan and Agnes McKean McGaughey. He married Margaret Laughlin. Together they had at least 7 children—6 daughters and 1 son-- David Smith Carnahan. Joseph died fairly young, in 1847, at age 46, leaving his only son, David Smith, at 8 years old, the sole male in the household. Joseph was interred in Hopewell Cemetery, New Bedford, Lawrence County, Pennsylvania.

Questions:

1. How did Joseph die?
2. Did he serve the military in any wars?
3. Is there a Find A Grave memorial for Joseph Carnahan or other burial record? Is there an obituary or funeral card?

I do not know much of Margaret Laughlin other than what the Census records reveal. She was born about 1804 in Pennsylvania. She married Joseph Carnahan about 1824 or 25. They were living in Mahoning, Mercer County, Pennsylvania, at the 1830 U.S. Federal Census and at the 1840 Census as well.

In the 1850 U.S. Federal Census, Margaret was the head of the household. Daughters, Mary and Martha, were 23 and 18; David was 11; and the younger daughters, Sarah and Isabell, were 8 and 7. Margaret's mother, Jane Laughlin, 83, completed the household. They were living in Pulaski, Lawrence County, Pennsylvania.

Margaret next showed up in the 1860 U.S. Federal Census, still living in Pulaski, Lawrence County, Pennsylvania, but now with her son, David, and his bride of one month, Susan Stevenson. Margaret's youngest daughters, Sarah and Isabell, completed the household.

She apparently stayed behind in Pennsylvania when David migrated to Illinois as she died 19 April 1876, in New Bedford, Mercer County, Pennsylvania. She was interred in Hopewell Cemetery, New Bedford, Lawrence, County, Pennsylvania.

Questions:

1. How did Margaret Laughlin Carnahan support the family after Joseph died?

2. How did she meet Joseph?
3. What denomination did she belong to?
4. Are there any church records on her available?
5. Who were her parents?
6. Is there a Find A Grave memorial or other funeral or death certification information available?

The Wife of David Smith Carnahan

Susan Stevenson

1842-1908

Susan Stevenson was born 5 April 1843, in Allegheny County, Pennsylvania. At the 1850 U.S. Federal Census for Ohioville, Beaver County, Pennsylvania, Susan Stevenson was 8 years old. Her father, Samuel M. Stevenson, 37; mother, Nancy A., 35; her older sisters were Catharine, 12; and Ellen, 10; and her younger brothers were Homer, 5; James W., 3; and Cyrus, 7 months, completed her family. Her father was a chair maker.

By the 1860 U.S. Federal Census, much had occurred in her young life. She had moved to Pulaski, Lawrence County, Pennsylvania, she had married David Smith Carnahan on 6 June 1860, just 1 month before the Census taker arrived at her house, and she was sharing her home with David's 2 youngest sisters, one of whom was just 1 year older than she was, and the other 1 year younger than she, plus his widowed mother, Margaret. David was working as a farmer. There are no records that I've been able to locate about her parents, Samuel Moore and Nancy Ann Dawson Stevenson, after 1855.

At the 1870 U.S. Federal Census, the Civil War had finished, and she was living in Voila, Mercer County, Illinois. David was a carpenter, while Susan was keeping house. Susan probably had her hands full with 5 children under age 10 including: Mary, 9; Margaret Anna, 7; Minnie, 5; Martha Emma, 2; and Robert Audley, 6 months. The family had real estate valued at $400 and personal property valued at $300.

From 1878 onward, we have a fascinating and revealing story about their move to Kansas written by Susan's youngest daughter, Mabel Pearl. The story, I Remember, reprinted below, is a journal of how the family settled their 160 acre homestead and 160 timber claim out on the native prairie land of Stafford County, Kansas.

I REMEMBER

By Mabel Pearl Carnahan Stevens

David S. Carnahan, and his wife, Susan Stevenson, living in Roseville, Illinois, decided in 1878 to go west and homestead in Kansas to benefit his health and that of their third daughter.

Father came earlier and filed on a homestead and timber claim in Stafford County: S E 1/4 of 22 and N.E. 1/4 of 27, TWP 25, Range 14 west, 6 PM.

The first shelter was a small sod room with a sod roof, a sod fireplace, and an opening for a door. Next, a sod house 12x24' inside with shingled gable roof, three windows, two doors and a dirt floor was built. It had a sleeping room upstairs with two small windows. They hung a rag carpet up to make a partition.

A well seventeen feet deep was dug and water was drawn with a bucket and rope over a pulley. A furrow was plowed to mark a trail.

In September, 1878, Mother and five children came to Kansas by train to Sterling, about 60 miles from the homestead. Among the things they brought from Illinois were a charter oak cook stove, a big Seth Thomas clock, and a looking glass. I still have the rolling pin Mother bought in 1860.

Two of the girls, Mary and Anna, found work in homes, and Minnie went to live with friends at Reno Center. She went to school and learned to play the organ. Mary, the oldest girl, had prepared to teach school, but she died Thanksgiving Day in1879.

Mother had a horse, Old Seal, to ride and a side saddle. She sometimes rode to Sterling. The first day she rode to Stafford--a collection of sod shanties--spent the night, then continued on to Sterling.

Father found work as a carpenter in Topeka. The west wing on the state capitol was being built. His first test was to make a sixteen foot straight edge. He did the finishing work on the main stairway.

There were buffalo, coyotes, antelope and thousands of rattle snakes. Buffalo chips and wild plum brush was used for fuel. Mother wouldn't buy coal, but did buy a cow. Corn was grown and all but the stubs and roots were fed to the cow. The stubs and roots were saved for fuel. Mother, Emma, and Audley lived one time for two weeks on green corn.

The first sermon and Sunday School was held in our sod house. The first post office was at Voxburg, two and one half miles west and one mile south. Later there was a post office, store, and school, No.7, at Livingston, seven miles away. Audley and Emma walked to that school every day for six months. The next school built was No. 12, one mile east and two miles north.

My sister, Anna, and Columbus Graff were married November 1, 1880.

Father came home in 1881 to plant the ten acres of trees on the timber claim. He bought a yoke of oxen to do the heavy work. They were also used to drive to Larned, 38 miles away, for supplies. The trip took several days. Second year cuttings of cotton wood were put in with a spade. Other trees were box elder, ailanthus, a few walnut, and one honey locust with horrible thorns. Peach seeds were planted to start an orchard. There had to be the required number of trees per acre to prove up.

We had a melon called a pie melon which was made into a butter spread with sorghum and spice. Pumpkins, squash, and beans, we always seemed to have, as well as wild plumbs. Potatoes grew good and were buried to keep from freezing.

Whenever Father was expected home, a lantern was hung in the north gable. When Duke and John saw the light, they made a "bee line" for it. Duke was a cantankerous old bull and John a lazy steer.

There was a great disappointment April 21, 1882, when a baby girl was born. Everyone wanted a boy. She was named Ruby Bell. On July 24, 1883, when another girl was born, an old maid aunt said, "Let the little thing die. It's only another one to keep." I got here long before I was expected. The mid-wife, Miriam McHenry, soaked me in a dishpan of warm water and did everything she knew. I was named Mabel Pearl. We must have been jewels to rate these names. Dr. Dix, a homesteader, did all he could for Mother and me. Dr. Dix, his wife, and daughter soon moved to Pratt where he practiced several years.

Sister Anna had a second child born August 5, 1883, and named Ralph. Her first one, Mary Grace, was born November 14, 1881. We all grew up together.

A wagon train of Mormons came driving along the trail one day and they saw a nice well-rounded hill. They stopped and settled there and built a church upon the hill. This became the city of St. John.

Water used to stand around the house after heavy rains and it would fill up the open well. Once there were several inches in the house. The dirt floor had worn down below the ground level so much I had great difficulty getting over the door sill. One of our neighbors had a sod house also, but with a board floor, and a sod roof. That roof gave way after a heavy rain and killed their two little girls. One time when Ruby was threatened with punishment she waded outside in the water and sat down in it then dared anyone to come and get her.

Morning worship was as regular as sunrise and breakfast. Father would read the Bible, then we all knelt by our chairs and Father prayed. Sometimes Mother would read and pray. Her prayer always had, "We thank Thee that it is as well with us as it is." No meal ever started until father or mother asked the blessing. We were to bow our heads and close our eyes. Once Ruby accused me of having my eyes open. HOW DID SHE KNOW??

School was held a few months of the year and the teacher studied along with the advanced pupils. It was held in a sod school house until Father and Will Goodman built the building which we attended through our school years.

Another settler, Ezra Webber, built a water powered mill in 1875 to grind meal for the settlers. When someone had no money to pay, he would take part of the meal as toll for payment.

We would bring sacks of corn into the house and shell it by hand for meal and wheat was cleaned and made into graham flour. Father and Audley planted a field of sorghum cane, and when it was ready, it was cut and taken to Macksville for squeezing. We then had a fifty gallon barrel of sorghum stored in the milk house. Ruby said it was no harm to worship that because there is nothing like it in heaven above or the earth beneath.

To learn to sew, I was allowed to use the sewing machine. The first dress I made had a blue check waist and sleeves and a brown check skirt. I had to have help with the sleeves. I had heard how ropes were stretched across a bed frame, so I made a doll bed that way.

One day there was talk about an organ; but what on earth was an organ? One day a man drove up in a spring wagon to deliver the organ. The thing was lifted out of the wagon and set in the middle of the room. He showed off how much he could play and sing. "When troubles come, I'll snap my thumb; For its all the same to Uncle Sam." When he was gone, Minnie played and we all sang "Jesus loves me, this I know, for the Bible tells me so." We all knew this one. Then the singing went on and on. The older ones sang all four parts: Father, the bass; Audley, tenor; and the girls, the other parts. Mother sang one song to us, "A Stone that is Rolling Gathers No Moss." A favorite hymn was, "I Need Thee Every Hour."

When I could reach the pedals of the organ, I learned a five finger exercise with words: "If at First you don't Succeed, Try, Try, Again. Then at Last if you Prevail, You Will Never, Never, Fail; If You Try, Try, Again."

~~~~~~

The hymn, "I Need Thee Every Hour," 1. I need thee every hour, Most gracious Lord; No tender voice like thine, Can peace afford. CHORUS: I need thee, O I need thee; Every hour I need thee! O bless me now, my Savior, I come to thee. 2. I need thee every hour, Stay thou nearby; Temptations lose their power, When thou art nigh. Chorus. 3. I need thee every hour, In joy or pain; Come quickly and abide, Or life is vain. Chorus. 4. I need thee every hour, Teach me thy will; Thy promises so rich, In me fulfill. Chorus. 5. I need thee every hour, Most Holy One; O make me thine indeed, Thou blessed Son.

~~~~~~

Father told us jokes and stories, one about two frogs: Long before dawn a farmer milked the cows and hitched his team to the wagon to take the milk to town and sell it. One can was not quite full, so he stopped at the creek and dipped up enough water to fill it, then went happily along. Two frogs found themselves in the can of milk. One said to the other, "No need struggle." So he went to the bottom. The other said, "I won't quit," so he kept on struggling. The farmer stopped to deliver some milk. Taking off the lid, there sat the frog on a chunk of butter croaking triumphantly, "Rivet---rivet---rivet."

Father made us a set of double six dominoes and there was a croquet set too.

In 1887, a new five-room house was built on a hill, and part of it was one and a half stories high with two bedrooms upstairs. We had a well close by the house with a pump. The old sod house was abandoned and the roof removed and used in a barn

I don't remember anything about the 1887 blizzard, but Father and Audley had to go out and break ice off of the noses of the cattle so they would not smother.

Father would get to coughing and he coughed so hard I thought he would surely cough up chunks of his lungs. Then Dr. Wilcox, a Civil War surgeon and doctor, moved on a farm near Livingston.

There was a big grove of cotton wood trees five miles from home, planted by the Neelands family. It was a fine place for picnics and camp meetings. About 1889, a Presbyterian church was organized and the preacher rode a horse from his farm near Belfont. He had been a chaplain in the Civil War and the horse was in the war with him. He was the shortest, fattest man you ever saw, and I wondered if he had had a bath since before the War.

My first school teacher was Stephen Frazee, and he taught vocal music in singing schools. My sister, Emma, and Tom Culbreath were married August 7, 1890, and it was surely a big day.

The next wedding was when Audley, my brother, and Annie Ketcham were married at her home August 27, 1891. He taught our school that year and there were about sixty-five pupils. We sat 3 in a seat. 1 sat between an 18 and a 20 year old and we shared one set of books. We valued our head marks in oral spelling. When any one missed a word, the one down the line spelling it went ahead. Once at the head of the line, you went to the foot and started over.

I don't think we burned much corn for fuel because we had wood brush and some coal, but we gave some to the neighbors to burn.

We picked hard shell potato bugs to earn money and got one cent per hundred. One summer I earned thirty five cents. When the soft shelled ones came, the vines were sprinkled with Paris green. Father said if we would milk a cow, he would give us a penny for each time until we got a dollar. Then we were supposed to know how. We also got a penny for Sunday School. One day a girl swallowed hers.

One time Father traded a registered pig to Dr. Wilcox for two hound dogs. They were brindle tan and named Fritz and Kaiswe. One day when Mother turned her back and the table was ready for dinner, they cleaned off everything, and she saw Fritz leaving with all the butter. She demanded screen doors and windows, and she got them.

In 1892 and 1893, Audley taught 8th and 9th grades in St. John. I was sick during vacation and did not go to school during the rest of the year. Mother went to care for Audley and Annie's first baby, and I went along. The baby, Lester Kent, only lived 7 months. That was the first death I knew in our family.

The follow spring I went fishing with Anna and Columbus. I seemed to catch a cold playing in the creek, and afterward, I had dreadful pains in my legs and they swelled up. Dr. Wilcox came and said it was inflammatory rheumatism. He gave me horrible tasting stuff and wrapped my legs with cotton. Sometime later, Father carried me downstairs for supper. Ralph came by, and he was sick also, with measles, so I got measles, too.

During that summer I couldn't make my left arm and leg work right. Father took me to see Dr. Wilcox, and with his help and a lot of will power, I outgrew all this. That summer was the first time I knew what it was to stay home from Sunday School.

Politics was a big issue and rallies were lively. Republicans were jubilant when Harrison was elected and the crops were good. In the campaign of 1892, we rode horses in the parade at St John. The township Albano got a big flag for the largest delegation. The Populists made a big hit in 1896 and about swallowed the divided Democrats. Jerry Simpson defeated Chester I. Long for Congress, and he didn't know enough to wear socks. Long was very capable. When Cleveland was elected the second time I never heard the vice president mentioned, although he was Mother's first cousin.

Minnie and George Culbreath were married in February 1896. It was his second marriage, and he had three children; the oldest ten years old.

In 1897 and 1898 we had a teacher whom the school board paid $22.00 per month, and he sure wasn't worth it.

Ruby and Enoch S. Davison were married February 20, 1898, and I didn't go to school the rest of the year. Mother was sick with rheumatism and arthritis. In September 1898, I went with my brother, Audley, and his wife, Annie, and two children, Carroll and Elsie, to go to school at Emporia. Father tried to keep someone to do the work for Mother. We went by train from Pratt. I stayed with friends near W. A. White's red rock home. We went to Buffalo Bill's Wild West Show. Buffalo Bill with the Wild West Riders chased buffalo around the grounds. Then riding at full gallop, Buffalo Bill and Annie Oakley came, he tossing glass balls into the air, and with a rifle, she hit every one.

When we were settled, I entered the Lewis Academy in connection with the College of Emporia. My brother was taking a course preparing for the ministry. There was so much memory work in the course; it was very easy for me.

A surprise to lots of folks: 1900 was not a leap year. We add one day to the fourth year, but a year is 365 days, 5 hours, 48 minutes and 46 seconds. So, leap year was left out to take up the slack.

Note: A leap year is a year whose number is exactly divisible by four, or in the case of century years, by 400. 1900/400=475 1896/4=474 2000/4005."

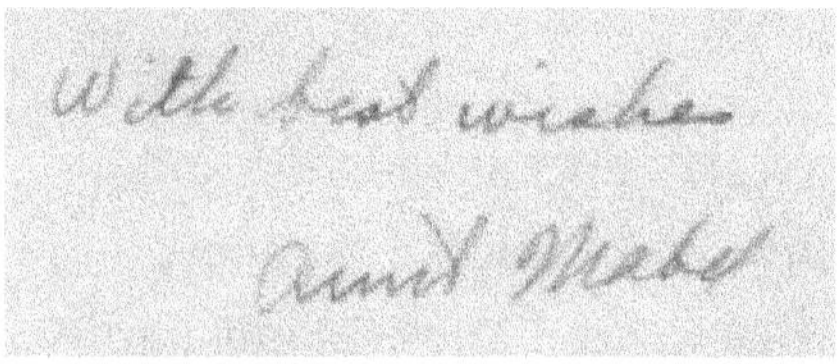

Charter Oak Cook Stoves were originally known as the Excelsior Stove Works and were the makers of the famous Charter Oak Cooking Stoves. In 1895, it was reorganized under the name of Charter Oak Stove and Range Co.

Although the train to Great Bend and Larned was already operating, the family disembarked in Sterling, Kansas, which was 60 miles from the homestead, while Great Bend was just 38 miles. Perhaps they had business there or friends. Mabel Pearl states

Susan rode her horse, Old Seal, to Sterling from time to time. She probably followed an early trail. Here's the former train station in Sterling.

Left, Sterling train station, destination of Susan Stevenson Carnahan and 5 children in 1878. Right, Piled up bleached buffalo bones marked the local trails to homesteaders' cabins, accessed at: http://boingboing.net/2012/09/13/the-grisly-business-of-buffalo.html

Local trails did not exist. If a pioneer wanted to find his way back to his sod house or dug out, he had to plow a furrow and stack bleached buffalo bones to mark the path.

Campaign button 1896 for Adlai Stevenson, supposed first cousin to Susan Stevenson Carnahan

The year the family arrived in Stafford County, Kansas, is described in the book, No Cyclone Shall Destroy, by Clelland Cole and Helen Malin Reuber, with Verl Manwarren; illustrations by Brent Ronen, 1981. Read the book at the link below.
https://openlibrary.org/books/OL3878443M/No_cyclone_shall_destroy

p. 8 -- "Eighteen hundred seventy eight was an especially trying year on the prairie; the wind, the drought, and the blizzards were discouraging. Not all of the newcomers stayed. Some of the wives, having a look at the dugouts and sod houses, and learning that under the weight of heavy snow some roofs had been known to collapse, returned to the east. Reports tell that no rain of any consequence fell from July 2, 1878, to August of 1879, and that such moisture as fell "warn't enough to wet a man's shirt."

A typical dugout which was built into the side of a hill.

That first year, 1878 and '79, with no crops yet producing food, they must have had a very difficult time. Susan was responsible for putting food on the table in David's absence. Here's a description of 1878 again from No Cyclone Shall Destroy, p. 9: "Money was scarce. Buffalo bones were hauled to Larned and sold for three to six dollars a ton, but the last buffalo hunt in the county took place in the spring of 1879. Many families in 1879 lived on jackrabbits, sand hill plums, and milk from the family cow."

Still, they did stay. Susan was evidently a hard worker. She raised 7 children on the prairie without benefit of much medical care. She ran the family farmstead much of the time while her husband was away doing carpentry work in Topeka. In fact, court records indicate that David Smith Carnahan transferred the family farmstead into Susan's name. She appeared on the plat map as the owner of the homestead, while David's name appeared on the plat map as the owner of the timber claim.

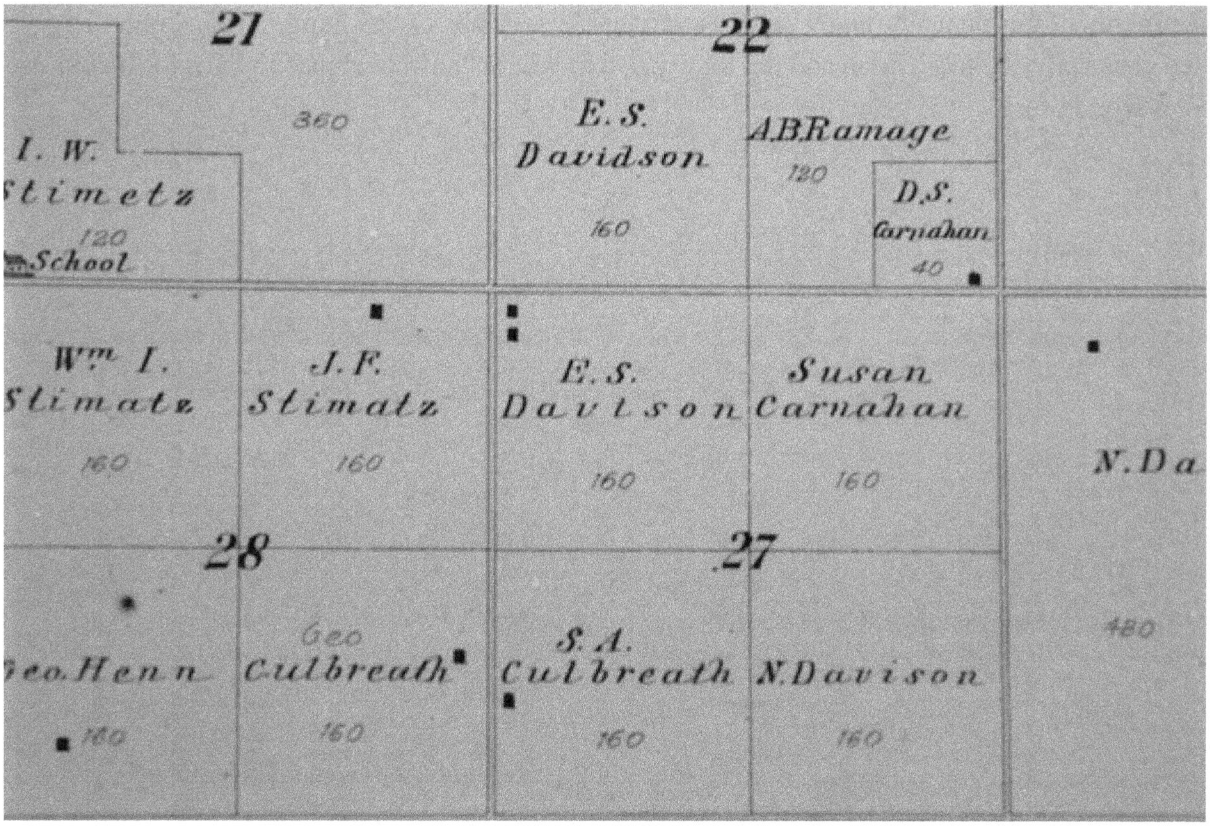

Plat map showing Sections 27 and 22 which contained Susan's 160 acre homestead and David Smith Carnahan's 160 acre timber claim. He apparently had sold part of the timber claim by the time of this plat map's issuance. Also note their sons-in-law, Logan (S.A.) and George Culbreath, plus Enoch Sylvester Davison had homesteads nearby.

In 2013, I watch home improvement shows on television, and when the home buyer is checking out prospective new houses, I hear the typical complaints, "Oh, no, there's only one sink in the bathroom…..I don't like the color of that granite counter top; it will have to be changed…..These hardwood floors are ugly; they will have to be replaced…..I don't want to paint over that hideous purple bedroom; I want a move-in ready house…..The kitchen is way too tight, it doesn't have a big enough island, and it's only got 6 upper cabinets; it's a total gut job…..Ugh, what's that wall doing there? I have to have an open concept living room and kitchen…..There's no formal dining room; I can't seat 16 people for Thanksgiving in that small space."

Yes, we do live in 2013; not 1880, and people think they have to have these hallmarks of an "American dream" house. Still, I can't help but compare my great, great grandmother's "American dream" home on the Kansas prairie of 1880 with our modern dwellings. Susan had a sod house. Basically, these were built of dank smelling bricks of prairie sod cut from the earth and chinked with a homemade mortar to keep out the cold. They did not keep out the rain completely, the dirt constantly sifted down through the sod roof sprinkling everything inside, there was no indoor plumbing, water came from a 17' well which was pulled up in a bucket over a pulley, it was super-hot in the summer, the biting cold winds of winter could take one's breath away, rattle snakes slithered their way through the sod walls to the inside threatening all who abided within, persistent packs of wolves were capable of destroying the walls of a sod house if one wasn't on guard with a shot gun, food was often scarce as they were at the mercy of the elements, and 9 people lived inside the walls of this humble sod abode. They didn't have electricity. In fact, Susan and the family had to gather "buffalo chips" to burn for fuel or use corn cobs or wood brush.

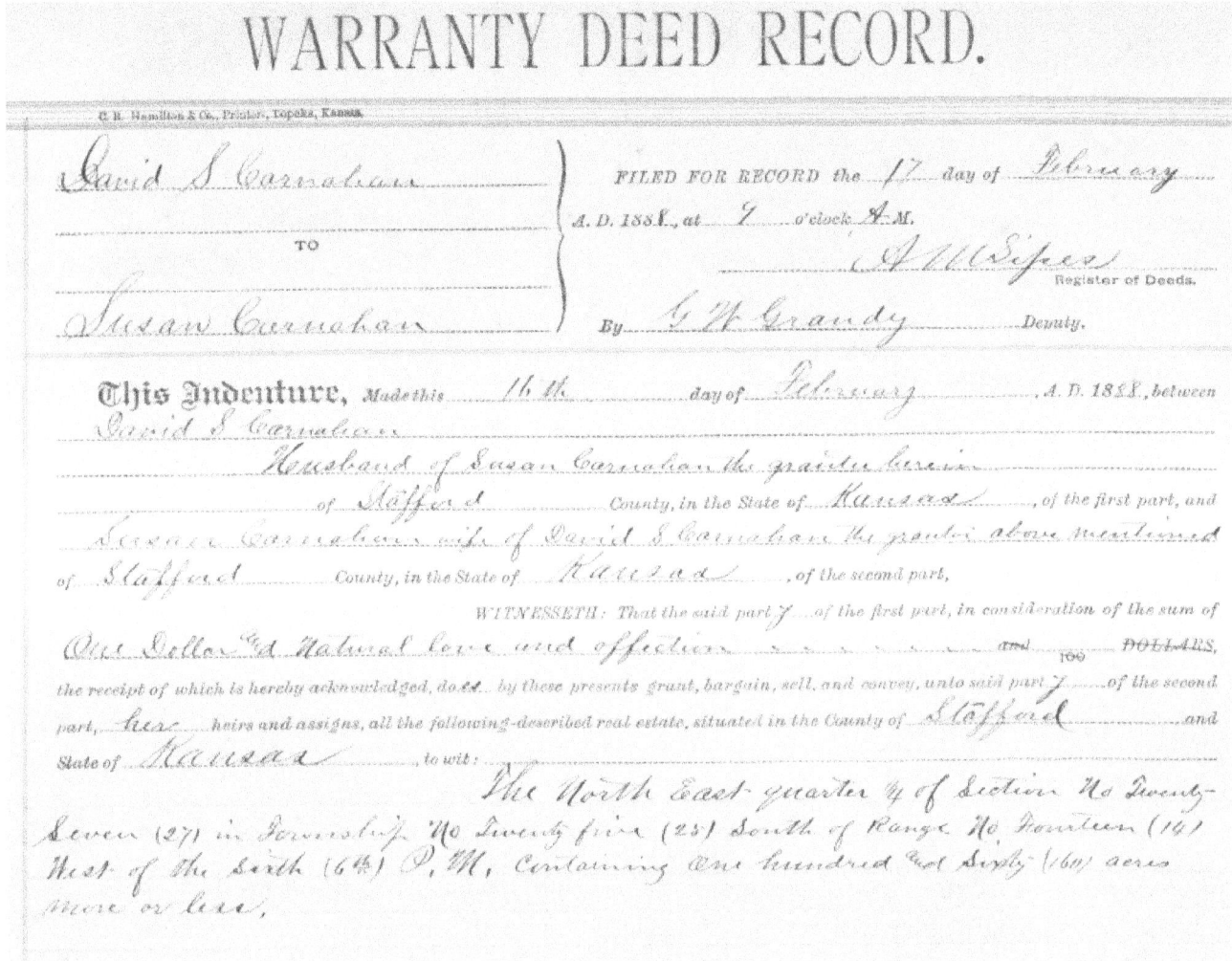

WARRANTY DEED RECORD.

G. H. Hamilton & Co., Printers, Topeka, Kansas.

David S Carnahan

TO

Susan Carnahan

FILED FOR RECORD the 17 day of February A. D. 1888, at 9 o'clock A.M.

A W Sipes
Register of Deeds.

By G W Grandy Deputy.

This Indenture, Made this 16th day of February, A. D. 1888, between David S Carnahan Husband of Susan Carnahan the grantee herein of Stafford County, in the State of Kansas, of the first part, and Susan Carnahan wife of David S Carnahan the grantor above mentioned of Stafford County, in the State of Kansas, of the second part,

WITNESSETH: That the said part y of the first part, in consideration of the sum of One Dollar and natural love and affection and 100 DOLLARS, the receipt of which is hereby acknowledged, does by these presents grant, bargain, sell, and convey, unto said part y of the second part, her heirs and assigns, all the following-described real estate, situated in the County of Stafford and State of Kansas, to wit:

The North East quarter ¼ of Section No Twenty-Seven (27) in Township No Twenty five (25) South of Range No Fourteen (14) West of the Sixth (6th) P. M. Containing One hundred and Sixty (160) acres more or less,

David Smith Carnahan deeded the family farmstead to his wife Susan Stevenson Carnahan for $1 and natural love and affection.

They didn't have separate bedrooms for each child; not even the parents had a private space. Before they sat to eat their daily meals, the entire family would kneel on the sugar sand floor of their sod home as David Smith Carnahan gave thanks to God Almighty for all He had provided for him and his family. Susan would pray when David was absent from the home. God's name was revered; not used flippantly or defiantly as in our 2013 culture. I believe that I'm a product of the faithfulness of my ancestors who recognized that all they were able to accomplish through hard work and business savvy was because they were enabled by their Creator and Savior, and for this heritage, I'm truly thankful.

Anyone for a buffalo chip? Photo from Stafford County History, 1870-1990
Compiled by Stafford County Historical and Genealogical Society, 1990

It is unclear what religious denomination Susan and David belonged to. We do know, from Mabel Pearl's journal, that faith in God was important to them as the first Sunday School in the community was held inside their sod house. The Carnahan name is Scottish in origin. If they descended from Scottish heritage, it is possible they were Presbyterians. Methodists were present in the area, and Susan's son-in-law's father, Nick Davison, was instrumental in the building and establishment of at least 2 different churches in the community: the Antrim Methodist Church and Emerson Presbyterian Church.

Left, This chandelier hanging in the Antrim Methodist Church, was made from glass plates which traveling ministers would use to tell Bible stories. Chandelier made by Roger Russell
Right, Stained glass window in Antrim Methodist Church made by Roger Russell

Antrim Methodist Church, Stafford County, Kansas

By the 1880 U.S. Federal Census, the Carnahans had been living on their homestead for just over a year. I wonder how many improvements they had managed to make in that short time. We know from I Remember, that much of this time David Smith was gone working in Topeka as a carpenter, so Susan was establishing the farmstead. We know that she grew corn, as that was the most popular crop in the early days of settlement. Corn produced about 40 bushels per acre. Corn kept the family fed and the livestock as well. We read in the journal how Susan and a few of the children lived on a diet of green corn once for a period of time. Later on, wheat became an important crop producing about 14 bushels an acre. Winter wheat produced gluten flour which was handy for bread and pastry. The first flour mill in Stafford County was Ezra Webber's grist mill in Albano Township. It was powered by a lake fed from underground springs. Other crops that were grown included milo, alfalfa, soybeans, barley, and oats, in addition to corn and wheat. In the early days settlers kept cattle, horses, poultry, hogs, and sheep. In 2013, mostly cattle were kept as a source of income.

Wheat milling continued in 2013. One of the most important mills in Stafford County produces a variety of flour called Hudson Cream because of its smooth silky texture. The modern packaging even has a QR code imprinted on the front. That's a far cry from the original cloth flour sacks which many a child growing up on the prairie recognized as their underwear!

At the 1885 Kansas State Census, daughter, Margaret Anna, had married Columbus Graff. Susan was left to farm with the help of daughter, Minnie, 20; Martha Emma, 17; only son, Robert Audley, 15; and she had to care for 2 small children, Ruby Isabel, 2; and Mabel Pearl, 1.

I wonder if she ever had time to just think about and remember her oldest, Mary Celestia, who had been taken from her on Thanksgiving Day, 1879. How did she react every Thanksgiving when the anniversary of that sad event rolled around? Was she thankful for all she had been granted, or was she sadly remembering the loss of her first born? I want to think that she was grateful; after all, God himself lost his only Son so that we all may have abundant life with Him. Surely He understood her pain and could provide a comfort for Susan in her own loss.

By the 1900 U.S. Federal Census, Susan was 58 years old. All her children except her youngest, Mabel Pearl, had married. They had 2 servants and 1 farm hand living with them. Living nearby was Audley and wife, Annie, and 3 children; Ruby Isabel and husband, Enoch Sylvester Davison, with 1 daughter; Ella Arminda (Minnie) and her husband, George Culbreath, with 6 children and 2 farm hands; daughter Margaret Anna and husband, Columbus Graff, and 7 of their children; and daughter Martha Emma and husband, Thomas Sherman Culbreath, with 3 of their children. I doubt that Susan was lonely.

After many years of hard work and suffering from arthritis and rheumatism, Susan passed away on 2 November 1908. She was interred in Neelands Cemetery near to her granddaughter, Ferne Davison, daughter of Ruby Isabel Carnahan and Enoch Sylvester Davison, who died as an infant.

Above, Entrance to Neelands Cemetery

Right, Susan Stevenson Carnahan, photo taken by Miss O. M. Shira photographer, St. John, Stafford County, Kansas in 1889.

A rope bed used in the 1870s. The ropes had to be tightened each night otherwise they would sag under the sleeper's weight, thus the expression, "Sleep tight; don't let the bed bugs bite."

Susan Stevenson Carnahan's former farmstead as it appeared in 2013

Former Carnahan farmstead and timber claim on either side of the road

Questions:

1. What, if any, was her connection to Vice President Adlai Stevenson? She herself claimed to be a first cousin.
2. What happened to her parents after 1855?
3. How did she meet David Smith Carnahan?
4. Did her father leave a will naming her or her siblings?
5. Why did she move to Pulaski?
6. When exactly did they move to Illinois, and did they live anywhere else in between Pennsylvania and Illinois?
7. Why did they move to Illinois?
8. What are possible routes and modes of transportation they may have taken to Illinois?
9. What inspired the family to move to Kansas?
10. Why did they choose their destination for their train migration as Sterling, Kansas, which was 60 miles away from the homestead, when there was a train all the way to Great Bend, Kansas, only 38 miles from the homestead?
11. What denomination did they belong to?
12. Where is Susan's oldest daughter, Mary Celestia Carnahan, buried?
13. Why did Susan go to Sterling often? Was it to visit friends, possibly visit her daughter's grave, go shopping, or some other reason.

The Children of Susan Stevenson and David Smith Carnahan

Mary Celestia Carnahan

1860-1879

Born 4 December 1860, in Pulaski Township, Lawrence County, Pennsylvania, Mary Celestia was the first child of Susan Stevenson and David Smith Carnahan. According to the family history account by her youngest sister, Mabel Pearl, I Remember, says that Mary found work in a home after the family arrived in Kansas. She also had prepared to become a teacher, but, unfortunately, she died on Thanksgiving Day in 1879, just a year after the family arrived in Kansas. Nothing else is known about her.

Questions:

1. Why did she die?
2. Where was she living at the time of her death?
3. Where is she buried?

Margaret Anna Carnahan

1863-1941

Margaret Anna was born 22 February 1863, in Pulaski Township, Lawrence County, Pennsylvania, to David Smith and Susan Stevenson Carnahan. She joined her older sister, Mary Celestia. She migrated to Illinois and then on to Kansas where, just 2 years after her arrival, on 1 November 1880, she married Columbus Graff who was farming the quarter section just south of her family's homestead. Columbus' land grant was described as: "S.E. Quarter of Section 27, Township 25 South, Range 14 West." The grant was recorded in Kansas Vol. 226, p. 278, and dated 24 January 1889, for 160 acres.

PROBATE COURT.

MARRIAGE LICENSE RECORD.

Marriage License.

State of Kansas, Stafford County, ss.

To any Person Authorized by Law to Perform the Marriage Ceremony, Greeting:

You are Hereby Authorized to Join in Marriage Columbus Graff aged 26 years, and Anna Carnahan aged years, and of this License you will make due return to my office within thirty days.

Probate Judge

CERTIFICATE OF MARRIAGE

State of Kansas, County, ss.

I the Undersigned, a Minister of the Gospel of the in said County, do hereby certify that in accordance with the authorization of the within License, I did, on the 7th day of November A. D. 1880 in said County, join and unite in Marriage the within named Columbus Graff Anna Carnahan

Witness my hand, the day and year above written.

Official Title: Rev

State of Kansas, Stafford County, ss. I the Undersigned, Probate Judge of said County, do certify the above to be a correct copy of the original Marriage License by me issued on the day first above written, together with a copy of the return endorsed on such license by the person performing the marriage ceremony.

Probate Judge

Columbus Graff and Margaret Anna Carnahan Marriage License

Together Anna and Columbus Graff had 12 children. The first of these children was born 14 November 1881, Mary Grace, and the second, Ralph Carleton, was born 5 August 1883. These 2 children grew up with their aunts, Ruby Isabel and Mabel Pearl Carnahan, also born in the early 1880s. Another child, Cephas Graff, died as an infant in 1887, and was interred in the Neelands Cemetery in Stafford County, Kansas, along with other members of his extended family.

At the 1900 U.S. Federal Census, Anna indicated she had given birth to 9 children, and 8 were living at the Census time. Children in the home included: Ralph Carleton, Harry Sylvester, Audley Columbus, David Eugene, Susan Katharine, Ethel Estelle, and Christian O. Graff. Perhaps Christian O. was known as Orley in the family history booklet, Love, Purity, Fidelity, The Carnahans, Culbreaths, Graffs.

In the 1910 U.S. Federal Census, the Graff family was living in Wayne, Edwards County, Kansas, on Lewis Street. Children in the home were: Susan, Ethel, and Orley as in the last Census, and newly added to the household were Cecil, John, and Ruby. Columbus was supporting the family doing odd jobs as a laborer. They were renting their home.

At the 1925 Kansas State Census, Columbus was working as a drayman, which, according to Dictionary.com, is a person who operates a dray which is a low, strong cart without fixed sides, for carrying heavy loads; a sledge or sled; or any vehicle, such as a truck, used to haul heavy goods; usually used to convey goods for short distances. I guess he was working as an early version of a trucker. The 2 youngest children were still in the home.

By the 1930 U.S. Federal Census, son, John, was the only child living in the household. He was working in a drug store.

Life during the 1930s Great Depression was difficult for everyone all over the country. It was especially difficult for those farmers in the Midwest where they had to contend with the Dust Bowl. I wonder if these 2 events caused Columbus and Margaret Anna to move off their farm and into the city. At any rate, for Columbus, it must have been discouraging and difficult to adjust to driving a cart around a town when he had been used to managing his own 160 acres of land since young adulthood. I believe this must have been the experience for a number of our ancestors.

Columbus Graff died in 1935 and was interred in Wayne Cemetery in Lewis, Edwards County, Kansas. His Find A Grave Memorial No. is 75741234. Margaret Anna Carnahan Graff passed away 28 March 1941, in Lewis, Edwards County, Kansas. Her burial place is not known to me as of 2013. It is presumed she may be next to Columbus.

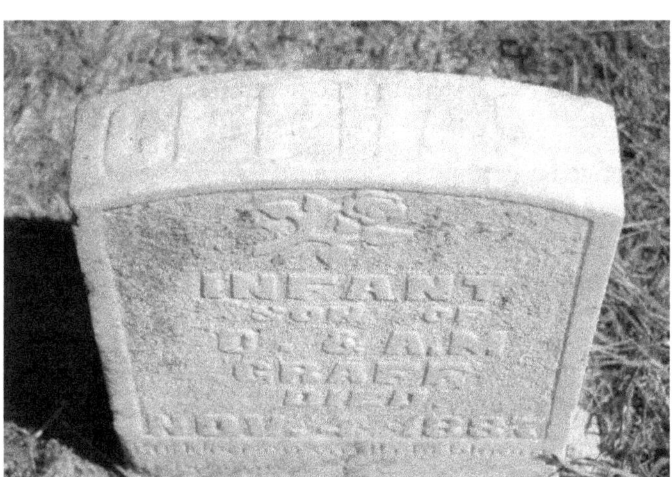

Cephas Graff's gravestone in Neelands Cemetery, Stafford County, Kansas. This tombstone is inscribed: "Infant Son of C. & A. M. Graff, Died November 4, 1887"

When in 2013 I visited the area just south of Stafford, the Gypsum Hills of Kansas, I saw many abandoned early 1900s era farmsteads like this one I photographed below.

Abandoned homestead in the Gypsum Hills area of Kansas along U.S. highway 160 between Coldwater and Medicine Lodge, Kansas

Gypsum Hills area of Kansas

Questions:

1. Where is Margaret Anna Carnahan Graff buried?

2. When and why did they sell their family farm?

3. What happened to their children and descendants? Where are they today?

4. What was the name of the denomination of the minister who performed their marriage ceremony as shown on their marriage license on pg. 280?

Ella Arminda "Minnie" Carnahan

1865-1907

Ella Arminda Carnahan was born in April 1865, after her family had relocated to Illinois from Pennsylvania. Known as Minnie, Ella was the third child of Susan Stevenson and David Smith Carnahan.

When the family came to settle in Stafford County, Kansas, Minnie went to live in Reno Center, presumably the next county to the east of Stafford. There she went to school and learned to play the organ according to her younger sister, Mabel Pearl's, family history journal, I Remember.

In the 1880 U.S. Federal Census, Ella Arminda was enumerated with her family in Clear Creek Township, Stafford County, and was listed as being a "hair worker". It's unclear if this is some kind of industry she was engaged in, or if she was working as a type of early beautician. She was 15 years old at the time and the only one of her siblings to have an occupation listed other than "at home", which was the standard classification for children who worked on the family farm.

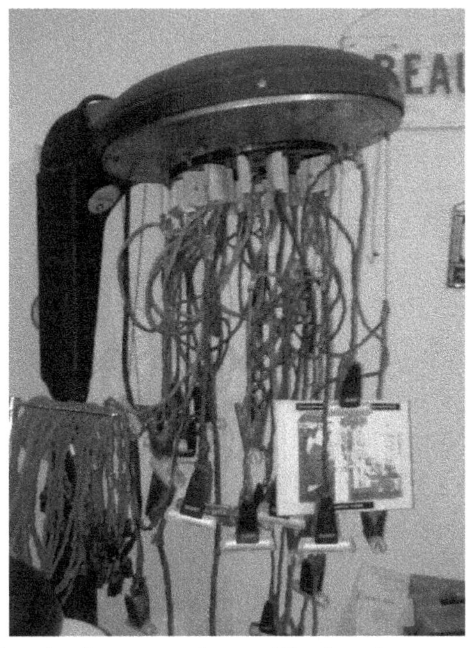

Ladies lucky enough to afford a day out at the beauty salon could look forward to drying their hair under this Helene Curtis electric hair dryer, or could be "tortured" under this contraption that curled the hair. It's a wonder the weight of the curlers didn't pull one's hair completely out!

In 1896, Ella married George Culbreath. Ella was 30 years old and George 35. He was a widower with 3 children, the oldest being 10 years old. Together George and Minnie gave birth to 6 children including: Lenna May Culbreath, born 1897, married James E. Burke; Mark C. Culbreath, born 1898, married Elsie; Aletta Mabel, born 1900, married Dr. Harry A. West; Ethel Beatrice, born 1903, married Herbert Berger; Goldia Anna, born 1905, married Dean Burleigh; and Helen Eliza, born 1907, married Willard Dunagan. Ella also functioned as step mother to George's 3 surviving children from his first marriage: Etta Mary, born 1884; Charles W., born 1888; and Grace Pearl., born 1890.

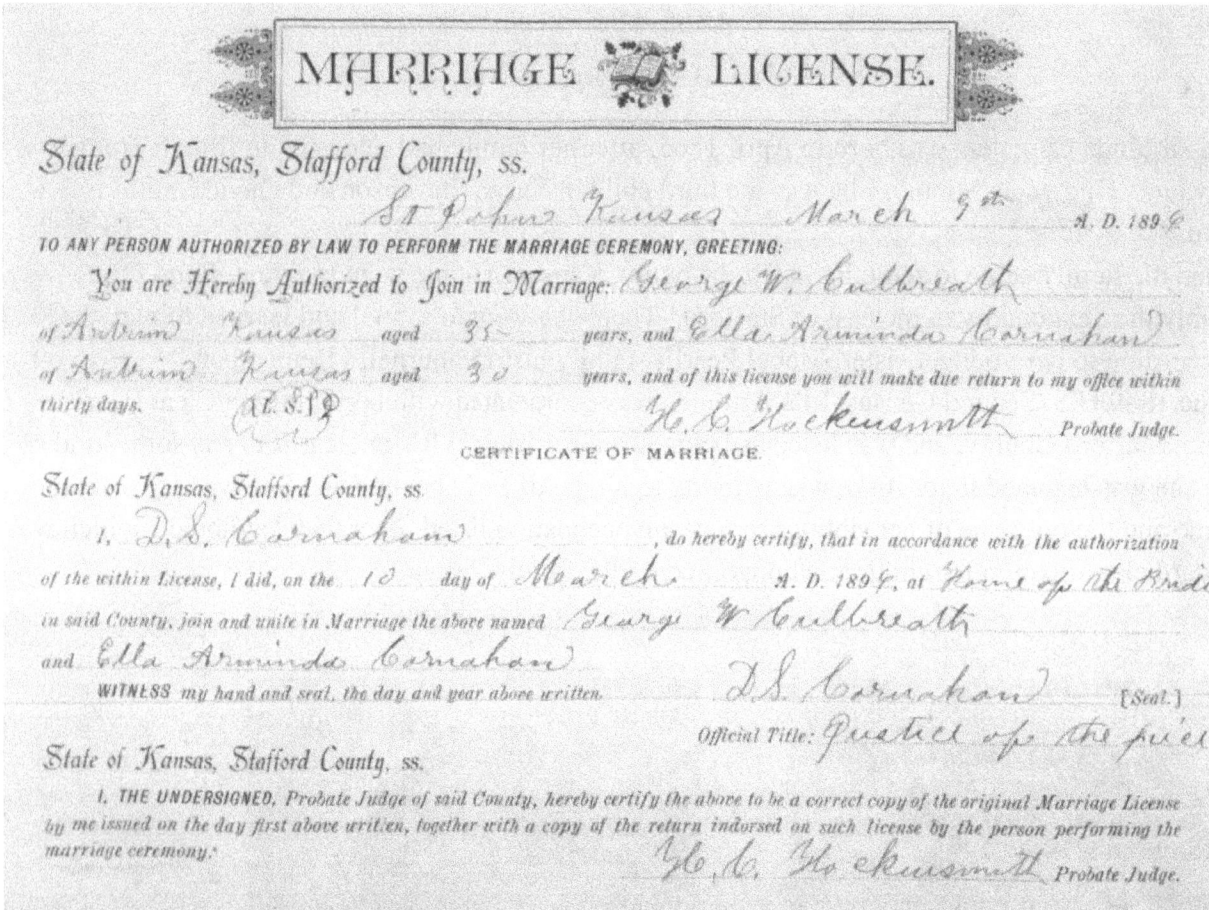

MARRIAGE LICENSE.

State of Kansas, Stafford County, ss.

St John Kansas March 9th A. D. 189[illegible]

TO ANY PERSON AUTHORIZED BY LAW TO PERFORM THE MARRIAGE CEREMONY, GREETING:

You are Hereby Authorized to Join in Marriage: George W. Culbreath of Antrim Kansas aged 35 years, and Ella Arminda Carnahan of Antrim Kansas aged 30 years, and of this license you will make due return to my office within thirty days.

H. C. Hockensmith Probate Judge.

CERTIFICATE OF MARRIAGE.

State of Kansas, Stafford County, ss.

I, D. S. Carnahan, do hereby certify, that in accordance with the authorization of the within License, I did, on the 10 day of March A. D. 1894, at Home of the Bride in said County, join and unite in Marriage the above named George W Culbreath and Ella Arminda Carnahan

WITNESS my hand and seal, the day and year above written. D. S. Carnahan [Seal.]

Official Title: Justice of the Peace

State of Kansas, Stafford County, ss.

I, THE UNDERSIGNED, Probate Judge of said County, hereby certify the above to be a correct copy of the original Marriage License by me issued on the day first above written, together with a copy of the return indorsed on such license by the person performing the marriage ceremony.

H. C. Hockensmith Probate Judge.

Marriage License of Ella Arminda Carnahan and George W. Culbreath

Of interest on the Marriage License, is that Ella's father, D. S. Carnahan, performed the ceremony in his capacity as Justice of the Peace.

Ella succumbed to an early death at age 42 in 1907 from consumption. Her obituary appeared in the 15 November 1907 issue of The Saint John News. See page 167, and for more on Ella.

She is interred in Fairview Park Cemetery, St. John, Stafford County, Kansas. Although George had a first wife and a third wife after Minnie, he is buried beside Minnie. Her Find A Grave Memorial No. is 104334313. On her gravestone is inscribed this sentiment: "God in His wisdom has recalled, The Boon his love had given, And though the body slumbers here, The soul is safe in heaven."

Lenna May Culbreath Burke, oldest daughter of Ella Arminda Carnahan and George W. Culbreath Photo taken 1917, St. John, Kansas, Gray's Studio

Questions:

1. Where exactly is Ella buried?

2. Did she work as a beautician as the Census record indicates?

3. What became of her children and descendants?

4. There is a photo in the historic collection of Gray's Studio photos of a woman with 3 children. Each person was photographed separately and later put together into one print. It's labeled, "Mrs. Culbreath and children." Is this photo of Ella and some of her children or is it George Culbreath's first wife, Rosa Matilda Peggs and the 3 children of hers who survived at her death?

William Carnahan

1866-1866

Some researchers list a child named William who was born and died in 1866, which would have been in Illinois as that is where the family was living in 1866. Apart from the fact that Susan Stevenson stated on the 1900 U.S. Federal Census that she was the mother of 8 children born with 6 living, I have found no other evidence for William or another unnamed child. That question would be one for further research.

Question:

1. Was there an eighth child born to Susan Stevenson and David Smith Carnahan? If so, where, when, what was the sex of the child, and why did the child die?

Martha Emma Carnahan Culbreath photo taken in O. M. Shira Studios in St. John, Stafford County, Kansas, circa 1890s.

Martha Emma Carnahan

1868-1946

Born to David Smith and Susan Stevenson Carnahan, Martha Emma was the fourth daughter born 9 January 1868, in Voila, Illinois. Before the Civil War, Viola was still on the edge of unsettled Indian territory. It's not clear why her family migrated there from Pennsylvania, but a check of land grants from the government reveals a number of Carnahan names received land grants—some in exchange for military service.

David Smith Carnahan was in the military. Additionally, children of deceased veterans were able to get their father's land. So far, however, I've found no record that Martha Emma's father, David Smith Carnahan, had land in Illinois. David's father, Joseph Carnahan, had died before the Civil War. I have not found other military service for Joseph to date, which may qualify David Smith for his father's land.

David Smith Carnahan listed his occupation as a carpenter in the 1870 U.S. Federal Census, though he possibly moved to Illinois with other Carnahan relatives who were farmers.

On 4 August 1890, Martha Emma Carnahan married T. S. Culbreath. The ceremony was conducted by a Presbyterian minister.

Martha Emma's sister, Mabel Pearl, wrote a family history account entitled I Remember which detailed the move from Illinois to Kansas where her family homesteaded. The photo of the farmstead following shows the family farm near Antrim in Albano Township, Stafford County, Kansas. Supposedly the picture shows Martha Emma hiding behind the wagon, her husband T. S. Culbreath, and sons Chal, Hobart, and Harlan. Since I have found no record of T. S. Culbreath owning land in Stafford County to date, it is my belief that this picture was possibly taken on Martha Emma's father, David Smith Carnahan's, farm, and that perhaps Martha Emma and her family were farming her father's land.

Family farmstead near Antrim in Rose Valley Township, Stafford County, Kansas, circa 1900-1910

Further evidence for their residence as being Antrim can be found inside Martha Emma's Bible.

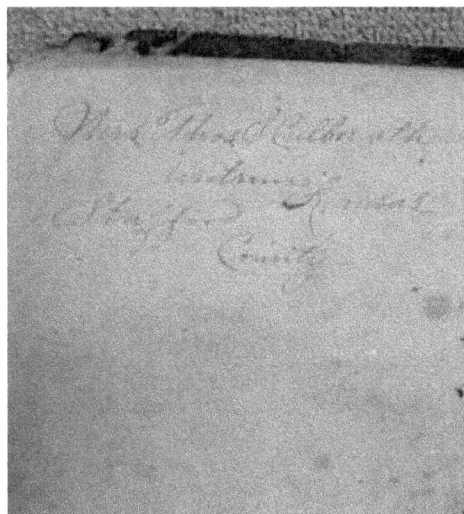

Martha Emma Carnahan Culbreath's Bible, left, and inside cover with her name inscribed in her handwriting, right

Inside of Martha Emma's Bible with a Merry Christmas card, left.

Martha Emma apparently trained her children in family worship according to a letter Alberta wrote to Hobart's wife, Dessie. Somehow I ended up with Martha Emma's prayer book she sent to her daughter, Alberta Anna Bell Culbreath Kinney. Printed in 1944 while the nation was embroiled in the Second World War, over one third of the book's prayers are devoted to prayer for the nation and the servicemen.

Here are 2 example pages:

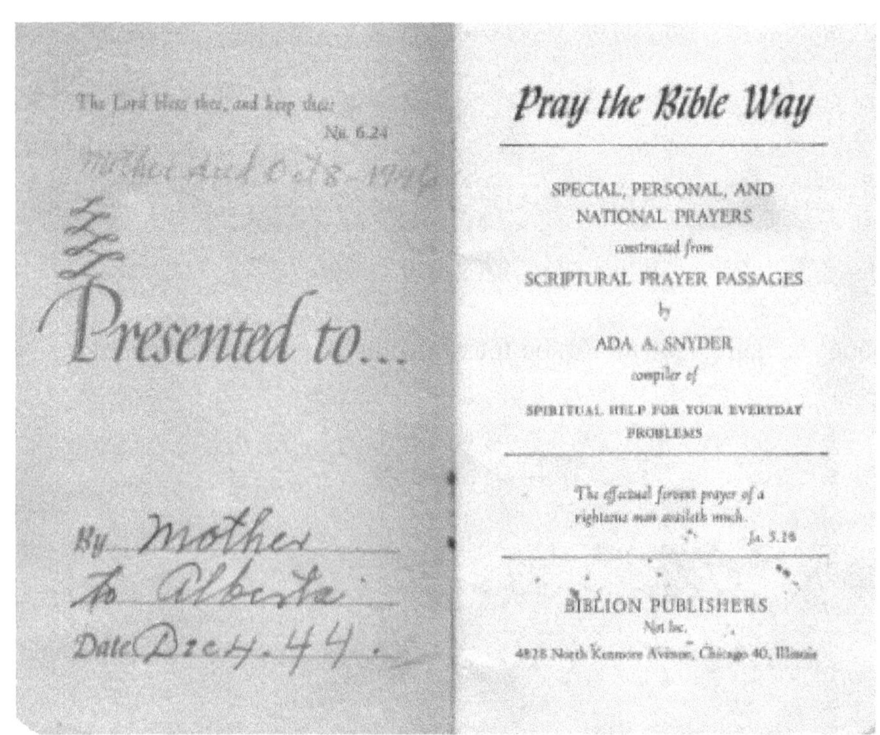

The Lord bless thee, and keep thee:
Nu. 6.24

Presented to...

By Mother
to Alberta
Date Dec 4. 44.

Pray the Bible Way

SPECIAL, PERSONAL, AND NATIONAL PRAYERS
constructed from
SCRIPTURAL PRAYER PASSAGES
by
ADA A. SNYDER
compiler of
SPIRITUAL HELP FOR YOUR EVERYDAY PROBLEMS

The effectual fervent prayer of a righteous man availeth much.
Ja. 5.16

BIBLION PUBLISHERS
Not Inc.
4828 North Kenmore Avenue, Chicago 40, Illinois

God is our refuge and strength, a very present help in trouble. Ps.46.1

For Strength

O Lord, thou art my God; I will exalt thee, . . . for thou hast done wonderful things; . . . thou hast been a strength to the poor, a strength to the needy in his distress, a refuge from the storm, a shadow from the heat,

. . . O Lord God, remember me, I pray thee, and strengthen me, . . . Strengthen ye the weak hands, and confirm the feeble knees. . . . Hold thou me up, and I shall be safe: . . . Incline not my heart to any evil thing,

O God the Lord, the strength of my salvation, . . . I can do all things through Christ which strengtheneth me. . . . according to his glorious power, Amen.

32

. . . Deal courageously, and the Lord shall be with the good. 2 Ch.19.11

For Courage

Think upon me, my God, for good, . . . I know that thou canst do everything, and that no thought can be withholden from thee. . . . For with God nothing shall be impossible.

Fearfulness and trembling are come upon me, . . . Hear my voice, O God, in my prayer: preserve my life from fear. . . . O send out thy light and thy truth: let them lead me; . . . The Lord is my light and my salvation; whom shall I fear? the Lord is the strength of my life; of whom shall I be afraid?

. . . I will trust, and not be afraid: . . . My times are in thy hand: . . . let thy lovingkindness and thy truth continually preserve me. Amen.

33

The inside of the prayer book says, "The Bible is the greatest prayer book ever written. It contains the greatest prayers for every occasion and situation in life." The topics for prayer are arranged around Scripture, for example: prayers for protection, healing, gratitude, forgiveness, tolerance, victory in war, justice, and The Lord's Prayer.

Marriage License.

...te of Kansas, Stafford County, ss. St. John,
Aug. 4" A. D. 1890. To any Person Authorized by Law to Perform the Marriage Ceremony, Greeting:
You are Hereby Authorized to Join in Marriage: Thomas S. Culbreath
Stafford County aged 23 years, and Martha E. Carnahan
" " aged 22 years, and of this License you will make due return to my office within
... days. [L. S.]
{Seal} J. R. Guernsey Probate Judge.

CERTIFICATE OF MARRIAGE

...te of Kansas, Stafford County, ss.
I the Undersigned, Wm. V. Howell of in said County, do hereby certify,
... accordance with the authorization of the within License, I did, on the 7th day of August A. D. 1890,
... in said County, join and unite in Marriage the within named Thomas S. Culbreath
Martha E. Carnahan
Witness my hand, the day and year above written.
Wm. V. Howell
Official Title: Presbn. Minister

...te of Kansas, Stafford County, ss. I the Undersigned, Probate Judge of said County,
certify the above to be a correct copy of the original Marriage License by me issued on the day first above written, together with a copy of the return indorsed ... license by the person performing the marriage ceremony.
{Seal} J. R. Guernsey Probate Judge.

Marriage License of Martha Emma Carnahan and Thomas S. Culbreath

For more on Martha Emma Carnahan Culbreath, see page 198.

Robert Audley Carnahan

1869-1955

Robert Audley Carnahan was the only son of Susan Stevenson and David Smith Carnahan. At the 1870 U.S. Federal Census, he was 6 months old and living with his family in Viola, Mercer County, Illinois. He had 4 older sisters including: Mary, Anna, Minnie, and Emma. Robert Audley was born 26 December 1869.

At age 9, he migrated with his family from Illinois to Stafford County, Kansas. As the youngest child, but the only boy, I wonder if he felt pressure to grow up quickly. When the family first arrived in Kansas, they needed an income, so David Smith Carnahan left the farm under the management of his wife, Susan Stevenson, while he went to Topeka to find work as a carpenter. During this time, Audley did not have his father's influence in his everyday life.

Audley and his older sister, Martha Emma, attended school at No. 7 in Livingston, which was 7 miles from the house. They walked both directions each day. When I visited Stafford County in 2013, the roads were just like beach sand. It's quite difficult to walk on beach sand for any distance, so I'm sure their calves got a super workout everyday going back and forth to school. Since school was only held a few months of each year, there was plenty of time to work on the farm. Once, Audley helped D. S. plant sorghum cane. This was taken to Macksville, squeezed, and the sorghum was stored in the milk house.

During the blizzard of 1887, Audley had to break ice off of the noses of the cattle so they would not smother to death.

Audley married Annie Estelle Ketcham 27 August 1891. During that school year, Audley taught the 65 students in the school where Mabel Pearl attended. He continued teaching in 1892 and 1893, but instead of the one-room school house, he had the eighth and ninth grades in Saint John.

Audley and Annie's first child was Lester Kent. He lived just 7 short months. He is interred in the Needlands Cemetery, along with his sister, Audley and Annie's daughter, Anna Esther, who lived from 1900-1901. The 18 August 1893 issue of The Saint John News, communicated the news about Lester Kent: "Died. Last Friday morning, the infant son of Mr. and Mrs. Audley Carnahan. The burial was on Saturday at the Neeland Cemetery, conducted by Rev. H. B. Johnson. This poem appeared in the paper.

Lester Kent and sister, Anna Esther, in Neelands Cemetery

"Only a baby dead—He left me in the early hours of a cloudy morn; And far, to the light of the Holy City, My babe was borne. Oh baby mine! In your soul's pure whiteness Forever beyond the dark, cold tide; At home in the light of the Lamb's own brightness; You never died."

Marriage License.

State of Kansas, Stafford County, ss. St John Kas
Aug 25 A. D. 1891.
To any Person Authorized by Law to Perform the Marriage Ceremony, Gree[ting]
You are Hereby Authorized to Join in Marriage: R A Carnahan
of Antrim, Stafford Co. Kas aged 21 years, and Annie E Ketcham
of Emerson " " " aged 25 years, and of this License you will make due return to my office wi[thin]
thirty days. [L. S.]
John B. Wilcox Probate Ju[dge]

CERTIFICATE OF MARRIAGE

State of Kansas, Stafford County, ss.
I the Undersigned, John S. Glendenning in said County, do hereby cer[tify]
that in accordance with the authorization of the within License, I did, on the 27 day of August A. D. 189[1]
at Emerson Postoffice in said County, join and unite in Marriage the within named R A Carnahan
and Annie E Ketcham
Witness my hand, the day and year above written.
John S Glendenning
Minister of the Gosp[el]

State of Kansas, Stafford County, ss. I the Undersigned, Probate Judge of said Cou[nty]
hereby certify the above to be a correct copy of the original Marriage License by me issued on the day first above written, together with a copy of the return indo[rsed]
on such license by the person performing the marriage ceremony.
John B. Wilcox
Probate Ju[dge]

Marriage License for Robert Audley Carnahan and Annie Estelle Ketchum

In 1898, Audley entered the College of Emporia to study for the ministry. He took his younger sister, Mabel Pearl, to Emporia with him and his family to finish her education.

At the 1900 U.S. Federal Census, Audley was enumerated in Albano Township, Stafford County, where he listed his occupation as farmer and student.

In 1902, Audley and Annie lived at 623 Arundel, Emporia, Kansas, according to the Emporia City Directory.

Emporia College, Emporia, Kansas

Audley must have completed his education by 1905, because in the Wisconsin State Census, he was listed as residing in Beloit, Rock County. His occupation was a Presbyterian Minister. They had 3 children: Chester Carroll, Elsie Estelle, and Marjorie R.

In the 1910 U.S. Federal Census, the family was still in Wisconsin, but had relocated to Mauston, Juneau County. They had welcomed another son, Robert A. Carnahan, Junior. Annie had given birth to 6 children with 4 living. Robert was still a minister. The family lived on Oak Street.

Audley was part of the Committee on Finance as reported in "The Minutes of the General Assembly of the Presbyterian Church in the USA, in August 1913." He was also pastor of the Presbyterian Church USA in Mauston, Wisconsin.

Audley and Annie's oldest son, Chester Carroll, also became a minister. This account of his wedding appeared in the 11 September 1919 issue of The Weekly News, Saint John, Kansas: "Early Autumn Wedding -- Under the above heading The Sauk County News, published at Praire du Sac, Wisconsin, under date of August 28th, had this to say regarding the marriage of Rev. C. Carroll Carnahan, a son of Rev. and Mrs. R. A. Carnahan, former residents of Albano Township, this county:

"An early autumn wedding took place at the home of Mr. and Mrs. N. W. Stephens of this city on Wednesday afternoon, August 27, at 4 o'clock. The younger daughter, Miss Ida, became the bride of the Rev. C. Carroll Carnahan, eldest son of the Rev. and Mrs. R. A. Carnahan, of Waukesha. Only the immediate families and a few intimate friends witnessed the ceremony.

The home was prettily decorated for the occasion, in a color scheme of orange and white, those being the Carroll College colors. Ribbon, crepe paper and flowers, golden glow and daisies were used.

The color scheme was even carried out in the three-course cafeteria luncheon which was served by Mrs. Mary Schwartz of this city, assisted by the Misses Irene Schubring of Madison and Mildred and Helen Cole of West Point.

The bride was attired in a gown of sheer white voile trimmed with clusters of tucks and imported French Valenciennes lace and wore a veil of silk bridal illusion caught with satin ribbon and swansonia. She carried a shower bouquet of white bridal roses and swansonia.

At the appointed hour Miss Blanche Hulbert, accompanied by Miss Marjorie Carnahan, younger sister of the groom, introduced the service by singing two favorite love songs, "The Nightingales Song" and "I Asked the Sun." While the groom and his father, the officiating clergyman, proceeded to their places in the living room, Miss Carnahan played, D'Hardelot's "Because." With the approach of the bride, Miss Ruth Haylett sang most impressively the words to "Because." The Episcopal ring service was used and just before the prayer, Miss Haylett sang very softly Blomfield's "O Perfect Love."

Congratulations and a brief social hour followed the ceremony. After the luncheon the newlyweds left by way of Baraboo for Chicago and other points in Illinois, before making final preparations to sail to their future home in Bahia, Brazil, South America.

Those who attended the wedding from away were: Rev. and Mrs. R. A. Carnahan, Misses Elsie and Marjorie Carnahan and Master Robert and David Carnahan of Waukesha; Miss Blanch Hulbert of Barron, Wisconsin, Miss Ruth Haylett of Evansville, Wisconsin, and Douglas O. Anderson of Milwaukee.

The bride was graduated from the local high school with the class of 1911, since which time she has completed a four year's course in English and dramatic literature at Carroll College and taught several years in the state. The groom is also a graduate of Carroll College and recently of McCormick Theological Seminary. He was ordained to the gospel ministry by Milwaukee Presbytery in May of this year.

Mr. and Mrs. Carnahan were the recipients of many beautiful gifts and have the best wishes of many friends as they go to a great work in the Central Brazil Mission under the direction of the Presbytery Board of Foreign Missions."

On the 30 June 1921, issue of The Saint John News, we read of another wedding in Audley and Annie Carnahan's family: "Miss Carnahan Weds – A very pretty home wedding took place at 4 o'clock this afternoon at the home of Rev. and Mrs. R. A. Carnahan, 309 East College Avenue, when their eldest daughter, Elsie, became the bride of Herbel A. Lange, son of Mr. and Mrs. Albert Lange, 711 Merrill Avenue, Beloit, Wisconsin. The ceremony was performed by the bride's father, in the presence of the immediate relatives and friends of the bride and groom, and took place before the fireplace, which was banked with ferns, roses and sweet peas, while the house decorations were carried out in pink and white.

The bride, who was unattended, wore a dress of ivory georgette and satin with a bodice of lace and satin. The veil was caught with pink rose buds. She carried a shower bouquet of white roses and swansonia.

Miss Marjorie Carnahan, younger sister of the bride, sang "I Asked the Sun," which was followed by Guy d'Harlot's "Because." She was accompanied by Miss Virginia Spillman.

Little Miss Mary Jane Humbert, daughter of Prof. and Mrs. T. A. Humbert, Waukesha, Wisconsin, dressed in pink organdie, acted as ring bearer.

Following the ceremony, a light luncheon was served by the Misses Jeanette Rodgers, Pearl Boortz, Ruth Bostwick and Daphne Bullard. The bridal couple leave this evening for a short wedding trip. They will be at home after July 10, at 844 Lincoln Avenue, Beloit, Wisconsin.

The bride was a member of the class of Carroll graduating in 1919, and is a member of the Theta Pi Delta sorority. The year following her graduation she taught in the English department of the Medford high school.

The groom has spent nearly his whole life in Beloit, graduating from the Beloit High School in the class of 1914 and receiving his degree from the college of mechanical engineering, University of Wisconsin, last year. He is a member of Lambda Chi Alpha fraternity. He served over two years in the World War, most of the time with the Thirty-second division, being eighteen months overseas. After the armistice he was sent to the University of Edinburgh, Scotland. At present, he is employed in the experimental department, Fairbanks Morse Company, Beloit.

The Waukesha guests present were Rev. and Mrs. C. E. Bovard, Mr. and Mrs. T. G. Breaw and Mrs. T. A. Humbert.

The out-of-town guests were Miss Elizabeth Stroh of Lake Forest, Miss Pauline Liebig, Mayville, Rev. and Mrs. C. H. Gesselbrecht, Milwaukee, Mr. and Mrs. Albert Lange, Miss Gladys Lange, Lytle Serivens and Harold Gordon of Beloit. – Waukesha Wisconsin Daily Freeman.

Rev. Audley Carnahan, father of the bridge, formerly lived in Albano Township and is well known here."

~~~~~~

In the Present Day . . . Carroll College bills itself as the oldest college in Wisconsin, established in 1846, as a 4-year private nonprofit college associated with the Presbyterian U.S.A. denomination. They are located in Waukesha, Wisconsin, just outside of Milwaukee.

~~~~~~

After living a number of years in Wisconsin, we find Audley and Annie in 1925 at 1116 South College Avenue, Tulsa, Oklahoma. Daughter, Marjorie, and son, Robert Junior, were living with their parents. Marjorie was a teacher and Robert Junior a student. Audley was still listed as Rev.

In the 1926 Tulsa City Directory, Audley was now a traveling representative. I wonder if he was associated with Oral Roberts University as later in life, most all of their children are shown to have died at the Oral Roberts Retirement Home in Tulsa.

Audley and Annie remained in Tulsa at least through 1933 as they were listed in the Tulsa City Directory continuously through 1933.

By 1935, they had relocated to Valley Township, Greensburg, Kiowa County, Kansas where they remained at the 1940 U.S. Federal Census. Annie died 18 August 1941, in Greensburg.

Audley married again in April 1946, to Olive Arbell Williams. He passed away in Pasadena, Orange County, California, at the age of 85 on 3 May 1955. As of 2013, his place of burial was unknown to me.

Questions:

1. Where is Audley buried?
2. What caused him to go into the ministry?
3. Did his other children marry?
4. Did he work in recruitment for Oral Roberts University?

Ruby Isabel Carnahan

1881-1967

Thirteen years after the birth of son, Audley, Susan Stevenson and David Smith Carnahan had another girl, Ruby Isabel, born 21 April 1882, in Stafford County, Kansas. Apparently, the family was all hoping for a boy. Ruby had 5 older siblings including 1 who had died 3 years before Ruby's birth.

Ruby married a neighbor, Enoch Sylvester Davison, on 20 February 1898. The marriage took place at the Carnahan home. The write-up in the newspaper was just a single sentence in the 25 February 1898 issue of The Saint John News: "E. S. Davidson and Miss Ruby Carnahan were united in wedlock Sunday at the home of the bride's parents, Mr. and Mrs. D. S. Carnahan."

David Smith Carnahan again performed the marriage ceremony for his daughter, Ruby Isabel, in his capacity as Justice of the Peace. What is very revealing, however, is that the name of his daughter is listed as Ruth P. Carnahan. Surely, a father knows his own daughter's correct legal name. So, what is her correct name: Ruth P. or Ruby Isabel?

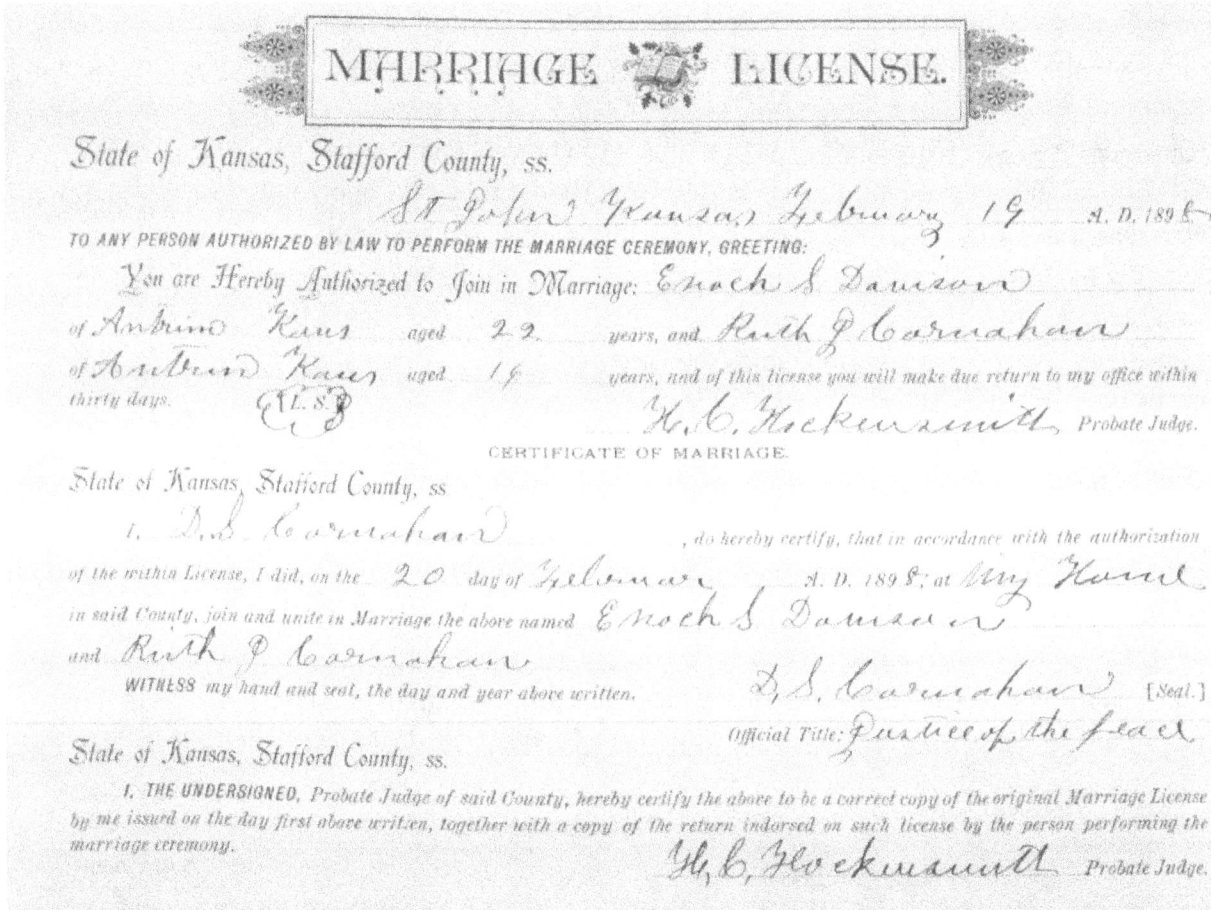

MARRIAGE LICENSE.

State of Kansas, Stafford County, ss.

St John Kansas February 19 A. D. 1898

TO ANY PERSON AUTHORIZED BY LAW TO PERFORM THE MARRIAGE CEREMONY, GREETING:

You are Hereby Authorized to Join in Marriage: Enoch S. Davison of Antrim Kans aged 22 years, and Ruth J Carnahan of Antrim Kans aged 16 years, and of this license you will make due return to my office within thirty days. (L. S.)

H. C. Hockensmith Probate Judge.

CERTIFICATE OF MARRIAGE.

State of Kansas, Stafford County, ss

I, D. S. Carnahan, do hereby certify, that in accordance with the authorization of the within License, I did, on the 20 day of February A. D. 1898, at My Home in said County, join and unite in Marriage the above named Enoch S. Davison and Ruth J Carnahan

WITNESS my hand and seal, the day and year above written. D. S. Carnahan [Seal.]

Official Title: Justice of the Peace

State of Kansas, Stafford County, ss.

I, THE UNDERSIGNED, Probate Judge of said County, hereby certify the above to be a correct copy of the original Marriage License by me issued on the day first above written, together with a copy of the return indorsed on such license by the person performing the marriage ceremony.

H. C. Hockensmith Probate Judge.

Marriage License for Ruby Isabel Carnahan and Enoch Sylvester Davison

Enoch Sylvester was 6 years older than Ruby Isabel. His family farmed next door to the Carnahan family. They arrived in Stafford County around the same time in 1878 or 1879 as D. S. and Susan. Enoch's parents were George Nicholas "Nick" Davison and Mary Elizabeth Ackley. As many men who homesteaded discovered, they had to work off of the farm to make ends meet, particularly in the early years when the family was just getting started. Nick, too, worked away from his homestead driving freight wagons from Independence to Dodge City.

Enoch had 10 siblings: 7 brothers and 3 sisters. Tragedy struck the Davison family when Enoch was just 8 years old. After a hard rain, the ridgepole supporting the sod roof of their house collapsed killing 2 of his sisters, Buena Vista and Elizabeth "Bessie" May. Then Enoch's third sister, Margaret Ellen, died when she was just 1 year old. They were all buried in the Neelands Cemetery in Stafford County. This event wiped out the last of the Davison daughters.

In the 1895 Kansas State Census, Enoch was still living with his parents. He was 19 years old and had 7 younger brothers including: Sam, George, Rosco, David, John, Eugene, and William. Enoch Sylvester and all his brothers, except William, farmed in Albano Township for many years. William was an attorney in St. John for 51 years and was Stafford County Attorney for 12 years.

Another story about Enoch's family as reported in The Saint John Advance, is told in the book, No Cyclone Shall Destroy, by Helen Malin Reuber & Dorothy Cole, 1981, p. 140:

"On Wednesday evening last week Sam Davidson was stabbed in the back by Robert Hensley. Sam is the second oldest son of Nick Davidson, Albano Township, and young Hensley is a resident of Pratt Center.

The boys were at schoolhouse No. 33 attending a Literary when the affair took place. The particulars of the affair as was reported are as follows: About two weeks ago young Hensley and two associates came to the Literary at the same place slightly intoxicated, and behaved in a very ungentlemanly manner, and finally began talking aloud and smoking during the exercises. Young Davidson asked the boys to desist, but they flatly refused and young Hensley made some very uncomplimentary remarks to Davidson which the latter resented by slapping young Hensley. This ended the trouble for the evening. But last Wednesday evening it seems Hensley returned for the purpose of giving his enemy a genuine thrashing. Davidson was standing near the stove when young Hensley came in, and without the least warning hit Sam with a pair of knuckles which came near laying him out, but Davidson soon regained his feet and in a short time a few minutes of a "rough house" was indulged in. Finally the boys were separated and young Hensley left the room, but Davidson remained in the house. He was standing facing the front of the room when Hensley slipped back into the house, and without the slightest warning, sprung upon his victim and stabbed him in the back…..Fortunately the wound was not fatal, but a gash some five inches in length was laid open to the bone. Had it not been for a pair of leather suspenders the stab would have been a great deal more serious."

Left, Enoch Sylvester Davison taken in Gray's Studio, St. John, Kansas. Notice the hat is too small for his head. The studio kept various props for their clients to use to enhance their photographs. Perhaps this hat is one of those props.

Right, Davison daughters Buena Vista, Bessie May, and Margaret E. in Neelands Cemetery, Stafford County, Kansas

One would think that Enoch's family would become bitter with so many tragedies befalling them. I believe their faith in God probably sustained them during these difficult times. I say this regarding their faith and dedication to God because of another story that's told about Enoch's father, Nick Davison.

The Antrim Methodist Church building was constructed during 1898 and 1899. The dedication service was held on February 12, 1899. The pastor was a circuit riding preacher, but he rode the rails instead of the horse trails. The day before the dedication service was to be held, he left Hutchinson on the train and it was 17 degrees below zero. There was a strong blizzard blowing, so only the train's engine and coal car were able to make the journey with the passengers all huddling inside the engine compartment to keep warm. On Sunday, the temperature was 29 degrees below zero for the dedication service. Nick Davidson waded through the snowy fields 2 miles to attend the service and to turn in his second $50 pledge to the building fund. The church was completely paid for that day with the funds that were contributed. The church in America of 2013 could take some inspiration from these hardy, dedicated pioneers who gave sacrificially. Their faithful efforts were rewarded as the church building still stands in 2013, more than 100 years later, and the congregation is still composed of the descendants of those early pioneers who laid the cornerstone and built on a lasting foundation.

It is unclear to me which church Mabel Pearl and the D. S. Carnahan family attended, but in Mable's sister, Martha Emma Carnahan Culbreath's Bible, there is the word "Antrim" inscribed on the front page. Perhaps they attended here at some point, or perhaps that inscription was just a reference to the area in which they lived. After all, the closest post office to their farm was called Antrim.

Left, Mable Davison, oldest child of Enoch Sylvester and Ruby Isabel Carnahan Davison, August 1908, photo taken in Gray's Studio, St. Johns, Kansas
Right, Three of the Davison children

In the 1910 U.S. Federal Census, Enoch and Ruby were living in Albano Township, Stafford County. Enoch was a farmer, in fact, they were farming next door to the Carnahan homestead. They had given birth to 6 children including: Mary Mabel, 11; Kenneth Wayne, 9; Emmett Sylvester, 8; Ruby Irene, 3; Nicholas David, 1, and Ferne. Now there's one of the saddest stories ever told in The Saint

John News. The 13 October 1905 headline read: "**A Sad Accident** – A very sad accident occurred at the home of E. S. Davison. In Albano Township, Saturday afternoon, October 7th, Ferne, the youngest daughter, fell in a milk pail which contained about 5 inches of milk, and was drowned. The little one was playing on the back porch while her mother and sister, Mabel, were upstairs. They were gone perhaps 15 minutes when Mabel came down and found her little sister in the sad plight. Mrs. Davison came immediately attracted by her cries. All efforts to revive here were in vain. Dr. Adams was called, but could do nothing. The little one was 11 months and 1 day old.

The funeral services were held at the home, conducted by Rev. E. N. Quist, Sunday afternoon. Burial at the Neeland Cemetery. Father, mother, 1 sister, 2 brothers, and very many relatives and friends mourn her loss for everyone loved little Ferne.

Sweet little darling, light of the home,
Looking for someone, beckoning come:
Bright as a sunbeam, pure as the dew,
Anxiously looking, Mother, for you.
By -- D. S. CARNAHAN"

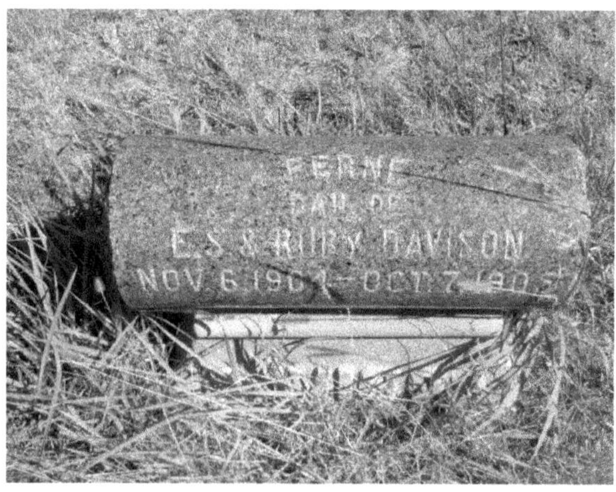

Ferne's gravestone in Neelands Cemetery next to her grandfather, D. S. Carnahan, who wrote the poem for her above.

By the 1915 Kansas State Census for Albano Township, Enoch was 39, Ruby, 32, Mabel, 16; Wayne, 14; Emmett, 12; Ruby Irene, 8; and Nicholas, 6.

World War I was looming and threatening to disrupt the family's lives. Enoch's 12 September 1918 World War I Draft Registration Card showed that he was 42, born 23 January 1876, he was a self-employed farmer, and was living at RFD No. 1, St. John, Stafford County, Kansas. He was of medium height and build, with dark brown eyes and dark brown hair.

At the 1920 U.S. Federal Census, they were still living in Albano Township. They had considerable land holdings. It appears that they had taken over Ruby's father, D. S. Carnahan's lands according to a 1916 plat map and court records.

April 1915 – Davison Family: the older couple on the front row, 2nd and 3rd from the right, is D. S. Carnahan and his second wife, Mary Rosanne. This is obviously a family gathering, but the occasion is unknown.

The end of the 1920's would spell the end of an era for many a mid-west farmer. With the crash of the stock market, the prices for food plummeted. In just a few short years, the Great Depression, coupled with the Dust Bowl, would put farmers out of business for good. For a family who had known nothing but farming, and who had considerable land holdings, these were disastrous times.

By the 1930 U.S. Federal Census, they had added another son, Audley Carnahan Davison, to the family. Changes had come as they were now living in Center Township, Washington County, Arkansas. Enoch was still farming, but son Nicholas, 21, was a cook in a restaurant. So, what happened to the family farms in Kansas? Why was the family in Arkansas? These questions intrigue me.

Dust Bowl era in Kansas. For more images, see the following website http://images.search.yahoo.com/yhs/search?_adv_prop=image&fr=yhs-att-att_001&va=free+images+of+the+the+dust+bowl+in+kansas&hspart=att&hsimp=yhs-att_001

Left, Enoch Sylvester and Ruby Isabel Carnahan Davison farm house in Stafford County, Kansas, as it appeared abandoned in 2013

Right, Rusting away on the former Davison homestead

Enoch Davison home while they were living there.

In 1939, we find them living in Fayetteville, Arkansas, living at 148 South Hill Avenue. Enoch was no longer farming, but was a broom maker working in a broom factory. I wonder what that did for his sense of self-worth.

In the 1940 U.S. Federal Census, we see they were still living in Fayetteville, Arkansas. Youngest son, Audley Carnahan Davison, 16, indicated he'd been born in Arkansas. If so, then the family must have left Kansas sometime before 1924.

~~~~~~

Back in the Day . . . Broom corn is a type of sorghum with open seed heads. It was sturdy and had stiff stalks making it the ideal choice for constructing brooms. It was grown in Illinois and other Midwest states. Factories making brooms from broom corn were concentrated in Oklahoma during the Great Depression, because the broom corn grew particularly well there. According to Stafford County History 1870-1990 , page 18, in Albano Township, broom corn was grown on the DeSelms farm located on the S.E. Quarter of Section 26. This was just a mile from the Carnahan homestead. Mr. DeSelms made brooms by hand from his harvested broom corn.

~~~~~~

We know they didn't stay in Arkansas either because Ruby Isabel Carnahan Davison passed away 10 December 1967, in Riverside, California. She followed Enoch Sylvester, who died 15 March 1966, also in Riverside. Where they are interred is unknown to me.

Enoch and Ruby Davison with grandchildren Timmy and Susan Israel, 1959

Questions:

1. When did Enoch and Ruby leave the farm?

2. What did they do with their lands? Did they sell to family or to others?
3. Where are they buried?
4. How did they die?
5. Are there obituaries or death certificates available?
6. What became of their children and descendants?

Mabel Pearl Carnahan

1883-1968

Mabel Pearl Carnahan, the last daughter of Susan Stevenson and David Smith Carnahan, was born 24 July 1883, at the family homestead in Stafford County, Kansas. She described her birth in her journal, I Remember: "July 24, 1883, when another girl was born, an old maid aunt said, "Let the little thing die. It's only another one to keep." I got here long before I was expected. The mid-wife, Miriam McHenry, soaked me in a dishpan of warm water and did everything she knew. I was named Mabel Pearl. We [Ruby Belle and Mabel Pearl] must have been jewels to rate these names. Dr. Dix, a homesteader, did all he could for mother and me."

Her mother, Susan Stevenson Carnahan, was probably 41or 42 years old when Mabel Pearl was born. Mabel Pearl was recorded with her family in the 1885 Kansas State Census living in Clear Creek, Stafford County, Kansas. She enjoyed the company of 3 siblings, all old enough to have been her mother or father, and 1 sibling just 1½ years older than her.

According to her I Remember journal, Mabel Pearl attended school. She stated she attended a sod school house and then her father, D. S. Carnahan, and a neighbor, Will Goodman, built a school building which she attended for the rest of her school years. She also mentioned several of her teachers including: Stephen Frazee, who also taught in singing schools; a teacher who "sure wasn't worth it" [the $22 a month he was paid]; her brother, Audley Carnahan; and the Lewis Academy, which she attended in Emporia, Kansas. She accompanied Audley and Annie who went there to complete a ministerial course in the College of Emporia.

In addition to her regular schooling, Mabel Pearl faithfully attended Sunday School. In fact, she stated that the first sermon and Sunday School in the area was held inside the Carnahan sod house. She would receive a penny for the offering plate. One day she observed that a girl swallowed hers. In her journal she mentions a Presbyterian church being started near their home about 1889, with a minister who had been a chaplain in the Civil War. Her comments about his appearance were less than complimentary.

Mable Pearl also suffered quite a few illnesses and ailments. She described catching a cold after playing in a creek which caused her legs to swell. The only creek around was called Rattlesnake Creek. It was a couple of miles from their home. Perhaps this is the creek she was playing in when she got sick.

Rattlesnake Creek, Stafford County, Kansas

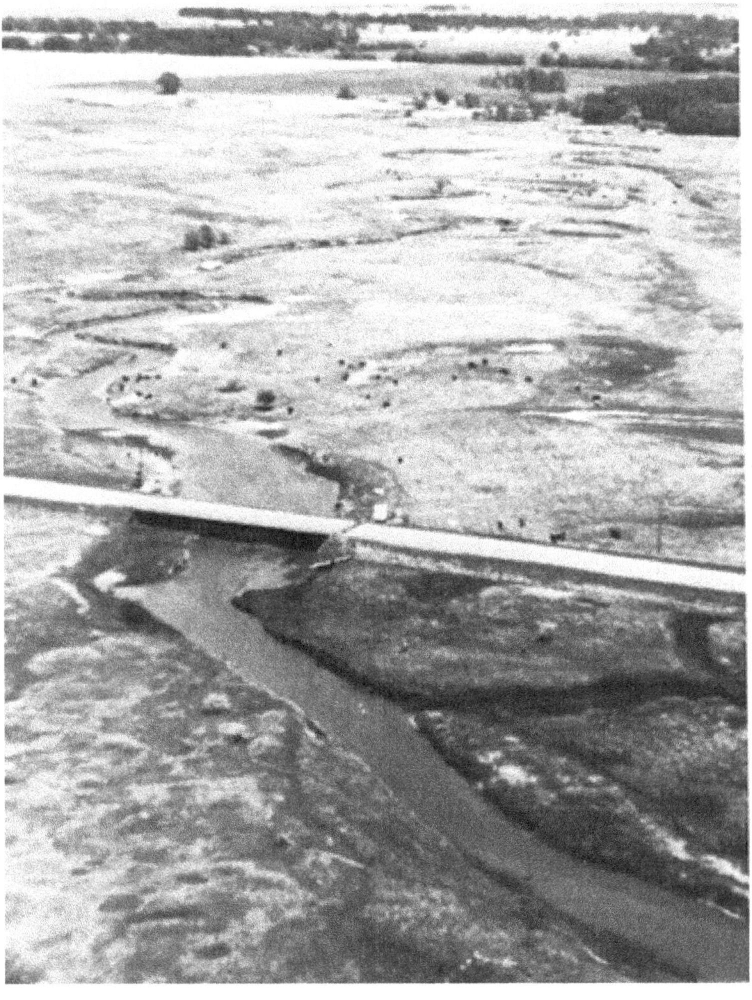

She also contracted measles at the same time. Later, she couldn't get her left arm and leg to work properly, but she outgrew these conditions with a lot of attention from the local doctor.

She also talked about politics, particularly in 1896, when Chester I. Long was running for Congress. Apparently, he was defeated by Jerry Simpson, who, according to Mabel Pearl, "didn't know enough to wear socks." Mabel Pearl thought Chester I. Long was very capable. So did the St. John Weekly News in the issue of 11 September 1896: "Congressman Chester I. Long is doing wonderful work in this congressional district. His speeches are full, good, sound everyday business arguments, and of the type that furnishes an abundant supply of food for his eager hearers to reflect upon. He is making votes in every city he visits, Democrats, Populists and free silver Republicans have publicly expressed themselves as intending to stand up for his country by voting for the Barber County statesman, and for McKinley and honest money. His talks are wholly and purely argumentative; entirely free from abuse. They are made up exclusively of just what the people are seeking for in this campaign—knowledge."

~~~~~~

Back in the Day . . . Free silver was a Central United States policy issue in the late 19th century. Its advocates were in favor of an inflationary monetary policy using the "free coinage of silver" as opposed to the less inflationary gold standard; its supporters were called "Silverites". The Silverites promoted bimetallism, the use of both silver and gold as currency at the ratio of 16 to 1 (16 ounces of silver would be worth 1 ounce of gold). Because the actual ratio was about 32 to 1 at the time, most economists warned that the cheaper silver would drive the more expensive gold out of circulation. Everyone agreed that free silver would raise prices; the question was whether or not this inflationary measure would be beneficial. The issue peaked from 1893 to 1896, when the economy was in a severe depression—called the Panic of 1893—characterized by falling prices (deflation), high unemployment in industrial areas, and severe distress for farmers.

http://en.wikipedia.org/wiki/Free_Silver

~~~~~~

Mabel Pearl also mentioned in her journal that her mother, Susan Stevenson, was first cousin to the Vice President, Adlai Stevenson. As of 2013, I've not found a specific connection between Susan and Adlai.

By the 1900 U.S. Federal Census, Mabel Pearl was the only child still living in the family home. D. S. had 1 servant and 2 farm hands living with them, probably to help with the work, as Susan was suffering from rheumatism. Incidentally, D. S. Carnahan was the Census enumerator that year. Below we can see his signature and handwriting at the top of the Census page on which his family appeared:

TWELFTH CENSUS OF THE UNITED STATES.

SCHEDULE No. 1.—POPULATION.

albano Township [Insert name of township, town, precinct, district, or other civil division, as the case may be. See instructions.] *Name of Institution,*

, within the above-named division,

umerated by me on the 13 *day of June, 1900,* D S Carnahan

In 1904, Mabel Pearl married William Henry Stevens, as we read in the 5 August 1904 edition of The Saint John News: **"Carnahan—Stevens Wedding – On Monday, August 1st**, Miss Mabel Pearl Carnahan, daughter of commissioner D. S. Carnahan of Albano township, was married to Mr. William Henry Stevens of St. Louis, Missouri. The wedding took place at six p.m. The Rev. L. E. McNeill of Antrim, performed the ceremony. It was a pretty, but very quiet wedding, owing to the invalid state of the bride's mother; for this cause the guests were confined to the nearest relatives and a very few friends.

The bride was dressed in a very pretty white Persian Lawn and lace costume. Miss Ethel Fry of Emporia and Mr. Steadman Aldis of Antrim, were the bridesmaid and best man. Miss Fry was dressed in white Persian Lawn with rose pink trimmings. After the ceremony, ice cream and cake were served.

The newly married couple received many nice and useful presents. They will remain in this neighborhood for the present."

The wedding was conducted by a Methodist Episcopal minister. It is difficult to ascertain just what the denominational preference was for the Carnahan family. We see ministers from 2 different denominations performing 2 of the Carnahan children's wedding ceremonies.

We learn from the above article that D. S. Carnahan was a Commissioner for Albano Township. He was also a Justice of the Peace.

At the 1910 U.S. Federal Census, the couple had been married 5 years and had 2 children: son, William D., 4; and daughter, Margaret T., 2. Mabel's husband, William H. Stevens, was a farmer. He had immigrated from England in 1889.

In 1905, he was enumerated as farming with his father-in-law, David Smith Carnahan, in the agricultural report completed as part of the Kansas State Census.

His World War I Draft Registration Card of 12 September 1918, indicated he was an alien declarant of Great Britain. His physical description was short, medium build, with blue eyes and light brown hair. Their address was Route 2, St. John, Stafford County, Kansas.

Mabel Pearl was active in a women's club called "The Civic and Study Club," organized in 1916. The 25 members studied various topics including American literature during their first year of organization. Mabel apparently stayed active in this club until she moved from Stafford County.

PROBATE COURT.

MARRIAGE LICENSE RECORD.

MARRIAGE LICENSE.

State of Kansas, Stafford County, ss.

St John Kansas, August 1st A.

TO ANY PERSON AUTHORIZED BY LAW TO PERFORM THE MARRIAGE CEREMONY, GREETING:

You are Hereby Authorized to Join in Marriage: Wm. H. Stevens of Stafford County Kansas aged 30 years, and Mabel Carnahan of Stafford County Kansas aged 21 years, and of this license you will make due return to my of thirty days. [L. S.] J S Lewis Sr Prob

CERTIFICATE OF MARRIAGE.

State of Kansas, Stafford County, ss.

I, L. E. McNeil, do hereby certify, that in accordance with the au of the within License, I did, on the 1 day of August A. D. 1894, at J S Car in said County, join and unite in Marriage the above named Wm H Stevens and Mabel Carnahan

WITNESS my hand and seal, the day and year above written.

L. E. McNeil

Official Title: M. E. Minister

State of Kansas, Stafford County, ss.

I, THE UNDERSIGNED, Probate Judge of said County, hereby certify the above to be a correct copy of the original Marr by me issued on the day first above written, together with a copy of the return indorsed on such license by the person per marriage ceremony.

J S Lewis Sr Pr

The Marriage License Record for Mabel Pearl Carnahan and William Henry Stevens, Stafford County, Kansas

By the 1920 U.S. Federal Census, they were still living in Albano and had added 2 more children: daughter, Marianna, 4 years, 11 months; and son, Robert L., 1 year, 11 months.

In the 1925 Kansas State Census, for some reason, they were living in Smith, Lincoln County, Kansas. They continued farming, and all 4 children were still living in the home.

At the 1930 U.S. Federal Census, the family was back living in Albano Township, farming, and the 3 youngest children were still living in the home. It appears that William H. Stevens had not become a naturalized citizen.

Left, Mabel Pearl Carnahan Stevens and her husband, W. H. Stephens, 1917, Photo taken in Gray's Studio, St. Johns, Kansas

Right, One of Mabel's sons. Funny, the dog looks remarkably like the same dog in Hobart Culbreath's photograph. I wonder if it were a family dog or a dog belonging to the photographer, Mr. Gray. See page 214 to compare dog pictures.

A Stevens baby, 1915, Gray's Studio

Gray's Studio equipment can be seen in the Stafford County Historical Society Museum. There is a contraption that closes like a claw around the baby to hold it upright while blankets are placed over the device to hide it from view. Having seen this claw-like piece of equipment, I can envision this baby being held in its grip for the photo.

In the 1940 U.S. Federal Census, we see that they were living on a rented farm in Harrison Township, Wallace County, Kansas. William was still farming, although he was 66 years old.

Both Mabel Pearl and husband William H. Stevens died in 1968. They are interred in Fort Wallace Cemetery in Wallace, Wallace County, Kansas. Their Find A Grave Memorial Nos. are: 40789470 and 40789501 respectively.

Questions:

1. Was Susan Stevenson the first cousin to Vice President Adlai Stevenson? If so, what is the exact connection?
2. Did Mabel write any other pieces of family history?
3. How did she die?
4. Why did she leave Stafford County and go to Wallace County?
5. Did they own land in Wallace County?
6. What became of their children and descendants?
7. Did they continue to attend church? If so, what denomination were they affiliated with?
8. Which children were pictured in the Gray's Studio photograph on pg. 302?

7
Famous Family Connections Confirmed and Denied

Who doesn't want to be connected with someone famous? It's part of our make-up—to want to be connected. For many years now, there have been rumors that the Vernon Haven Kinney family is related to Jesse James, the infamous outlaw, and his brother, Frank James. Several in the family vehemently swear to this connection. So, what's the answer? Are we or aren't we related to Jesse James?

Jesse James Family Connection to the Vernon Haven Kinney Family

After researching the James Family genealogy online and finding no definitive connection, I turned to other possible explanations for the idea that these 2 families were related.

I interviewed all family members who were alive in 2013 which had heard rumor of the Kinney family's connection to the family of Jesse James, to see who was told what and from whom. The general consensus was that, "Grandma Anna Rachel Fox Kinney Anderson said that Jesse James was a cousin, or something."

Only 1 family member offered a different answer. Anna Rachel Fox Kinney Anderson's grandson, Lawrence Kinney, once stated that his father, Vernon Haven Kinney, had told him that after one of the James Gang's bank robberies, Frank James hid out on one of our family's farms disguising himself as a farm laborer. When our ancestor learned his true identity, Frank was asked to leave, which he did without incident.

This sounded like a more plausible explanation for the belief that the Kinney family was kin to the James Gang. So, I decided to research. The next question I had to answer was: 'Which family member could have owned the farm where Frank James allegedly hid out?' There were 4 different possibilities of ancestors who had farms in the vicinity of where the Gang was originally from, and where some of their bank robberies took place. I compiled the information into a chart to study the possibilities. My conclusions are listed below in no specific order.

Left, Frank James, brother of Jesse James
Right, Entrance to one of the pie-shaped individual jail cells in the infamous Squirrel Cage Jail in Gallatin, Daviess County, Missouri

James Vernon Fox and/or John D. Haven Farm

James Vernon Fox was the father of Anna Rachel Fox and John D. Haven was her maternal grandfather. These 2 farmed together in Daviess County, near Gallatin, Missouri, where the first daylight bank robbery in U.S. history was committed by the James Gang. John D. Haven's farm was on the outskirts of Gallatin, and John D. Haven also fought on the Confederate side during the Civil War. Jesse James and his gang were Southern sympathizers. This farm is a likely candidate just because of its very close proximity to the location of the Gallatin bank robbery.

The James Gang were daring and reckless. They robbed banks and trains with no thought for their victims. For example, this building is where a bank employee was gunned down and killed. That was audacious enough, but what the photo doesn't show, is that the bank sits kitty corner from the County Courthouse on the square in Gallatin, Missouri.

Former bank building Gallatin, Daviess County, Missouri where the Jesse James Gang executed the first daylight bank robbery in U.S. history.

Site of bank robbery Gallatin, Daviess County, Missouri by the Jesse James Gang

Squirrel cage jail in Daviess County, Missouri, where Frank James was held while awaiting trial for bank robbery

View of the front side of the homestead of the Jesse and Frank James Family in Kearny, Missouri

James Patrick Kinney Farm

James Patrick Kinney was the father-in-law of Anna Rachel Fox Kinney. He farmed in Worth and Harrison Counties in Northwestern Missouri during the time when the James Gang was most active. During the Civil War, James Patrick Kinney served in the Union Army and was very proud of that fact for the rest of his life. His farm would be a likely candidate because he probably would have been opposed to the James Gang's Southern sympathies, therefore would have probably been anxious for Frank to leave his farm, once Frank's identity was known. Also, James had a son named Jesse who's name could possibly have, over time, become replaced with Jesse James adding to the legend that the 2 families were related.

William Abner Fox Farm

William Abner Fox was the paternal grandfather of Anna Rachel Fox Kinney. He was a Southern sympathizer who owned businesses and farms in Platte County, Missouri, during the Civil War. Platte County is adjacent to Clay County where the James Family was from. William Abner Fox had strong feelings for the rebel cause. He followed Colonel John Winston into battle for the South. As a Southern sympathizer, it is presumed he probably knew who Jesse and Frank James were, so it is less likely that his farm was the one where Frank James hid out as Frank's identity was probably known to William Abner Fox.

Founding Father, President George Washington

During early 2013, I noticed numerous persons on Ancestry.com were saving a specific document which I'd posted on my tree to their trees. I wondered what was so popular about the document in question and decided to scrutinize it further.

The document was entitled, "Sons of the American Revolution Application for Membership for a descendant of John Eskridge, Patriot of Virginia. The following text from the document caught my attention: "Registrar Notes: The Eskridge family in Virginia were noted for their patriotism, and at least seven members are recorded in the military annals of that state as holding commissions in the Patriot Army; said commissions graduating from that of Lieutenant to that of Lieutenant-Colonel. All of the above mentioned Eskridge Continental officers, converge in George Eskridge, the pioneer, noted herein. George Eskridge, the pioneer, is mentioned specifically in the will of Mrs. Hewes, in which she makes him the guardian of Mary Ball who became the mother of General George Washigtnon, and it is assumed that General Washington was named for George Eskridge who had acted in place of a father to Mary Ball. George Eskridge was a Vestryman at old Christ Church in Alexandria where Washington worshipped. Bronte A. Reynolds, Registrar for Sacramento Chapter, S.A.R.

Note: With reference to the last will of Mrs. Mary Hewes, the exact words read, "…..my said daughter, Mary Ball…..to be under the tutelage and government of Captain George Eskridge, during her minority."

For the full record, see: http://interactive.ancestry.com/2204/32596_242246-00088/559285?backurl=http%3a%2f%2fsearch.ancestry.com%2fcgi-bin%2fsse.dll%3findiv%3d1%26db%3dSARMemberApps%26new%3d1%26MSAV%3d1%26msT%3d1%26gss%3dangs-d%26gsln%3deskridge%26dbOnly%3d_F0006399%257c_F0006399_x%26uidh%3d6r4%26rank%3d1%26pcat%3d39%26fh%3d3%26h%3d559285%26recoff%3d%26ml_rpos%3d4%26hovR%3d1&ssrc=&backlabel=ReturnRecord#?imageId=32596_242246-00089

Here is the connection between the Colonel George Eskridge and the grandchildren of Vernon Haven Kinney:

Colonel George Eskridge (1672 - 1735)
is your 7th great grandfather

Samuel Eskridge (1702 - 1747)
son of Colonel George Eskridge

John Ashton Eskridge (1737 - 1803)
son of Samuel Eskridge

Lucinda Lucy Eskridge (1797 - 1876)
daughter of John Ashton Eskridge

William Abner Fox (1814 - 1891)
son of Lucinda Lucy Eskridge

James Vernon Fox (1853 - 1923)
son of William Abner Fox

Anna Rachel Fox (1877 - 1956)
daughter of James Vernon Fox

Vernon Haven Kinney (1902 - 1984)
son of Anna Rachel Fox

Lawrence Sherman Kinney (1928 -)
son of Vernon Haven Kinney

Barbara Kinney Black
daughter of Lawrence Sherman Kinney

When I first discovered we had a legal connection to George Washington, I almost couldn't believe it. My brother and I spent a weekend researching to make sure of what we had discovered. It was undeniable. To think that my 7th great grandfather influenced the first President of the United States is quite an honor.

The following is from the Virginia Historical Society website, accessed 24 June 2013 at http://www.vahistorical.org/dynasties/georgeeskridge.htm. Per Virginia Historical Society George Eskridge, c. 1715 Unidentified artist, Oil on canvas, Gift of Peter C. Rust, 1914. This portrait is significant for its unusually early date, its provenance that firmly identifies the sitter, and the political prominence of George Eskridge (d. 1735). The canvas is dated by an inventory of the sitter's estate that also lists a portrait of his wife Rebecca, who died in 1715, a terminus ad quem for the pair of paintings. These canvases remained in the Eskridge family until they were given to the Society nearly a century ago. For thirty years, from 1705 to 1735, George Eskridge served with distinction in the House of Burgesses. He was appointed to important committees—Public Claims, Propositions and Grievances, Courts of Justice, Elections and Priviledges—and often was selected to prepare bills for the House and convey, in writing, the views of the House to the governor, his Council, or London. Eskridge's elegant dress and impressive wig were expected accoutrements of the emerging gentry of the colony. Unlike many of his contemporaries in England and his successors in Virginia, he is not, however, presented as a haughty aristocrat, but instead is shown to be concerned with other matters. To judge from the contents of his library, those were intellectual and spiritual. Eskridge collected some two dozen books about law, nearly a dozen on world history, and twice that number of religious treatises. The sober, thoughtful reader of those volumes is captured here on canvas. It is little wonder that so capable and solemn a man was selected by Mary Hewes (by means of her will) to provide "tutelage" for her soon-to-be-orphaned daughter, Mary Ball, later the mother of George Washington. By Eskridge family tradition, Mary Ball named her son out of devotion to George Eskridge."

So, we can see that there is not a blood connection between the 7 times great grandchildren of Colonel George Eskridge and President George Washington, but there was a legal connection between Colonel George Eskridge and the mother of President George Washington, Mary Ball.

General Robert E. Lee

The statement which began this investigation was a simple 3-line paragraph from the book Annals of Platte County, Missouri, by William McClung Paxton, p. 606-607:
"THE ESKRIDGES. Mrs. James Fox was an Eskridge. Her mother was a Moxley, who was descended from the Lee family, of Virginia. Three of Mrs. Fox's brothers were killed in the Revolutionary War, on the patriot side; and two others fought throughout the bloody struggle."

The relationship between Robert Edward Lee and the grandchildren of Vernon Haven Kinney is 1st cousin 2x removed of husband of 1st cousin 7x removed, again, very distant, but interesting all the same.

Robert Edward Lee (1807 - 1870)

Henry Lee III (1756 - 1818)
father of Robert Edward Lee

Henry Lee II (1729 - 1787)
father of Henry Lee III

Henry Lee I (1691 - 1747)
father of Henry Lee II

Richard Lee II (1647 - 1715)
father of Henry Lee I

Thomas Lee (1690 - 1750)
son of Richard Lee II

Thomas Ludwell Lee (1730 - 1778)
son of Thomas Lee

Mary Aylett (1738 - 1836)
wife of Thomas Ludwell Lee

Elizabeth Eskridge (1716 -)
mother of Mary Aylett

Colonel George Eskridge (1672 - 1735)
father of Elizabeth Eskridge

Common ancestor. George Eskridge is father to Samuel Eskridge, below, and father to Elizabeth Eskridge, above.

Samuel Eskridge (1702 - 1747)
son of Colonel George Eskridge

John Ashton Eskridge (1737 - 1803)
son of Samuel Eskridge

Lucinda Lucy Eskridge (1797 - 1876)
daughter of John Ashton Eskridge

William Abner Fox (1814 - 1891)
son of Lucinda Lucy Eskridge

James Vernon Fox (1853 - 1923)
son of William Abner Fox

Anna Rachel Fox (1877 - 1956)
daughter of James Vernon Fox

Vernon Haven Kinney (1902 - 1984)
son of Anna Rachel Fox

Lawrence Sherman Kinney (1928 -)
son of Vernon Haven Kinney

Barbara Kinney Black
daughter of Lawrence Sherman Kinney

Photo of General Robert E. Lee accessed from:
https://www.google.com/search?q=robert+e.+lee+images&tbm=isch&source=iu&imgil=a4fcLUNXj7x6QM%253A%253Bhttps%253A%252F%252Fencrypted-tbn0.gstatic.com%252Fimages%253Fq%253Dtbn%253AANd9GcS1M4jaHu02j3D167WEyJILp2_g7G4pybb9aL2FKIIIN7pLkIJd%253B677%253B860%253BDUicZAnGZx_-9M%253Bhttp%25253A%25252F%25252Fwww.paintingsilove.com%25252Fimage%25252Fshow%25252F208619%25252Fgeneral-robert-e-lee-acrylic&sa=X&ei=G06zUsPpDoW42gWI2YHYCg&sqi=2&ved=0CEkQ9QEwDg&biw=1280&bih=608#facrc=_&imgdii=a4fcLUNXj7x6QM%3A%3BlaiHUsYnPxnqxM%3Ba4fcLUNXj7x6QM%3A&imgrc=a4fcLUNXj7x6QM%3A%3BDUicZAnGZx_-9M%3Bhttp%253A%252F%252Fpic.pilpix.com%252F25%252F25716%252Fgeneral-robert-e-lee-acrylic.jpg%3Bhttp%253A%252F%252Fwww.paintingsilove.com%252Fimage%252Fshow%252F208619%252Fgeneral-robert-e-lee-acrylic%3B677%3B860

Adlai Stevenson the First, Vice-President to President Grover Cleveland

A single line in Mabel Pearl Carnahan's journal, I Remember, started this search: "When Cleveland was elected the second time I never heard the vice president mentioned although he was Mother's first cousin."

Susan Carnahan's maiden name was Stevenson, so Mabel Pearl Carnahan was referencing Adlai Stevenson the First, who was the Vice-President to President Grover Cleveland during his second term in office, 1896.

Research to date, 2013, has not yet uncovered a definitive connection between Susan Stevenson Carnahan and Adlai Stevenson. Additional research is needed.

When Adlai Stevenson, descendant of Adlai I, was running for President during the 1950s, he made a campaign stop at Eastern Airlines in Miami, Dade County, Florida. He entered the mechanic shop where Lawrence Sherman Kinney was repairing a landing gear. Adlai walked right over to Lawrence and said, "I want to shake your hand." Lawrence replied, "My hands are all dirty." To which Adlai responded, "That's o.k. My hands are dirty, too. I'm a politician."

Left, Adlai Stevenson the First.

President James Buchannan

While following the George Eskridge line, I made a very interesting discovery which is outlined below.

James Buchanan II (1791 -)
brother-in-law of 2nd cousin 6x removed

James Buchanan
father of James Buchanan II

Jane Buchanan (1793 - 1839)
daughter of James Buchanan

Elliott Tolley Lane (1784 - 1841)
husband of Jane Buchanan

Mary Newton (1745 -)
mother of Elliott Tolley Lane

Sarah Eskridge (1707 - 1753)
mother of Mary Newton

Colonel George Eskridge (1672 - 1735)
father of Sarah Eskridge

Common Ancestor – George Eskridge is father to Sarah above, and Samuel below.

Samuel Eskridge (1702 - 1747)
son of Colonel George Eskridge

John Ashton Eskridge (1737 - 1803)
son of Samuel Eskridge

Lucinda Lucy Eskridge (1797 - 1876)
daughter of John Ashton Eskridge

William Abner Fox (1814 - 1891)
son of Lucinda Lucy Eskridge

James Vernon Fox (1853 - 1923)
son of William Abner Fox

Anna Rachel Fox (1877 - 1956)
daughter of James Vernon Fox

Vernon Haven Kinney (1902 - 1984)
son of Anna Rachel Fox

Lawrence Sherman Kinney (1928 -)
son of Vernon Haven Kinney

Barbara Kinney Black
daughter of Lawrence Sherman Kinney

Portrait of President James Buchanan accessed at: https://www.google.com/search?q=president+james+buchanan&tbm=isch&tbo=u&source=univ&sa=X&ei=DlGzUqWtB8jg2gXu54BY&ved=0CKcBEIke&biw=1280&bih=608#facrc=_&imgdii=_&imgrc=UqPYJ0lDGkjYjM%3A%3B0xbbZOaIIrrNQM%3Bhttp%253A%252F%252Fupload.wikimedia.org%252Fwikipedia%252Fcommons%252F9%252F98%252FJamesBuchanan_crop.jpg%3Bhttp%253A%252F%252Fen.wikipedia.org%252Fwiki%252FWilliam_R._King%3B1216%3B1546

Yes, I admit, brother-in-law of 2nd cousin 6x removed, is quite a distant relationship! What intrigued me, however, was the niece of President James Buchanan, Harriett Rebecca Lane, who served as the bachelor President's first lady. She was my third cousin five times removed, as shown below.

First Lady Harriett Rebecca Lane

Harriett Rebecca Lane (1830 - 1903)
is your 3rd cousin 5x removed

Elliott Tolley Lane (1784 - 1841)
father of Harriett Rebecca Lane

Mary Newton (1745 -)
mother of Elliott Tolley Lane

Sarah Eskridge (1707 - 1753)
mother of Mary Newton

Colonel George Eskridge (1672 - 1735)
father of Sarah Eskridge

Common Ancestor is George Eskridge
He is father to Sarah above, and Samuel below.

Samuel Eskridge (1702 - 1747)
son of Colonel George Eskridge

John Ashton Eskridge (1737 - 1803)
son of Samuel Eskridge

Lucinda Lucy Eskridge (1797 - 1876)
daughter of John Ashton Eskridge

William Abner Fox (1814 - 1891)
son of Lucinda Lucy Eskridge

James Vernon Fox (1853 - 1923)
son of William Abner Fox

Anna Rachel Fox (1877 - 1956)
daughter of James Vernon Fox

Vernon Haven Kinney (1902 - 1984)
son of Anna Rachel Fox

Lawrence Sherman Kinney (1928 -)
son of Vernon Haven Kinney

Barbara Kinney Black
daughter of Lawrence Sherman Kinney

The biography of Harriet Rebecca Lane was a fascinating read as accessed from the following Internet site: http://www.firstladies.org/biographies/firstladies.aspx?biography=16
What I was most impressed with was the huge impact she made in so many people's lives ranging from ill children to the royalty of Great Britain.

Portrait of Harriet Rebecca Lane accessed at:
http://www.firstladies.org/biographies/firstladies.aspx?biography=16

Name Index

A—

B—

C—

F—

K—

L—

M—

N—

O—

P—

Q—

R—

ABOUT THE AUTHOR

Barbara Kinney Black is a passionate family history researcher who wants to experience the lives of her ancestors through as many means possible. In her research she wasn't satisfied with mere photographs and Internet research. Like a detective or a reporter, she hunted down their stories on site. Armed with GPS, notebooks, pencils, digital camera, hand held scanner, maps, and a list of local historic societies and libraries, she discovered her ancestors in the pages of courthouse documents, dug up dirt samples from their former farmsteads, photographed any crumbling building that looked 100 years old or more, and interviewed anyone who would talk with her about "back in the day". When she isn't researching and writing, Barbara is an ESL professor and enjoys meeting international students and traveling. This may be her first book, but it certainly won't be her last.

www.ingramcontent.com/pod-product-compliance
Lightning Source LLC
Chambersburg PA
CBHW081412270326
41931CB00015B/3247